Developing Competence in Teaching Reading

Developing Competence in Teaching Reading

Instructional Modules in Reading Education

Colden Garland
Temple University

wcb
Wm. C. Brown Company Publishers
Dubuque, Iowa

To the children
of the School
District of
Philadelphia

Contents

Preface

The history of teacher education is the account of a continuous search for increasingly effective approaches to the preparation of teachers who will have the competence both to understand and to meet the diverse learning needs of the children with whom they interact. The development of the modules included in *Developing Competence in Teaching Reading* represents an effort to contribute to that search.

The original modules were developed as one component of the Competency-Based Teacher Education Program of the Department of Early Childhood and Elementary Education, College of Education, Temple University. They have been field-tested by teacher education students working with children in elementary schools within the School District of Philadelphia. Their implementation, in a variety of University contexts and classroom settings, has resulted in the revision and redesign of those original modules. These changes are reflected here. I hope that as they are implemented in other settings, those who use these modules will further revise and redesign them to meet the needs of specific groups of students and of the children they teach. In this way, the search for more effective strategies for teacher education will continue.

Throughout the process of developing the modules, many colleagues found time to discuss ideas and offer suggestions. To them I extend my appreciation for their interest.

I am particularly grateful to the following for their contributions to the development of the modules:

Dr. Charlotte Epstein, Professor of Education, Temple University, for the story "The Mists of Change";

Teresa Richardson, for her invaluable assistance, through careful attention to detail and thoughtful suggestions, in the carrying out of the variety of tasks essential to the preparation of the manuscript;

Lynne Landers Benedict, Dennis Esposito, Dorothy McNamee, Teresa Richardson, and Jodi Silverstein, students in the College of Education, Temple University, for the lesson plans and the Informal Reading Inventory included in the modules.

Introduction

The modules included in *Developing Competence in Teaching Reading* were developed in an effort to achieve one objective: to provide students with experiences that will enable them to develop the competencies they will need as teachers to insure that each child's *right to read* is realized in *success in reading*. The framework within which the modules were developed represents an approach to teacher education in which the focus is the identification of the competencies students will be developing, and the ways in which their achievement of these competencies will be assessed. Because the focus in this approach is student performance, the modules are designed to encourage students to become actively involved, at each stage of their progress, in the process of (1) internalizing concepts and generalizations, and (2) using these understandings in the development and demonstration of specific teaching competencies.

The organization of the modules, suggestions for their use in programs of preservice and of inservice teacher education, and procedures which students may find helpful in working with the modules, are presented in the following sections of this introduction.

Organization of the Modules

An instructional module is defined here as a set of competencies, learning experiences, and measures for assessing acquisition of the competencies. The components of each module are organized in the following sequence.

Overview: Introduces the content of the module through the presentation of a selected article; identifies the overall purposes in the module; and explains the relationship of the instructional activities to the module competencies.

Competencies:	Identifies those understandings and skills which students will be able to demonstrate upon completion of the module.
Instructional Activities:	Presents a set of learning experiences which are designed to enable students to develop the competencies specified for the module.
Preassessment and Postassessment:	Identifies one or more measures to be used in assessing students' progress in acquiring the module competencies. Performance criteria are specified for each measure.

Suggestions for Instructors

Using the Modules for Preservice Teacher Education

The modules were designed for flexible use in teacher education programs representative of different types of organizational patterns. The instructional settings described here are provided as illustrations of the variety of ways in which the modules can be used.

1. Individualized Instructional Program
   a. The instructor provides students with an orientation to a module through an introductory seminar. At this time, students who want to complete the Knowledge and/or Performance Levels of the preassessment and postassessment in order to demonstrate previous acquisition of the module competencies can arrange with the instructor to do so.
   b. Following the orientation seminar, students select, on the basis of interest, previous experience, and learning style, those activities that they feel will enable them to develop the module competencies. They may, in addition, design activities of their own. Students then work independently to complete the activities they have selected and/or designed.
   c. Activities which involve school settings (e.g., teaching and observing lessons) may be completed in classrooms in which students are working with children on a regular basis (one day a week, for example).
   d. If field placements are not included in the program, students can arrange peer teaching sessions in which they can complete those activities that focus on teaching specific lessons.

e. Each student contacts the instructor when he feels that he is ready to complete each level of the postassessment. The Performance Level component can be completed in peer teaching sessions if classroom settings are not available.

f. If a student is unable to demonstrate one or more of the module competencies at the level specified in the performance criteria, the instructor and student diagnose the difficulty together and plan experiences that will enable the student to demonstrate the competencies successfully.

2. Combined Class and Individualized Instructional Program

a. The instructor meets with students for part of the regularly scheduled class time (e.g., one hour a week, two hours a week). During this time students complete instructional activities selected by the instructor or selected on the basis of instructor-student planning. Small groups and individuals may complete different activities and share the results of their work with others in the class.

b. During the nonscheduled class time, students complete additional activities of their selection independently. If arrangements can be made for field placements, students may use this time to complete activities involving interaction with children and with teachers. If field placements are unavailable, students can participate in peer teaching.

c. Students complete the Knowledge Level component of the postassessment during a class session. The Performance Level component may be completed through peer teaching or with children in classroom settings.

d. The instructor develops plans for additional learning experiences with students who are unable to demonstrate acquisition of the module competencies.

3. Class Instructional Program

a. The instructor meets with students during all regularly scheduled class times. Students complete instructional activities identified by the instructor or identified through instructor-student planning. Activities involving peer teaching can be completed during class sessions.

b. Students complete the Knowledge Level component of the postassessment during a class session. The Performance Level component is completed during class sessions through the use of peer teaching.

c. Plans for additional learning experiences are developed with students who are unable to demonstrate acquisition of the module competencies.

Using the Modules for Inservice Teacher Education

The competency-based approach reflected in the modules is particularly well suited for use with inservice teacher education programs. On the basis of their experiences with children, teachers can identify the areas in which they want to increase their competence. The preassessment measures can also be used as a means of helping teachers identify the areas in which they want to concentrate. Each teacher can then focus specifically on those modules which include the competencies he or she has identified. Teachers who have selected the same module(s) can work together in completing the module activities. Such groups can provide the context for peer teaching, for example, if teachers want to refine new procedures in this setting before they use them in their classrooms. The Knowledge Level components of the postassessments can be administered in individual or group sessions as the participants indicate their readiness to complete them. Competence at the Performance Level can be demonstrated by teachers in their own classrooms, or in peer teaching settings. When the modules are used in the way described here, individuals are working to meet their own needs, rather than participating in a prescribed program in which all teachers are provided with the same learning experiences regardless of differences in levels of competence.

In concluding this section concerning ways in which the modules can be used, two additional points should be made. First, it may prove more effective, in certain contexts, to use the modules in a sequence other than the one suggested here. With minor adjustments, this sequence can easily be adapted to the structure of a particular program or to the needs of a specific group of students. The second point is concerned with the lesson plans included in the modules. These plans were developed by teacher education students for use with children in actual classroom settings. In this respect, they do not represent the "model" lesson plans often found in textbooks. Frequently, students view such plans as being too abstract or unrealistic to be of help to them. It is hoped, therefore, that the inclusion of plans that students have used successfully will encourage other students in their efforts to plan effective learning experiences for children.

Correlation of the Modules with Selected References

A matrix which indicates the correlation of the modules with selected references is located at the end of this introduction. This matrix is provided to facilitate the use of additional reference material. Using the matrix makes it possible to determine quickly and easily which chapters in the selected texts correspond to each of the modules.

The focal point in the set of modules provided for you in *Developing Competence in Teaching Reading* is the development of your ability to help each child you teach to experience success in learning to read. Each module identifies a set of specific competencies (understandings and skills) that will contribute to your ability to provide effective reading experiences for children. Each module also identifies the ways in which you will demonstrate your acquisition of the module competencies and the criteria which you and your instructor will use to evaluate your performance. The advantage for you in using this competency-based approach is that you will know exactly what is expected of you, and the ways in which you will be asked to demonstrate that you can meet those expectations. As a result, you may find that you are learning not only more effectively, but also more efficiently than you have in other contexts.

In the first section of this introduction, "Organization of the Modules," an instructional module is defined as a set of competencies, learning experiences, and measures for assessing acquisition of the competencies. Reread that section in order to develop an understanding of the module components and the sequence in which they are organized. The sequence is repeated here for your convenience:

Overview
Competencies
Instructional Activities
Preassessment and Postassessment

Before suggesting a procedure for using the modules, it may be helpful to point out several overall features of the modules that have been included in order to facilitate your work with them. First, because the focus of the modules is your performance, they are designed to encourage you to become actively involved in the process of developing understandings and skills. As you engage in activities that go beyond just *reading* about the teaching of reading, you will be able to evaluate your progress toward the development of the module competencies and your readiness for demonstrating the competencies in the ways identified in the postassessment. Second, in order to make your reading as meaningful as possible, a set of *purposes for reading* is provided whenever you are asked to read specific material. These purposes (in the form of questions) can be helpful both in guiding your reading, and in assessing your comprehension of the material after you have read it. Third, in order to illustrate procedures for teaching specific reading skills, lesson plans are included in the modules.

These plans were developed by students for use with children in actual classroom settings. It is hoped that as you examine lessons that were planned and used successfully by other students, you will develop confidence in your ability to provide equally effective learning experiences for children.

Procedure for Using the Modules

The procedure you follow in working with the modules will depend, in part, upon the organizational structure of the course or program in which you are participating. Because individuals organize their learning experiences in different ways, the procedure will depend, also, upon the learning style that has proven to be most effective for you. If you are participating in a program of individualized instruction, it is suggested that you follow the procedure outlined here initially. As you gain experience in working with the modules, you may find ways of adapting this procedure so that it more closely dovetails with your particular learning style.

Step 1. Read the reprinted article, included in the "Overview" section, through which the module is introduced. Use the questions that precede the article as your purposes for reading. When you have completed the article, assess your comprehension of it by responding to these questions.

Step 2. Complete the "Overview" section of the module. The overall purposes in the module and the relationship of the activities to the module competencies are identified in the subsections "Module Competencies" and "Instructional Activities."

Step 3. Read the "Competencies" section of the module. The statements included there identify the understandings and skills that you will be able to demonstrate upon completion of the module.

Step 4. Read the "Preassessment and Postassessment" section of the module. If you feel that you can complete either the Knowledge Level or the Performance Level successfully, in terms of the performance criteria, indicate to your instructor your readiness to do this. If you are going to complete the Knowledge and Performance Levels as a postassessment rather than as a preassessment, understanding what is included in this assessment can serve as a focus for your work with the module activities.

Step 5. Read the "Instructional Activities" section of the module. On the basis of your interests, previous experience, and preference for particular types of learning experiences, select and complete those activities which you feel will enable you to achieve the module competencies. If you find that you are interested in obtaining additional information related to an activity you are completing, consult the list of selected references at the end of the module.

Step 6. When you feel that you are ready to complete the postassessment successfully, in terms of the performance criteria, indicate to your instructor your readiness to do so. Complete the postassessment following the procedure indicated.

Correlation of the Modules with Selected References

A matrix which indicates the correlation of the modules with selected references is located on pages 8 and 9. This matrix is provided in order to facilitate your use of additional reference material. As you work with the modules and find that you want to consult other sources, using the matrix will enable you to determine quickly and easily which of the references include material that is relevant to each module, and the pertinent chapter numbers in each case.

Correlation Matrix
Correlation of Modules with Chapters in Selected Texts

Textbooks—With Chapter Numbers	1 Readiness for Beginning Reading Instruction	2 Approaches to Reading Instruction	3 Developing Phonic Analysis Skills	4 Developing Structural Analysis Skills	5 Developing Comprehension Ability	6 Planning Directed Reading Lessons	7 Adjusting Instruction to Individual Differences	8 Reading in the Content Fields	9 Evaluating Growth in Reading Ability
Bond, Guy L., and Wagner, Eva Bond. *Teaching the Child to Read*. 4th ed. New York: Macmillan Company, 1966.	2	5, 6	8	8	9	7	16	11, 13	15
Bush, Clifford L., and Huebner, Mildred H. *Strategies for Reading in the Elementary School*. New York: Macmillan Company, 1970.	3	10	4	4	5	11	10	6	14
Dallmann, Martha; Rouch, Roger L.; Chang, Lynette Y. C.; and DeBoer, John J. *The Teaching of Reading*. 4th ed. New York: Holt, Rinehart and Winston, 1974.	4A, 4B	15	5A, 5B	5A, 5B	6A, 6B		12, 13	8A, 8B, 10	12
Durkin, Dolores. *Teaching Them to Read*. 2d ed. Boston: Allyn & Bacon, 1974.	5, 6, 7	2	9, 10, 11	12	14		3	15	16
Harris, Albert J., and Sipay, Edward R. *Effective Teaching of Reading*. 2d ed. New York: David McKay Company, 1971.	2	3	8, 9	9	11	3	7	12	6
Heilman, Arthur W. *Principles and Practices of Teaching Reading*. 3d ed. Columbus, Ohio: Charles E. Merrill Publishing Company, 1972.	4	5, 6	7	7				13, 14	8
Karlin, Robert. *Teaching Elementary Reading: Principles and Strategies*. New York: Harcourt Brace Jovanovich, 1971.	3	4	5	5	6	4	9	7	2
May, Frank B. *To Help Children Read*. Columbus, Ohio: Charles E. Merrill Publishing Company, 1973.	7	9	2	4	6		5, 9	8	

Reference									
Otto, Wayne; Chester, Robert; McNeil, John; and Myers, Shirley. *Focused Reading Instruction.* Reading, Mass.: Addison-Wesley Publishing Company, 1974.	5	12	7	7	9		11	8	11
Russell, David H. *Children Learn to Read.* 2d ed. Waltham, Mass.: Blaisdell Publishing Company, 1961.	6	5	10	10		5	15	11	16
Smith, Nila Banton. *Reading Instruction for Today's Children.* Englewood Cliffs, N. J.: Prentice-Hall, 1963.		5	8, 21	8, 21			6	10, 23	
Spache, George D., and Spache, Evelyn B. *Reading in the Elementary School.* 4th ed. Boston: Allyn & Bacon, Inc., 1977.	6, 7	2, 3, 4, 5	11	11	13	2	14	9	
Stauffer, Russell G. *Teaching Reading as a Thinking Process.* New York: Harper & Row, Publishers, 1969.	7	5, 8	9	9	2	2, 3			11
Tinker, Miles A., and McCullough, Constance M. *Teaching Elementary Reading.* 3d ed. New York: Appleton-Century-Crofts, 1968.		1	8	8	9, 10	23	18	13, 24	17
Veatch, Jeannette. *Reading in the Elementary School.* New York: Ronald Press Company, 1966.			11	11			5, 7	10	12
Walcutt, Charles C.; Lamport, Joan; and McCracken, Glenn. *Teaching Reading.* New York: Macmillan Company, 1974.		14	28		20			25	16
Wallen, Carl J. *Competency in Teaching Reading.* Chicago: Science Research Associates, 1972.	4, 5	18	6, 7	8, 9	10, 11, 12, 13, 14, 15, 16, 17	5	19		
Zintz, Miles V. *The Reading Process: The Teacher and the Learner.* 2d ed. Dubuque, Iowa: Wm. C. Brown Company Publishers, 1975.	8	9	10	10	11, 13	5	4, 5	12	21

Readiness for Beginning Reading Instruction

Overview

The "readiness for learning" concept is of concern to all teachers. At each age or grade level, and in each area of the curriculum, children must be provided with the skills and understandings that are prerequisite to the effective learning of new skills and understandings. The focus in this module is one specific dimension of readiness: that combination of abilities and experiences that will provide for each child the maximum opportunity for success as he engages in the complex process of learning to read.

The module is introduced through Dolores Durkin's article, "Reading Readiness."[1] Durkin traces the origin of the readiness concept to the 1920s, and points up the influence of the work of Arnold Gesell in establishing the viewpoint that children experience difficulty in reading when instruction is begun before they are "ready." Durkin discusses the traditional interpretation of readiness and then proposes an interpretation which focuses on the relationship between the child and the opportunities for learning that are provided for him. Within this framework, she describes the kinds of experiences that can be offered to children as they begin learning to read. When reading Durkin's article, use the following questions as your purposes for reading:

1. How did the belief of the 20s and 30s that a child was not ready for reading until he reached a mental age of about 6.5 years affect beginning reading programs?

---

1. Dolores Durkin, "Reading Readiness," *The Reading Teacher* 23 (March 1970): 528-34, 564.

2. How does Durkin support the position that readiness is not just a product, but rather ". . . a product in relation to a given set of circumstances"?[2]
3. How does providing children with opportunities for learning to read when they enter school aid the teacher in assessing readiness for reading?
4. What is Durkin's position regarding any attempt to establish the one best age, method, and set of materials for beginning reading?

Reading Readiness
Dolores Durkin

To understand how "reading readiness" got into professional vocabularies and then into the school curriculum, it is necessary to go back to the 1920's. That decade is relevant because it was characterized by the beginning of so-called "scientific" measurements of human behavior. Among the results of what became almost a craze to measure everything was the appearance of school surveys. Of special relevance to reading readiness is a finding common to many of the survey reports which indicated that large numbers of children were failing first grade, most often because of insufficient achievement in reading.

Within a short time—this was still the 1920's—concern about the finding became as widespread as the finding itself, and for at least two reasons. Successful teaching of reading, then as now, was considered uniquely important among elementary school responsibilities. In addition, the failures that were occurring resulted in first-grade classrooms populated by many "over age" children. Behavior problems blossomed, and so did concern about why first graders were having difficulty learning to read.

Logically, it would seem, a study of reading problems—whether carried on in the 1920's or now—would look to such multiple and commonsense causes as overly large classes, inappropriate materials, inadequate teacher preparation, lack of motivation on the part of the children, and so on. However, in the study of beginning reading problems that went on in the 1920's and 1930's, the factor given singular attention is to be found in a pronouncement appearing with great frequency in the professional literature of that period: First graders are having difficulty learning to read because they were not ready when the instruction started. Why beginning reading problems were attributed so exclusively to a lack of readiness and, secondly, why delaying instruction was soon proposed as *the* solution, can be understood only when the psychological setting of the 1920's and 1930's is brought into focus.

Described briefly, and therefore incom-

Reprinted from *The Reading Teacher* 23 (March 1970): 528-34, 564, with permission of Dolores Durkin and the International Reading Association.

2. Ibid., p. 347.

pletely, the 1920's and 1930's was a period in which the ideas of Arnold Gesell dominated. As a physician, Gesell was especially interested in children's physical and motor development. Resulting from his work and his prolific writing about it came the notion that these aspects of development "unfold in stages." Or, to put it another way, a young child grows and develops as a result of maturation, not learning. Acceptance of this point of view would suggest that if a child is unable to perform some particular motor task—crawling, for example—it is because he has not yet reached that point or stage of development which allows him to crawl. Thus, he is unready. The solution? According to Gesell and his disciples it was to let time pass. That is, let additional maturity occur and then the child will be ready and he will be crawling.

Intellectual Skills Merged with Motor Skills

Had Gesell and his followers confined their descriptions and explanations to motor skills, there would be little reason to quarrel with them because much about a child's physical development does depend upon maturation and, therefore, the passing of time. However, this is not what happened. Instead, prominent educators were soon using Gesell's explanation of motor skills to explain the development of intellectual skills. In fact, nowhere was this highly questionable merger more apparent than in the field of reading.

When, in the 1920's, school surveys revealed that children were failing first grade because of insufficient achievement in reading, the one "explanation" to get attention was that these first graders had problems because they were not ready when school instruction began. The solution? Still following the Gesell school of thought about motor development, some very influential educators were soon advocat-

ing that reading instruction be postponed so that the passing of additional time would insure a readiness for it. And so was born the doctrine of postponement. This doctrine fostered the notion that (a) getting children ready to read and (b) teaching them to read occur at distinctly different times in the school curriculum.

Such a notion is reflected, of course, in the long entrenched practice of having a readiness program followed by a reading program. In fact, and not many years ago, it was very common to find the first six or eight weeks of first grade given over to the goal of "readiness." This practice apparently assumed that a child could be "unready" for reading on, for example, Friday of the sixth week of school but quite "ready" on Monday of the seventh week. "What a week-end!" is one possible reaction to such an assumption. A less sarcastic and certainly more helpful response, however, is to think more carefully about what it means to help a child get ready to read and, secondly, what it means to teach him to read.

Traditional Interpretation of Reading Readiness

Readiness—whether applied to reading or some other kind of learning—is an unquestionably valid psychological concept with permanent relevance. However, what is considerably less permanent and always open to question is how it is interpreted. Applied to reading, the concept of readiness was for a long time interpreted to mean that children become ready as a result of maturation. Or, to phrase this traditional interpretation somewhat differently, readiness for learning to read was thought to constitute a certain maturational stage in the child's development. Because this interpretation came into existence at a time when great efforts were being made to be objective and quantitatively precise about every description of human behavior—these were the decades of the 1920's and 1930's—it was very natural for educators of that period to seek out a quantitative and precise description of the stage of development which they believed constituted readiness for reading. The end result was the proclamation that a mental age of about 6.5 years defines readiness.

How seriously this proclamation was taken by the man who had much to do with promoting it can be seen in a 1936 article. It was written by Carleton Washburne, then superintendent of the Winnetka, Illinois, public schools and, more importantly, a leader of the Progressive Education Movement. In the article Washburne[3] noted: "Nowadays each first grade teacher in Winnetka has a chart showing when each of her children will be mentally six-and-a-half, and is careful to avoid any effort to get a child to read before he has reached this stage of mental growth."

Washburne's comments are useful now because, in capsule form, they portray the once widely held belief that *getting* ready to read and *being* ready occur at completely separate points on some time line. It was just such a belief, of course, that led to the practice of having a readiness program at one point in the child's school life and a reading program at some later date.

Another Interpretation

With the initial or traditional interpretation, readiness was viewed as a product; specifically, a product of maturation. Viewing readiness as a product is very defensible, but current knowledge indicates that it is the product of both maturation *and* learning. Within such a framework, readiness can be defined as various combinations of abilities which result from, or are the product of, nature and nurture interacting with each other.

A view of readiness which sees it as a product is defensible: yet, to view it only as a product is incomplete. What must be added is that dimension which brings into focus a relationship, a relationship between a child's particular abilities and the kind of learning opportunities made available to him. Within this framework readiness is still a product, but a product in relation to a given set of circumstances. Or, to use another's words, readiness is "the adequacy of existing capacity in relation to the demands of a given learning task".[1]

This interpretation, if accepted, offers three important reminders to educators:

1. Readiness is not one thing. In fact, the variety of abilities, both in kind and amount, which add up to readiness suggests that a more accurately descriptive term would be "readinesses"—awkward, to be sure, but also accurate.
2. Although what makes one child ready for reading might be different from what makes another ready, *both* are ready because of the interplay of nature and nurture. This is a recognition that children are ready because of hereditary and maturational factors, but also because of the learning opportunities in their particular environment.
3. Because readiness depends not only upon a child's abilities but also upon the kind of learning opportunities made available to him, it is possible for a child to be ready when one type of reading program is offered, but unready when other kinds are available.

This dependence of readiness upon the type and quality of instruction that will be offered also has some implications for assessing a child's readiness. What it highlights right away, for example, is the inadequacy of any attempt to assess it apart from the kind of reading instruction that will be available. In positive terms the implication is: If readiness is "the adequacy of existing capacity in relation to the demands of a given learning task," then the best and even only way to assess a child's readiness for reading is to give him varied opportunities to begin to read.

Providing Reading Opportunities

When should these learning opportunities be offered. In responding to such a query, it is of initial importance to remember that the practice of starting children to read in first grade and at the age of six is the result of convention, not of any evidence that there is something about six-year-old children which makes this a particularly productive time to start teaching reading. With such a reminder in the background, it seems appropriate to suggest—but with a little reservation—that since kindergarten is the first level of public school education now offered, kindergarten is the time to learn about children's readiness by giving them varied and interesting opportunities to begin to read.

The "little reservation" is rooted in the knowledge that some kindergartens are now bombarding children with whole-class, drill-oriented instruction. Knowing that this unfortunate practice is spreading, it seems wise to repeat the recommendation: Give kindergarten children *varied* and *interesting opportunities* to begin to read.

The wording for such a recommendation was carefully selected. For example, the emphasis on "opportunities" is there because it implies that with some children in some kindergartens the opportunities might not "take." Acceptance of this is of basic importance. It frees the kindergarten teacher from thinking that every child *must* learn to read and so, in turn, also frees her from feeling any need "to put the pressure on." Today, unfortunately, some kindergarten teachers *are* "putting the pressure on" with their whole-class use of drill

and workbooks. Predictably, in the years to come, there will be a reaction against this—a reaction which is not likely to make a distinction between a timing that might be just right, and a methodology that is all wrong.

The need for *varied* opportunities is emphasized because the easiest way to become a reader is probably different for different children. Consequently the "varied" refers to opportunities for learning to identify whole words, but also opportunities to learn to print and spell and, too, opportunities to begin to learn about letters and the sounds they record. The end result of such varied efforts would be insight into the readiness of the children and, too, very specific information about the way into reading that seems easiest for each child. Of course, another result is that some of these kindergarten children would be reading.

Probably the best way to clarify "kindergarten opportunities to learn to read" is to describe some. Through these few examples it should become app rent that readiness instruction and reading instruction are not always two different things.

In the kindergarten, because five-year-olds love nobody quite as much as they love themselves, reading opportunities of a whole-word identification type might begin with attention to the children's names. Since attendance-taking is a daily routine, it could also become a source of daily "practice" as children tuck their names into a card holder when they arrive and, later, read all the name cards—at first with much assistance from the teacher—to find out who is present and who is absent. Other opportunities to learn to read other words of interest—days of the week, months of the year, and so on—could be provided too. How the children respond to such opportunities and what they learn from them will offer a teacher much information about their readiness to read *via,* in this case, a whole-word approach.

Art projects can often be a vehicle for assessments because, in this case, they provide occasions for children to learn to print labels or even short captions for their pictures. Such activities have direct relevance for readiness assessment because some young children who have no interest in reading *per se* are found to be very interested in printing.[2] With this in mind, the kindergarten teacher who offers opportunities to learn to print is providing herself with the opportunity to identify children whose way into beginning reading ought to be through writing and spelling. In addition, however, she is also becoming aware of other children for whom the motor skill of writing is a formidable task.

Because many young children seem to enjoy playing with the sounds of language, it also makes sense to provide kindergarten opportunities for learning about letters and the sounds they record. For example, it might happen that the word *magnet* takes on special interest. Perhaps it was first introduced in a story, and then simple experiments were done to show magnets, to demonstrate magnetism, and so on. The end result is that the word *magnet* is written many times for the children to see and thus—for some—to learn to read. With *magnet* written on the chalkboard, a teacher might one day say to the children, "You know some other words that start with the same letter. Who knows the name of this letter . . . Who remembers some other words that start with an *m*?" Quickly, children like Martha and Michael proudly offer their names as examples. And then another child recalls the word *Monday*.

The end result is a list of *m* words, but also the teacher's opportunity to introduce letter-sound associations. In this case, for instance, the teacher might read the list, point out again that all the words begin with *m*, then repeat the words—this time asking the children to try to hear how they all begin with the same sound. A natural follow-up question would be, "Can you think of some other words that begin

with the sound that you hear at the beginning of these words? Listen. I'll say them again and then maybe you can think of other words that begin with the same sound."

As a result of this plus other instances of attention to letters and sounds, a teacher has the chance to learn which children are unable to name letters and, what will be more common, which are unable to hear initial sounds in words. At the same time, however, she is also learning that other children know the names of many letters and even are successful in hearing and distinguishing among beginning sounds.

These very few illustrations of "kindergarten opportunities to learn to read" hardly describe a total program. However, they ought to be sufficient to exemplify the main points suggested. They have illustrated, for example, that the assessment of readiness and the teaching of reading can result from the very same situation. Thus, the teacher's use of the children's name in attendance-taking was a chance for her to learn about their readiness to read whole words. In addition, though, for the children who were in fact "ready" it was the start of their learning to read—in this instance, children's names.

The few examples also ought to have shown that a single teaching procedure will be readiness instruction for some children, but reading instruction for others. For instance, the use that was made of the word *magnet* could result in beginning learning in phonics for some. Yet, for other less ready children, the teacher's questions about a particular group of words beginning with *m* would only be the first step in a series of steps which will finally result—perhaps during kindergarten—in the ability to hear and distinguish among initial sounds in words. For these latter children, the teacher was carrying on a type of readiness instruction. However, with the children who were very ready to grasp the connection between *m* and a certain sound, reading instruction was taking place.

In summary, then, three points seem particularly important:

1. Readiness for reading should not be viewed as comprising a single collection of abilities which will be the same for all children. Actually, what makes one child ready might be quite different from what makes another ready.
2. Whether or not a child *is* ready depends upon his particular abilities, but also upon the reading instruction that will be offered. This type of dependence means that readiness can be assessed only when a child is given varied opportunities to learn to read.
3. What a child is able to learn as a result of these opportunities offers very specific information about his readiness. With some children, a particular opportunity will result in reading ability and so, quite obviously, these children were ready. With others, however, the same opportunity will not "take," and so for them it is a type of readiness instruction. That the same teaching procedure can be reading instruction for some children and readiness instruction for others suggests serious flaws in school practices which seem to go out of their way to create an artificial separation between a readiness program and a reading program. A much more defensible way of working is to view readiness instruction as reading instruction in its early stages.

Acceptance of these views about readiness also entails acceptance of a variety of challenges for educators. Probably the major one has to do with the need for greater flexibility in the way schools handle beginning reading. Within the context of this view of readiness, for instance, there would be no room for thinking that there is one best age for starting reading; no room for thinking there is one best methodology and one best set of materials. Nor, certainly, is there a place for thinking that all children must accomplish the same learning at the same time.

Another and briefer way of stating these challenges is to insert the reminder that the important question for educators is not, "Are these children ready to learn to read?" but, rather, "Are we ready to teach them at a time, at a pace, and in a way that is just right for each child?"

References

1. Ausubel, D. P. "Viewpoints from Related Disciplines: Human Growth and Development," *Teachers College Record*, 60 (1959), 245-254.
2. Durkin, Dolores. *Children Who Read Early*. New York: Teachers College Press, Columbia University, 1966.
3. Washburne, C. "Ripeness," *Progressive Education*, 13 (1936), 125-130.

Module Competencies

The purpose in this module is to provide you with opportunities to develop understandings and skills related to specific dimensions of readiness: factors related to readiness for reading, assessing readiness, and providing readiness experiences for children. These understandings and skills are identified as the competencies you will be able to demonstrate as a result of working through this module.

The "Preassessment and Postassessment" section of the module identifies the ways in which your acquisition of the competencies specified for this module will be assessed. For each means of assessment, performance criteria are identified. Use these criteria as guides in evaluating your ability to complete both levels of the postassessment successfully.

Instructional Activities

The instructional activities provided in this module are designed to enable you to progress to the point of successful completion of the postassessment, thereby demonstrating your achievement of the module competencies. Whether the activities involve reading, examining or evaluating materials, or teaching children or peers, each is directly related to one of the module competencies. The material in activity 2 describes the relationships between abilities in several categories and readiness for beginning reading (competency 1). Activities 3 and 4 focus on the assessment of readiness through formal and informal means (competency 2). Activities 5, 6, 7, and 8 are concerned with the teaching of readiness skills through the use of a variety of activities and materials (competency 3). Activity 9 is directed toward helping you understand how teachers use the information available to them in making decisions regarding children's readiness for reading instruction (competency 4). In activity 10 you are encouraged to design activities of your own that will enable you to develop the module competencies.

Competencies

1. Describe social and emotional, intellectual, physical, and educational factors related to readiness for beginning reading.
2. Contrast formal and informal measures of readiness for reading.
3. Develop activities and materials which enable children to develop specific readiness skills.
4. Assess children's readiness for beginning reading instruction.

Instructional Activities

Select from the following learning experiences those which you feel will enable you to achieve the competencies stated for this module:

Activity 1
Attend a seminar for orientation to this module.

Activity 2

As Durkin points out in her article, readiness for beginning reading consists of a variety of abilities. In assessing each child's readiness, it is important for the teacher to understand those factors that contribute to success in beginning reading. Bond and Wagner identify four categories of factors that need to be considered in assessing readiness. Read the discussion of these readiness factors that follows (adapted from Bond and Wagner[3]), using these two questions as your purposes for reading:

1. Which abilities can the teacher most directly help children to develop?
2. Under what circumstances might two children have different combinations of the abilities described here, yet both be ready for reading nevertheless?

Readiness Factors

1. Intellectual development. The variation in mental ability among children will be reflected in their progress in beginning reading. It is important that the teacher provide for these mental ability differences by (1) using a variety of materials and procedures, and (2) fitting the length of the readiness program to the needs of the individual child.
2. Physical factors. Several specific physical factors are related to children's ability to succeed in the beginning reading program.
   a. Visual acuity. Clear vision is an important factor for children involved in the process of learning to read. If a child exhibits behavior which may indicate a vision problem, that child should be referred for a complete visual examination. In the classroom, the teacher will need to make seating and other adjustments to minimize the difficulties encountered by the child with a vision problem.
   b. Visual discrimination. When they enter school, children vary in their ability to detect likenesses and differences in letters and words. Because of the importance of visual discrimination in learning to read, it is necessary for the teacher to provide instruction in the development of visual discrimination skills for those children who need it, through the use of commercial readiness programs and a variety of teacher-prepared activities and materials.
   c. Auditory acuity. Children with hearing problems can encounter difficulty in learning to read. It is essential that the teacher

3. Guy L. Bond and Eva Bond Wagner, *Teaching the Child to Read*, 4th ed. (New York: Macmillan Company, 1966), pp. 25-48.

refer for a hearing test any child whose lack of attention and failure to understand suggests a hearing problem. The teacher should make certain that a child with a hearing problem fully understands directions and procedures so that the child's opportunities for learning are maximized.

d. Auditory discrimination. The ability to detect likenesses and differences in sounds as they occur in the beginning, medial, or ending positions in words is essential in learning to read. Since children differ in their ability to make the auditory discriminations necessary for reading, opportunities for developing these skills will need to be provided for some children. Both formal readiness programs and informal activities can be used by the teacher to help children in the sequential development of skills in auditory discrimination.

e. Speech problems. Children who have speech difficulties which appear to be the result of physical or emotional factors should be referred for diagnosis and treatment. Children with speech difficulties that have been learned (poor enunciation, inaccurate pronunciation) can be helped in speech improvement through the use of a tape recorder, and by having their attention focused on the speech they hear on radio and television. If they demonstrate readiness in other areas, children with speech problems should begin reading. The method used with them, however, should not emphasize oral reading.

f. Health problems. The child who evidences symptoms of poor health should be referred for examination and treatment. While the problems are being diagnosed and treated, the teacher must adjust the learning environment so that the demands placed on the child are not excessive.

3. Social and emotional development. Children entering school vary as to the level of social and emotional development they have reached. Some will need much more time to adjust to the new interpersonal relationships they face than will others. Opportunities for learning new skills can further the adjustment of such children by increasing their confidence in their ability to succeed.

4. Educational factors. Children differ in the extent to which they have acquired specific skills associated with success in beginning reading. Opportunities need to be provided that will enable each child to acquire the skills he or she does not have, and to further the child's growth in skills that have already begun to develop.

a. Interpreting pictures. Learning to "read" pictures for such purposes as finding details and determining sequence provides the foundation for the development of comprehension skills in beginning reading.

b. Establishing a left-to-right orientation. Children must develop the habit of looking at material from left to right before they encounter experiences in reading.

c. Extending vocabulary and experiential background. By using concrete experiences and a wide range of materials, the teacher can help children develop the concepts and vocabulary necessary for understanding what they read.

d. Increasing the ability to use oral language. As they are provided with a variety of opportunities to express themselves, children can be helped to increase their ability to use sentences effectively and, through the development of this skill, to increase their ability to comprehend what they read.

e. Developing skill in recalling sequence and in following directions. The ability to recall a sequence of events is essential to an understanding of what is read. Skill in following a sequence of directions is necessary for working with the variety of materials the child encounters in the beginning reading program. These skills can be developed through providing classroom activities in which remembering sequence and following directions are necessary for the completion of a task.

f. Using classroom materials. Many children enter school having had previous experiences in using such classroom materials as books, paper, pencils, and scissors. Others, however, who have had limited prior experiences or who lack the necessary coordination, will need many and varied opportunities for learning to work with these materials effectively.

Read one or more of the following discussions of readiness and the factors related to it. Compare each with the material presented in this activity (2). Is there general agreement concerning the factors related to readiness for reading?

Smith, Nila B. *Reading Instruction for Today's Children.* Pt. 4, "Beginning Reading Instruction." Englewood Cliffs, N. J.: Prentice-Hall, 1965.

Spache, George D., and Spache, Evelyn B. *Reading in the Elementary School.* 4th ed. Chap. 6, "Readiness and Reading for Young Children." Boston: Allyn & Bacon, 1977.

Stauffer, Russell G. *Teaching Reading as a Thinking Process.* Chap. 7, "Readiness for Reading." New York: Harper & Row, Publishers, 1969.

Tinker, Miles A., and McCullough, Constance M. *Teaching Elementary Reading.* 3d ed. Chap. 4, "Getting Ready to Read." New York: Appleton-Century-Crofts, 1968.

Activity 3

One means of assessing a child's readiness for reading is through the use of standardized reading readiness tests. Each test has several subtests which are designed to measure abilities which contribute to success in beginning reading. A comparison of the subtests of four widely used readiness tests is presented in table 1.1. Which abilities are measured by all tests? How much range is there in the number of subtests provided by each test?

Although standardized readiness tests are widely used, many limitations of these tests have been identified. Several of these limitations are discussed by Spache and Spache:

> There are several basic limitations in the use of most reading readiness tests. First, most tests are limited in the sampling of abilities they include. Some measure only auditory vocabulary; others omit any evaluation of such significant factors as visual or auditory discrimination, articulation, or auditory comprehension. A second common limitation in readiness tests is the tendency to depend upon measures of preschool learning such as matching or even reading words and letters. Because of this content, many readiness tests are not much more than concealed measures of intelligence determined by sampling the child's preschool learning. Finally, most readiness tests do not yield very accurate predictions of later reading success. Their correlations with reading are usually about 0.5 or 0.6, a relationship which gives a prediction 25 to 30 percent better than sheer chance. Is it surprising that careful teacher observation and judgment often yield predictions just as accurate as any readiness test?[4]

In their discussion of readiness tests, Harris and Sipay identify additional limitations:

> . . . readiness tests do not measure all of the factors associated with success in learning to read. Although correlations between total readiness test scores and reading scores at the end of first grade are high enough to allow good prediction for a group, they are not high enough to allow accurate predictions for individuals. These two facts indicate that a high degree of faith should not be placed in readiness test scores when making decisions about individuals.
>
> Not all reading readiness tests are equally valid in predicting success in reading, nor are they equally reliable. Furthermore, it is quite possible that two subtests which supposedly measure the same skill (e.g., auditory discrimination) in fact measure different skills. Selecting the best test for a

---

4. George D. Spache and Evelyn B. Spache, *Reading in the Elementary School,* 3d ed. (Boston: Allyn & Bacon, 1973), pp. 78-79.

Table 1.1

A Comparison of the Abilities Measured by Subtests of Selected Reading Readiness Tests.

	Visual Discrimination	Auditory Discrimination	Shape Completion	Word Meaning	Using Information	Listening Comprehension	Following Instructions	Sentence Copying	Letter Recognition
Clymer-Barrett Prereading Battery (Princeton, N. J.: Personnel Press, 1969)	X	X	X					X	X
Metropolitan Readiness Test (New York: Harcourt, Brace and World, 1966)	X			X	X				
Murphy-Durrell Diagnostic Reading Readiness Tests (New York: Harcourt, Brace and World, 1964)	X	X							
Gates-MacGinitie Reading Tests: Readiness Skills (New York: Teachers College Press, Columbia University, 1966)	X	X				X	X		X

particular school involves careful study and tryout. Some readiness tests provide only a total score while others provide separate norms for each part of the test. The latter procedure is preferable because, although the subtests are usually not highly reliable, an examination of each child's performance on the subtests should assist the teacher in determining if he shows particular strengths and weaknesses.[5]

Because of the limitations of readiness tests, it is important for the teacher to exercise caution in interpreting and using test results. The results of readiness testing can be used effectively if they are viewed as providing *one* source of information in diagnosing children's needs and planning appropriate learning experiences.

The readiness test items reproduced in figure 1.1 illustrate the ways in which three abilities are measured by subtests of the *Gates-MacGinitie Reading Tests: Readiness Skills* (New York: Teachers College Press, Columbia University, 1966).

It is possible for the same ability to be measured in different ways on different readiness tests. Select a specific readiness ability from table 1.1 and compare the way it is measured on two or more tests (specimen sets of tests can often be found in the college library or instructional materials center). How is the child asked to demonstrate his mastery of the ability on each test?

Activity 4

Standardized readiness tests do not measure the wide range of abilities discussed in activity 2. For this reason, teachers use a variety of informal measures to obtain additional information concerning each child. By observing the child's interaction with others, his use of language and his response to the materials and activities presented him, the teacher can gain much information that will be useful in assessing the child's readiness for reading. Teachers often find it helpful to record this information on a readiness checklist or inventory. The readiness inventory shown in figure 1.2 and the readiness checklist shown in figure 1.3 represent two types of readiness inventories. Analyze them using the following questions:

1. In what ways are the inventories alike?
2. In what ways do they differ?
3. Which inventory would you prefer to use?
4. Is there a way in which you could take parts of each inventory and combine them to develop another inventory?

5. Albert J. Harris and Edward R. Sipay, *Effective Teaching of Reading*, 2d ed. (New York: David McKay Company, 1971), pp. 37-38.

FIGURE 1.1.

Item A: Auditory discrimination. In this item, the teacher names both pictures (MAIL-NAIL) and then instructs the child to "Put an X on MAIL."

Item B: Visual discrimination. The teacher tells the child that three of the words in each line are alike. The child is to put an X on the word that is different.

Item C: Following directions. In this item, the child is instructed to "Put an X on the tall girl who is wearing a hat and another X on the little girl who doesn't have any hat."

Reproduced from the *Gates-MacGinitie Reading Tests: Readiness Skills* (New York: Teachers College Press, Columbia University, 1966) by permission of the publisher.

Item A

Item B

food	foot	food	food
held	held	cold	held
real	rest	real	real
hit	hat	hat	hat

Item C

Informal Readiness Inventory

FIGURE 1.2. Informal Readiness Inventory. From George D. Spache, *Toward Better Reading* (Champaign, Illinois: Garrard Publishing Co., 1963), p. 15. By permission of the publisher.

	Poor	Average	Good
Vision			
Binocular visual acuity, near			
Binocular visual acuity, far			
Binocular coordination			
Shift focus easily			
Free from symptoms of strain			
Color vision			
Coordination in cutting and drawing			
Visual discrimination			
Hearing			
Acuity			
Discrimination among sounds			
Speech			
Articulation of common sounds			
Free from stuttering or lipsing			
Free from monotony or high-pitch			
General Health			
General responsiveness			
Large muscle coordination			
Free from undue fatigue			
Nutritional status			
Social and Emotional Readiness			
Feelings of adequacy and security			
Cooperation with group			
Ability to lead or follow			
Acceptance of authority			
Free from infantile behaviors			
Language Readiness			
Fluency and choice of words			
Skill in conversation and with audience			
Breadth of verbal concepts			
Listening			
Ability to attend and recall			
Following of directions			
Follow sequence of story			
Mental Readiness			
Attention span			
Interest in signs and symbols			
Independent work habits			
Care of self and materials			

FIGURE 1.3 From *Manual for Teaching the Reading-Readiness Program* of THE GINN BASIC READERS, REV. ED., by David H. Russell and others, © Copyright, 1957, 1953, 1948, by Ginn and Company (Xerox Corporation). Used with permission.

Checklist for Reading Readiness

Physical Readiness

	Yes	No

1. Eyes:
   a. Do the child's seem comfortable? (Does he squint, rub eyes, hold material too close or too far away from eyes?) _____ _____
   b. Are the results of clinical test or an oculist's examination favorable? _____ _____
2. Ears:
   a. Does he respond to questions or directions, and is he apparently able to hear what is said in class? _____ _____
   b. Does he respond to low-voice test of twenty feet, a whisper test of fifteen inches? _____ _____
   c. Is his audiometer test normal? _____ _____
3. Speech:
   a. Does he speak clearly and well? _____ _____
   b. Does he respond to correction readily? _____ _____
4. Hand-eye coordination:
   a. Does he make his hands work together well in cutting, using tools, or bouncing a ball? _____ _____
5. General health:
   a. Does he give an impression of good health? _____ _____
   b. Does he seem well nourished? _____ _____
   c. Does the school physical examination reveal good health? _____ _____

Social Readiness

1. Cooperation
   a. Does he work well with a group, taking his share of the responsibility?
   b. Does he cooperate with the other children in playing games? _____ _____
2. Sharing:
   a. Does he share materials without monopolizing their use? _____ _____
   b. Does he share his home toys with others? _____ _____
   c. Does he wait his turn in play or games? _____ _____
   d. Does he await his turn when classwork is being checked by the teacher? _____ _____
3. Self-reliance:
   a. Does he work things through for himself? _____ _____
   b. Does he work without asking teacher about the next step? _____ _____
   c. Does he take care of his clothing and materials? _____ _____
   d. Does he find anything to do when he finishes an assigned task? _____ _____
4. Good listening:
   a. Is he attentive?
   b. Does he listen rather than interrupt? _____ _____

c. Does he listen to all of a story with evident enjoyment so that he can re-tell all or part of it? _____ _____
d. Can he follow simple directions? _____ _____
5. General:
a. Does he take good care of materials assigned to him? _____ _____
b. Does he follow adult leadership without objection or show resentment? _____ _____
c. Does he alter his own methods to profit by an example set by another child? _____ _____

Emotional Readiness

1. Adjustment to task:
a. Does the child see a task (such as drawing, preparing for an activity, or cleaning up) through to completion? _____ _____
b. Does he accept changes in school routine calmly?
c. Does he appear to be happy and well adjusted in school work, as evidenced by good attendance, relaxed attitude, pride in work, eagerness for a new task? _____ _____
2. Poise:
a. Does he accept a certain amount of opposition without crying or sulking? _____ _____
b. Can he meet strangers without unusual shyness? _____ _____

Psychological Readiness

1. Mind set for reading:
a. Does the child appear interested in books and reading? _____ _____
b. Does he ask the meanings of words or signs? _____ _____
c. Is he interested in the shapes of unusual words? _____ _____
2. a. Does the child's mental test show him sufficiently mature to begin reading? _____ _____
b. Can he give reason for his opinions about work of others or his work? _____ _____
c. Can he draw something to demonstrate an idea as well as children of his own age? _____ _____
d. Is his memory span sufficient to allow memorization of a short poem or song? _____ _____
e. Can he tell a story without confusing the order of events? _____ _____
f. Can he listen or work an average length of time without restlessness? _____ _____
g. Can he dramatize a story imaginatively? _____ _____
3. Mental habits:
a. Has the child established the habit of looking at a succession of items from left to right? _____ _____
b. Does he interpret pictures? _____ _____

FIGURE 1.3. Continued.

  c. Does he grasp the fact that symbols may be associated with pictures or subjects? ————— —————

  d. Can he anticipate what may happen in a story or poem? ————— —————

  e. Can he remember the central thought as well as important details? ————— —————

4. Language:

  a. Does he speak clearly? ————— —————

  b. Does he speak correctly after being helped with a difficulty by the teacher? ————— —————

  c. Does he speak in sentences? ————— —————

  d. Does he know the meaning of words that occur in preprimers and primers? ————— —————

  e. Does he know certain related words such as up and down, top and bottom, big and little? ————— —————

The following references contain additional examples of readiness inventories. Compare these inventories with those in figures 1.2 and 1.3.

Harris, Albert J., and Sipay, Edward R. *Effective Teaching of Reading.* 2d ed. Chap. 2, "Readiness for Learning to Read," p. 43. New York: David McKay Company, 1971.

Spache, George D., and Spache, Evelyn B. *Reading In The Elementary School.* 4th ed. Chap. 6, "Readiness and Reading for Young Children," p. 168. Boston: Allyn & Bacon, 1977.

Activity 5

Included in each basal reading series (a set of books and related materials designed to be used for teaching reading skills at successive levels of development) is a workbook or set of activities for developing readiness skills. Each workbook focuses on the sequential development of those specific skills needed for beginning reading in the series to which it belongs. The exercises shown in figures 1.4 and 1.5 are illustrative of the types of activities provided for children in the readiness workbooks of two basal reading series.

Examine the readiness workbooks of several basal reading series, using the following questions:

1. Which skills are developed in all the workbooks?

2. Are certain skills emphasized more in one workbook than in others?

Select one skill (e.g., visual discrimination, auditory discrimination, language development, etc.) and follow the sequential development of it

EXERCISE A

EXERCISE B

FIGURE 1.4.
Visual discrimination. From *Something Special,* Teacher's Edition Kindergarten by Katherine B. Wingert and Barbara Ann Pearson. Copyright © 1976 by Scott, Foresman and Company. Pp. 6, 41. Reprinted by permission of the publisher.

In Exercise A the children are asked to identify the objects in the first row and to describe them using as many attributes as they can (shape, taste, etc.). The teacher then explains that three of the objects are alike in some way and that one is different. The children decide which object does not belong in the group and place an X on it. This procedure is repeated with the second and third rows. In Exercise B the children discriminate between letter forms; this requires a finer degree of discrimination than is needed for Exercise A. The children's attention is directed to the first box and they are asked to identify the capital letter on the T-shirt the child is wearing. They are then asked to look at the other letters in this box and to point to the letter that is just like the capital letter on the T-shirt. The children circle this letter. This procedure is repeated with the other boxes on the page, moving from left to right.

Readiness for Beginning Reading Instruction

FIGURE 1.5.
Listening for beginning sounds; making letter-sound associations. From M. Lucile Harrison, William K. Durr, and Paul McKee, *Getting Ready to Read,* Teacher's Edition (Boston: Houghton Mifflin Company, 1974), pp. 10, 12. Reproduced by permission of the publisher.

In Exercise A the children are helped to differentiate beginning sounds. The teacher says *fish, fork* as he points to the first two pictures in the long box. The children are told to notice that both words begin with the same sound. Next the teacher says *fish, fork* and *fairy* and asks the children what they can tell him about the way the words begin. After the four pictures in the box have been identified in this way, the children are asked to find other objects on the page having names that begin with /f/ (the sound that the letter f stands for). In Exercise B the teacher identifies the small f and the capital F with the children and reminds them that the picture of the fish with the f will help them remember the sound that f stands for. As they name the pictures in each box, the children decide whether the name begins with the sound that the letter f stands for.

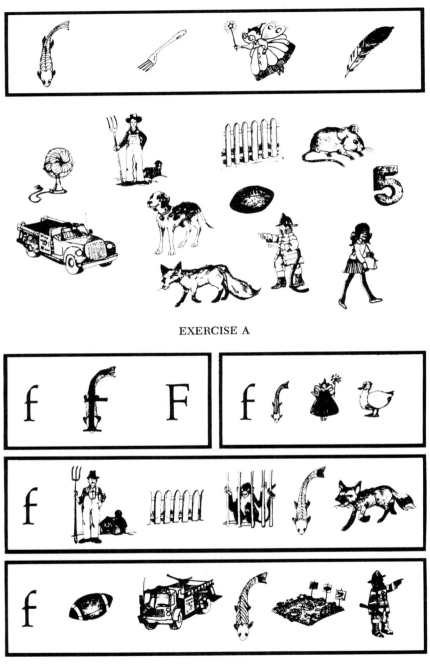

EXERCISE A

EXERCISE B

throughout one workbook. On the form shown in figure 1.6, record several exercises that illustrate this sequential development.

Activity 6

Much of the readiness program consists of materials and activities developed by the teacher. These learning experiences are used to (1) provide background for activities children will encounter in the readiness workbook; (2) reinforce workbook activities; and (3) develop skills in those areas that are not included in the readiness workbook. The following activities are illustrative of the variety of activities that can be provided:

Visual Discrimination

Collect pictures which contain various fundamental shapes. Mount these on oaktag or stiff paper. Children will enjoy observing closely to see how many squares, circles or other shapes can be found in each picture.[6]

A large tree is made from colored paper. In the green section of the tree cut small slits. Make lollipops by attaching colored circles to wooden sticks. On one side of the lollipops print letters of the alphabet. The children take turns picking lollipops from the tree. If they can name the letter on the back, they get to keep the lollipop. The child with the most lollipops wins.[7]

Auditory Discrimination

The group closes their eyes and listens while the teacher or another child does the following: (1) tears paper, (2) crumples paper, (3) bounces a ball, (4) taps table with pencil. Children try to discriminate what is being done.[8]

Vocabulary Development

Having children draw pictures illustrating such "new words" as *funnel, burrow, tractor.*[9]

Taking children on excursions and helping them become familiar with terms that give more meaning to their trip, like *cash register, sales, customer.*[10]

Introducing songs and poems that contain new words.[11]

---

6. Evelyn Spache, *Reading Activities for Child Involvement* (Boston: Allyn & Bacon, 1972), p. 29.
7. Ibid., p. 33.
8. Ibid., p. 37.
9. Martha Dallmann, Roger L. Rouch, Lynette Y. C. Chang, and John J. DeBoer, *The Teaching of Reading*, 4th ed. (New York: Holt, Rinehart and Winston, 1974), p. 84.
10. Ibid., p. 85.
11. Ibid.

FIGURE 1.6.

Readiness Skill Development

Name _____ Date _____

Name and publisher of series _____

Title of readiness workbook _____

Readiness skill selected _____

Describe briefly several exercises that illustrate the sequential development of the readiness skill you selected:

Recalling Sequence

After the teacher or a pupil has told a story, the teacher may ask such questions as: "What was the first thing Nancy did when she saw that her dog had followed her?" "What did she do next?"[12]

The teacher might place on a flannel board, in mixed-up order, a series of pictures illustrating a story known to the boys and girls and then ask the pupils to rearrange the pictures in correct order.[13]

Develop a lesson for teaching a readiness skill in any of the areas discussed in this module. Teach the lesson to a group of children who are involved in a readiness program or to a group of peers. You may find it helpful to use the Lesson Plan Format shown in figure 1.7.

The following references are excellent sources of ideas for activities:

Dallmann, Martha; Rouch, Roger L.; Chang, Lynette Y. C.; and DeBoer, John J. *The Teaching of Reading.* 4th ed. Chap. 4B, "Developing Readiness for Reading." New York: Holt, Rinehart and Winston, 1974.

Russell, David H., and Karp, Etta E. *Reading Aids Through the Grades.* Second Revised Edition by Anne Marie Mueser. Section 2, "Reading Readiness Activities." New York: Teachers College Press, Columbia University, 1975.

Smith, Nila Banton. *Reading Instruction for Today's Children.* Chap. 18, "Preparing and Using Experience Charts." Englewood Cliffs, N. J.: Prentice-Hall, 1963.

Spache, Evelyn B. *Reading Activities for Child Involvement.* Chap. 2, "Reading Readiness." Boston: Allyn & Bacon, 1972.

Activity 7

The following lesson plan illustrates the way in which teacher-prepared activities and materials can contribute to the development of readiness skills. Read the plan using the following questions as a guide:

1. Which readiness skill is being developed?
2. Why do you think the student who developed this lesson decided to use comic strips?
3. What value is there in having the children tell their stories to others in the group?
4. What additional activities might be used to further the development of this skill?

12. Ibid., p. 90.
13. Ibid., p. 91.

FIGURE 1.7.

Lesson Plan Format

Name   Date

Module   Activity no.

Level   Size of group

    I. Behavioral Objectives

   II. Procedure

      A. Introduction

      B. Development

      C. Conclusion

  III. Evaluation

I. Behavioral Objective

The students will be able to place a series of pictures in a logical sequence.

II. Procedure

A. Introduction
1. How many of you read the comic strips in the newspaper?
2. What are some of your favorite comics?
3. Today, boys and girls, we are going to make some of these comic strips.
B. Development
1. Show students a sample of one comic strip that has been cut apart into individual picture panels.
2. I'm going to give each of you a package of pictures. When you get your package, lay the pictures down and spread them out. Then look at the pictures and decide which picture shows what happened first, which picture shows what happened next (and so on).
3. Have each student paper clip his pictures on oaktag in the sequence he has decided on. Note: paper clips are used so that the comic strips may be reused.
C. Conclusion
1. Have each child who wants to, come up to the front of the class and tell a story that will explain his sequence of pictures.
2. After the preceding activity is complete: Now, when you go home tonight, look through your favorite comic strips and have Mommy or Daddy cut them out for you and bring them to school tomorrow and maybe we'll make some others.

III. Evaluation

If the students are able to present a story in a logical sequence, the objective will be met.

Activity 8

Observe one or more lessons in developing readiness skills. Use the following questions as your guide:

1. Which readiness skill is the focus of the lesson?
2. How does the teacher provide for individual differences as the lesson progresses?
3. Through what means is the teacher able to evaluate each child's acquisition of the skill (oral responses, completion of a worksheet, etc.)?

Activity 9

In making decisions concerning children's readiness for reading, it is important that the teacher evaluate carefully each child's pattern of development in the abilities discussed in this module. Read the following description of the way in which a teacher evaluated one child's strengths and limitations in order to reach a decision regarding his readiness for reading. Do you agree with the teacher's decision?

> One child, for example, may seem, in comparison with the class as a whole, to be advanced in such things as background of experience, ability to handle equipment, ability to follow directions, and mental age, but he may actually have trouble expressing himself. Perhaps he comes from a home where a foreign language is spoken. His linguistic patterns may be poor. The teacher, after weighing these facts, may plan to start book reading with him because he is nevertheless high in many other fundamental factors. The teacher recognizes, however, that instruction must go rather cautiously and that much attention must be given to the development of his oral language. Thus, for this child, instruction in book reading must proceed slowly. Many opportunities must be given him to talk about his reading experiences so that his linguistic capabilities may be improved. The reading experience provides excellent opportunities for the development in language to proceed rather rapidly. Consequently, this boy should receive oral-language instruction as reading instruction progresses.[14]

Activity 10

Design activities of your own that will enable you to achieve the competencies stated for this module.

---

14. Bond and Wagner, *Teaching the Child to Read*, p. 52.

Preassessment and Postassessment

A. Knowledge level

1. Describe the relationship to readiness for beginning reading of one factor in each of the following categories: social and emotional, intellectual, physical, and educational.

   Criteria for successful performance:
   a) the relationship to readiness for beginning reading of each factor is accurately described;
   b) each factor is correctly identified with the appropriate category.

2. Identify two ways in which formal and informal measures of readiness differ. Give one example of a formal measure and one example of an informal measure.

   Criteria for successful performance:
   a) formal and informal measures of readiness are accurately differentiated in two ways;
   b) both examples given are correct.

3. Read the following case studies. Each one provides information concerning the background and development of one child. Decide, for each child, whether he is ready to begin formal reading instruction or needs additional readiness activities. State the reasons for your decisions.

   Criteria for successful performance:
   a) each decision is defensible;
   b) the reasons given adequately support each decision.

Robin

Robin appears to have had only limited opportunities for developing experiential background during her preschool years. She seldom contributes to discussions. When the teacher is reading to the class, Robin finds it difficult to sit and listen for more than a brief time, but she enjoys interacting with the other children in physical activities. She is well coordinated. Intelligence test results indicate that her mental ability is above average.

David

Because some aspects of David's behavior indicated the possibility of a vision problem, he was given a complete eye examination. He now wears glasses, and the earlier symptoms are no longer apparent. In informal activities with other children, David finds it difficult to share, and often cries when he can't have his own way. David is highly successful in any activity which focuses on auditory discrimination. He enjoys looking at books and talking about stories the teacher has read. He often brings his own books to school. His mental ability is average.

B. Performance level
  1. Planning the lesson
    a) Plan lessons for two activities which will contribute to the development of two specific readiness skills. Design your own materials for these activities.
    b) Criteria for successful performance:
      (1) the objectives are stated in terms of pupil behavior;
      (2) the instructional procedures are developed in ways that are appropriate for the skill being taught;
      (3) the material is appropriate for the skill being taught;
      (4) the procedures for the evaluation of pupil achievement are identified.

  2. Teaching the lesson
    a) Arrange to teach the lessons to small groups of children. When you teach the lessons, either
      (1) have the instructor or cooperating teacher observe, or
      (2) tape the lessons.
    b) Criteria for successful performance:
      (1) there is evidence that the pupils have achieved the objectives;
      (2) the student has demonstrated the ability to adapt his teaching procedures, as necessary, in response to pupil needs during the lesson.

  3. Evaluating the lesson
    a) After the lessons have been taught, write an evaluation of each one. Respond to the following questions in your evaluations.
      (1) Did the pupils achieve the objectives? Support your answer with specific evidence.
      (2) If there were pupils who did not achieve the objectives, can you identify the experiences they still need in order to reach the objectives?
      (3) Are there elements of the lesson you would approach differently if you were to teach that lesson again?
    b) Follow one of these procedures:
      (1) If the instructor has observed the lessons, schedule a conference to discuss both plans and lessons.
      (2) If the cooperating teacher has observed the lessons, ask for written evaluations and then schedule a conference with the instructor to discuss the plans, the lessons, and the cooperating teacher's evaluations.
      (3) If the lessons have been taped, schedule a conference with the instructor to discuss the plans and the taped lessons.

References

Bond, Guy L., and Wagner, Eva Bond. *Teaching the Child to Read*. 4th ed. Chap. 2, "Preparing the Child for Instruction." New York: Macmillan Company, 1966.

Bush, Clifford L., and Huebner, Mildred H. *Strategies for Reading in the Elementary School*. Chap. 3, "Readiness for Reading." New York: Macmillan Company, 1970.

Dallmann, Martha; Rouch, Roger L.; Chang, Lynette Y. C.; and DeBoer, John J. *The Teaching of Reading*. 4th ed. Chap. 4A, "Readiness for Reading"; chap. 4B, "Developing Readiness for Reading." New York: Holt, Rinehart and Winston, 1974.

Durkin, Dolores. *Teaching Them to Read*. 2d ed. Chap. 4, "Readiness for Reading"; chap. 6, "Preschool Reading"; chap. 7, "Reading in the Kindergarten." Boston: Allyn & Bacon, 1974.

Harris, Albert J., and Sipay, Edward R. *Effective Teaching of Reading*. 2d ed. Chap. 2, "Readiness for Learning to Read." New York: David McKay Company, 1971.

————. *How to Increase Reading Ability*. 6th ed. Chap. 2, "Readiness for Reading." New York: David McKay Company, 1975.

Heilman, Arthur W. *Principles and Practices of Teaching Reading*. 3d ed. Chap. 4, "Assessing and Developing Readiness for Reading." Columbus, Ohio: Charles E. Merrill Publishing Company, 1972.

Herr, Selma E. *Learning Activities for Reading*. 2d ed. Chap. 38, "Reading Readiness." Dubuque, Iowa: Wm. C. Brown Company Publishers, 1970.

May, Frank B. *To Help Children Read*. Module 7, "Getting Children Ready to Read." Columbus, Ohio: Charles E. Merrill Publishing Company, 1973.

Otto, Wayne; Chester, Robert; McNeil, John; and Myers, Shirley. *Focused Reading Instruction*. Chap. 5, "Prerequisites to Reading." Reading, Mass.: Addison-Wesley Publishing Company, 1974.

Russell, David H. *Children Learn to Read*. 2d ed. Chap. 6, "The Readiness Program." Waltham, Mass.: Blaisdell Publishing Company, 1961.

Russell, David H., and Karp, Etta E. *Reading Aids Through the Grades*. Second revised edition by Anne Marie Mueser. Chap. 2, "The Readiness Program." New York: Teachers College Press, Columbia University, 1975.

Shankman, Florence. *Games and Activities to Reinforce Reading Skills*. New York: MSS Information Corporation, 1972.

Smith, James A. *Creative Teaching of Reading in the Elementary School*. 2d ed. Chap. 5, "The Creative Teaching of Beginning Reading in the Primary Grades." Boston: Allyn & Bacon, 1975.

Smith, Nila Banton. *Reading Instruction for Today's Children*. Chap. 15, "Changing Concepts of Beginning Reading"; chap. 16, "Appraising Beginning Reading Maturity"; chap. 17, "Laying Skill Foundations in Kindergarten and First Grade"; chap. 18, "Preparing and Using Experience Charts." Englewood Cliffs, N. J.: Prentice-Hall, 1965.

Spache, Evelyn B. *Reading Activities for Child Involvement*. Chap. 2, "Reading Readiness." Boston: Allyn & Bacon, 1972.

Spache, George D., and Spache, Evelyn B. *Reading in the Elementary School*. 4th ed. Chap. 6, "Readiness and Reading for Young Children"; chap. 7, "Readiness Training." Boston: Allyn & Bacon, 1977.

Stauffer, Russell G. *Teaching Reading as a Thinking Process*. Chap. 7, "Readiness for Reading." New York: Harper & Row, Publishers, 1969.

Tinker, Miles A., and McCullough, Constance M. *Teaching Elementary Reading*. 3d ed. Chap. 4, "Getting Ready to Read." New York: Appleton-Century-Crofts, 1968.

Walcutt, Charles C.; Lamport, Joan; and McCracken, Glenn. *Teaching Reading*. Chap. 10, "Methods of Evaluation"; chap. 11, "The Kindergarten Year." New York: Macmillan Company, 1974.

Wallen, Carl J. *Competency in Teaching Reading.* Chap. 4, "Testing strategies for word-attack readiness: discrimination skills"; chap. 5, "Teaching strategies for word-attack readiness: discrimination skills." Chicago: Science Research Associates, 1972.

Zintz, Miles V. *The Reading Process: The Teacher and the Learner.* 2d ed. Chap. 8, "The Assessment of Prereading Skills." Dubuque, Iowa: Wm. C. Brown Company Publishers, 1975.

2

Approaches to Reading Instruction

Overview

The number of reading programs available to schools has increased dramatically in recent years. In his book, *Approaches to Beginning Reading*, Aukerman classifies one hundred or more programs under ten categories, each program representing an "approach" to the teaching of reading.[1] Because of the variation among programs in assumptions, materials, and methods of implementation, Aukerman contends that, "It is quite obvious . . . that it is not possible to conclude 'which one is best.' "[2] The current trend in selecting reading programs for school systems appears to support Aukerman's contention. Teachers, reading specialists, and administrators are selecting programs that are directed toward the needs of specific groups of children, rather than attempting to find the *one* program that will be best for all children. As a result, it is not uncommon to find a variety of reading programs being used within a single school system.

The foundation upon which every approach to teaching reading is based is a set of assumptions concerning the nature of the reading process. Before examining approaches to reading instruction, then, it is essential to consider the basic question, "What is reading?" Clymer points out the relationship between the teacher's definition of reading and his reading program:

> A clear concept of reading is not just an academic concern. The teacher's definition of reading influences every action he takes in his reading program.

1. Robert C. Aukerman, *Approaches to Beginning Reading* (New York: John Wiley and Sons, 1971).
2. Ibid., p. 5.

In addition, if the teacher lacks a clear idea of what reading is, he cannot know when his students have attained the goals of the instructional program.[3]

In order to help you develop a concept of reading, the module is introduced through John B. Carroll's article, "The Nature of the Reading Process."[4] Carroll describes the dimensions of the reading process as they function for the mature reader. He then identifies the components of learning to read that must be acquired by children in order to develop mature reading ability. The controversy about how reading should be taught is, according to Carroll, a disagreement about the order in which skills should be introduced. He identifies two main points of view regarding this disagreement, and then suggests that a third approach currently exists. In his conclusion, Carroll lists what he considers to be the most important questions and problems that still confront us in our attempts to understand more precisely the nature of the reading process. Use the following questions as your purposes for reading Carroll's article:

1. How do the eyes function during the reading process?
2. How does the process of comprehension appear to influence eye movements during reading?
3. What does Carroll consider to be the *essential* skill in reading?
4. What components of reading skill does Carroll identify?
5. What positions does Carroll identify regarding the order in which reading skills should be introduced?
6. What questions concerning the ordering of the components of reading skill does Carroll suggest need be answered?

3. Theodore Clymer, "What Is 'Reading'?" *Teachers' Edition, for The Dog Next Door and Other Stories* of the READING 360 series by Theodore Clymer and others (Lexington, Mass.: Ginn and Company, Xerox Corporation, 1969), p. 8.
4. John B. Carroll, "The Nature of the Reading Process," in *Theoretical Models and Processes of Reading*, ed. Harry Singer and Robert B. Ruddell (Newark, Del.: International Reading Association, 1970), pp. 292-303.

The Nature of the Reading Process

John B. Carroll
Educational Testing Service
Princeton, New Jersey

As you silently read this very paragraph, what are you doing? If you are a skilled reader and are attending carefully to what this paragraph is trying to say, you will notice the following. First, what are your eyes doing? Moving together in a swift and well-coordinated way, your eyes are making a series of fixations, jumping from place to place on the page of print. The jumps are exceedingly rapid; you see little while your eyes are jumping. What is important are the fixations, when your eyes come to rest. Most of these fixations are actually on or close to the line of print, but unless you are reading quite slowly you cannot easily predict or control where your eyes will fixate. The fixations are usually quite short in duration; each one will last about one-quarter of a second on the average.

Usually the fixations progress from left to right along the first line of print, then back to the beginning of the next line and again from left to right across the line, and so on. For the average adult reader there will be about two fixations per inch of ordinary type like this. Some of these fixations may be very brief, amounting to minor adjustments in order to bring the print better into view. During most of the fixations, you receive an impression of a certain amount of printed material; that is, you instantaneously perceive and recognize one or more words, perhaps up to four or five in some cases. You are more likely to recognize the words that are in the immediate area of fixation; words outside this immediate area may be less well recognized, but some of them have been recognized in a previous fixation, and others may be more clearly recognized in a future fixation. Some of the words may never be clearly recognized, but you apprehend enough of the stimulus to fill them in from the general drift of what you are reading.

Let us just think about this process of instantaneous word recognition. Most of the words you see are words you have seen many times before; even though in actuality they may be relatively rare, they are familiar enough to you to permit "instantaneous" recognition. Of course recognition is not really instantaneous; it takes a certain amount of time. Experiments in which words are exposed very briefly show that common words can be recognized quite accurately in less than 1/10 of a second; even words that are quite rare can be recognized with at least 50 percent accuracy in exposures of about 1/5 of a second. During the average fixation lasting 1/4 of a second it is often possible to take in several words. The point is that most words are recognized extremely rapidly. If you are a skilled reader you do not have to stop to figure out the pronunciation of a familiar word from its spelling; you are hardly conscious of the spelling at all. Still less do you attend to the particular phonetic values of the letters; in reading the word *women* it would scarcely occur to you to note that the

Prepared by the author for the Advisory Committee on Dyslexia and Related Reading Disorders. From John B. Carroll, "The Nature of the Reading Process," in *Theoretical Models and Processes of Reading*, ed. Harry Singer and Robert B. Ruddell (Newark, Del.: International Reading Association, 1970), pp. 292-303. Reprinted with permission of John B. Carroll and the International Reading Association.

Approaches to Reading Instruction

"o" in the first syllable stands for a sound that rhymes with /i/ in *whim.* The printed word *women* is a gestalt-like total stimulus that immediately calls to mind the spoken word that corresponds to it—or if not the spoken word itself, some underlying response which is also made when the word is spoken. As a skilled reader, you can consider yourself lucky to have a large "sight" vocabulary.

The actual process by which we recognize words is not well understood, simply because the whole process of "pattern perception," as it is called, is one of the most mysterious problems in psychology. How, for example, do we recognize a table, a goblet, or a flagpole for what it is, regardless of the angle of regard? Nevertheless, it is a simple fact that we *can* learn to recognize words even though the words may be printed in different typefaces or written in different cursive styles, and in different sizes. Now even though word recognition is rapid, it obviously depends to a large extent on cues from the letters composing the word. There is little confusion among such highly similar items as *cob, rob, mob,* and *nob* even in fast single exposures. We do know that in recognizing longer words, the letters standing at the beginning and end are more critical than letters in the middle, for in fast exposures these middle letters can sometimes be altered or replaced without this being noticed by the reader. In ordinary reading we frequently fail to notice words that contain printer's errors. But there is little evidence to support the idea that a mature reader recognizes words merely by their outlines or general shape. It is unlikely that if you see the shape ⬡ you will recognize the word *dog;* you might just as well think it to be *day* or *dug.* Beginning readers sometimes use mere shape cues in trying to recognize words, but they will be overwhelmed with confusion if they depend solely on such cues apart from the recognition of the letters themselves. In the mature reader the process

of rapid word recognition seems to depend upon his ability to integrate the information provided by the separate letters composing the word, some letters being more critical as cues than others. Because the recognizability of a word is apparently correlated rather highly with its frequency of use, word perception seems to be a skill that depends upon large amounts of practice and exposure.

Suppose, however, that the skilled reader comes to a word that he has never seen before, like *dossal, cunctation,* or *latescent,* or an unfamiliar proper name like *Vukmanovich* or *Sbarra.* Though the skilled reader can hardly be said to "recognize" a word he has never seen before, he nevertheless recognizes elements of it—letters and patterns of letters that give him reasonably good cues as to how the word should be pronounced. *Dossal* may be recognized as similar to *fossil* and pronounced to rhyme with it, the first letter cuing the /f/ sound. *Cunctation* may give a little more difficulty but be recognized as somewhat similar to *punctuation* and at the same time to *mutation;* by following the total pattern of cues the reader may be able to infer the correct pronunciation. *Latescent* will probably be recognized not as a compound of *late* and *scent,* but as a member of a family of words like *quiescent, fluorescent,* etc. Somewhat the same principles apply to the reading of foreign proper names; even if he is not familiar with the foreign language involved, the skilled reader will be sensitive to the possible values of the letters and letter-combinations in the name, and come up with a reasonable pronunciation.

It should be noted that thus far we have been speaking of the recognition of words as particular combinations of letters. Actually, in English there are numerous instances of homographs—words that are pronounced in different ways depending on their use. The word "read" is an interesting example: in the context *to read* it rhymes with *bead,* but in the context *to have read,* it rhymes with *bed.* The skilled reader instantaneously interprets the word in its proper "reading" or pronunciation depending upon the context—i.e., the surrounding words and their meanings.

This takes us, in fact, to the next stage of our analysis of the reading process. As you take in material recognized in the succession of rapid fixations that is characteristic of skilled reading, it somehow merges together in such a way as to build up in your mind an impression of a meaningful message—a message that is in many ways analogous to the message you would apprehend if someone read the paragraph aloud to you, with all its proper inflections and accents. Some people report that as they read they can "hear" (in the form of internal auditory images) the message as it might be spoken; at least they report that they "hear" snatches of such a message. Other readers feel that they apprehend a meaning from the printed message directly—that is, without the intervention of any auditory images. In slow readers, or even in skilled readers reading very difficult material, one may notice slight articulatory movements that suggest that the reader is trying to pronounce the words subvocally.

The process of scanning a paragraph for a meaningful message does not, of course, always run smoothly. As one reads, there may be momentary lapses of attention (which can be due to lack of interest, distractions, or even stimulation from the content itself), or of comprehension (which can be due to the difficulty of the material, poor writing, or other conditions). The process of comprehension seems to have some influence on the movements of the eye: when the reader fails to attend or comprehend, his eyes may "regress," moving back to fixate on a portion of the material already scanned. Difficulties in recognizing particular words may cause the eyes to dwell on or around a particular point in the text longer than the usual amount of time. There are large differences among individuals in all the reading processes we have mentioned. Some readers can read with markedly fewer fixations per line; some read with an abnormally high number of fixations per line and exhibit many more regressions than normal. Few individuals have the same pattern of eye movements, even when they read at approximately the same speed. Obviously, there are wide individual differences in rate and accuracy of comprehension.

The *essential* skill in reading is getting meaning from a printed or written message. In many ways this is similar to getting meaning from a *spoken* message, but there are differences, because the cues are different. Spoken messages contain cues that are not evident in printed messages, and conversely. In either case, understanding language is itself a tremendous feat, when one thinks about it. When you get the meaning of a verbal message, you have not only recognized the words themselves; you have interpreted the words in their particular grammatical functions, and you have somehow apprehended the general grammatical patterning of each sentence. You have unconsciously recognized what words or phrases constitute the subjects and predicates of the sentence, what words or phrases modify those subjects or predicates, and so on. In addition, you have given a "semantic" interpretation of the sentence, assigning meanings to the key words in the sentence. For example, in reading the sentence "He understood that he was coming tonight" you would know to whom each "he" refers, and you would interpret the word *understood* as meaning "had been caused to believe" rather than "comprehended." Somehow you put all these things together in order to understand the "plain sense" of what the message says.

Even beyond getting the simple meaning of the material you are reading, you are probably reacting to it in numerous ways. You may be trying to evaluate it for its truth, validity, significance, or importance. You may be checking it against your own experience or knowledge. You may find that it is reminding you of previous thoughts or experiences, or you may be starting to think about its implications for your future actions. You may be making inferences or drawing conclusions from what you read that go far beyond what is explicitly stated in the text. In doing any or all of these things, you are "reasoning" or "thinking." Nobody can tell you exactly what to think; much of your thinking will be dependent upon your particular background and experience. At the same time, some thinking is logical and justified by the facts and ideas one reads, while other kinds of thinking are illogical and not adequately justified by the facts and ideas one reads. One aspect of a mature reader's skill consists in his being able to think about what he reads in a logical and well-informed way. This aspect of reading skill sometimes takes years to attain.

We have described the process of reading in the skilled reader—a process that is obviously very complex. How is this process learned or attained?

As in the case of any skill, reading skill is not learned all at once. It takes a considerable amount of time. Furthermore, the process of learning to read is *not* simply a slow motion imitation of the mature reading process. It has numerous components, and each component has to be learned and practiced.

There are probably a great many ways to attain reading skill, depending upon the order in which the various components are learned and mastered. It may be the case that some ways are always better than others. On the other hand, children differ in their aptitudes, talents, and inclinations so much that it may also be the case that a particular way of learning is better for one child while another way is better for another child. It all depends upon which components of reading skill a given

child finds easier to learn at a given stage of his development. In referring to different orders in which component skills would be learned, we do not mean to imply a lockstep procedure in which the child first learns and masters one skill, then goes on to learn and master another skill, and so on. Actually, a child can be learning a number of skills simultaneously, but will reach mastery of them at different periods in his development. From the standpoint of the teacher, this means that different skills may need to be emphasized at different periods, depending upon the characteristics of the individual child. This is particularly true in the case of the child who is having difficulty in learning to read.

Let us try to specify the components of reading skill. Some of these components come out of our analysis of the mature reading process; others out of a further analysis of *those* components.

1. *The child must know the language that he is going to learn to read.* Normally, this means that the child can speak and understand the language at least to a certain level of skill before he starts to learn to read, because the purpose of reading is to help him get messages from print that are similar to the messages he can already understand if they are spoken. But language learning is a lifelong process, and normally there are many aspects of language that the individual learns solely or mainly through reading. And speaking and understanding the language is not an absolute prerequisite for beginning to learn to read; there are cases on record of children who learn to read before they can speak, and of course many deaf children learn the language only through learning to read. Foreign-born children sometimes learn English mainly through reading. Children who, before they begin to read, do not know the language, or who only understand but do not speak, will

very likely require a mode of instruction specially adapted to them.

2. *The child must learn to dissect spoken words into component sounds.* In order to be able to use the alphabetic principle by which English words are spelled, he must be able to recognize the separate sounds composing a word and the temporal order in which they are spoken—the consonants and vowels that compose spoken words. This does not mean that he must acquire a precise knowledge of phonetics, but it does mean that he must recognize those aspects of speech sound that are likely to be represented in spelling. For example, in hearing the word *straight,* the child must be able to decompose the sounds into the sequence /s, t, r, ey, t/.

3. *The child must learn to recognize and discriminate the letters of the alphabet in their various forms (capitals, lower case letters, printed, and cursive).* (He should also know the names and alphabetic ordering of the letters.) This skill is required if the child is to make progress in finding correspondences between letters and sounds.

4. *The child must learn the left-to-right principle by which words are spelled and put in order in continuous text.* This is, as we have noted, a very general principle, although there are certain aspects of letter-sound correspondences that violate the principle—e.g., the reverse order of *wh* in representing the sound cluster /hw/.

5. *The child must learn that there are patterns of highly probable correspondence between letters and sounds, and he must learn those patterns of correspondence that will help him recognize words that he already knows in his spoken language or that will help him determine the pronunciation of unfamiliar words.* There are few if any letters in English orthography that always have the same sound values; nevertheless, spellings tend to give good clues to the pronunciation of words. Often a letter will have highly predictable sound values if it is considered in conjunction with surrounding letters. Partly through direct instruction and partly through a little-understood process of inference, the normal child can fairly readily acquire the ability to respond to these complex patterns of letter-sound correspondences.

6. *The child must learn to recognize printed words from whatever cues he can use—their total configuration, the letters composing them, the sounds represented by those letters, and/or the meanings suggested by the context.* By "recognition" we mean not only becoming aware that he has seen the word before, but also knowing the pronunciation of the word. This skill is one of the most essential in the reading process, because it yields for the reader the equivalent of a speech signal.

7. *The child must learn that printed words are signals for spoken words and that they have meanings analogous to those of spoken words. While decoding a printed message into its spoken equivalent, the child must be able to apprehend the meaning of the total message in the same way that he would apprehend the meaning of the corresponding spoken message.* As in the case of adult reading, the spoken equivalent may be apprehended solely internally, although it is usual, in early reading efforts, to expect the child to be able to read aloud, at first with much hesitation, but later with fluency and expression.

8. *The child must learn to reason and think about what he reads, within the limits of his talent and experience.*

It will be noticed that each of these eight components of learning to read is somehow involved in the adult reading process—knowing the language, dissecting spoken words into component sounds, and so forth. Adult reading is skilled only because all the eight components are so highly practiced that they merge together, as it were, into one unified performance. The well-coordinated, swift eye movements of the adult reader are a result, not a cause, of good reading; the child does not have to be *taught* eye movements and therefore we have not listed eye-coordination as a component skill. Rather, skilled eye movements represent the highest form of the skill we have listed as 4—the learning of the left-to-right principle. The instantaneous word recognition ability of the mature reader is the highest form of the skill we have listed as 6—recognition of printed words from whatever cues are available, and usually this skill in turn depends upon the mastery of some of the other skills, in particular 5—learning patterns of correspondence between letters and sounds. The ability of the adult reader to apprehend meaning quickly is an advanced form of skill 7, and his ability to think about what he reads is an advanced form of skill 8.

The "great debate" about how reading should be taught is really a debate about the *order* in which the child should be started on the road toward learning each of the skills. Few will question that mature reading involves all eight skills; the only question is which skills should be introduced and mastered first. Many points of view are possible. On the one hand there are those who believe that the skills should be *introduced* in approximately the order in which they have been listed; this is the view of those who believe that there should be an early emphasis on the decoding of print into sound via letter-sound relations. On the other hand, there are those who believe that the skills should be introduced approximately in the following order:

1. The child should learn the language he is going to read.

6. The child should learn to recognize printed words from whatever cues he can use, but initially only from total configurations.
7. The child should learn that printed words are signals for spoken words, and that meanings can be apprehended from these printed words.
8. The child must learn to reason and think about what he reads.
4. The child should learn the left-to-right principle, but initially only as it applies to complete words in continuous text.
3. The child should learn to recognize and discriminate the letters of the alphabet.
2. The child should learn to dissect spoken words into component sounds.
5. The child should learn patterns of correspondence between letters and sounds, to help him in the advanced phases of skill 6.

This latter view is held by those who argue that there should be an early emphasis on getting the meaning from print, and that the child should advance as quickly as possible toward the word-recognition and meaning-apprehension capacities of the mature reader. Skills 2, 3, and 5 are introduced only after the child has achieved considerable progress towards mastery of skills 4, 6, 7, and 8.

These are the two main views about the process of teaching reading. If each one is taken quite strictly and seriously, there can be very clear differences in the kinds of instructional materials and procedures that are used. It is beyond our scope to discuss whether the two methods differ in effectiveness. We would emphasize, rather, that methods may differ in effectiveness from child to child. Furthermore, it is possible to construct other reasonable orders in which the various components of reading skill can be introduced to the child. There is currently a tendency to interlace the approaches distinguished above in such a way that the child can attain rapid sight recognition of words at the same time that he is learning letter-sound correspondences that will help him "attack" words that he does not already know.

For the child who is having difficulty in learning to read, it may be necessary to determine exactly which skills are causing most difficulty. The dyslexic child may be hung up on the acquisition of just one or two skills. For example, he may be having particular trouble with skill 3—the recognition and discrimination of the letters of the alphabet, or with skill 2—the dissection of spoken words into component sounds. On determining what skills pose obstacles for a particular child, it is usually necessary to give special attention to those skills while capitalizing on those skills which are easier for the child to master.

Uncertainties and Research Problems

The above description of the nature of the reading process is based on the findings of nearly three-quarters of a century of research. A good deal is known about reading behavior, yet there are many questions that have not been answered with precision and certainty. We shall list the most important of these.

Questions About the Mature Reading Process

1. How does the individual's ability to recognize words instantaneously develop? What cues for word recognition are most important? How and when does awareness of spelling clues and inner speech representation recede, if at all? What is the extent of the sight vocabulary of the mature reader? (It should be noted that most studies of word recognition processes have been conducted with adults; there is need for developmental studies in which word recognition processes would be investigated over different chronological age levels.)
2. How do skilled readers process unfamiliar words? To what extent, and how, do they use patterns of letter-sound correspondences?
3. How do skilled readers find the proper readings of homographs and other types of ambiguous words?
4. What are the detailed psychological processes by which skilled readers comprehend the simple meaning of what they read? In what way do lexico-semantic, syntactical, and typographical factors interact to yield this comprehension?
5. How are eye movements controlled by comprehension processes, and how does the individual develop skill in scanning print?
6. How does the mature reader acquire skill in reasoning and inferential processes?
7. What are the major sources of individual differences in rate and accuracy of comprehension in mature readers?

Questions About Certain Components of Reading Skill as They Affect Learning

1. In what way does knowledge of the spoken language interact with learning to read? What kinds and amounts of competence are desirable before the child undertakes any given task in learning to read?
2. What is the nature of the ability to discriminate sounds in the spoken language and to dissect words in terms of these sounds? How does it develop, and what role does it play in the beginning reader's learning of letter-sound correspondences? How can this ability be taught?
3. How do children learn to recognize and discriminate alphabetic letters in their various forms? When children have difficulty with letter recognition, how can these difficulties be overcome?
4. How do children learn the left-to-right principle in orthography, both as applied to individual words and to the order of words

in continuous text? Are there children with special difficulties in learning this component of reading skill?

5. Exactly what are the most useful and functional patterns of letter-sound correspondence in English orthography, and in what order should they be learned? How, indeed, *are* they learned? Is it better to give direct instruction in them, or is it better to rely upon the child's capacity to infer these patterns from the experience he acquires as he learns to read? Should the characteristics of particular children be taken into account in deciding this?

6. When a child has acquired the ability to recognize words and read them in order, yet does not appear to comprehend the message as he would if it were spoken to him, what is the nature of the difficulty?

Questions About the Ordering of the Components of Reading Skill in the Teaching Process

1. In what way are the various skills prerequisite for each other? What aspects of each skill are necessary to facilitate progress in another skill?

2. Is there one best order in which to introduce the components of reading skill in the learning process, or are there different orders depending upon characteristics of individual children or groups of children? If so, how can these individual or group characteristics be determined?

3. On the assumption that there is an optimal ordering of skills for any given child, how much mastery of a given skill is desirable before another skill is introduced?

Module Competencies

The first competency specified for this module focuses on the development of your understanding of the similarities and differences that exist among current approaches to the teaching of reading. The second module competency is directed toward your ability to analyze approaches to reading instruction in relation to different points of view regarding the process of teaching reading.

The postassessment for the first competency identifies specific approaches to be compared and contrasted and the dimensions to be included in your discussion of each approach. In the postassessment for competency two, you are asked to select two approaches to reading instruction and identify the point of view regarding the process of teaching reading that is reflected in each approach.

Instructional Activities

The instructional activities in this module are designed to help you analyze current approaches to the teaching of reading. The material presented in activity 2 provides you with a basis for identifying the essential characteristics of four approaches to reading instruction (competency 1).

You are asked, as you consider these approaches, to relate them to the points of view regarding the process of teaching reading identified by Carroll in the article which introduces this module (competency 2). You are also encouraged in this activity to examine approaches other than the four presented in this module. The focus in activity 3 is on the differences among approaches as to the way in which introductory vocabulary words are selected (competency 1). The findings of the first grade reading studies sponsored by the United States Office of Education are considered in activity 4 (competency 1). The interview format presented in activity 5 provides you with a means of collecting data regarding teachers' perceptions of the effectiveness of the reading programs they are using (competency 1). In activity 6 you are encouraged to design other learning experiences that will enable you to analyze current approaches to reading instruction.

Competencies

1. Compare and contrast approaches to reading instruction.
2. Analyze approaches to reading instruction in terms of current positions regarding the process of teaching reading.

Instructional Activities

Select from the following learning experiences those which you feel will enable you to achieve the competencies stated for this module.

Activity 1

Attend a seminar for orientation to this module.

Activity 2

As Carroll indicates in his article, the viewpoint from which the process of teaching reading is regarded affects the materials and procedures used. The major characteristics of the basal reading, individualized, language experience, and linguistic approaches are identified in the material that follows. Each approach reflects specific assumptions regarding the process of teaching reading. Use the following questions as your purposes for reading this discussion of the four approaches:

1. What are the major elements of the (a) rationale, (b) materials, and (c) procedures of each approach?
2. With which of the three positions regarding the order in which the skills should be introduced, as identified by Carroll, does each of the approaches seem most consistent?

Basal Reading Approach

Rationale The assumption which underlies the basal reading approach, as discussed by William D. Sheldon, is that there is a set of skills fundamental to learning to read and that these skills can be systematically presented to children through a series of sequentially developed books and workbooks. The focus of this approach is providing children with essential skills in word comprehension and interpretation—skills they can apply in reading the wide range of materials they will encounter in life.

Materials Each basal reading series includes a set of books through which reading skills are presented sequentially. At each level a workbook is also provided. Each workbook is correlated with the book for that level, and is designed to reinforce and review the word recognition and comprehension skills that are being introduced. Additional related materials often provided in basal programs include word cards, phonics charts, recordings, and supplementary readers.

A teachers' guide accompanies the materials designed for each level in the basal series. The guide describes the overall philosophy of the program, and presents specific procedures for teaching each selection in the reader. Explanations for the use of the workbook and supplementary materials are also included. In addition to providing detailed plans for using the program, guides typically include a wide range of suggestions for activities to further skill development and for enrichment.

A major emphasis of the basal program is on the controlled introduction and continuous review of vocabulary. The words selected are those which have a high frequency of occurrence in English. New words are introduced for each reading selection, and children are given many opportunities to use the words in varied contexts.

In response to widespread criticism, the content of basal readers has undergone change in recent years. Critics claimed that the selections reflected primarily a white, middle-class culture, were unrealistic, and lacked nonfiction content. As a result of these criticisms, basal readers now present a more multiracial orientation, give more attention to realistic situations, particularly in urban settings, and include content other than stories, myths, and folktales.

Procedures The procedures characteristic of basal reading programs are designed to integrate the teaching of vocabulary and skills in word recognition and comprehension at each level. As children progress beyond the initial stages, this integrative approach expands to include reading in content areas, the development of study skills, and the appreciation of literature.[5]

A specific plan for teaching each reading selection is provided in the teachers' guide. The following outline, taken from one basal series teachers' guide, is illustrative of the overall teaching procedure characteristic of basal programs:

Preparation for Reading

Introducing the Vocabulary

This section gives detailed suggestions for presentation of vocabulary. Not all words are presented at all levels, depending on the type of word and the maturity of the pupil.

Story Background for the Teacher

Information and details helpful to pupils in achieving a good understanding of the selection are provided. This aid is given only where essential.

Leads to Motivation

Suggestions for arousing interest and enthusiasm for the selection are described.

Reading the Story

Purpose for Reading

Overall purposes are established with the pupils to guide comprehension of the selection.

Guided Reading

In certain cases, depending upon the selection, the teacher's goals, and the ability of the pupils, these questions designed to promote comprehension may be omitted. These optional questions are designed for use during reading or as a follow-up after reading is completed.

Discussion of Purposes

Comprehension of the total selection is promoted through discussion of the general purposes which were set as the pupils began their reading of the selection.

Purposeful Rereading

Occasionally pupils will be helped by reading the selection with a new purpose in mind. Suggestions for such rereading are given in this section of the lesson plan.

---

5. Adapted from William D. Sheldon, "Basal Reading," in *First Grade Reading Programs*, Perspectives in Reading, no. 5, ed. James Kerfoot (Newark, Del.: International Reading Association, 1965), pp. 28-44.

Related Language Activities

Further development of language skills is provided through suggestions for activities related to theme or content of the selection.

Supplementary Materials

Other useful materials are listed. The emphasis is upon readily usable and available items.

Developing Reading Skills

In this section of the lesson plans, specific activities for extending reading skills are provided. These activities develop decoding skills, comprehension abilities, vocabulary, language skills, study-skills, and creativity. Many of the activities can be completed independently. Others require teacher direction.[6]

In classrooms using the basal approach, teachers typically divide the total class into small groups for reading instruction. Children are placed in groups according to their reading levels. Teachers use previous records, test results, and informal reading inventories to determine the reading level of each child. Many basal series provide informal reading inventories or placement tests that can be used to determine children's reading levels.

Individualized Reading

Rationale The individualized approach to reading, as discussed by Groff, is built on the assumption that instruction should be adjusted to provide for individual differences. Each child is seen as having specific needs that can best be met by providing him with learning experiences that focus on his abilities and interests. This affords the child maximum opportunities for success and continued growth. Because he is developing skills through reading material that interests him, he finds learning to read a meaningful process. The foundation of the individualized approach is the belief that each child can be successful in learning to read if his abilities, interests, and natural motivation to learn form the basis of the instructional program.

Materials Since each child selects his own reading material according to his interests, a large quantity of varied materials is an essential component of an individualized program. Materials typically provided include trade books, basal readers, textbooks, newspapers, magazines, reading kits, and stories and other material written by children. The availability of a school library or instructional materials center, in addition to

---

6. From *Teachers' Edition, Skills Handbook, for Seven Is Magic* of the READING 360 series by Theodore Clymer and others, © Copyright, 1969, by Ginn and Company (Xerox Corporation), p. 27. Used with permission.

the classroom library, greatly increases children's opportunities to satisfy their reading interests.

In selecting materials for inclusion in the program, the teacher must be aware of the range in levels of reading ability that exists in his classroom so that a variety of materials can be provided for each reading level. In addition to providing a variety of types of materials, it is also essential to be certain that there is variety of content. Many types of materials within the areas of both fiction and nonfiction must be available so that children can both satisfy and expand their interests.

Procedures While the individualized approach emphasizes flexibility of instruction, there are certain concepts and practices that provide an overall framework. The concepts of self-selection and self-pacing, suggested by Olson, are reflected in practice as each child selects his own reading material, and as the teacher aids each child in selecting material that is at an appropriate level for him.[7]

During the reading period, children in an individualized program engage in a variety of activities. Some children continue to read the books or other materials they have previously selected. Others, having completed their current selections, complete a record of what they have read and develop a plan for sharing their books with others in the class. Following this, they begin the process of selecting the next material they will read.

During each reading period, the teacher holds individual conferences with several children. These teacher-pupil conferences are essential to the effective functioning of the program. During the conference, the teacher asks the child to read orally from his current selection and to respond to questions which evaluate his comprehension of the material. Through this procedure, the teacher assesses the child's progress and diagnoses his specific needs in word recognition and comprehension. The conference also provides the opportunity for the teacher to determine the child's reading interests, and to encourage the child to expand his range of interests if this seems appropriate.[8]

The information gained from the individual conference is recorded by the teacher in the child's folder, thereby providing a cumulative record of the child's progress and specific difficulties. The checklists shown in figures 2.1 and 2.2 illustrate the way in which information gained through conferences can be organized and recorded.

7. Willard C. Olson, "Seeking, Self-Selection, and Pacing in the Use of Books by Children," in *Individualizing Your Reading Program*, ed. Jeannette Veatch (New York: G. P. Putnam's Sons, 1959), pp. 89-98.
8. Adapted from Patrick Groff, "Individualized Reading," in *First Grade Reading Programs*, Perspectives in Reading, No. 5, ed. James Kerfoot (Newark, Del.: International Reading Association, 1965), pp. 7-27.

FIGURE 2.1.
Pupil Checklist (Skills).
From Arthur W. Heilman, *Principles and Practices of Teaching Reading*, 3d ed. (Columbus, Ohio: Charles E. Merrill Publishing Company, 1972), p. 400. Reprinted by permission of the publisher.

Pupil Checklist (Skills)

NAME: _____

AGE: _____ GRADE: _____ DATE: _____

I. *Basic Sight Vocabulary*   Test Used: _____

    No. of Words Tested _____ No. of Words Missed _____

    Words Not Known _____

II. *Difficulties Noted*

___Reads Word by Word   ___ Easily Distracted

___ Omits Words*   ___ Guesses Words

___ Poor Phrasing   ___ Word Analysis Poor**

___Does Not Profit from Punctuation***   ___ Errors Not Corrected

    ___ Little Help From Context Clues

___"Service Words" Missed****

___(Other)

         *Examples:
         **Examples:
         ***Examples:
         ****Examples:

III. *Study Skills and Effective Use of Textbooks*
Understands and Effectively Uses:

	Yes	No	Comments
A. Index	___	___	
B. Table of Contents	___	___	
C. Glossary	___	___	
D. Appendix	___	___	
E. Card Catalogue	___	___	
F. (Other)	___	___	

Comprehension Checklist

FIGURE 2.2. Comprehension Checklist. From Arthur W. Heilman, *Principles and Practices of Teaching Reading*, 3d ed. (Columbus, Ohio: Charles E. Merrill Publishing Company, 1972), p. 401. Reprinted by permission of the publisher.

NAME: _____

AGE: _____ GRADE: _____ DATE: _____

Book Title and Author: _____

Date Started: _____ Finished: _____ No. Pages: _____ Level: _____

Recall of Material Read

1. Level of Language Usage:

2. Following Sequence of Story:

3. Recall of Details: (unaided) _____
   with Questions: _____

4. Knowledge of Word Meanings (special connotations, figurative language, etc.)

   Examples Tested: _____

   _____

   _____

   _____

   _____

   _____

5. Examples of Pupil Responses:
   A. Describing Particular Character:
   B. Main Point of Story:
   C. Part Liked Best:
   D. Ability to Draw Inferences:
   E. Evaluation of Book (Does he recommend it highly—why or why not?): _____

   _____

   _____

   _____

   F. Ideas Expressed by Pupil:

6. Pupil Interest in Reading (teacher judgment):
7. Does pupil need guidance in selection of material?

The teacher may decide, as a result of information gained from individual conferences, to bring together several children who are having difficulty with the same skill. The teacher then works with these children as a group until they have acquired the skill. Temporary groups can also be formed so that children who have read the same book can work together in planning a way of sharing it with the remainder of the class.

Language Experience Approach[9]

Rationale   According to Stauffer, the language experience approach to beginning reading has two major facets: (1) the integration of the four dimensions of language (listening, speaking, writing, and reading), and (2) the utilization and extension of the child's experiences, interests, and understandings. One basic assumption underlying this approach is that individual differences must be provided for by pacing the teaching of reading skills so that each child has the opportunity to learn and to apply them. A second assumption is that reading is a communication process, and therefore involves the deriving of meaning, not merely the pronouncing of words. It is important that the vocabulary and concepts children use in oral communication become associated with the written words that will elicit the same concepts. The fundamental objective of this approach is to demonstrate to children that reading is really talk written down. In order to accomplish this, the child's own language is used as the foundation on which the reading program is built.

Materials   It is considered essential that the language in the materials of a language experience program closely parallels the oral language of children. One way of ensuring this is by developing experience charts or stories that are dictated by the children. After experiencing a common event or situation, children share their reactions and observations among themselves. As the children dictate their responses, the teacher records them on a large sheet of chart paper. The completed story provides meaningful material through which to develop a variety of reading skills. The following story resulted from children's experiences with the white mouse they were keeping in their classroom.

9. Adapted from Russell G. Stauffer, "Language Experience Approach," in *First Grade Reading Programs*, Perspectives in Reading, no. 5, ed. James Kerfoot (Newark, Del.: International Reading Association, 1965), pp. 86-118.

Snow White

Dick said: "Snow White scratched around in his cage." Jane said: "Snow White has pink eyes." Alice said: "She stood up on her hind legs and looked at us." Jerry said: "Her tail is two feet long." Bill said: "Snow White ran around on the table." Nancy said: "Snow White is soft and furry."[10]

Individual, group, and total class experience charts provide a continuous supply of relevant material. The content ranges widely in any classroom, and may include stories related to special events, holidays, field trips, and the activities of individual children. Charts can also evolve from children's experiences in such areas as science, social studies, and creative expression.

Because of the emphasis on integrating all aspects of language, children are encouraged to write their own experience stories as soon as they are able to do so. Children are motivated to develop writing skills in order to communicate their ideas in written form for others to read.

The materials of a language experience program for beginning reading include more than just charts and stories. The classroom must contain a wide range of trade books and other materials so that children can broaden their reading to include a variety of types of material and areas of content.

Procedures The procedures characteristic of the language experience approach include both individual and group instruction. Experience charts and stories are used in a variety of ways to develop beginning reading skills. Following the dictation of a class experience story, the teacher reads the story to the children, pointing to each word as it is said, and then has the children read the story with him. As they do this, the children are beginning to discriminate between letter forms and to develop a left-to-right orientation. They are also seeing that their words can be written down and read.

Based on his assessment of individual skills, the teacher typically divides the class into groups for their ongoing work in the reading program. As the teacher works with a group, each child is given the opportunity to dictate a story. As each child finishes his story, he works independent-

10. Ibid., p. 88.

ly rereading it and underlining the words he knows, while the teacher records the individual stories of others in the group. During this time, others in the class may be selecting library books, illustrating stories, or reading to each other.

As each child begins to acquire a stock of words he recognizes, the teacher puts these words on small cards which become the child's *word bank*. The cards can then be arranged by the child to produce a variety of sentences and stories. Children can also work together, using their cards in such visual discrimination activities as matching initial consonants, blends, digraphs, and whole words.

In the language experience approach, many opportunities are provided for teaching word recognition skills in meaningful contexts. Auditory and visual discrimination skills develop as children read the stories they have dictated. As the child learns specific words, these words can be used to teach single letter-sound relationships. As more words are acquired, the teacher moves to the relationships involving letter combinations. The emphasis in the language experience approach is on teaching these skills, not in isolation, but rather through experiences and materials that are meaningful and real to children.

Linguistic Approaches[11]

Rationale According to Charles C. Fries, reading programs designated as "linguistic approaches" to the teaching of reading are based upon certain assumptions concerning the nature of language development and its relationship to reading. In linguistic programs, learning to read is viewed as the process of transferring the ability to derive meaning from oral language to the ability to derive the same meaning from seeing the written representation of this same language. Linguists, those who study the nature of human language, contend that by the time they reach the age of five, children have acquired a more complete control of their language than has generally been assumed by those outside the field of linguistics. At this stage, the child's receptive language control (his understanding of what is said to him) is greater than his productive language control (his production of language), and it is this receptive language control that is the primary focal point in teaching the child to read. From the linguistic standpoint, the reading program must build upon the language control that children have already achieved. Word recognition, then, means "a recognizing of the 'word' as it appears spelled in letters as the same 'word' that the child knows in his 'talk'."[12]

11. Adapted from Charles C. Fries, "Linguistic Approaches," in *First Grade Reading Programs*, Perspectives in Reading, No. 5, ed. James Kerfoot (Newark, Del.: International Reading Association, 1965), pp. 45-55.
12. Ibid., p. 46.

As he begins the process of learning to read, the child develops habits of recognizing the words he sees, as they appear in specific spelling patterns, as being the same words he knows when he hears them spoken.

Materials While there is variation among linguistic programs in the materials provided, there are common features that can be identified. Vocabulary is introduced by presenting groups of words that conform to spelling patterns which reflect the regularities of English writing. Through repeated presentations of a specific spelling pattern, children learn not only to recognize the words used to illustrate the pattern, but also to identify new words that fit the pattern. In linguistic materials, words are presented in sequences of sentences, not in isolation. Through this type of presentation, children develop habits of "reading for meaning." This emphasis on meaning is illustrated in the following sequence which appears at the beginning of one linguistic series.

cat	Nat is a cat.
Nat	Is Nat fat?
fat	Nat is fat.
	Nat is a fat cat.[13]

Linguistic programs typically include a series of sequentially developed readers, accompanied by teachers' guides which present an explanation of the program and specific procedures for implementing it. Workbooks and additional supplementary materials may also be provided.

Procedures The initial procedure in preparing children for reading is to help them develop instant recognition of individual letters. In addition, children learn to identify letters as they appear in a left-to-right sequence. Words are then introduced through specific spelling patterns. Following its introduction, each spelling pattern is constantly repeated in contrast to other spelling patterns. "Reading with expression" receives attention from the initial stages of the program. The teacher determines, through the intonation patterns children use in their oral reading, whether they are getting meaning from what they read or are just pronouncing words. In contrast to other types of reading programs, the procedures characteristic of linguistic programs do not include the use of pictures as an aid in identifying words or obtaining meaning from a selection. Proponents of these programs contend that pictures distract children's attention from the task of learning spelling patterns and getting meaning from the material they read.

13. Ibid., p. 52.

Activity 3

As you begin to differentiate approaches to reading instruction, you may find it useful to identify what seem to you to be the essential elements of each approach. Table 2.1 can be used to develop summaries of the approaches presented in this activity, as well as of additional approaches you examine.

Using one or more of the following references, identify the rationale, materials, and procedures of approaches to reading other than the four presented in this activity:

Aukerman, Robert C. *Approaches to Beginning Reading.* New York: John Wiley and Sons, 1971.
Kerfoot, James F., ed. *First Grade Reading Programs.* Perspectives in Reading, no. 5. Newark, Del.: International Reading Association, 1965.
Spache, George D., and Spache, Evelyn B. *Reading in the Elementary School.* 3d ed. Chap. 8, "Innovations and Recent Research." Boston: Allyn & Bacon, 1973.
Vilscek, Elaine C., ed. *A Decade of Innovations: Approaches to Beginning Reading.* Newark, Del.: International Reading Association, 1968.

Activity 4

One of the most significant differences among approaches to reading instruction is the way in which the words that are first presented to children are selected. The authors of one basal reading series, for example, conducted a computerized study of children's library books in order to identify high-frequency words. The rationale and findings of the study are discussed in the following excerpt.

A Computerized Study of Children's Library Books

In order to determine precisely which words are most essential for today's young readers, a computerized vocabulary analysis was made of a selected list of library books proven to be of high interest to primary-grade children. In a total number of running words that amounted to more than 105,000, the total number of different words—not counting inflected or compounded forms separately, proper names, or purely onomatopoeic words— proved to be only 3,220. Of these 3,220 different words, just over 200 were found to account for nearly 70 percent of all the running words.

These facts made it clear that as soon as children could develop instant recognition of those 200 or so high-frequency words and also master the decoding strategy taught in this reading system, they should have the power to read—independently and with a minimum of trouble—any reading matter written for children of ages six to nine. This would be true because their recognition vocabulary would give them instant control over at least seven out of every ten words and their word perception or decoding ability would

Table 2.1

**Summary of the Major Characteristics of
Selected Approaches to Reading Instruction**

Approach	Major Characteristics		
	Rationale	Materials	Procedures
Individualized			
Language Experience			
Basal			
Linguistic			

give them control over practically all other words they would be likely to meet.

Please note that in this program the word *recognition* refers only to knowledge of a previously identified word and is not used to refer, as it sometimes is, to the act of perceiving the identity of an unknown word. What is sometimes called word recognition in reading tests might better be called word perception since it covers two sorts of words: (1) those which are being recognized instantly, and (2) those which are being identified or re-identified through the use of contextual and phonological clues.[14]

Based on this vocabulary analysis, these words were selected for introduction through the prereading program and the first preprimer (this list does not include proper names, inflected forms, compounds, or contractions):

a	get	in	see	where
and	go	is	stop	will
are	have	it	the	with
can	he	me	this	you[15]
cat	help	not	to	
come	here	on	want	
fish	I	real	we	

Additional words of relatively low frequency are also introduced because they are essential to the telling of specific stories:

bus	rocket	truck	zoo[16]
hide	tigers	TV	

Using the teachers' editions of the beginning books in several reading series, compare the introductory vocabulary and the bases for vocabulary selection. The chart shown in table 2.2 can be used to summarize the results of your vocabulary analysis.

Activity 5

During the 1964-65 school year, the United States Office of Education sponsored twenty-seven research projects designed to evaluate approaches to teaching reading in first grade. These studies comprised the Coopera-

---

14. From *Teachers' Edition, for Tigers* of *The Houghton Mifflin Readers*. Copyright © 1971 by Houghton Mifflin Company, pp. 20-21. Reprinted by permission of the publisher.
15. Ibid., p. 46.
16. Ibid.

Table 2.2

Vocabulary Analysis

Name and Publisher of Reading Program	Examples of Introductory Vocabulary	Basis for Selection of Vocabulary

tive Research Program in First-Grade Reading Instruction. The studies were conducted in different school systems across the country, and each one compared two or more approaches. No study duplicated another study. The approaches that were compared included Basal, Basal plus Phonics, i. t. a., Linguistic, Language Experience, and Phonic/Linguistic.

A Coordinating Center was established for the purpose of initiating and maintaining communication among the project directors. Meetings were held at which the directors made decisions regarding the common reading measures to be used, the types of information to be collected, and the common experimental controls that would be needed. At the completion of the studies, data from each of the twenty-seven projects were sent to the Coordinating Center where they were organized, analyzed, and interpreted.[17]

The results of the data analyses were extensive and detailed. Among the findings reported, Tinker and McCullough suggest the following as most significant:

1. No one method can be called the best approach.
2. In most instances, teacher skill, enthusiasm, and dedication appear to be more important than the particular method employed.
3. Boys need not do less well than girls in reading improvement.
4. The better performance in certain experimental groups could be due, partially and perhaps wholly, to a reading drive on the part of the teacher. . .
5. Reports of the continuation of the program in the second grade [14 of the 27 studies were extended through second and third grade] revealed no marked differences from what was found in the first-grade studies.[18]

Summaries of twenty of the twenty-seven first-grade reading studies were reported in the May 1966 issue of *The Reading Teacher*. Based on his analysis of the studies reported, Russell Stauffer suggests that because of the large number of variables that were not uniformly controlled, caution must be exercised in attempting to draw conclusions from the studies. Stauffer identifies the following limitations inherent in the studies:

1. The methods cannot be compared because they were not sharply and clearly different.
2. Methods that were given the same label were often not the same.

17. Guy L. Bond and Robert Dykstra, "The cooperative research program in first-grade reading instruction," *Reading Research Quarterly* (Newark, Del.: International Reading Association, 1967), pp. 27-28.
18. Miles A. Tinker and Constance M. McCullough, *Teaching Elementary Reading*, 3d ed. (New York: Appleton-Century-Crofts, 1968), p. 123.

3. Reading instruction time could not be defined in a way that was acceptable to all studies.
4. The statistical procedures used were not uniform from study to study.
5. The reporting of findings was not uniform.
6. The extent of the operation of the Hawthorne effect must be considered, since in almost every instance the gains made by the experimental populations were significantly greater than the gains made by the control populations.[19]

Read several reports of the first-grade reading studies, keeping in mind the limitations pointed out by Stauffer. Use the following questions as a guide in analyzing the studies you select:

1. Are the methods clearly defined in terms of rationale, procedures, and materials?
2. Are the same labels given to methods that appear to be not the same?
3. What differences do you find in statistical procedures used, and in the reporting of findings?
4. Did the experimental group make significantly greater gains than the control group in each study?

The following references contain reports of the first-grade reading studies, and of those studies that were extended beyond first grade:

United States Office of Education. "First Grade Reading Studies." *The Reading Teacher* 19 (May 1966).
———. "First Grade Reading Studies." *The Reading Teacher* 20 (October 1966).
———. "The Second Grade Extension of First Grade Reading Studies." *The Reading Teacher* 20 (May 1967).

Activity 6

One source of information regarding the effectiveness of different approaches to reading instruction is the perceptions of teachers who are using the programs. Read the teachers' guide for the program used in the school in which you are teaching in order to obtain the following information: (1) rationale of the program, (2) basic and supplementary materials provided, and (3) procedures for implementing the program. When you feel that you understand the program, request interviews with teachers at several grade levels. After explaining your purpose in requesting the interviews, ask each teacher to respond to the following questions:

19. Russell G. Stauffer, "The Verdict: Speculative Controversy," *The Reading Teacher* 19 (May 1966):563-64.

1. By whom was the program selected (e.g., administrators, teachers, reading specialists)?
2. What do you consider to be the strengths and limitations of the program?
3. In what ways do you attempt to overcome the limitations of the program?
4. Do you find the program equally effective for all the children in your classroom? If not, for which children does the program appear to be most effective? For which children does it appear to be least effective? In what ways do you adapt the program in order to increase its effectiveness?

Use the data collected in your interviews to answer the following questions:

1. Do teachers at different grade levels find the program equally effective? If not, at what levels does the program appear to be most effective? At what levels does it appear to be least effective?
2. In what ways are teachers adapting the program so that it more effectively meets children's needs?

Compare the results of your interviews with the results obtained from interviews by others with teachers using different programs.

Activity 7

Design activities of your own which you feel will enable you to achieve the competencies stated for this module.

Preassessment and Postassessment

A. Knowledge level
1. Compare and contrast the following approaches to reading instruction: basal reading, individualized, language experience, and linguistic. Include the following dimensions in your discussion of each approach: (a) rationale of the approach, (b) materials, and (c) teaching procedures.
   Criteria for successful performance:
   a) the dimensions of each approach are accurately identified;
   b) the similarities and differences among approaches are clearly specified.
2. Select two approaches to reading instruction. For each ap-

proach (a) identify the point of view regarding the process of teaching reading (refer to the Carroll article in "The Overview") that is reflected in the approach, and (b) support your decision with references to specific aspects of the approach.

Criteria for successful performance:

a) the identification of a point of view regarding the process of teaching reading as being reflected in a specific approach is defensible for each approach.

b) each decision is supported by accurate reference to specific aspects of the approach.

References

Aukerman, Robert C. *Approaches to Beginning Reading.* New York: John Wiley and Sons, 1971.

Bond, Guy L., and Wagner, Eva Bond. *Teaching the Child to Read.* 4th ed. Chap. 5, "Current Approaches to Reading Instruction;" chap. 6, "Reading Program and Materials of Instruction." New York: Macmillan Company, 1966.

Bush, Clifford L., and Huebner, Mildred H. *Strategies for Reading in the Elementary School.* Chap. 10, "Organization of the Reading Program." New York: Macmillan Company, 1970.

Dallmann, Martha; Rouch, Roger L.; Chang, Lynette Y. C.; and DeBoer, John J. *The Teaching of Reading.* 4th ed. Chap. 15, "Approaches to Reading Instruction." New York: Holt, Rinehart and Winston, 1974.

Durkin, Dolores. *Teaching Them to Read.* 2d ed. Chap. 2, "Instructional Materials." Boston: Allyn & Bacon, 1974.

Harris, Albert J., and Sipay, Edward R. *Effective Teaching of Reading.* 2d ed. Chap. 3, "Beginning to Read." New York: David McKay Company, 1971.

————. *How to Increase Reading Ability.* 6th ed. Chap. 3, "Beginning Reading Instruction." New York: David McKay Company, 1975.

Heilman, Arthur W. *Principles and Practices of Teaching Reading.* 3d ed. Chap. 5, "Beginning Reading: pt. 1;" chap. 6, "Beginning Reading: pt. 2." Columbus, Ohio: Charles E. Merrill Publishing Company, 1972.

Kerfoot, James F., ed. *First Grade Reading Programs.* Perspectives in Reading, no. 5. Newark, Del.: International Reading Association, 1965.

May, Frank B. *To Help Children Read.* Module 9, "Organizing and Managing Your Reading Program." Columbus, Ohio: Charles E. Merrill Publishing Company, 1973.

Otto, Wayne; Chester, Robert; McNeil, John; and Myers, Shirley. *Focused Reading Instruction.* Chap. 12, "Individualization by objective." Reading, Mass.: Addison-Wesley Publishing Company, 1974.

Russell, David H. *Children Learn to Read.* 2d ed. Chap. 5, "Overview of the Whole Reading Program: Methods and Materials." Waltham, Mass.: Blaisdell Publishing Company, 1961.

Smith, James A. *Creative Teaching of Reading in the Elementary School.* 2d ed. Chap. 3, "The Creative Teaching of Reading." Boston: Allyn & Bacon, 1975.

Smith, Nila Banton. *Reading Instruction for Today's Children.* Chap. 5, "Approaches Differ." Englewood Cliffs, N. J.: Prentice-Hall, 1963.

Spache, George D., and Spache, Evelyn B. *Reading in the Elementary School.* 4th ed. Chap. 2, "Using the Basal Reader Approach;" chap. 3, "Using the Individualized Approach;" chap. 4, "Using the Linguistic Approaches;" chap.

5, "Using the Language Experience Approach." Boston: Allyn & Bacon, 1977.

Stauffer, Russell G. *Teaching Reading as a Thinking Process*. Chap. 5, "Individualized Reading Instruction;" chap. 8, "The Language-Experience Approach." New York: Harper & Row, Publishers, 1969.

Tinker, Miles A., and McCullough, Constance M. *Teaching Elementary Reading*. 3d ed. Chap. 1, "Reading: Nature, Goals, Teaching Methods." New York: Appleton-Century-Crofts, 1968.

U. S. Office of Education, "First Grade Reading Studies." *The Reading Teacher* 19 (May 1966).

———. "First Grade Reading Studies." *The Reading Teacher* 20 (October 1966).

———. "The Second Grade Extension of First Grade Reading Studies." *The Reading Teacher* 20 (May 1967).

Vilscek, Elaine C., ed. *A Decade of Innovations: Approaches to Beginning Reading*. Newark, Del.: International Reading Association, 1968.

Walcutt, Charles C.; Lamport, Joan; and McCracken, Glen. *Teaching Reading*. Chap. 14, "Approaches and Programs." New York: Macmillan Company, 1974.

Wallen, Carl J. *Competency in Teaching Reading*. Chap. 18, "Using testing and teaching strategies with three types of reading methods." Chicago: Science Research Associates, 1972.

Zintz, Miles V. *The Reading Process: The Teacher and the Learner*. 2d ed. Chap. 9, "Teaching Beginning Reading." Dubuque, Iowa: Wm. C. Brown Company Publishers, 1975.

Developing Phonic Analysis Skills

As you read, you use a variety of techniques to identify words. Because reading has become an automatic process for you, you are probably seldom aware of the particular technique you are using to identify a specific word. In the following excerpt, Gray describes the word recognition techniques we use as we encounter both familiar and unfamiliar words:

How Printed Words Are Identified

In efficient, rapid word perception the reader relies almost wholly on context clues and word-form clues. Awareness of sentence context (and often of general context) and a glance at the general configuration of a word enable the reader to respond instantly with the meaning the author had in mind when he wrote the word. This type of word perception occurs in most of the reading done by experienced, mature readers. For example, you had no difficulty perceiving the words in this . . . paragraph. You did not stop to study the form of separate words. Nor did you analyze words by consciously noting root words, prefixes, and suffixes or by "sounding them out," syllable by syllable. It is highly unlikely that you consulted a dictionary for the pronunciation or the meaning of any word. Why not? Every word was familiar—you have used each one yourself and have seen it in print thousands of times; you know its meaning (or meanings). Therefore you were free to comprehend the ideas conveyed by the words, react to these ideas, and add them to what you already know about the subject, providing of course you consider them worthwhile.

Suppose, however, you encounter this sentence: "The annulet on his coat of arms proclaimed him a fifth son." Unless the word *annulet* is in your vocabulary, it probably stops you, at least momentarily. From sentence context you infer that an annulet is some kind of symbol; in short, you use context clues to get a general meaning for the word. Because a glance at the word does not reveal a word that you know, you may try word analysis. But study of the word form reveals no familiar ending, prefix, suffix, or root (structural analysis); so you divide the word into syllables and determine vowel sound and accent (phonic analysis). When you arrive at a pronunciation, you wonder about it, since you cannot remember ever seeing or hearing this word. If you are in a hurry, you may be satisfied with your tentative pronunciation and with a general meaning ("some kind of symbol"). Nevertheless your perception of the word *annulet* is uncertain and incomplete. To find out exactly what it means and to check its pronunciation, you will have to consult the dictionary.[1]

The focus in this module is helping children develop and apply skills in phonic analysis. This involves providing them with opportunities to acquire and use knowledge concerning relationships between significant speech sounds and the letters or combinations of letters that represent them as *one* means of identifying unfamiliar words.

The module is introduced through Jack Bagford's article, "The Role of Phonics in Teaching Reading."[2] As Bagford points out, attempts to define the role of phonics in reading instruction have generated considerable controversy over the years. After identifying the areas of disagreement that exist today, Bagford discusses current views regarding approaches to phonics instruction and the content of phonics programs. In the final sections of the article, he (1) identifies factors which he feels need to be considered in developing phonics programs, and (2) proposes overall guidelines to be used by teachers in establishing a balance between phonics and other aspects of the reading program. As you read Bagford's article, use the following questions as your purposes for reading:

1. What current areas of disagreement regarding phonics instruction does Bagford identify?
2. What are the essential differences between *analytic* and *synthetic* approaches to the teaching of phonics?
3. What difficulties does Bagford suggest may result for children who learn phonics through a synthetic approach?
4. What criteria does Bagford suggest teachers use in selecting content for phonics programs?

1. William S. Gray, "How Printed Words are Identified," in *On Their Own in Reading*, rev. ed. (Chicago: Scott, Foresman and Company, 1960), pp. 14-15.
2. Jack Bagford, "The Role of Phonics in Teaching Reading," in *Reading and Realism*, ed. J. Allen Figurel. (Newark, Del.: International Reading Association, 1969), pp. 82-87. Reprinted with permission of Jack Bagford and the International Reading Association.

5. In what ways should teachers adjust phonics instruction to differences among children?
6. On what basis does Bagford propose that teachers be actively involved in determining the role of phonics in reading instruction?

The Role of Phonics in Teaching Reading
Jack Bagford

In the past, there has been much controversy among teachers concerning the value of phonics to the teaching of reading. Some have argued that phonics has limited usefulness because of the relatively unphonetic character of the English language; others have felt that such knowledge is not only a useful but necessary part of the reading program. Fortunately, there are now some limited agreements about the use of phonics in the teaching of reading.

There is no longer any serious doubt about *whether* phonics content should be included in the reading program; teachers and reading specialists almost universally accept it as an indispensable tool for teaching children to read. Disagreements concerning phonics are still very much in evidence, but they have now centered largely on questions of (a) how phonics should be presented, (b) what content should be included, and (c) when should it be emphasized. Though space will not permit a penetrating analysis of these questions, an attempt will be made to raise some basic issues regarding the manner in which these questions may be answered and to provide reading teachers with guidelines for action until results of research and practice answer them more adequately.

How Should Phonics Be Taught

Historically, there have been several different approaches to the teaching of phonics.

In recent decades it has been customary to categorize them into two main types, analytic approaches and synthetic approaches.

The *analytic approaches* to teaching phonics are those approaches in which the teacher first teaches a limited number of sight words, possibly 75 to 100, and then teaches the reader to utilize these known words to infer letter-sound associations for unknown words. In presenting phonics analytically, a teacher might teach a number of sight words, including, for example, *bat, bill,* and *bug.* Then by *analyzing* the words and noting that they all begin with the same sound, the students learn the letter-sound association for *b.* Subsequently, when unknown words such as *basket, bitter,* and *bundle* occur in his reading, the student will know the *b* sound and will thus have a clue to help him identify the words.

The *synthetic approaches* to teaching phonics are those approaches in which the teacher first teaches the sounds which certain letters represent and then teaches the pupil to combine (or synthesize) the sounds into words. Following one of the synthetic approaches, a teacher would first present the sounds represented by the printed form of the letters: for example, *p* usually sounds like *puh; a* sounds like *a;* and *t* sounds like *tuh.* When

From *Reading and Realism*, IRA Conference Proceedings, 1969, pp. 82-87. Reprinted with permission of Jack Bagford and the International Reading Association.

the sounds are blended, the word is *pat*. Later on, when the student meets words like *pen* and *pig*, he will know that they begin with the *p* sound and thus he will have a clue to their identification.

Since the early 1930's, those who favored analytic approaches have been in the majority, but there has been continuous support for the synthetic approaches. Recently, since linguistic scholars have focused attention on "breaking the code" as the prime emphasis for early reading instruction, the synthetic approaches have gained remarkably in their popularity. Beginning with the Boston studies in the mid-fifties (7) and continuing with the Sparks-Fay study (11), the Bear study (3), the Bliesmer-Yarborough study (4), and the USOE First and Second Grades Studies (8), evidence has been presented to support the contention that synthetic approaches provide a more rapid start in reading than analytic approaches do.

Chall (5) recently presented a convincing case for those reading programs which make use of the synthetic approaches. Under a grant from the Carnegie Foundation, she has made a searching analysis of the major research findings related to problems of beginning reading instruction. One of her major conclusions was that "code emphasis" approaches (synthetic approaches) proved superior, at least in the primary grades, to "meaning emphasis" approaches (analytic approaches).

There does appear to be some question about whether early gains made by synthetic approaches can be maintained as the children progress through the reading program (11). Further longitudinal research is needed on this very important point, but one would think that intermediate grade teachers and curriculum workers could find ways of maintaining reading gains achieved by primary grade teachers, almost regardless of the manner in which the gains were achieved.

This assumption, however, may be en-
tirely contrary to fact. Children taught by synthetic methods may over-learn some word-analysis habits which later militate against reading growth: they may learn to concentrate so intently on word analysis that attention to meaning is impeded; they may acquire habits that slow down the reading rate and thus make it difficult to comprehend rapidly; they may grow to believe that reading is a process of drill on seemingly meaningless sounds and thus grow to dislike reading. If in their zeal for phonics mastery, primary grade teachers have overemphasized habits that will need to be unlearned at a later date, then it does seem probable that children taught by the more moderate or the more analytic approach would become the better readers.

With present knowledge teachers still must rely somewhat on their own judgment about what is best. It is comforting to note that children do learn to read by any of several methods. At this point in time a reasonable course seems to be (a) teach letter-sound associations relatively early in the reading program with a synthetic emphasis while at the same time considering interest and comprehension as prime goals and prime guides for teaching procedures, and (b) after the child has progressed sufficiently in his word recognition ability, shift the emphasis rather rapidly to comprehension while at the same time trying to foster high interest in reading.

What Phonic Content Should Be Taught

Through the years much information has been compiled concerning speech sounds and their written representations. It is a generally accepted fact that some of the information is helpful in teaching reading and some of it is not. In fact, this matter is implied by the way phonics is defined. *Phonetics* is generally defined as the science of speech sounds, while *phonics* is defined as that portion of phonetics which is applicable in teaching children to read. For the purpose of teaching reading, it is neither feasible nor desirable to try to teach all that is known about phonetics.

One of the basic reasons for including any phonetic knowledge in a reading program is to improve the efficiency of the teaching process. To accomplish this good, programs should concentrate on content which occurs frequently in reading, is easy to teach, and is relatively regular in its application.

Studies by Clymer (6), Fry (10), Bailey (2), and Emans (9) have investigated the question of "what content" by making use of one or more of the preceding criteria in judging the value of selected phonic content. They have found that at least some of the phonic content that is usually included in reading programs is not adequately justified by these criteria. These studies need to be expanded and amplified into other pertinent areas, but they do provide some substantial data which should prove extremely helpful as teachers concern themselves with problems of what phonics content *should* and *should not* be included in the reading program.

Some Basic Considerations

In determining the proper role of phonics in a reading program one needs to consider underlying factors which relate to this role. Some of the basic considerations follow.

Children differ in their ability to benefit from a sound-oriented approach to the teaching of reading. It seems plausible to assume that some children learn better from a method which emphasizes a whole-word approach to word recognition while others probably learn better from a method which emphasizes sound-symbol correspondence. To put it another way, some children probably learn better through visual means while others learn better through auditory means. Generally speaking, teaching

materials are designed with the underlying assumption that all children learn equally well with all modalities. This assumption may or may not be correct. Thus it seems logical to advise that whenever a child is experiencing difficulty with learning to read, the teacher should investigate the possibility that he may be emphasizing the least effective modality for the child in question.

Research studies that arrive at generalizations about which method works best for *large* groups of children miss a very basic point: i.e., methods which produce significantly higher mean scores for the total group do not necessarily work best for each individual student in the group. Certain individuals may profit more from a method which has been shown to produce significantly lower mean scores than another. Teachers should recognize this possibility and adjust their teaching accordingly.

It seems likely that some words are more easily learned by a phonic method than by a sight method, while others are more easily learned by the sight method. High frequency, but irregularly sounded, words probably are more efficiently taught by a sight method while phonetically regular words and words which contain easily learned sounds probably are better taught by a phonic method. Learning the word recognition skills is a step in a developmental process, one of the goals of which is to know a large number of words by sight. Accomplishing this goal by the most efficient method is important. Sometimes the most efficient method is determined by the nature of the word itself.

A given child may be able to utilize a sound-oriented approach better at one age than another. The concept of reading readiness suggests that there is an optimum time in the developmental process for a child to learn any given skill. Presumably, attempts to teach a skill prior to this optimum time will prove unsuccessful and may even cause emotional or psychological problems which seriously retard normal growth. Also, it is assumed that if instruction is postponed until later than this optimum time, the skill involved is not as readily learned as it would have been at the optimum time.

In a like manner, each child may have an optimum time in his total development for learning phonics content. For some phonic readiness may be achieved relatively early in school while others may take considerably longer. In presenting phonics content, teachers should consider the natural growth patterns of the pupils.

How the teacher feels about the teaching procedure which he is following seems to make a difference in the effectiveness of the teaching method. If children can learn to read by any of several approaches, which apparently they can, then how the teacher feels about the method may well be one of the most important factors in determining its success. If the teacher is philosophically committed to the method he is using, then he is likely to do a good job of teaching reading regardless of how good or how bad the method might be. When selecting a particular phonics program or determining degree of emphasis on content or methodology, one of the key factors to be considered should be what the teachers think about it.

Interest may not be directly related to method. It is doubtful that one method is inherently more interesting than another. Enthusiastic teachers can take very dull content and make an interesting lesson out of it. Others can take what seems to be very interesting material and create pure drudgery for children. Whether a method is interesting is probably less related to method than it is to other factors related to the teaching-learning situation.

Two factors which influence pupil interest are variety of presentation and appropriateness of teaching level. If presentations are varied within a method, interest is not likely to be lacking. Likewise, if a child is given a learning challenge, but at a level where he has a relatively good chance for success, he will seldom lose interest. The important point related to phonics is that approaches probably should not be accepted or rejected because of interest or lack of it. Rather, *effective* approaches should be selected for use and then adjustments made in the teaching situation to maintain a high interest level.

Guidelines for the Reading Teacher

In teaching phonics, the major task which confronts today's reading teacher is how to maintain a proper balance between attention to phonics and attention to other important reading goals. The myriad of research results and the verbal wranglings of reading "experts" are likely to confuse the average teacher about the proper course of action as he performs the daily tasks of teaching reading. The following are suggested as broad guidelines to follow as teachers attempt to determine the role of phonics in the teaching of reading.

Phonics content is taught so that children have a tool to identify words which are known in the spoken form but not in the printed form. All decisions concerning the use of phonics should reflect this purpose. Teachers should regularly ask themselves whether the phonic content being taught and the methods being employed in teaching it contribute to the accomplishment of this major purpose. If not, the teacher should adjust accordingly.

Phonics is but one aspect of word recognition; word recognition is but one goal of the reading program. Phonics is best used in conjunction with other word recognition skills. As a child learns to read, he gradually learns several ways to identify words. Ideally, he learns them in such a manner so that he can coordinate and combine their use as he attacks unknown words. The ability to use sound-symbol relationships is one of the more important reading skills, but it is just one and should be so considered.

The second aspect of this guideline has to do with the relationship of word recognition skills to the total reading program. Word identification techniques should be taught in a manner that facilitates, not hampers, the attainment of other important reading goals. Intensive attention to phonics can seriously impair progress toward goals of speed, interest, and meaning; teachers need to recognize this possibility so that emphasis can be adjusted to best serve the total reading program.

The teacher is the key person in determining the success of a reading program. Whether children learn better by one method than another is largely determined by the skill and enthusiasm of the teacher. In recent years, research has consistently shown that the quality of the teacher in the classroom is the most important variable relating to how well the pupils in a class learn to read. Effective functioning in such a key role requires that a teacher know as much as possible about (a) phonics and research related to phonics, (b) the total reading process, and (c) the pupils' reading abilities and needs.

Acting in terms of the preceding guidelines leads one directly to the next. *Teachers should take an active part in determining the role of phonics in the reading program.* On the whole, modern-day teachers are well-trained, competent people who are capable of determining the reading needs of pupils and adjusting the program to meet these needs. Caring for individual differences is a constant job, and only teachers are in a position to know these needs well enough to adjust instructional procedures to meet them; teachers should be encouraged to do so.

This guideline means, for example, that teachers should adjust content and method for children who are slow learners or fast learners; for children who have speech and hearing problems; and for those who learn better through visual means than through auditory means. It means that teachers need to recognize and adjust for the fact that some phonic content is learned by all pupils without any direct teaching.

It is recognized that adjusting for individual differences is an age-old problem that has no easy solutions. Nevertheless, with the wide variety of high quality materials available to today's teachers, intensive efforts toward recognizing differences and providing for them can produce rich benefits for the pupils.

Relatively speaking, phonics should be taught fairly early in the reading program. Basically, the two major goals of a reading program are *word recognition* and *comprehension*. These goals can hardly be separated, but for instructional purposes it is probably better to place the heavy emphasis on one and then the other. Early in the process of learning to read, word recognition (including phonics) should receive major attention; and as progress is made, the emphasis should be shifted to comprehension.

Summary

Phonics has an extremely important role to play in the teaching of reading. In this paper it is assumed that phonic analysis is best used in conjunction with other word-identification techniques for the purpose of unlocking words which are known in their spoken form but unknown in their written form. It is known that the pupils can learn to read by any of a number of methods. Thus teachers, rather than method, are the most important variable in the teaching process. Teachers are encouraged to know research relating to methods and materials and to utilize their knowledge in adjusting their procedures to the individual needs in their own classrooms. Guidelines for making these adjustments are provided.

References

1. Bagford, Jack. *Phonics: Its Role in Teaching Reading*. Iowa City: Sernoll, 1967.
2. Bailey, Mildred Hart. "The Utility of Phonic Generalizations in Grades One through Six," *Reading Teacher*, 20 (February 1967), 413-418.
3. Bear, David. "Phonics for First Grade: A Comparison of Two Methods," *Elementary School Journal*, 59 (April 1959), 394-402.
4. Bliesmer, Emery P., and Betty H. Yarborough. "A Comparison of Ten Different Beginning Reading Programs in First Grade," *Phi Delta Kappan*, 46 (June 1965), 500-504.
5. Chall, Jeanne. *Learning To Read: The Great Debate*. New York: McGraw-Hill, 1967.
6. Clymer, Theodore. "The Utility of Phonics Generalizations in the Primary Grades," *Reading Teacher*, 16 (February 1963), 252-258.
7. Durrell, Donald D. (ed.). "Success in First Grade Reading," *Journal of Education*. Boston University. (February 1958), 1-48.
8. Dykstra, Robert. *Continuation of the Coordinating Center for First-Grade Reading Instruction Programs*. USOE, Project Number 6-1651. Minneapolis: University of Minnesota, 1967.
9. Emans, Robert. "The Usefulness of Phonic Generalizations above the Primary Level," *Reading Teacher*, 20 (February 1967), 419-425.
10. Fry, Edward. "A Frequency Approach to Phonics," *Elementary English*, 41 (November 1964), 759-765.
11. Sparks, Paul E., and Leo C. Fay. "An Evaluation of Two Methods of Teaching Reading," *Elementary School Journal*, 57 (April 1957), 386-390.

Module Competencies

One purpose in this module is to help you develop an understanding of the linguistic concepts that provide the foundation for phonic analysis. A second purpose is to help you develop ways of teaching specific phonic analysis skills to children. Both purposes are reflected in the module competencies which identify the specific understandings and skills you will develop as you work with this module.

After reading the "Competencies" section of the module, read the "Preassessment and Postassessment" section. The means of assessment, and performance criteria, identified in those sections can serve as focal points for your work with the instructional activities.

Instructional Activities

The instructional activities in this module are designed to enable you to develop the module competencies through a variety of learning experiences. The material in activity 2 provides an overview of the field of linguistics, and differentiates linguistic concepts associated with phonic analysis. Also included in this activity are definitions and examples of linguistic terms that you will encounter as you work with children in the area of phonic analysis (competency 1). In activity 3, the inductive approach to teaching phonic analysis skills is introduced, and a specific procedure for using this approach is described (competency 2). Activities 4 and 5 focus on the application of the inductive approach in teaching phonic elements (competency 2). The results of research designed for the purpose of analyzing the usefulness of selected phonic generalizations are presented in activity 6 (competency 3). The focus of activities 7 and 8 is the use of the inductive approach in teaching phonic generalizations (competency 2). The classroom observations suggested in activity 9 can provide you with a variety of techniques for use with children as they learn and apply phonic analysis skills (competency 4). Examples of activities designed to help children apply the skills they are learning are provided in activity 10 (competency 4). In activity 11 you are encouraged to design activities of your own that will enable you to achieve the module competencies.

Competencies

1. Define and give examples of the following linguistic terms: consonant blend, consonant digraph, vowel digraph, diphthong, grapheme, phoneme, phonogram.
2. Develop plans for teaching phonic elements and generalizations inductively.
3. Identify generalizations whose inclusion in phonics programs is supported by research.
4. Develop activities that will enable children to apply phonic analysis skills.

Instructional Activities

Select from the following learning experiences those which you feel will enable you to achieve the competencies stated for this module:

Activity 1

Attend a seminar for orientation to this module.

Activity 2

Educators have long been aware that a relationship exists between the area of reading and the field of linguistics. Until fairly recently, this awareness has been only minimally reflected in the curriculum and materials of reading programs. In the past decade, however, the work of linguistic scholars has significantly influenced the procedures and materials of reading instruction. It would, in fact, be difficult today to find recent revisions of basal reading series, or other reading materials, that do not incorporate at least some linguistic findings.

Currently, there is a lack of agreement among linguists, and among reading educators, concerning the role that the field of linguistics should occupy in the development of reading programs. One view of the relationship between linguistics and reading is expressed by Roger Shuy, linguistic consultant for *Reading 360*, Ginn and Company's basal reading series:

> Linguistics is not the easy cure-all to the readers' difficulties. A great deal of what linguists concern themselves with is irrelevant to the development of reading material, and it goes without saying that other disciplines also have important things to say about reading. But linguists, as scholars in the field of language, do have some things to say about language which can be very useful for the teaching of reading, and a good reading series will benefit from the discoveries of modern linguistics. So far, the insights of linguists into problems of reading have been only partially applied in beginning reading materials, and it is safe to assume that many insights have been overlooked because of the primitive state of development of both the fields of reading and linguistics.[3]

In order to use current reading materials effectively in helping children develop phonic analysis skills, it is necessary for teachers to understand the linguistic concepts associated with phonic analysis. Basic to this understanding is an explanation of the overall field of linguistics. Shane suggests the following way of viewing linguistics:

> Perhaps, one of the most useful ways of explaining linguistics is to say that it is:
>
> 1. A *scholarly discipline* concerned with the nature of human language—with what speakers do with and know about their language—as well as with different grammar systems, dialects, and the like, AND . . .
> 2. A *behavioral science* with implications for classroom strategy in trying to induce behavioral change through the use of language, AND . . .
> 3. A *social science* as it establishes linkages between language and culture and culture and language.[4]

Following this explanation, Shane identifies the major divisions of the field of linguistics. These divisions are presented in figure 3.1.

---

3. Roger W. Shuy, "Some Relationships of Linguistics to the Reading Process," in *Teachers' Edition, for May I Come In?* of the READING 360 series by Theodore Clymer and others, Ginn and Company (Xerox Corporation), pp. 8-9.
4. Harold G. Shane, *Linguistics and the Classroom Teacher* (Washington, D.C.: Association for Supervision and Curriculum Development, 1967), p. 3.

FIGURE 3.1. "The Major Divisions of the Field of Linguistics." Harold G. Shane. "The Quiet English Reformation." *Linguistics and the Classroom Teacher*. Washington, D. C.: Association for Supervision and Curriculum Development, 1967, p. 4, Figure 1. Reprinted with permission of the Association for Supervision and Curriculum Development and Harold G. Shane. Copyright © 1967 by the Association for Supervision and Curriculum Development.

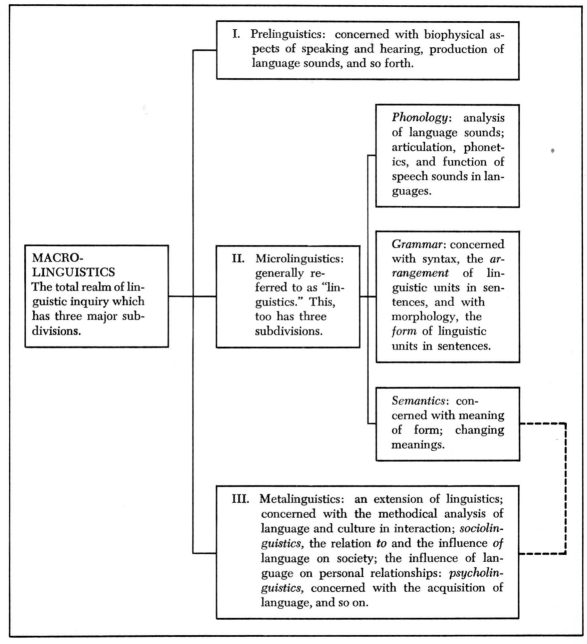

The division of linguistics with which this module is concerned is *phonology*. Within this area, it is important to differentiate three concepts: *phonetics, phonemics,* and *phonics*. Durkin differentiates *phonetics* and *phonemics*.

Phonetics is broad in the sense that it deals with the speech sounds that occur or can occur in human language. It is concerned with similarities and differences among these sounds, with their articulatory movements, and with the vibrations that account for their acoustic effect. Phonetics could thus be defined as the science of describing the sounds of human speech. Used to record these sounds is the International Phonetic Alphabet, along with other linguistic symbols. At least one symbol in the International Phonetic Alphabet, the schwa (ə), is familiar to teachers because it appears in phonics materials and represents a sound that occurs very frequently in English—for example, in initial position in words like *above, alone,* and *aware.* More specialized than phonetics is *phonemics,* for its scholars deal with one language at a time. Their aim is to identify the sounds in a particular language or dialect that are significant (that is, are phonemes) in that they account for words that are different in meaning but phonetically the same except for one sound. In our language, to cite some examples, the sounds associated with *d* and *t* each constitute a phoneme because they account for words like *dot, tot; dime, time.* In some other language they might not be functional or significant—that is, they might not be separate phonemes—because they do not make for differences in vocabulary.[5]

Harris and Sipay provide a definition of *phonics*:

. . . *Phonics* is knowledge about phonemes and graphemes; it involves the development of associations between phonemes and the graphemes that represent them, and an understanding of the principles governing the relationships of spoken words to written or printed words, which allows accurate translation of printed or written language into spoken language, and of spoken language into written or printed language.[6]

The "Definitions of Linguistic Terms" found in table 3.1 include terms that will be used in this module. An understanding of these terms will enable you to work with the variety of materials available today for teaching phonic analysis skills.

Read one or more of the following references which present additional information concerning linguistic concepts:

5. Dolores Durkin, *Teaching Them to Read,* 2d ed. (Boston: Allyn & Bacon, 1974), pp. 234-35.
6. Albert J. Harris and Edward R. Sipay, *Effective Teaching of Reading,* 2d ed. (New York: David McKay Company, 1971), pp. 445-46.

Table 3.1

Term	Definition	Examples
Allophone	The total members of a phoneme class. These are phonetically alike, and do not show contrasts in meaning.	The [d] at the end of *mind* and the [d] at the end of *seed* are both allophones of the phoneme /d/. (Slanted lines are typically used to indicate phonemes, whereas brackets are used to indicate allophones.)
Consonant Blend	Two or three consonant sounds that are blended or combined but retain their separate identity: *play,* st*reet,* a*sk.*	*bl, cl, fl, gl, pl, sl, br, cr, dr, fr, gr, pr, tr, sc, sk, sm, sn, sp, st, sw, spl, spr, str, thr, tw, sch, scr*
Consonant Digraph	Two successive consonant letters whose recorded phonetic value is a single sound: *sh*ip, *ch*urch.	*ch, gh, ph, sh, th, wh, ck, ng*
Vowel Digraph	Two successive vowel letters whose recorded phonetic value is a single sound: l*ea*d, s*ay*.	*ai, au, ay, ea, ee, ei, eu, ie, oa, oo*
Diphthong	Two vowel sounds combined: beginning with the first and gliding smoothly into the next: n*oi*se, b*oy*.	*oi, oy, ou, ow, ew*
Grapheme	The written symbols which record the particular sounds of a language: the letter(s) which represent(s) a phoneme. Orthography is the writing, in proper order, of graphemes to form morphemes.	*b, sh*
Phoneme	The minimal unit of sound which signifies meaning, or which provides the smallest unit of contrast in paired words.	*pit* vs. *pat* *put* vs. *pot*
Phonogram	Combinations of letters within words that function as pronounceable units: *take, fine, right.* In some material phonograms are called *graphemic bases.*	*all, ick, ight, ack, ine, it, ill*

Source: With the exception of the **terms** *consonant blend* and *phonogram*, the definitions used here are derived from Heath W. Lowry, "A glossary of terms—linguistics," *The Reading Teacher* 22 (November 1968): 136-43.

Durkin, Dolores. *Teaching Them to Read.* 2d ed. Chap. 9, "Linguistics"; chap. 10, "Phonics: The Content." Boston: Allyn & Bacon, 1974.

Heilman, Arthur W. *Principles and Practices of Teaching Reading.* 3d ed. Chap. 7, "Phonics Instruction." Columbus, Ohio: Charles E. Merrill Publishing Company, 1972.

Hull, Marion A. *Phonics for the Teacher of Reading.* Columbus, Ohio: Charles E. Merrill Publishing Company, 1969. A programmed text which presents detailed explanations and specific examples.

May, Frank B. *To Help Children Read.* Module 2, "Helping Children Develop Skill in Phonic Analysis." Columbus, Ohio: Charles E. Merrill Publishing Company, 1973.

Smith, Nila Banton. *Reading Instruction for Today's Children.* Chap. 8, "Word Identification", pp. 88-94. Englewood Cliffs, N. J.: Prentice-Hall, 1963.

Zintz, Miles V. *The Reading Process: The Teacher and the Learner.* 2d ed. Chap. 10, "Word Recognition Skills." Dubuque, Iowa: Wm. C. Brown Company Publishers, 1975.

Activity 3

As Bagford points out in the introduction to this module, differences of opinion exist with regard to the way in which phonic analysis skills should be presented to children. Because of its potential for increasing children's understanding of what they learn through active participation in the learning process, a procedure known as the *inductive* approach is being used in this module. In her discussion of approaches to phonics instruction, Durkin describes the inductive approach:

> A different approach for teaching phonics is commonly described as being *inductive.* Like any inductive process, this methodology begins with specifics and then moves to a generalization about them. With phonics, the specifics are words and the generalization is a description of some visual-auditory feature that is common to them.
>
> . . . an inductive approach employs known words to help children discover phonic generalizations. In each instance, words are selected that have a visual-auditory feature in common. It is about this feature that the generalization makes a statement. Subsequently, that statement can be used to decode unknown words.[7]

Durkin then goes on to identify advantages in using an inductive approach:

> . . . with the child who is just beginning to learn to read, the idea that words are comprised of blended sounds that are represented by letters is totally new. At this stage, therefore, inductive instruction can make a special con-

---

7. Durkin, *Teaching Them to Read*, p. 282.

tribution by helping him understand the very nature of our written language as known words are used to teach letter-sound relationships.

Inductive instruction also has the potential of providing children with a strategy for learning. It does this by encouraging them to look at written words in ways that can help them induce phonic generalizations not yet formally taught. It thus gives them an opportunity not only to be independent learners but also to experience what might be called the delight of discovery. Of course, not all of this will happen with all children; still, inductive instruction does have this important potential. Used with beginners in phonics, it can also pave the way for a better understanding of what is being done when deductive methods are followed later.[8]

A specific procedure for using the inductive approach is described by McCullough in "An Inductive Approach to Word Analysis" that follows. Use these questions as your purposes for reading McCullough's procedure:

1. What are the four steps identified in this procedure (generalization and application will be considered two steps even though McCullough includes them in the same heading)?
2. Why does the auditory exercise precede the visual exercise?
3. For the visual exercise, the teacher selects words that are in the children's reading vocabulary. How does the selection of words for the application step differ?

An Inductive Approach to Word Analysis

When I was on the threshold of my teens, I went to visit some friends on a farm. City-bred, I thought that horses that were white were older than horses that were gray. There was a lot for me to learn in those two weeks.

One experience of that visit impressed me more than any other. I helped to bring in the cows one night, and the next night asked for the privilege of bringing them in all by myself. Not realizing the density of the ignoramus with whom he was dealing, my host consented.

I went out alone, down to the pasture along the strip of woods, rounded up the cows, and got them started up the lane toward the barn. My bosom swelled with pride in my accomplishment and with affection toward the beasts that were cooperating so well. Full of confidence, I began to stride ahead of the herd. But when I reached the barn and looked back down the lane, I could see the swinging tails of cows headed for the pasture again.

I never think of the teaching of word analysis without remembering those cows, for they told me more in a short time about the relationship between . . . a teacher and a group of learners than a good deal of the research in reading. With all due apology to proud parents and fond teachers, I must report that children are much like cows. You never can tell where they

8. Ibid., pp. 283-84.

are in their thinking if you get ahead of them. You have to prod with questions and let them take the lead. Otherwise, chances are good that you will lose them and arrive at the barn—the end of the lesson or the end of the book —without them.

The essence of an inductive approach to teaching word analysis is just that. The teacher fences off the desired area and the children go up the lane; the children are the first to discover; the teacher encourages from the rear until everyone gets to the barn.

Auditory Exercise: Take the problem of teaching the sound of the initial consonant *b*. First, the teacher has to make sure that the children can discriminate between the sound of *b* and the sound of other letters. She says, "I am thinking of the name of a person in this room. It begins like *Billy* and *Bobby*. What do you suppose it is?" She hopes that someone will say *Betty* or *Bonita*. But perhaps little Milly will say, "Peter." The teacher will say, "Let's listen. Do these words begin alike: *Billy, Bobby, Peter?*" Milly, reading the teacher's face better than the sound of the initial consonant *b*, says, "No," but she's really not sure.

The teacher must spend a good many little game periods with Milly and her kind until Milly's batting average is championship level. It won't help if the teacher says, "Look, Chum; *Billy* and *Bobby* begin with the same sound as *Betty, Bernard,* and *Bonita*. Now, remember this." Milly will be memorizing instead of listening to initial sounds. No, the teacher must stay behind the cows. "I'm thinking of something that begins like *ball* and *bat* and it's a game." "I'm thinking of something that begins like *box* and *bag* and it is on the table." Something to eat, something to wear, whatever it is, the teacher must keep after the group until the children catch on. Perhaps teacher can work this into a game that reinforces some other learning—reminds the children of facts they are learning in other subject areas.

As seatwork, the children may draw pictures of words that begin with that sound. A chart may be made of such pictures. In meaning for the children, such a chart is superior to a chart the teacher makes of commercial pictures.

If the initial sound is *s* and a child says that *circus* begins like *see* and *say*, the teacher should accept this offering in the ear training exercise, for these words do, indeed, begin alike in sound.

Visual Exercise: When the children can hear the initial sound of *b*, they are ready to look at words containing that initial sound, and to determine the letter which makes it. Notice that the *ear* training *precedes* the *visual* lesson. Now that they have proved that they can distinguish the initial consonant sound *b* from other sounds, the teacher takes them on to the visual exercise.

Since children learn a new task better if that task involves known facts, it is better to use in the visual exercise, words the children have in their reading vocabulary—sight words familiar to them. This implies three things: 1. The visual exercise will not be undertaken unless and until the children have mastered by sight two, but preferably three or four or five words that start with *b*. (More words are preferable to fewer words because the more examples the children have of the principle they are trying to discover, the easier it will be to observe.) 2. Even though, on occasion, children who are invited to engage in the visual exercise are operating at different vocabulary levels, there will be an attempt on the part of the teacher to keep the vocabulary at the sight vocabulary level of the poorest reader in the group. Otherwise, the poorest reader will not be only the poorest reader but the one for whom the exercise is made deliberately more difficult by the use of words he does not know. Perhaps this suggests that, ordinarily, the first visual lesson should be administered to a relatively homogeneous group—a group reading at the same level of sight vocabulary—and that only later visual exercises should involve mixed groups. 3. Obviously, the children will have been reading for some time before such a visual exercise is undertaken, since the limited vocabulary of the beginning reading books does not start with a cluster of *b* words, such as: "Billy bumped his buttons on the back bench." When parents complain that their children are not learning phonics, this is the teacher's answer. The ingredients for the lesson are not yet assembled. One might just as well say, "Why haven't you baked that three-egg cake today?" Answer: "Not enough eggs yet."

Since children forget something they do not use, two other precautions should be taken in the use of the visual exercise: 1—The visual exercise should be introduced when it will be useful in the solution of new words. If the next story the children are to read will contain a *b* word, it is a good time to introduce the visual exercise. Then, 2—in introducing the next story the teacher will not tell the children the word. She will, rather, present it with a picture or put it into a revealing context: "The *baker* makes bread and cake," and let the children guess from the picture or verbal context, and from the initial consonant, what the word must be. By her encouragement of the use of the new learning, the teacher does not let it rust out.

The visual exercise goes something like this: The teacher says, "I am thinking of some words you have been reading. They begin like *ball* and *boy*. What are they?" As she says *ball*, she writes *ball* (in manuscript if the children are accustomed to manuscript) and stands so that all can see the word as she writes it. As she says *boy*, she writes *boy* under *ball*, so that the *b*'s are in a column, directly under one another:

ball

boy

This means that, as the teacher writes the *b* in each word, the children hear that sound in the teacher's pronunciation of *ball*, *boy*, or whatever word it is; the sight and sound of the letter occur simultaneously.

Jimmy volunteers, "*Box*." The teacher says and writes *box*, immediately under *boy*. "Now, let's all say these words and listen to hear whether Jimmy is right." The group says, "Ball, boy, box." Does *box* begin with the same sound as "*boy* and *ball?*" They agree that it does. Bobby offers, "*Baby*," and the teacher goes through the same procedure as with *box*.

When four or five words are in a column on the blackboard, the teacher decides to see whether or not the children are arriving at the barn. "Let's

say the words over together and listen to the beginning of each word again."
The children look and listen. "Does anyone notice anything alike about the
way the words *look?*" Algernon will say they are all short words. He is still
in the pasture. But, if the teacher is lucky and the children are ready, Joe
will say, "They all begin with the same letter." The teacher looks at him
as at a diamond stick-pin on the floor of the supermarket. "Say that again!"
Joe sticks out his chest two more inches and says it again. "How many of you
think you see what Joe sees in these words?" Those who see and those who
are good politicians indicate that they do. Algernon tries hard to come out
of the pasture, but he may not make it that day.

"Who would like to come up to the blackboard and draw a line under
the letter in the first word?" Joe had better have the honor. "Who would
like to draw a line under the letter in the second word?" Some children who
have not caught on up to this time may be helped by this stress. Meanwhile,
the opportunity to go up and find the right letter gives Joe and his ilk a great
deal of satisfaction. (A variation of this which emphasizes form is to overlay
the initial *b* in each word with colored chalk, different children doing this.)

Generalization and Application: Now to close the barn door: "Who
can tell me what he knows from this? When a word begins with this letter,
what do we know about its sound?" John, the philosopher, may come
through: "When a word begins like that, I know it begins like *ball* and *boy*
and *box* and *baby.*" Perhaps, to dramatize the statement, the teacher will
write a *b* above the words in the column on the blackboard. She may, in addition, engage the children for a few minutes in proving their point by finding other words beginning with *b,* on charts and signs about the room.
Young children enjoy the physical relief of this field trip off the chairs.

But, before dismissing the group, she says, "Let's see whether we can
use what we know. I shall write a sentence on the blackboard. Read it to
yourselves and see if you can recognize the new word." She writes a sentence in which all words are known to the children by sight except the new
b word: "Pony's home is in the barn." After time for silent reading, Martha
is selected to read the sentence. "How did you know, Martha?" Martha says,
"I knew because Pony's home *is* in a barn and because *barn* begins with the
same letter as *ball.*"

The follow-up can be one of several tasks. The teacher may have other
such sentences, which the children are to read, in which they are to underline the *b* in the strange word, and for which they are to draw a picture representing the new word. She may have sentences with the *b*'s left out, for
the children to insert. She may have them find sentences in their readers
containing *b* words. She may have them make a list of all the words they
know that begin with *b*. She may have them trace over the *b*'s that begin
certain words, using a bright color. Some of these exercises are better than
others, in that they stress meaning as well as form. The exercises in which
the children write or trace over the *b*'s are good because of the tactile experience with the shapes of the letters.

The next day the teacher may appear with a chart which the children
may call their *ball* chart:

b— *ball*

boy

box

baby

As the children learn new *b* words, they will add them to the chart.[9]

Activity 4

The following lesson plan illustrates the application of McCullough's inductive approach to the teaching of a consonant blend. Read the plan using these three questions as a guide:

1. Can you identify the four steps outlined by McCullough?
2. How does the introduction attempt to help children find meaning in what they are going to do?
3. How does the application step relate to the introduction?

Lesson Plan
Consonant Blend

Grade Level: Second

I. Behavioral Objectives

   A. The children will be able to state that all words beginning with the consonant blend represented by *bl* sound the same at the beginning.

   B. The children will be able to apply this statement in pronouncing unfamiliar words.

II. Procedure

   A. Introduction

   How many like to read? Well, today we are going to work with an activity that will allow us to become better readers. This activity, when completed, will allow us to read words which we have never seen before.

9. Constance M. McCullough, *Handbook for Teaching the Language Arts* (San Francisco, Calif.: Paragon Publications, 1963), pp. 69-71. Reprinted by permission of Constance M. McCullough.

B. Development
   1. Auditory
      a. Put the following words on the board:
         block

         blue

         blow
      b. Ask the children to read the words. What sound do you hear that is the same in all of the words? (The sound represented by *bl*)
   2. Visual
      a. How do all the words look the same? (All begin with *bl*)
   3. Generalization
      a. What things are the same about all these words?
      b. When we see a word that begins with *bl,* what will we know about the beginning sound? Who can say that in a sentence?
   4. Application
      a. Present sentences that contain unknown words that have *bl* at the beginning.
         I cut my finger, but it did not <u>bleed.</u>
         Mother cannot <u>blame</u> me for the broken glass.
      b. Ask the children to read the sentences and pronounce the underlined words. Ask them how they knew the underlined words.
      c. Use the context of each sentence to help the children understand the meanings of the new words.
C. Conclusion
   Now you will be able to read words that you were not able to read before. This will help you to learn more about the things that interest you.

III. Evaluation

The children's ability to state the generalization and pronounce the new words will indicate their achievement of the objectives.

Activity 5

Teach one or more phonic elements (single consonants, digraphs, blends, diphthongs) to a group of children or peers. Use the inductive procedure as outlined by McCullough.

If you teach a group of children, it is important that you select elements that are appropriate in terms of the children's level of skill development. The classroom teacher is, of course, your best source of information for identifying the specific needs of the children you will be teaching.

In addition to consulting the teacher, you may want to administer a phonics inventory. The phonics inventory developed by Botel is reproduced in figure 3.2. Administering this inventory will provide you with useful information concerning children's acquisition of specific skills (the section of the inventory dealing with syllabication need not be given; syllabication will be considered in the module on structural analysis).

Activity 6

Reading programs typically suggest that a number of *phonic generalizations* be taught to children as aids in the analysis of unknown words. Because of the lack of agreement among reading programs concerning the generalizations to be taught, several attempts have been made to determine which generalizations are most useful by comparing the numbers of words that conform with the numbers of words that are exceptions to specific generalizations.[10]

In her investigation, Bailey analyzed the forty-five phonic generalizations previously studied by Clymer. A list of 5,773 words was compiled from the vocabularies of eight basal reading series (grades one through six). Words that appeared in two or more of the series were included in the list, with the exception of place names, proper names, and foreign words.

The following data were collected for each of the forty-five generalizations:

1. the number of words in the list to which the generalization applied;
2. the number of words that conformed to the generalization;
3. the number of words that were exceptions to the generalization.

Finally, the percentage of utility was computed for each generalization. The results of Bailey's analysis are presented in figure 3.3. Bailey does not suggest a specific percentage of utility for judging the usefulness of a generalization. In his study, Clymer proposes that a criterion level of 75 percent utility be applied in determining which generalizations are most

---

10. Mildred Hart Bailey, "The Utility of Phonic Generalizations in Grades One Through Six," *The Reading Teacher* 20 (February 1967): 413-18; Theodore Clymer, "The Utility of Phonic Generalizations in the Primary Grades," *The Reading Teacher* 16 (January 1963): 252-58; Robert Emans, "The Usefulness of Phonic Generalizations Above the Primary Grades," *The Reading Teacher* 20 (February 1967): 419-25.

FIGURE 3.2.
"Phonics Mastery Test"
from *The Botel Reading
Inventory*, by Dr. Morton
Botel. Copyright © 1971
by Follett Publishing
Company. Used by per-
mission.

BOTEL READING INVENTORY A

Phonics Mastery Test

Level A

1. Consonant Sounds

Directions: Listen carefully as I read a group of words. Write the beginning letter of each word after the correct number on your answer sheet. (*Note:* Since this is a test on sounds, not on spelling, any answer in parentheses should be accepted.)

1. par	(p)	6. vamp	(v)	11. jade	(j)	15. lair	(l)
2. batch	(b)	7. terse	(t)	12. hulk	(h)	16. yacht	(y)
3. malt	(m)	8. soot	(s)	13. zest	(z)	17. keel	(k, c)
4. wean	(w)	9. deft	(d)	14. nape	(n)	18. gape	(g)
5. foil	(f)	10. ramp	(r)				

2. Consonant Blends

Directions: Now I shall read some other words. Listen carefully and write the first two letters of each word. (*Note:* Acceptable answers are in parentheses. Since this is a test on sounds, not on spelling, any indicated answer is correct.

1. blithe	(bl)	6. slink	(sl)	11. gripe	(gr)	16. snag	(sn)
2. clog	(cl)	7. bray	(br)	12. prance	(pr)	17. spike	(sp)
3. flounce	(fl)	8. crass	(cr)	13. trek	(tr)	18. stint	(st)
4. glum	(gl)	9. dredge	(dr)	14. scud	(sc, sk)	19. swap	(sw)
5. plush	(pl)	10. frisk	(fr)	15. smear	(sm)		

3. Consonant Digraphs

Directions: In the next group of words listen carefully and again write the first two letters: *shorn, chide, thence, thatch.* Now write the two letters that end this word: *sling.*

1. shorn	(sh)	3. thence	(th)	5. sling	(ng)
2. chide	(ch)	4. thatch	(th)		

4. Rhyming Words

Directions: There are four words printed on your paper. Write two or more words that rhyme with each word and have the same group of ending letters.

| 1. ball | 2. make | 3. get | 4. will |

Level B

1. Long and Short Vowels

Directions: Listen carefully to the vowel sound in these words. If the vowel is short, write the word *short* and the letter for the vowel sound. If the vowel is long, write the word *long* and the letter for the vowel sound. (Correct answers are in parentheses.)

1. bid	(short i)	6. stop	(short o)
2. eve	(long e)	7. bun	(short u)
3. flat	(short a)	8. mile	(long i)
4. note	(long o)	9. best	(short e)
5. cave	(long a)	10. cute	(long u)

2. Other Vowel Sounds

Directions: Sometimes two vowels work together and have one sound. Some of these vowels are *oo, oi,* and *oy.* Also certain consonants, such as *r* and *w,* after a vowel change the sound of the vowel. Listen carefully to the words I say. If a word has a vowel team, write the two vowel letters. If a word has a vowel changed by a consonant, write the vowel and the consonant letters. (Correct answers are in parentheses. Some sounds can be spelled more than one way. Since this is a test on sounds, not on spelling, any of the indicated answers should be accepted.)

1. nook	(oo)	4. jar	(ar)	7. boil	(oi, oy)
2. blouse	(ou, ow)	5. Troy	(oy, oi)	8. whirl	(ir, er, ur)
3. broom	(oo)	6. claw	(aw, au)	9. scorn	(or)

useful. Examine the data in figure 3.3 using the following questions as a guide:

1. What is the range in percentage of utility of the generalizations?
2. If 75 percent utility were used as a criterion level for selecting generalizations for inclusion in a phonics program, which generalizations would qualify?

Developing Phonic Analysis Skills

FIGURE 3.2.
Continued.

Level C

1. Number of Syllables

Directions: Listen carefully to the words I say. Circle the number that shows the correct num ber of syllables in each word. *(Note:* Correct answers are in parentheses.)

A.	excitement	(3)	F.	anticipate	(4)
B.	spice	(1)	G.	motel	(2)
C.	music	(2)	H.	mechanical	(4)
D.	whispering	(3)	I.	leaf	(1)
E.	orbit	(2)	J.	consider	(3)

2. Accented Syllable

Directions: Listen carefully and circle the num ber that shows the accented syllable in each word I say. *(Note:* Correct answers are in pa rentheses.)

A.	excitement	(2)	F.	anticipate	(2)
B.	spice	(1)	G.	motel	(2)
C.	music	(1)	H.	mechanical	(2)
D.	whispering	(1)	I.	leaf	(1)
E.	orbit	(1)	J.	consider	(2)

Nonsense Words

Directions: This is an individual test. Each stu dent should be asked to read the words aloud. *(Note:* Beyond the third grade, the test may be administered as a quick-screening test. If the student passes it successfully, he does not need to be given Levels A, B, and C.)

The phonetic respelling and stressed sylla bles are indicated in parentheses. Short vowels are not marked, and the schwa (ə) symbol is used for the short *u* sound in both stressed and unstressed syllables.

1. ringtrape (ring'trāp)
2. pegflitting (peg'flit·ing)
3. concealter (kən·sēl'tər)
4. flingle (fling'l)
5. decentively (dē·sent'iv·lē)
6. fragmil (frag'mil)
7. aggravement (ə·grāv'ment)
8. craminstate (kram·in·stāt')
9. jungulation (jəng·u·lā'shən)
10. sloapclinger (slōp'kling·ər)
11. whister (hwis'tər)
12. calcumvent (kal'kəm·vent)
13. tampillage (tam·pil'ij)
14. chumertracing (chəm·ər trās'ing)
15. donagrant (don'ə·grant)

Note: Generalizations 1, 2, 3 and 4 are often referred to in the following way:

1. VV (vowel-vowel) pattern
2. CVC (consonant-vowel consonant) pattern

3. CV (consonant-vowel) pattern
4. VCe (vowel-consonant-final *e*) pattern

Activity 7

Phonic generalizations can be taught inductively using the procedure outlined by McCullough (activity 3). The following lesson plan illustrates the application of the inductive approach in teaching phonic generalizations. Read the plan using the following questions as a guide:

1. Can you identify the auditory, visual, generalization, and application steps?
2. Why were the auditory and visual steps reviewed before the children were asked to state the generalization?
3. How does the context of each sentence in the application step help the children understand the *meaning* of the new word after they have pronounced it?

Lesson Plan
Phonic Generalization

Grade Level: Third

I. Behavioral Objectives
   A. The children should be able to form the following generalization: In words with *ay*, the *y* is silent and the *a* usually has a long sound.
   B. The children should be able to use this generalization to pronounce unfamiliar words to which it applies.

II. Procedure
   A. Introduction
     Today we are going to do something that will help you read faster and better. When we're finished you will know some new words. Then when you come across these words in a book, you'll be able to recognize them and read them.
   B. Development
     1. Put these words on the board.
        play
        day
        gray
        may
     2. Let's say these words aloud. What is the vowel? (*a*) What sound does the vowel have? (long) Do all these words have the same vowel sound?

FIGURE 3.3. Utility of Phonic Generalizations, Grades One Through Six. From Mildred Hart Bailey, "The Utility of Phonic Generalizations in Grades One Through Six," *The Reading Teacher* 20 (February 1967):415-17. Reprinted with permission of Mildred Hart Bailey and the International Reading Association.

The Utility of Phonic Generalizations in Grades One Through Six

Generalization	No. of Incidents	No. of Words Conforming	No. of Exceptions	Percent. of Utility
1. When there are two vowels side by side, the long sound of the first vowel is heard, and the second vowel is usually silent.	1732	586 (leader)†	1146 (breath)	34
2. When a vowel is in the middle of a one-syllable word, the vowel is short.	1021	730	291	71
Middle letter	430	335 (flank)	95 (her)	78
One of the middle two letters in a word of four letters	478	325 (glen)	153 (long)	68
One vowel within a word of more than four letters	113	70 (depth)	43 (knight)	62
3. If the only vowel letter is at the end of a word, the letter usually stands for a long sound.	38	29 (go)	9 (do)	76
4. When there are two vowels, one of which is final *e*, the first vowel is long and the *e* is silent.	578	330 (cradle)	248 (judge)	57
5. The *r* gives the preceding vowel a sound that is neither long nor short.	1604	1378 (depart)	226 (merit)	86
6. The first vowel is usually long and the second silent in the digraphs *ai, ea, oa,* and *ui.*	497	298	199	60
ai	121	87 (acclaim)	34 (plaid)	72
ea	259	143 (bean)	116 (create)	55
oa	66	63 (roam)	3 (broad)	95
ui	51	5 (pursuit)	46 (biscuit)	10
7. In the phonogram *ie,* the *i* is silent, and the *e* has a long sound.	88	27 (grieve)	61 (brier)	31
8. Words having double *e* usually have the long *e* sound.	171	148 (exceed)	23 (deer)	87

†Words in parentheses are examples, either of words following the rule or of exceptions, depending on the column.

Generalization	No. of Incidents	No. of Words Conforming	No. of Exceptions	Percent. of Utility
9. When words end with silent *e*, the preceding *a* or *i* is long.	674	340 (amaze)	334 (give)	50
10. In *ay*, the *y* is silent and gives *a* its long sound.	50	44 (spray)	6 (prayer)	88
11. When the letter *i* is followed by the letters *gh*, the *i* usually stands for its long sound, and the *gh* is silent.	35	25 (flight)	10 (weight)	71
12. When *a* follows *w* in a word, it usually has the sound *a* as in *was*.	78	17 (wand)	61 (sway)	22
13. When *e* is followed by *w*, the vowel sound is the same as represented by *oo*.	35	14 (shrewd)	21 (stew)	40
14. The two letters *ow* make the long *o* sound.	111	61 (flow)	50 (scowl)	55
15. *W* is sometimes a vowel and follows the vowel digraph rule.	180	60 (arrow)	120 (drew)	33
16. When *y* is the final letter in a word, it usually has a vowel sound.	518	462 (lady)	56 (key)	89
17. When *y* is used as a vowel in words, it sometimes has the sound of long *i*.	596	63 (ally)	533 (silly)	11
18. The letter *a* has the same sound (ô) when followed by *l*, *w*, and *u*.	346	119 (raw)	227 (laugh)	34
19. When *a* is followed by *r* and final *e*, we expect to hear the sound heard in *care*.	24	23 (flare)	1 (are)	96
20. When *c* and *h* are next to each other, they make only one sound.	225	225 (charge)	0	100
21. *Ch* is usually pronounced as it is in *kitchen*, *catch*, and *chair*, not like *sh*.	225	196 (pitch)	29 (chute)	87

FIGURE 3.3. Continued.

Generalization	No. of Incidents	No. of Words Conforming	No. of Exceptions	Percent. of Utility
22. When *c* is followed by *e* or *i*, the sound of *s* is likely to be heard.	284	260 (glance)	24 (ancient)	92
23. When the letter *c* is followed by *o* or *a*, the sound of *k* is likely to be heard.	428	428 (canal)	0	100
24. The letter *g* often has a sound similar to that of *j* in *jump* when it precedes the letter *i* or *e*.	216	168 (genius)	48 (eager)	78
25. When *ght* is seen in a word, *gh* is silent.	40	40 (tight)	0	100
26. When a word begins *kn*, the *k* is silent.	17	17 (knit)	0	100
27. When a word begins with *wr*, the *w* is silent.	17	17 (wrap)	0	100
28. When two of the same consonants are side by side, only one is heard.	826	809 (dollar)	17 (accept)	98
29. When a word ends in *ck*, it has the same last sound as in *look*.	80	80 (neck)	0	100
30. In most two-syllable words, the first syllable is accented.	2345	1906 (bottom)	439 (attire)	81
31. If *a, in, re, ex, de,* or *be* is the first syllable in a word, it is usually unaccented.	398	336 (reply)	62 (extra)	84
32. In most two-syllable words that end in a consonant followed by *y*, the first syllable is accented and the last is unaccented.	195	190 (pony)	5 (apply)	97
33. One vowel letter in an accented syllable has its short sound.	3031	1960 (banish)	1071 (fortune)	65
34. When *y* or *ey* is seen in the last syllable that is not accented, the long sound of *e* is heard.	449	0	449 (ferry)	0

Generalization	No. of Incidents	No. of Words Conforming	No. of Exceptions	Percent. of Utility
35. When *ture* is the final syllable in a word, it is unaccented.	22	21 (future)	1 (mature)	95
36. When *tion* is the final syllable in a word, it is unaccented.	102	102 (notion)	0	100
37. In many two- and three-syllable words, the final *e* lengthens the vowel in the last syllable.	430	198 (costume)	232 (welcome)	46
38. If the first vowel sound in a word is followed by two consonants, the first syllable usually ends with the first of the two consonants.	1689	1311 (dinner)	378 (maple)	78
39. If the first vowel sound in a word is followed by a single consonant, that consonant usually begins the second syllable.	1283	638 (china)	645 (shadow)	50
40. If the last syllable of a word ends in *le,* the consonant preceding the *le* usually begins the last syllable.	211	196 (gable)	15 (crackle)	93
41. When the first vowel element in a word is followed by *th, ch,* or *sh,* these symbols are not broken when the word is divided into syllables and may go with either the first or second syllable.	74	74 (fashion)	0	100
42. In a word of more than one syllable, the letter *v* usually goes with the preceding vowel to form a syllable.	184	119 (river)	65 (navy)	65
43. When a word has only one vowel letter, the vowel sound is likely to be short.	1105	759 (crib)	346 (fall)	69
44. When there is one *e* in a word that ends in a consonant, the *e* usually has a short sound.	149	137 (held)	12 (clerk)	92
45. When the last syllable is the sound *r,* it is unaccented.	761	601 (ever)	160 (prefer)	79

3. What letter comes after the *a*? (*y*) Do we hear the *y*? (*y* is silent)
4. Go back and review all that was said about the ways in which the words are alike.
5. What can we say about these kinds of words? What sound will we try when we see a word that ends in *ay*? How can we say this in a sentence? Who else would like to say it?
6. Put sentences on the board containing unfamiliar words that can be identified using the *ay* generalization. Ask the children to read the sentences and tell how they were able to pronounce the new words.
   a. stray
      The little boy looked all around for his <u>stray</u> dog.
   b. fray
      When your coat gets old, it might <u>fray</u>.
   c. display
      The children's art work was put on <u>display</u> in the classroom.
7. Ask the children how they knew the meanings of the new words.

C. Conclusion
   1. Can anyone think of other words that fit our generalization?
   2. Now you have just taught yourself something that will help you to read better.

III. Evaluation

If the children can state the generalization and pronounce the new words they will have achieved the objectives.

Activity 8

Teach one or more phonic generalizations to a group of children or peers using the inductive approach. If you teach a group of children, be certain that each generalization you select is appropriate in terms of the children's level of development.

The items reproduced in figure 3.4 are taken from the *Durkin-Meshover Phonics Knowledge Survey*. These test items illustrate one way of assessing children's knowledge of phonic generalizations.

Activity 9

Observe one or more lessons in the teaching of phonic analysis skills. Use the following questions as a guide:

FIGURE 3.4.

Items for testing knowledge of vowel generalizations. From Dolores Durkin and Leonard Meshover, *Phonics Knowledge Survey* (New York: Teachers College Press, 1964). Reprinted by permission of the publisher.

The items are reproduced from the form on which the teacher records the child's responses. Notice that in each item the teacher has the child point to the letter he is being asked about.

Part 4. VOWEL GENERALIZATIONS

GENERALIZATIONS ABOUT VOWEL SOUNDS ARE ENCLOSED IN BOXES.

SCORING: CHECK APPROPRIATE BLANK.

A When there are two vowels within a syllable, the first is usually long and the second is silent, as in *aid*.

aef

	RIGHT	WRONG

1. If the letters *a*, *e*, and *f* were a word, what sound would the letter *a* have in that word? (Have child point to the first letter in the nonsense word.)   1. Long *a* ____ ____

2. What would be the sound of *e*?   2. Silent *e* ____ ____

3. Why would *a* and *e* have these sounds?   3. Why? ____ ____

4. How would you say this word?   4. Blend ____ ____

B When there are two vowels in a syllable, the second of which is final *e*, the first is usually long and the final *e* is silent, as in *ice*.

ibe

	RIGHT	WRONG

1. If the letters *i*, *b*, and *e* were a word, what sound would the letter *i* have in that word? (Have child point to the first letter in the nonsense word.)   1. Long *i* ____ ____

2. What would be the sound of *e*?   2. Silent *e* ____ ____

3. Why would *i* and *e* have these sounds?   3. Why? ____ ____

4. How would you say this word?   4. Blend ____ ____

C When there is one vowel within a syllable, it is usually short, as in *end*.

em

	RIGHT	WRONG

1. If the letters *e* and *m* were a word, what sound would the letter *e* have in that word? (Have child point to the first letter in the nonsense word.)   1. Short *e* ____ ____

2. Why would the letter *e* have this sound?   2. Why? ____ ____

3. How would you say this word?   3. Blend ____ ____

D When there is one vowel, but it is at the end of a syllable, it is usually long, as in *be*.

bu

	RIGHT	WRONG

1. If the letters *b* and *u* were a word, what sound would the letter *u* have in that word? (Have child point to the second letter in the nonsense word.)   1. Long *u* ____ ____

2. Why would the letter *u* have this sound?   2. Why? ____ ____

3. How would you say this word?   3. Blend ____ ____

FIGURE 3.5.
Phonemic Analysis: Consonant Correspondences. From *Teachers' Edition, Skills Handbook, for A Duck Is A Duck* and *Helicopters and Gingerbread* of the READING 360 series by Theodore Clymer and others, © Copyright, 1969, by Ginn and Company (Xerox Corporation), p. 79.

Used with permission. After each animal has been identified, the children are directed to draw a line from each picture to the letter that represents the beginning sound of the animal's name.

Look for the Animals

Phonemic analysis: Correspondences /f/<u>f</u>, /h/<u>h</u>, /z/z, /l/<u>l</u>, /p/<u>p</u>, /b/<u>b</u>, /s/<u>s</u>, /k/<u>c</u>, /m/<u>m</u>, /t/<u>t</u> in initial position

How Is <u>Sat</u> Like <u>Did</u>?

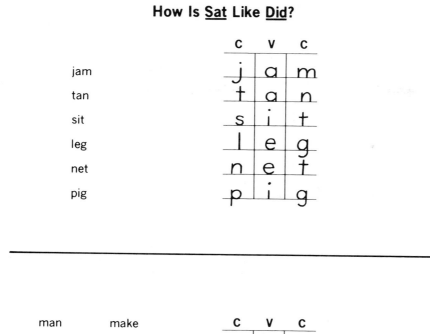

	c	v	c
jam	j	a	m
tan	t	a	n
sit	s	i	t
leg	l	e	g
net	n	e	t
pig	p	i	g

		c	v	c
man	make	m	a	n
let	men	l	e	t
like	eat	p	i	n
pin	he	m	e	n
beat				

<u>hat</u>	<u>did</u>	read	need
find	side	<u>ran</u>	<u>pet</u>
<u>can</u>	she	<u>sad</u>	ride
home	<u>wig</u>	rain	<u>ten</u>

Structural analysis: Unglided vowel sounds in the CVC spelling pattern

FIGURE 3.6. CVC Pattern. From *Teachers' Edition, Skills Handbook, for May I Come In?* of the READING 360 series by Theodore Clymer and others, © Copyright, 1969, by Ginn and Company (Xerox Corporation), p. 37. Used with permission.

The meaning of the letters CVC in this spelling pattern is reviewed. Then the children are instructed to (1) chart the words in the first section by writing their letters in the appropriate columns; (2) chart (only) the words in the second section that follow the CVC pattern; and (3) underline the words in the third section that follow the CVC pattern.

1. What phonic element or generalization is the focal point of the lesson?
2. Is the element or generalization being introduced or reviewed in this lesson?
3. If the element or generalization is being introduced, is an inductive approach being used?
4. What opportunities do the children have to *apply* the skill they have learned?

Activity 10

It is important that children be provided with activities which enable them to apply the phonic analysis skills they are learning. Two sources of such activities are the workbooks that accompany basal reading series and commercially produced games and kits. In using games and kits that are not correlated with specific reading programs, it is important for the teacher to be certain that the activities are appropriate for the level of skill development of the children. The exercises shown in figures 3.5 and 3.6 are examples of the kinds of workbook activities that provide children opportunities for using skills they have learned.

Activities and games developed by the teacher can also be used to help children apply the skills they are learning in a variety of contexts. The following activities are examples of the wide range of possibilities that exists:

> Motivation for individual practice with speech consonants and consonant blends may be provided with some simple games, such as Circle Wheels. Make one big wheel and attach a smaller one to it with a paper fastener. On the smaller wheel may be blends such as *ch*, *wh*, and *st*. On the larger wheel the word endings may be placed (*op*, *ip*, *ick*, and so forth). Children can make these from oak tag. By turning the small wheel inside the bigger one, new words are formed which children can sound out. Some of the words will be nonsense words, but careful planning will result in many recognizable words.[11]

Smith continues with other suggestions, as

> Well-chosen games such as the following provide interesting practice for phonics development. On three-by-five-inch cards print words with different vowel sounds, such as *pig*, *hat*, *wig*, *can*, *ran*, *sat*, and *big*. Shuffle the cards and give four to each child. A small pack should be left face down on the table. The first player reads a word from any of his four cards. If another player holds a card that contains a rhyming word, he must give the card to the player calling for it. The next player receives a chance to call any of his words. When a player fails to get a card from any of the others, he may draw

11. James A. Smith, *Creative Teaching of Reading in the Elementary School,* 2d ed. (Boston: Allyn & Bacon, 1975), p. 239.

from the pack on the table. If he still fails to get a rhyming word, or if he cannot read the card he has chosen, he must discard the card he called. The player with the most cards at the end is the winner.[12]

Develop one or more activities that children can use in applying phonic analysis skills. Assess the effectiveness of the activities after you have used them with children. The following references are good sources of ideas:

Dallmann, Martha; Rouch, Roger L.; Chang, Lynette Y. C.; and DeBoer, John J. *The Teaching of Reading.* 4th ed. Chap. 5B, "Developing Skills in Word Recognition." New York: Holt, Rinehart and Winston, 1974.

Herr, Selma E. *Learning Activities for Reading.* 2d ed. Dubuque, Iowa: Wm. C. Brown Company Publishers, 1970.

Russell, David H., and Karp, Etta E. *Reading Aids Through the Grades.* Second revised edition by Anne Marie Mueser. New York: Teachers College Press, Columbia University, 1975.

Shankman, Florence. *Games and Activities to Reinforce Reading Skills.* New York: MSS Information Corporation, 1972.

Smith, James A. *Creative Teaching of Reading in the Elementary School.* 2d ed. p. 57-58, 231-43. Boston: Allyn & Bacon, 1975.

Smith, Nila Banton. *Reading Instruction for Today's Children.* Chap. 8, "Word Identification," pp. 88-94. Englewood Cliffs, N. J.: Prentice-Hall, 1963.

Spache, Evelyn B. *Reading Activities for Child Involvement.* Chap. 4, "Word Perception." Boston: Allyn & Bacon, 1972.

Activity 11

Design activities of your own which you feel will enable you to achieve the competencies stated for this module.

Preassessment and Postassessment

A. Knowledge Level
1. Define and give one example of each of the following linguistic terms: consonant blend, consonant digraph, vowel digraph, diphthong, grapheme, phoneme, phonogram.
   Criteria for successful performance:
     a) the definition of each term is correct;
     b) the example given for each term is correct.
2. State three phonic generalizations that have a utility of at least 75 percent according to Bailey's analysis.
   Criteria for successful performance:
     a) each generalization is accurately stated;

12. Ibid., p. 243.

b) each generalization is correctly identified as having a utility of at least 75 percent.

B. Performance Level
  1. Planning the Lesson
     a) Develop plans for teaching (1) a phonic element (single consonant, digraph, blend, diphthong) and (2) a phonic generalization using the inductive procedure outlined by McCullough for each lesson. For both (1) and (2) devise an activity/material that will enable children to apply their knowledge of the phonic element or generalization you plan to teach.
     b) Criteria for successful performance:
        (1) the objectives are stated in terms of pupil behavior;
        (2) the instructional procedures outlined by McCullough are identifiable and in the correct sequence;
        (3) the activity/material devised is appropriate for the element and generalization being taught;
        (4) the procedures for the evaluation of pupil achievement are identified.

  2. Teaching the Lesson
     a) Arrange to teach the lessons to small groups of children. Arrange to
        (1) have the instructor or cooperating teacher observe the lessons, or
        (2) tape the lessons.
     b) Criteria for successful performance:
        (1) there is evidence that the pupils have achieved the objectives;
        (2) the student has demonstrated the ability to adapt his teaching procedures as necessary, in response to pupil needs, during the lesson.

  3. Evaluating the Lesson
     a) After the lessons have been taught, write an evaluation of each one. Respond to the following questions in your evaluations.
        (1) Did the pupils achieve the objectives? Support your answer with specific evidence.
        (2) If there were pupils who did not achieve the objectives, can you identify the experiences they need now in order to reach the objectives?
        (3) Are there elements of the lesson that you would approach differently if you were to teach the lesson again?
     b) Follow one of these procedures:
        (1) If the instructor has observed the lessons, schedule a conference to discuss both plans and lessons.

(2) If the cooperating teacher has observed the lessons, ask for written evaluations and then schedule a conference with the instructor to discuss the plans, the lessons, and the cooperating teacher's evaluations.

(3) If the lessons have been taped, schedule a conference with the instructor to discuss the plans and the taped lessons.

References

Bond, Guy L., and Wagner, Eva Bond. *Teaching the Child to Read.* 4th ed. Chap. 8, "Developing Word Recognition." New York: Macmillan Company, 1966.

Bush, Clifford L., and Huebner, Mildred H. *Strategies for Reading in the Elementary School.* Chap. 4, "Vocabulary Development." New York: Macmillan Company, 1970.

Dallmann, Martha; Rouch, Roger L.; Chang, Lynette Y. C.; and DeBoer, John J. *The Teaching of Reading.* 4th ed. Chap. 4, "Vocabulary Development." New York: Macmillan Company, 1970.

Durkin, Dolores. *Phonics and the Teaching of Reading.* 2d ed. New York: Teachers College Press, Columbia University, 1971.

———. *Teaching Them to Read.* 2d ed. Chap. 9, "Linguistics"; chap. 10, "Phonics: The Content"; chap. 11, "Phonics: Teaching Procedures." Boston: Allyn & Bacon, 1974.

Gray, William S. *On Their Own in Reading.* rev. ed. Chicago: Scott, Foresman and Company, 1960.

Harris, Albert J., and Sipay, Edward R. *Effective Teaching of Reading.* 2d ed. Chap. 8, "Learning to Recognize Words"; chap. 9, "Developing Independence in Word Recognition." New York: David McKay Company, 1971.

———. *How to Increase Reading Ability.* 6th ed. Chap. 14, "Developing Word-Identification Skills." New York: David McKay Company, 1975.

Heilman, Arthur W. *Principles and Practices of Teaching Reading.* 3d ed. Chap. 7, "Phonics Instruction." Columbus, Ohio: Charles E. Merrill Publishing Company, 1972.

Herr, Selma E. *Learning Activities for Reading.* 2d ed. Chap. 33, "Phonics." Dubuque, Iowa: Wm. C. Brown Company Publishers, 1970.

Hull, Marion A. *Phonics for the Teacher of Reading.* Columbus, Ohio: Charles E. Merrill Publishing Company, 1969.

Kottmeyer, William. *Decoding and Meaning.* Chap. 5, "Tactics in Teaching the Word Perception Skills." New York: McGraw-Hill Book Company, 1974.

May, Frank B. *To Help Children Read.* Module 2, "Helping Children Develop Skill in Phonic Analysis." Columbus, Ohio: Charles E. Merrill Publishing Company, 1973.

McCullough, Constance M. *Handbook for Teaching the Language Arts.* Pp. 66-75. San Francisco: Paragon Publications, 1963.

Otto, Wayne; Chester, Robert; McNeil, John; and Myers, Shirley. *Focused Reading Instruction.* Chap. 7, "Objectives for Word Attack." Reading, Mass.: Addison-Wesley Publishing Company, 1974.

Russell, David H. *Children Learn to Read.* 2d ed. Chap. 10, "A Developmental Word Recognition Program." Waltham, Mass.: Blaisdell Publishing Company, 1961.

Russell, David H., and Karp, Etta E. *Reading Aids Through the Grades.* Second revised edition by Anne Marie Mueser. New York: Teachers College Press, Columbia University, 1975.

Shane, Harold G. *Linguistics and the Classroom Teacher.* Washington, D. C.: Association for Supervision and Curriculum Development, 1967.

Shankman, Florence. *Games and Activities to Reinforce Reading Skills.* New York: MSS Information Corporation, 1972.

Smith, James A. *Creative Teaching of Reading in*

the Elementary School. 2d ed. Pp. 57-58, 231-43. Boston: Allyn & Bacon, 1975.

Smith, Nila Banton. Reading Instruction for Today's Children. Chap. 8, "Word Identification," pp. 88-94. Englewood Cliffs, N. J.: Prentice-Hall, 1963.

Spache, Evelyn B. Reading Activities for Child Involvement. Chap. 4, "Word Perception." Boston: Allyn & Bacon, 1972.

Spache, George D., and Spache, Evelyn B. Reading in the Elementary School. 4th ed. Chap. 11, "Word Recognition Techniques and Skills." Boston: Allyn & Bacon, 1977.

Stauffer, Russell G. Teaching Reading as a Thinking Process. Chap. 9, "Developing Skill in Word Recognition." New York: Harper & Row, Publishers, 1969.

Tinker, Miles A., and McCullough, Constance M. Teaching Elementary Reading. 3d ed. Chap. 8, "Word Identification and Recognition." New York: Appleton-Century-Crofts, 1968.

Walcutt, Charles C.; Lamport, Joan; and McCracken, Glenn. Teaching Reading. Chap. 28, "Phonics and Beginning Reading Instruction." New York: Macmillan Company, 1974.

Wallen, Carl J. Competency in Teaching Reading. Chap. 6, "Testing Strategies for Phonic Word-Attack Skills"; chap. 7, "Teaching Strategies for Phonic Word-Attack Skills." Chicago: Science Research Associates, 1972.

Zintz, Miles V. The Reading Process: The Teacher and the Learner. 2d ed. Chap. 10, "Word Recognition Skills." Dubuque, Iowa: Wm. C. Brown Company Publishers, 1975.

4

Developing Structural Analysis Skills

It is important that children develop a variety of skills to use in analyzing unfamiliar words. The focus in the preceding module was the development of skills in phonic analysis (analyzing words in terms of phoneme-grapheme relationships). The focus in this module is on the development of skills in structural analysis (analyzing words in terms of their meaningful units or morphemes). As Gray and McCullough point out, skills in phonic and structural analysis should be developed in parallel stages.[1] If this parallel development does not take place, and children acquire skills in only one of the areas, they will be handicapped when they attempt to apply techniques that are inappropriate in specific situations.

The module is introduced through Leo M. Schell's article, "Teaching Structural Analysis."[2] Schell raises critical questions concerning the validity of the content and instructional procedures found in structural analysis programs. He identifies questionable practices, and supports his criticisms with specific examples from a well-known basal reading series and from professional texts. On the basis of the evidence he presents, Schell calls for the development of more accurate content and better instruction than that found in current structural analysis programs. Read Schell's article, using the following questions as your purposes for reading:

1. William S. Gray, *On Their Own in Reading* (Chicago: Scott, Foresman and Company, 1960), p. 38; Constance M. McCullough, *Handbook for Teaching the Language Arts* (San Francisco: Paragon Publications, 1963), pp. 72-73.
2. Leo M. Schell, "Teaching Structural Analysis," *The Reading Teacher* 21 (November 1967); 133-37.

1. What problems can occur when children attempt to use their knowledge of the meanings of prefixes and suffixes?
2. What pronunciation difficulties do children encounter when they use principles of syllabic division based on dictionary vocabulary entries?
3. What steps does Schell suggest children use in applying structural analysis to unrecognized words?
4. How does Schell view the role of the teacher in relation to content and instruction in structural analysis programs?

Teaching Structural Analysis

Leo M. Schell

To teach children how to figure out the pronunciation and/or meaning of an unrecognized word through the use of phonic and structural analysis is one important goal of reading instruction. Yet Clymer (2) has shown that many phonic generalizations lack either validity or frequency of application and that consideration should be given to some possible revisions in the commonly taught content of phonic analysis. Recently, Winkley (13) has raised some similar disturbing questions about the worth of certain generalizations about accenting. It therefore seems a propitious time to examine some of the problems concerning the content of structural analysis as found in both professional methods textbooks and basal reading series.

The Meaning of Affixes

Methods textbooks typically list prefixes and suffixes which the elementary school pupil should know. Usually, it is not clear whether it is the pronunciation or meaning or both which pupils should know. If it is the meaning which is intended, some problems arise.

Few prefixes are valuable for meaning. Four prefixes commonly recommended to be taught—and their meanings—are:

con- .... together, with, very
ex- .... out of, from, beyond, without
pre- .... before in time
re- .... backwards, again

Yet, consider the plight of the intermediate grade pupil trying to apply what he has been taught to any of these words commonly found in elementary school textbooks: *conserve, exclaim, present,* and *resin.*

The obvious problem is that these prefixes have meaning to an elementary school child only when there is a known base word. Even though in Latin these prefixes were attached to base words, over the years these bases have lost their independent standing and the prefixes have become known as "absorbed prefixes." In such words, knowledge of the meaning of the prefix is virtually worthless.

Suffixes present difficulties in two ways. Many suffixes have multiple meanings; e.g., -ment may mean act, condition, or concrete instance. To use the suffix to help derive the word's meaning, the reader must (a) recall these three meanings, (b) choose the appropriate one, and (c) apply this meaning to the base form—a prodigious task for most elemen-

From *The Reading Teacher* 21 (November 1967): 133-37. Reprinted with permission of Leo M. Schell and the International Reading Association.

tary school pupils. Surely, there must be a *more efficient* procedure.

Suffixes are most valuable to the reader when they are affixed to a known base word; e.g., *development*. But, in some cases it does the reader little good to detach the suffix in order to locate the base word because the base changes forms when a suffix is added, e.g., *admission* and *deceptive*. In such instances, recognition and knowledge of the meaning of the suffix seem of little value in determining the meaning of an unrecognized word.

Inaccurate Instruction

Not only are there difficulties inherent in the construction and meaning of affixed words, but the accuracy of the content taught is sometimes questionable. Instructional techniques frequently fail to distinguish between reading and spelling. For example, one prominent reading specialist writes, "When a word ends in *y* following a consonant, *y* is usually changed to *i* when adding an ending as in *cried, ponies, tinier, happily*" (10). This rule goes from the base to the inflected form, a spelling sequence. The reading sequence should go from the inflected form to the base. Perhaps it isn't too confusing to children, but it seems to indicate some lack of understanding by those engaged in teaching teachers.

It appears that sometimes it is not clear whether pronunciation or syllabication comes first. The senior author of one of the best selling basal series writes in his professional text, "Lead pupils to note that the vowel sound (in "*paper*") is long and therefore, the first syllable is probably "*pa*" (5). Similarly, another basal series author writes in her professional text, "When two vowels come together and each keeps its own sound, they form separate syllables, as *pi-o-neer*" (7).

Both of these principles imply that the pupil must pronounce the word before he can syllabicate it. But, if he can already pronounce the word, why should he need to syllabicate it? Furthermore, the latter generalization is a tautology: the dependent and independent clauses say the same thing, just in different words. The definition of a syllable is such that this statement does not really tell one anything; it only masquerades as information.

Unfortunately, most principles of syllabic division are based on the vocabulary entry in the dictionary rather than on the respelling, a procedure excellent for composition but questionable for reading. Troup outlines the historical process by which the present system evolved and points out that

> The way a word is pronounced has nothing whatsoever to do with the way it is divided at the end of a line in writing. . . . Over the years, educators set up a kind of a phonics system based on a mechanical practice that was never intended to relate to speech. In any dictionary, for example, you will find the word *vision* divided *vi-sion* in the entry and respelled the only way it can be pronounced in English, the first syllable being *vizh* (11, p. 142).

Pupils are told that affixes form separate syllables and then asked to divide and pronounce words such as *building* which everyone pronounces in context as *bil-ding* rather than *bild-ing*. It is surprising there is not a complete generation of skeptics, unwilling to accept what is told them. Maybe teachers are lucky students do not take instruction too seriously!

Directions for how to use structural analysis to unlock an unrecognized word may be inefficient even if not inaccurate. One fourth grade basal workbook tells pupils to syllabicate the word and then look for affixes (8). Since affixes are predominantly monosyllabic, it seems easiest to locate known affixes first. This leaves only the base word to be syllabicated.

Practice exercises in workbooks, basal series, etc. leave much to be desired. One fifth grade workbook presents this principle, "If a word ends in *le* preceded by a consonant, the consonant is included in the last syllable," and then asks the pupil to apply it to the word *single* (9). A widely used methods text uses *donkey* as appropriate practice for the rule about dividing syllables between medial consonants (1). These words may follow the respective generalizations, but they would be of little help in pronouncing an unknown word.

Valuable Principles?

It may be a waste of pupils' time to teach them certain structural principles. One methods text recommends teaching this accenting generalization: "In multisyllabic words, the first or second syllable has either a primary or secondary accent (su'per-vi'sor, re-spon'si-bil'i-ty)" (6). If the reader syllabicates correctly and then accents incorrectly, is he at much of a disadvantage? The purpose for learning accenting principles is to allow the reader to recreate the sound of a word he already knows, to activate its auditory memory. Should the reader give the first rather than the second syllable a primary accent, it hardly seems that this minor deviation will hinder the desired recreation. Having children learn this principle seems to be the educational equivalent of "overkill."

From Here, Where?

The foregoing discussion was not intended to be a comprehensive survey of all the problems associated with the content and methodology of structural analysis. It was meant only to highlight, to call attention to, certain facets of the topic which deserve critical scrutiny. Some suggestions for dealing with these problems seem warranted.

That pupils should be made aware of the limited applicability of the meaning of prefixes seems an obvious first step. But, if it has ever been previously suggested, it has never been practiced systematically. Intermediate grade pupils should have a realistic perception of what they can—and cannot—do with their learnings. To help them attain this goal, after introducing and practicing on prefix meanings, it would be wise to present and discuss some common exceptions, e.g., *disaster, illusion,* and *uncouth.*

In dealing with the meaning of suffixes, perhaps it would be more efficient to stress the grammatical function of the suffixed word in the sentence than to teach the meaning of individual suffixes. For example, rather than teach that *-al* means "pertaining to" and that therefore *musical* means "pertaining to music," have pupils examine the location of "musical" in the sentence and note its relation to other words. In "We went to a musical comedy," the grammatical function of the word is an obvious cue to the grammatically informed that music had a dominant role in the play.

To rectify inaccurate instruction, there must be more precise understanding of how structural analysis aids in unlocking unrecognized words. Possibly better than teaching a set of separate and independent rules (tactics), concentration should be on a general technique (strategy) applicable to various situations. The first three steps of such an approach could be:

1. Visually locate and isolate any recognized affixes.
2. If the base word is not recognized, syllabicate it.
3. Determine the vowel sound in each syllable.

This approach begins with the affixed form and goes to the base form, a realistic reading procedure. It also treats syllabication as an integral part of phonics, which is its correct role.

It seems probable that linguists with their emphasis on the subordination of writing to speaking may provide a more functional set of principles governing syllabic division than those now used. Teachers need to know how best to handle the syllabication of words such as *connect* and how to cope with the problem of neutral (schwa) sounds in unaccented syllables.

The most practical way to teach accenting generalizations would seem to be to coordinate them with dictionary work rather than to present and practice them in isolation. This approach not only gives pupils independence with unrecognized words in their listening vocabulary, but also helps them pronounce words not already in their listening vocabulary—the two functions of accenting. "Two birds with one stone."

There must be studies using the techniques of Clymer (2) and Winkley (13) to provide information about as yet uninvestigated areas of structural analysis and to extend their ideas to other material and grade levels. However, twiddling collective thumbs until someone produces this information hardly seems the proper attitude. Teachers need to be selective in what they teach and how they teach it. They should feel free to omit a principle that has little applicability or to revise suggested procedures so they are correct and accurate. A teacher is primarily a decision maker and should not be shackled to suggestions in teachers' manuals.

And finally, we must consider the possibility that our total approach to the teaching of syllabication is wrong. I am not really convinced that calculating the percentage of utility of a rule and then using only those which meet some criteria—or possibly revising the rules to make them more useful—is much of an answer. Especially for below-average intelligence youngsters and definitely for retarded readers. Glass (3, 4) and Wardhaugh (12)

have penetratingly questioned some of our traditional assumptions about how we should teach children to syllabicate words. Glass can find no evidence that adults or children apply known principles of syllabication in sounding out an unrecognized multisyllabic word. He maintains that readers respond to clusters of letters rather than looking for places to divide a word according to certain principles. (To understand his contention, look at these two words, *phenylpuruvic, oligaphrenia.* Did you apply syllabication principles? Or did you look for pronounceable clusters of letters?) He outlines a program labeled "perceptual conditioning" which he says has been used with numerous children with gratifying success. The idea merits serious consideration. The prevailing attitude seems to be "Which rules are most valid?" and "How can we help children better learn these rules?" Perhaps we should ask, "Are there ways other than rules which can be equally efficacious?"

There seems to be sufficient evidence that some of the content of structural analysis is incorrect and seldom applicable and that some current methodology may be inefficient and questionable. All teachers must be aware of these shortcomings and must search for more accurate content and better methods of instruction.

References

1. Bond, G. L., and Wagner, Eva. *Teaching the Child to Read.* New York: Macmillan, 1966, p. 167.
2. Clymer, T. The utility of phonic generalizations in the primary grades. *The Reading Teacher,* January 1963, 16, 252-258.
3. Glass, Gerald G. The strange world of syllabication. *Elementary School Journal,* 67 (May 1967), 403-405.
4. Glass, Gerald G. The teaching of word analysis through perceptual conditioning. *Reading and Inquiry,* J. Allen Figurel, ed. Newark,

Del.: International Reading Association, 1965, 410-413.

5. Gray, W. S. *On Their Own in Reading.* Chicago: Scott, Foresman, 1960, p. 128.

6. Harris, A. J. *Effective Teaching of Reading.* New York: McKay, 1962, p. 369.

7. Hester, Kathleen. *Teaching Every Child to Read.* New York: Harper & Row, 1964, p. 149.

8. Russell, D. H., and McCullough, Constance M. *My Do and Learn Book to Accompany Roads to Everywhere.* Boston: Ginn, 1961, p. 23.

9. Russell, D. H., and McCullough, Constance M. *My Do and Learn Book to Accompany Trails to Treasure.* Boston: Ginn, 1961, p. 13.

10. Smith, Nila Banton. *Reading Instruction for Today's Children.* Englewood Cliffs, N. J.: Prentice-Hall, 1963, p. 225.

11. Troup, Mildred. Controversial issues related to published instructional materials. Controversial issues in reading and promising solutions. *Supplementary Educational Monographs,* No. 91, 1961, 135-144.

12. Wardhaugh, Ronald. Syl-lab-i-ca-tion. *Elementary English,* 43 (Nov. 1966), 785-788.

13. Winkley, Carol K. Which accent generalizations are worth teaching? *The Reading Teacher,* December 1966, 20, 219-224.

Module Competencies

The competencies that you will develop as you work with this module reflect two purposes. The first is to help you extend your knowledge of linguistic concepts to include those associated with structural analysis. The second is to enable you to develop techniques for working with children in the area of structural analysis.

The postassessments for this module identify the ways in which you will demonstrate your achievement of the module competencies and the criteria by which your performance will be evaluated.

Instructional Activities

The material presented in activity 2 defines the linguistic concepts you will encounter as you work with children in the area of structural analysis (competency 1). The application of the inductive approach in teaching the concept of *syllable* is illustrated in activity 3 (competency 2). Activities 4 and 5 focus on the teaching of specific structural elements inductively (competency 2). An analysis of the usefulness of eight generalizations concerning syllabication and accent is presented in activity 6 (competency 3). The focus of activities 7 and 8 is the use of the inductive approach in teaching syllabication generalizations (competency 2). The classroom observations suggested in activity 9 can provide you with a variety of teaching strategies that can be used with children as they learn and apply skills in structural analysis (competency 4). Examples of activities designed to help children apply the skills they are learning are provided in activity 10 (competency 4). In activity 11 you are encouraged to design activities of your own that will enable you to achieve the module competencies.

1. Define and give examples of the following linguistic terms: morpheme, root word, syllable, prefix, suffix, inflectional ending, compound word.
2. Develop plans for teaching structural elements and syllabication generalizations inductively.
3. Identify syllabication generalizations that can be considered for inclusion in structural analysis programs on the basis of percentage of utility.
4. Develop activities that will enable children to apply structural analysis skills.

Instructional Activities

Select from the following learning experiences those which you feel will enable you to achieve the competencies stated for this module:

Activity 1

Attend a seminar for orientation to this module.

Activity 2

The division of linguistics which underlies the area of structural analysis is *morphology*. This branch of linguistics is concerned with studying the meaningful units of a language. Shane defines the basic concepts within the division of *morphology*:

> Let us now turn to *morphology*. It comes from the Greek root *morph-* or *morpho-* meaning "form." It is the study of the forms of a language; of the meaningful units we call words.
>
> 1. *Morphophonemics* is concerned with the relation of syntax to phonemics —i.e., of word order to sound in language. In structural linguistics it applies to the phonemic modifications that accompany the addition or subtraction of morphemes. E.g., conspire-conspiracy in which "long i" becomes "short i."
> 2. *Morphemics* deals with the analysis of forms and how they enter into words.[3]

3. Harold G. Shane, *Linguistics and the Classroom Teacher* (Washington, D. C.: Association for Supervision and Curriculum Development, 1967), p. 14.

The definitions in table 4.1 include terms associated with structural analysis. You will find an understanding of these terms useful as you begin to examine materials and techniques used in teaching structural analysis skills.

Table 4.1

Definitions of Linguistic Terms

Term	Definition	Examples
Affix.	A bound morpheme which may be found either preceding or following a base. Prefixes are affixes before a base, and suffixes occur after a base.	*re*open work*able*
Allomorph.	An allomorph is a phonemic variation of a morpheme. It shares the same relationship to a morpheme as *allophone* does to *phoneme*.	*a* and *an* are examples of allomorphs of the one morpheme, *a*.
Compound Word.	A word composed of two or more words whose meanings are combined to form a different word.	*homework* *grandmother*
Inflectional Ending.	A suffix added to a word to indicate one of the following: plural, possession, comparison, third person singular, present participle, or change of tense.	boy*s*, dress*es*, Joan'*s* soft*er*, soft*est*, walk*s*, walk*ing*, work*ed*
Morpheme.	The minimal meaning unit of a language. It consists of some phonemes or combinations of phonemes, and may be described as "*free*" (e.g., ear, hare) or "*bound*" (e.g., pro-, est, etc.). It is indivisible without violating its meaning or remainders.	*tree* *re*make
Prefix.	A meaningful unit added to the beginning of a root word to modify its meaning.	*re*work, *over*pay
Root Word.	A base word that is not modified by a prefix, suffix, or inflectional ending.	*fill, car, boy, pay, soft*
Suffix.	A meaningful unit added to the end of a root word to modify its meaning.	care*ful*, home*less*
Syllable.	A word or part of a word which contains one vowel sound.	*meat, di vide,* *con tain ing*

Source: The definitions of *affix*, *allomorph*, and *morpheme* are derived from Heath W. Lowry, "A glossary of terms—linguistics," *The Reading Teacher* 22 (November 1968): 136-44.

Activity 3

The inductive approach described by McCullough which was presented in the module on phonic analysis can also be used in teaching skills in structural analysis. The following excerpt illustrates the application of this approach in helping children develop the concept of *syllable*. Read the suggested procedure using these two questions as a guide:

1. Can you identify the *auditory, visual,* and *generalization* steps?
2. Why doesn't the teacher *tell* the children that "There is a syllable for every *sounded* vowel?"

> *Syllabication*: The inductive approach may be applied to all phases of word analysis. In syllabication, for instance, the first job is ear training, the child's own discovery of the number of syllables in different words. "Let's tap out these words as I say them. How many taps can you give to beat out the word *re-turn?*" Ultimately, the teacher says, "These beats are called *syllables.*" She writes *syllables* as she says, "*Syl-la-bles.* (Some linguists advise the division should be syll-a-bles.) Let's all say it." One fine day, she puts several words of different lengths but of one syllable on the blackboard, directly under each other:
>
> catch
>
> go
>
> mitt
>
> bat

She asks how many syllables are in the first word, and so on, and after each word she has a child indicate the number of syllables. Then she asks how many vowels they hear in each word. The blackboard record becomes:

Word	Syllables	Vowels
catch	1	1
go	1	1
mitt	1	1
bat	1	1

"Can you tell the number of syllables in a word by something else besides tapping out the words?" "Yes;" someone says, "there is a syllable for every vowel." The teacher wants, "There is a syllable for every *sounded* vowel," but the exercise does not warrant that conclusion. Another day can be devoted to words like *came, strange,* and *toe;* another day to words like *boil* and *mouth.* In *came,* the *e is* silent (a marker); in *tail,* only the *a* is sounded; and in *boil* and *mouth,* the two vowels form a single, new sound. As children mature, the generalizations which they make about word analysis may well be expressed on the charts they make recording their knowledge of word parts.[4]

Activity 4

In the article which introduces this module, Schell identifies the problems intermediate grade children can encounter as they attempt to apply their knowledge of prefixes and suffixes.[5] Spache and Spache point out that a variety of criteria is used in selecting a syllabus of roots, prefixes, and suffixes for the intermediate grades.[6] On the basis of their evaluation of several suggested lists of elements, they propose that two lists of these structural elements be developed. One list would include items having only one meaning. The second list would include those items that function as common units or syllables. Children could be taught the pronunciations of these units, and would learn to recognize them visually, but would not need to learn their multiple meanings.[7] The elements that would comprise these two lists are shown in figure 4.1.

The following lesson plan illustrates the way in which the inductive approach can be used in teaching structural elements. Notice that the element being taught appears on the syllabus shown in figure 4.1. Use the following questions as a guide in reading the plan:

1. Why does the lesson begin with words the children know?
2. In the application step, how does the context of each sentence aid the children in determining the meaning of the unfamiliar word?

Lesson Plan
Structural Element (Prefix)

Grade Level: Fifth

    I. Behavioral Objectives

        A. The students will be able to state the generalization that when the prefix *over* is added to a word, the meaning of the word is changed to "too much" plus the root word.

        B. Using this generalization, the students will be able to define words that are unfamiliar to them.

4. Constance M. McCullough, *Handbook for Teaching the Language Arts* (San Francisco: Paragon Publications, 1963), pp. 71-72.
5. Schell, "Teaching Structural Analysis," p. 194.
6. George D. Spache and Evelyn B. Spache, *Reading in the Elementary School*, 3d ed. (Boston: Allyn & Bacon, 1973), pp. 488-89.
7. Ibid., p. 489.

A Syllabus of Roots and Affixes

Meaningful Units

Combining Forms
auto- (*self*)
homo- (same, alike)
micro- (small)
omni- (all, entire)
phono- (sound)
poly- (much, many)
pseudo- (false)
tele- (far off)

Prefixes
circum- (around)
extra- (outside, beyond)
in- (in, into)
intra-, intro- (inside)
mal- (bad)
mis- (wrong)
non- (not, the reverse)
out- (more than, beyond)
over- (too much)
self-
syn- (together)
under- (below)
up- (up, above)

Suffixes
-self
-wise (manner)

Visual Units

aqua-
audio-
bene-
cred-
junc-
mit-
pon-, pos-
scrib-, scrip-
vert-, vers-
vide-, vis-

a-, ab-   *per-*
ad-   *peri-*
ante-   *post-*
anti-   *pre-*
con-, com-, col- *pro-*
contr-   *re-*
de-   *sub-*
dis-, di-   *super-*
e-, ex-   *trans-*
inter-

Noun
   -ance, -ence, -tion, -cion, -sion, -ism,
   -ment, -al, -ic, -meter, -scope, -fet, ity,
   -gram, -graph
Agent ("one who")
   -eer, -ess, -ier, -ster, -ist, -stress, -trix
Adjectival
   -est, -fic, -fold, -from, -wards, -less,
   -able, -ible, -ble, -most, -like, -ous,
   -ious, -eous, -ose, -ful, -way, -ways

FIGURE 4.1.
A Syllabus of Roots and Affixes. From George D. Spache and Evelyn B. Spache, *Reading in the Elementary School*, 3d ed. (Boston: Allyn & Bacon, 1973), p. 490. Reprinted by permission of the publisher.

II. Procedure

  A. Introduction

    When you come to a word you don't recognize, what are some of the things you could look for in the word that would give you a clue to its meaning? (prefixes, suffixes, root words, etc.) How do these help you discover the meaning?

  B. Development

    1. These known words are on the board:

      a. The boss was afraid the men would become tired if they continued to <u>overwork</u>.

      b. For the little amount of work he finishes, she really does <u>overpay</u> him.

      c. If you continue to <u>overeat</u>, you will only gain weight.

      d. The game was tied when the quarter ended, so they went into <u>overtime</u>.

    2. Have the sentences read and discuss the meanings of the underlined words.

    3. What is the root word in each of the underlined words? With what prefix does each word begin?

    4. How did adding the prefix *over* change the meanings of the words?

    5. Now what can we say about the meanings of words that begin with the prefix *over*? Who can say that in a sentence? Let's say it together.

    6. These sentences, containing unfamiliar words, are on the board:

      a. Because he had never driven in winter, the new driver became <u>overanxious</u> at the thought of driving on the icy road.

      b. Saying that there were fifty thousand people on the bus was a definite <u>overstatement</u>.

      c. The racers' <u>overeagerness</u> caused them to start before the gun was sounded.

    7. Discuss the meanings of the underlined words. What clues helped you know the meanings of these words? (*over* and the way the word was used in the sentence)

  C. Conclusion

    Are there any other root words to which we can add the prefix *over*? How are the meanings of the words changed when *over* is added?

III. Evaluation

  If the students can state the generalization and give the definitions for the unfamiliar words, they have satisfied the objectives.

Activity 5

Teach two or more structural elements (inflectional endings, prefixes, suffixes, roots, compound words) inductively to a group of children or peers. If you teach a group of children, be certain that the elements you select are appropriate in terms of the children's level of skill development. The subtest shown in figure 4.2 represents one way of assessing children's knowledge of selected affixes. You may want to use this or a similar test with the children you will be teaching.

Activity 6

Materials and procedures for teaching children to use *syllabication generalizations* in analyzing unknown words are typically included in the structural analysis component of reading programs. Recently, questions have been raised regarding the practice of teaching these generalizations. In the introduction to this module, Schell gives specific examples of the problems children can encounter in attempting to use principles of syllabic division.[8] Other writers are voicing the same criticisms of current practices in teaching syllabication.[9] Waugh and Howell emphasize the responsibility of teachers who are confronted by this growing controversy.

> . . . Some resolution of the controversies will no doubt be forthcoming. In the meantime, teachers must continue evaluating instruction to determine which activities facilitate achievement of the end goal and which ones are merely traditional and may even be detrimental.[10]

Because of the difficulties surrounding their use, it is evident that if syllabication generalizations are going to be taught, only those which appear to be most useful should be considered for inclusion in the structural analysis program. One means of assessing the usefulness of syllabication generalizations is to follow the same procedure that has been used in analyzing phonic generalizations. Included within Bailey's analysis of phonic generalizations (activity 6 in Module 3 dealing with phonic analysis skills) are eight generalizations concerning syllabication and accent. The analysis of these generalizations is presented in table 4.2. Examine this analysis using the questions on page 124 as a guide.

8. Schell, "Teaching Structural Analysis," pp. 195-96.
9. Dorothy Z. Seymour, "Word division for decoding," *The Reading Teacher* 27 (December 1973): 275-83; R. P. Waugh and K. W. Howell, "Teaching modern syllabication," *The Reading Teacher* 29 (October 1975): 20-25; L. V. Zuck, "Some questions about the teaching of syllabication rules," *The Reading Teacher* 27 (March 1974): 583-88.
10. R. P. Waugh and K. W. Howell, "Teaching Modern Syllabication," *The Reading Teacher* 29 (October 1975):20.

FIGURE 4.2.
Root Words in Affixed
Forms. From *McCullough Word-Analysis Tests,* by Constance M. McCullough, © Copyright, 1962, 1960, by Ginn and Company (Xerox Corporation). Used with permission.

TEST VII   Root Words in Affixed Forms

N<small>AME</small> --

This is a test of your ability to see the prefix or suffix of a word as separate from its root. In the word *return,* you see the prefix *re* and the root *turn.* In the word *turning,* you see the root *turn* and the suffix *ing.* Look at each word in the test. Think which part of the word is the prefix or suffix and draw a circle around it. Do the two parts of the sample first.

SAMPLE: return   turning

1. thankful	16. fasten
2. darkness	17. transport
3. unbend	18. seventy
4. react	19. mistake
5. sorting	20. endear
6. export	21. natural
7. certainly	22. depart
8. starvation	23. commend
9. frosted	24. invite
10. speechless	25. ability
11. discourage	26. memorize
12. porter	27. improve
13. foolish	28. conserve
14. lovable	29. produce
15. dangerous	30. obtain

HIJ 765

PRINTED IN THE UNITED STATES OF AMERICA

Table 4.2

Generalizations Concerning Syllabication and Accent

Generalization	No. of Incidents	No. of Words Conforming	No. of Exceptions	Percent of Utility
1. In most two-syllable words, the first syllable is accented.	2345	1906 (bottom)	439 (attire)	81
2. If *a, in, re, ex, de,* or *be* is the first syllable in a word, it is usually accented.	398	336 (reply)	62 (extra)	84
3. In most two-syllable words that end in a consonant followed by *y*, the first syllable is accented and the last is unaccented.	195	190 (pony)	5 (apply)	97
4. If the first vowel sound in a word is followed by two consonants, the first syllable usually ends with the first of the two consonants.	1689	1311 (dinner)	378 (maple)	78
5. If the first vowel sound in a word is followed by a single consonant, that consonant usually begins the second syllable.	1283	638 (china)	645 (shadow)	50
6. If the last syllable of a word ends in *le,* the consonant preceding the *le* usually begins the last syllable.	211	196 (gable)	15 (crackle)	93
7. When the first vowel element in a word is followed by *th, ch,* or *sh,* these symbols are not broken when the word is divided into syllables and may go with either the first or second syllable.	74	74 (fashion)	0	100
8. In a word of more than one syllable, the letter *v* usually goes with the preceding vowel to form a syllable.	184	119 (river)	65 (navy)	65

1. What is the range in percentage of utility of the generalizations?
2. If 75 percent utility were used as a criterion level for selecting the generalizations to be taught, which generalizations would be excluded?

Note: Generalizations 4 and 5 are often referred to in the following way:

4. VCCV (vowel-consonant-consonant-vowel) pattern
5. VCV (vowel-consonant-vowel) pattern

Spache and Spache point out that although the fifth generalization does not reach the criterion level of 75 percent utility, many writers suggest retaining it because it functions more efficiently in total vocabularies and is useful as a complement to the fourth generalization.[11]

Activity 7

Syllabication generalizations can be taught inductively using the procedure outlined by McCullough. The following lesson plan illustrates the application of this procedure in teaching a syllabication generalization. Read the plan using the following questions as a guide:

1. Can you identify the auditory, visual, generalization, and application steps?
2. Why is it necessary for the auditory step to precede the visual step?
3. This lesson illustrates the relationship between phonic and structural analysis. Which of the phonic generalizations in Bailey's analysis do the children need to know in order to respond to the questions in step 3 of the Development?

Lesson Plan
Syllabication Generalization

Grade Level: Fourth

I. Behavioral Objectives

    A. The students will be able to state the generalization that when the first vowel sound in a word is followed by two consonants, the first syllable usually ends with the first of the two consonants.

    B. The students will be able to pronounce unknown words by applying this generalization.

11. Spache and Spache, *Reading in the Elementary School*, p. 493.

II. Procedure

    A. Introduction

    We have been learning different ways to divide words into syllables. How does this help you when you are reading and come to a word you don't know? Today you are going to learn another rule that will help you divide words into syllables.

    B. Development

      1. Have these words on the board:

> winter
> children
> picnic
> pencil

      2. Everyone say these words together. For each of the words ask what sound the first vowel has. (short)

      3. Where do you think the first syllable will end in the word *winter*? Why? (Because the vowel is short and a short vowel comes in the middle of a syllable.) Have a student draw the line on the board to show the division. Repeat this procedure for the three remaining words.

      4. How many consonants follow the first vowel in *winter*? Where does the first syllable end? (With the first consonant following the vowel.) Repeat this procedure for the three remaining words.

      5. When you see a word that has two consonants after the first vowel, where will you divide the word into syllables? Who can say this in a sentence? Would someone else like to say it in a sentence? After you divide the word into syllables, what sound will you give the first vowel? (short)

      6. Have sentences, each containing an unknown word, on the board. Have students read the sentences and tell how they knew how to pronounce the new words in each sentence. Ask the students how the other words in each sentence helped them figure out the meaning of the new word.

        a. The <u>bandit</u> pointed a gun at the man and took his money.

        b. Peter blew his whistle as a <u>signal</u> to start the race.

        c. There are only fifty houses in the <u>hamlet</u> where I live.

        d. Mary won the <u>contest</u> because she had more words spelled correctly than anyone else.

    C. Conclusion

    Now you have one more rule to use when you need to divide words into syllables.

Developing Structural Analysis Skills

III. Evaluation

If the students can state the generalization and pronounce the un-known words, the objectives have been achieved.

Activity 8

Teach one or more syllabication generalizations to a group of children or peers using the inductive approach. If you teach a group of children, be certain that each generalization you select is appropriate in terms of the children's level of development.

The items shown in figure 4.3 comprise the syllabication subtest of the *Durkin-Meshover Phonics Knowledge Survey.* You may want to use this test to assess the syllabication knowledge of the children you will be teaching.

Activity 9

Observe one or more lessons in the teaching of structural elements and syllabication generalizations. Use the following questions as a guide:

1. What structural element or syllabication generalization is the focus of the lesson?
2. Is the element or generalization being introduced or reviewed in this lesson?
3. If the element or generalization is being introduced, is an inductive approach being used?
4. What opportunities do the children have to *apply* the skill they have learned?

Activity 10

It is important that teachers provide children with a variety of opportunities to apply the structural analysis skills they are learning. Because of current criticisms of many types of activities included in structural analysis programs, however, it is necessary for teachers to examine materials carefully and select only those activities which will provide meaningful experiences for children. Both commercial and teacher-developed materials should be evaluated in terms of their contribution to children's ability to arrive at the meanings of words through the use of structural analysis.

The following activities suggested by Duffy emphasize the way in which structural elements serve as signals of meaning in communicating messages:

FIGURE 4.3.
Items for testing knowledge of syllabication. From Dolores Durkin and Leonard Meshover, *Phonics Knowledge Survey* (New York: Teachers College Press, 1964). Reprinted by permission of the publisher.

The items are reproduced from the form on which the teacher records the child's responses. For each item the child is presented visually with the whole word, e.g., *idfer*.

Part 15. SYLLABICATION

GENERALIZATIONS ABOUT SYLLABICATION ARE ENCLOSED IN BOXES.
SCORING: CHECK APPROPRIATE BLANK

A When two consonants are between two vowels, a syllable division is usually made between the consonants, as in *un der.*

idfer

1. In this section we will be talking about syllables in words. If the letters *i, d, f, e,* and *r* were a word, where would you divide it into syllables?

	RIGHT	WRONG
1. id fer	___	___

2. Why would you divide it between those letters?

	RIGHT	WRONG
2. Why?	___	___

B When a single consonant appears between two vowels, that consonant is usually in the same syllable as the vowel following it, as in *pu pil.*

nefut

1. If the letters *n, e, f, u,* and *t* were a word, where would you divide it into syllables?

	RIGHT	WRONG
1. ne fut	___	___

2. Why would you divide it between those letters?

	RIGHT	WRONG
2. Why?	___	___

C When *x* is preceded and followed by vowels, the *x* is in the same syllable as the preceding vowel, as in *tax i.*

uxot

1. If the letters *u, x, o,* and *t* were a word, where would you divide it into syllables?

	RIGHT	WRONG
1. ux ot	___	___

2. Why would you divide it between those letters?

	RIGHT	WRONG
2. Why?	___	___

D When a word ends in *le* preceded by a consonant, that consonant is in the same syllable as the *le,* as in *can dle.*

rinfle

1. If the letters *r, i, n, f, l,* and *e* were a word, where would you divide it into syllables?

	RIGHT	WRONG
1. rin fle	___	___

2. Why would you divide it between those letters?

	RIGHT	WRONG
2. Why?	___	___

List a group of words on the chalkboard. Ask the children for the meaning of these words. Then add the plural/s/ to the words:

$$girl + s = girls$$

$$horse + s = horses$$

$$apple + s = apples$$

Guide the children to generalize that the addition of an /s/ signals a change in the meaning of a noun. Have the children define the meaning of the /s/, and let them practice changing other nouns in a similar manner. Work also with /es/.

Plan activities designed to help children understand the manner in which suffixes such as "-er," "-ful," "-less," and "-ly" can change the meaning and function of a root word. For instance, using verbs such as "play," "teach," and "drive," add "-er" to the words and guide children to generalize that the words are now nouns. Similarly, by adding "-ful" or "-less" to nouns, such as "hope," we can change the word to an adjective, while the addition of "-ly" to the new word ("hopeful") makes it an adverb.

Using verbs, such as "make," "tie," and "write," show pupils how the meanings of these words can be changed by the addition of prefixes such as "re-." Encourage children to state this phenomenon as a principle of word building, and plan activities for them in which they develop new words from known roots by adding common prefixes.[12]

Seymour suggests that the following elements be included in activities dealing with the division of multisyllabic words:

1. Present *only* words the pupils has not read before.
2. Be sure the words are made up of structural and phonological parts the pupil has been taught.
3. Give the pupil an opportunity to decode each new word by dividing it into known structural parts, decoding each part, and combining the parts into a word.
4. Check on whether the pupil has really decoded the words by requiring their use in sentences.[13]

The exercise shown in figure 4.4 is an example of one type of activity that gives children the opportunity to apply the syllabication skills they have learned.

Develop one or more activities that will provide children with opportunities to apply the structural analysis skills they have learned. Assess

12. Gerald G. Duffy, *Teaching Linguistics* (Dansville, N. Y.: Instructor Publications, 1969), p. 21.
13. Seymour, "Word division for decoding," p. 279.

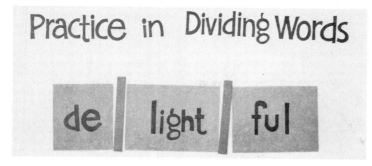

FIGURE 4.4.
Syllabication. From *Teachers' Edition, Skills Handbook, for With Skies and Wings* of the READING 360 series by Theodore Clymer and others, © Copyright, 1969, by Ginn and Company (Xerox Corporation), p. 24. Used with permission.

1. Divide the underlined words into parts to decode them. Tell which rule you used by putting its number on the line.
2. Now look at the two words that follow the underlined word. Choose one of these words which best completes the sentence. Write it on the blank.

1. mo|dern, modest, model   (Rule _4_)

   My brother is building a ___*model*___ airplane.

2. tur|ban, turnip, turpentine   (Rule _3_)

   The painter mixed ___*turpentine*___ with his paint.

3. cor|ner, cornet, correct   (Rule _3_)

   My big brother plays a ___*cornet*___ in the band.

4. la|dy, label, labor   (Rule _4_)

   Mother puts a ___*label*___ on each glass of jam she makes.

5. a|live, aloft, alert   (Rule _4 or 2_)

   Two big kites flew ___*aloft*___ in the breeze.

6. con|test, consonant, concert   (Rule _3_)

   Our class sang two songs in the school ___*concert*___.

Structural analysis: Syllabication

the effectiveness of the activities after you have used them with children. The following references are good sources for ideas:

Dallmann, Martha; Rouch, Roger L.; Chang, Lynette Y. C.; and DeBoer, John J. *The Teaching of Reading*. 4th ed. Chap. 5B, "Developing Skills in Word Recognition." New York: Holt, Rinehart and Winston, 1974.

Herr, Selma E. *Learning Activities for Reading*. 2d ed. Dubuque, Iowa: Wm. C. Brown Company Publishers, 1970.

Russell, David H., and Karp, Etta E. *Reading Aids Through the Grades*. Second revised edition by Anne Marie Mueser. New York: Teachers College Press, Columbia University, 1975.

Shankman, Florence. *Games and Activities to Reinforce Reading Skills*. New York: MSS Information Corporation, 1972.

Smith, Nila Banton. *Reading Instruction for Today's Children*. Chap. 21, "Practice and Maintenance Activities in Word Identification." Englewood Cliffs, N. J.: Prentice-Hall, 1963.

Spache, Evelyn B. *Reading Activities for Child Involvement*. Chap. 4, "Word Perception." Boston: Allyn & Bacon, 1972.

Activity 11

Design activities of your own which you feel will enable you to achieve the competencies stated for this module.

Preassessment and Postassessment

A. Knowledge Level
1. Define and give one example of each of the following linguistic terms: morpheme, root word, syllable, prefix, suffix, inflectional ending, compound word.
   Criteria for successful performance:
   a) the definition of each term is correct;
   b) the example for each term is correct.
2. State three syllabication generalizations that have a utility of at least 75 percent according to Bailey's analysis.
   Criteria for successful performance:
   a) each generalization is accurately stated;
   b) each generalization is correctly identified as having a utility of at least 75 percent.
B. Performance Level
1. Planning the Lesson
   a) Develop plans for teaching (1) a structural element (root word, prefix, suffix, inflectional ending), and (2) a syllabica-

tion generalization using the inductive approach for each lesson. For both (1) and (2) devise an activity/material that will enable children to apply their knowledge of the structural element or syllabication generalization you plan to teach.

b) Criteria for successful performance:
   (1) the objectives are stated in terms of pupil behavior;
   (2) the instructional procedures of the inductive approach are identifiable and in the correct sequence;
   (3) the activity/material devised is appropriate for the element or generalization being taught;
   (4) the procedures for the evaluation of pupil achievement are identified.

2. Teaching the Lesson
   a) Arrange to teach the lessons to small groups of children. Arrange to
      (1) have the instructor or cooperating teacher observe the lessons or
      (2) tape the lessons.
   b) Criteria for successful performance:
      (1) there is evidence that the pupils have achieved the objectives;
      (2) the student has demonstrated his ability to adapt his teaching procedures as necessary, in response to pupil needs, during the lesson.

3. Evaluating the Lesson
   a) After the lessons have been taught, write an evaluation of each one. Respond to the following questions in your evaluations.
      (1) Did the pupils achieve the objectives? Support your answer with specific evidence.
      (2) If there were pupils who did not achieve the objectives, can you identify the experiences they still need in order to reach the objectives?
      (3) Are there elements of the lesson that you would approach differently if you were to teach the lesson again?
   b) Follow one of these procedures:
      (1) If the instructor has observed the lessons, schedule a conference to discuss both plans and lessons.
      (2) If the cooperating teacher has observed the lessons, ask for written evaluations and then schedule a conference with the instructor to discuss the plans, the lessons, and the cooperating teacher's evaluations.
      (3) If the lessons have been taped, schedule a conference with the instructor to discuss the plans and the taped lessons.

References

Bond, Guy L., and Wagner, Eva Bond. *Teaching the Child to Read*. 4th ed. Chap. 8, "Developing Word Recognition." New York: Macmillan Company, 1966.

Bush, Clifford L., and Huebner, Mildred H. *Strategies for Reading in the Elementary School*. Chap. 4, "Vocabulary Development." New York: Macmillan Company, 1970.

Dallmann, Martha; Rouch, Roger L.; Chang, Lynette Y. C.; and DeBoer, John J. *The Teaching of Reading*. 4th ed. Chap. 5A, "Word Recognition"; chap. 5B, "Developing Skills in Word Recognition." New York: Holt, Rinehart and Winston, 1974.

Duffy, Gerald G. *Teaching Linguistics*. Dansville, N. Y.: The Instructor Publications, 1969.

Durkin, Dolores. *Phonics and the Teaching of Reading*. 2d. ed. Pp. 45-50, 74-78. New York: Teachers College Press, Columbia University, 1971.

———. *Teaching Them to Read*. 2d ed. Chap. 12, "Teaching Structural Analysis." Boston: Allyn & Bacon, 1974.

Gray, William S. *On Their Own in Reading*. Rev. ed. Chicago: Scott, Foresman and Company, 1960.

Harris, Albert J., and Sipay, Edward R. *Effective Teaching of Reading*. 2d ed. Chap. 9, "Developing Independence in Word Recognition." New York: David McKay Company, 1971.

———. *How to Increase Reading Ability*. 6th ed. Chap. 14, "Developing Word-Identification Skills." New York: David McKay Company, 1975.

Heilman, Arthur W. *Principles and Practices of Teaching Reading*. 3d ed. Chap. 7, "Phonics Instruction." Columbus, Ohio: Charles E. Merrill Publishing Company, 1972.

Herr, Selma E. *Learning Activities for Reading*. 2d ed. Chap. 35, "Prefixes"; chap. 44, "Suffixes"; chap. 45, "Syllabication." Dubuque, Iowa: Wm. C. Brown Company Publishers, 1970.

Hull, Marion A. *Phonics for the Teacher of Reading*. Columbus, Ohio: Charles E. Merrill Publishing Company, 1969.

Kottmeyer, William. *Decoding and Meaning*. Chap. 4, "Sound-Symbol Relationships in Elementary School Vocabulary." New York: McGraw-Hill Book Company, 1974.

May, Frank B. *To Help Children Read*. Module 4, "Helping Children Develop Other Word Recognition Skills." Columbus, Ohio: Charles E. Merrill Publishing Company, 1973.

McCullough, Constance M. *Handbook for Teaching the Language Arts*. Pp. 66-75. San Francisco: Paragon Publications, 1963.

Otto, Wayne; Chester, Robert; McNeil, John; and Myers, Shirley. *Focused Reading Instruction*. Chap. 7, "Objectives for Word Attack." Reading, Mass.: Addison-Wesley Publishing Company, 1974.

Russell, David H. *Children Learn to Read*. 2d ed. Chap. 10, "A Developmental Word Recognition Program." Waltham, Mass.: Blaisdell Publishing Company, 1961.

Russell, David H., and Karp, Etta E. *Reading Aids Through the Grades*. Second revised edition by Anne Marie Mueser. New York: Teachers College Press, Columbia University, 1975.

Shane, Harold G. *Linguistics and the Classroom Teacher*. Washington, D. C.: Association for Supervision and Curriculum Development, 1967.

Shankman, Florence. *Games and Activities to Reinforce Reading Skills*. New York: MSS Information Corporation, 1972.

Smith, James A. *Creative Teaching of Reading in the Elementary School*. 2d ed. Pp. 58-59, 244-47. Boston: Allyn & Bacon, 1975.

Smith, Nila Banton. *Reading Instruction for Today's Children*. Chap. 8, "Word Identification"; chap. 21, "Practice and Maintenance Activities in Word Identification." Englewood Cliffs, N. J.: Prentice-Hall, 1963.

Spache, Evelyn B. *Reading Activities for Child Involvement*. Chap. 4, "Word Perception." Boston: Allyn & Bacon, 1972.

Spache, George D., and Spache, Evelyn B. *Reading in the Elementary School*. 4th ed. Chap. 11, "Word Recognition Techniques and Skills." Boston: Allyn & Bacon, 1977.

Stauffer, Russell G. *Teaching Reading as a Thinking Process*. Chap. 9, "Developing Skill in Word Recognition." New York: Harper & Row, Publishers, 1969.

Tinker, Miles A., and McCullough, Constance M. *Teaching Elementary Reading*. 3d ed. Chap. 8, "Word Identification and Recognition." New York: Appleton-Century-Crofts, 1968.

Wallen, Carl J. *Competency in Teaching Reading*. Chap. 8, "Testing Strategies for Structural and Syllabic Word-Attack Skills"; chap. 9, "Teaching Strategies for Structural and Syllabic Word-Attack Skills." Chicago: Science Research Associates, 1972.

Zintz, Miles V. *The Reading Process: The Teacher and the Learner*. 2d ed. Chap. 10, "Word Recognition Skills." Dubuque, Iowa: Wm. C. Brown Company Publishers, 1975.

5

Developing Comprehension Ability

Overview

Every aspect of reading instruction is directed toward one objective: the development of each child's ability to "comprehend" what he reads. While concern for children's achievement of this objective is universally expressed, this concern has not been paralleled by the development of a clear, consistent definition of the concept of "comprehension." Writers of textbooks and instructional materials present definitions of the components of comprehension that are often imprecise, and that frequently reflect different points of view in approaching this complex concept. The result is confusion on the part of teachers as they attempt to develop a systematic approach to working with children in this area of comprehension.

The point of view presented in this module is that the teacher's approach to the concept of comprehension affects his teaching. That is, if the teacher's definition of comprehension is vague and ambiguous, this lack of clarity will be reflected in his attempts to help children develop the ability to comprehend what they read. The overall purpose in this module, then, is to help you not only to develop a clear concept of comprehension, but also to apply this understanding in the planning of a systematic approach to helping children develop the ability to comprehend what they read.

The module is introduced through Nila Banton Smith's article, "The Many Faces of Reading Comprehension."[1] Smith emphasizes the importance of helping children develop thinking skills, and suggests that teachers of reading have a vital role to play in the development of these intellec-

1. Nila Banton Smith, "The many faces of reading comprehension," *The Reading Teacher* 23 (December 1969): 249-59.

tual processes. She then identifies several needs that must be met if this important objective is to be achieved.

Smith traces the emergence of the concept of "comprehension" in the field of reading, and proposes that the varied and imprecise ways in which it has been defined have hindered the effective development of children's thinking skills in reading. She then presents four models or categories of skills which she feels teachers can use easily in providing opportunities for children to think about what they are reading. It is Smith's opinion that the systematic application of these models in the teaching of reading can contribute significantly to the development of children's thinking skills.

As you read Smith's article, use the following questions as your purposes for reading:

1. What needs does Smith suggest must be met as a basis for improving the teaching of thinking skills in reading?
2. What categories of skills are presented by Smith for use in developing children's reading comprehension? Do the categories appear to you to be precise and clearly differentiated?
3. How does Smith view the role of the teacher in the development of children's thinking skills in reading?

The Many Faces of Reading Comprehension
Nila Banton Smith

Confucious, the famous Chinese scholar and teacher, once wrote: "Learning without thought is labor lost; thought without learning is perilous."

It has been more than 2000 years since Confucious expressed these ideas about the relationships of thought and learning. Other great philosophers have expressed similar ideas throughout the ages. Yet the implementation of their recommendation has scarcely been discernible in the teaching of reading even as century after century has passed by.

At the present moment we have one era of reading instruction that is in full bloom, another that is well on the way, and a third that

is in the embryonic stage. Those who are helping to push the new era that is on its way are urging vigorously that we couple thought and reading, that we go far beyond the stage of picking up what the book *says* and use our higher mental processes in *thinking* about what it says. Contemporary educators are expressing themselves in dramatic and concrete ways in their attempts to spur us on in this direction.

From Nila Banton Smith, "The many faces of reading comprehension," *The Reading Teacher* 23 (December 1969):249-59. Reprinted by permission of Nila Banton Smith and the International Reading Association.

Edgar Dale (1969) says it dramatically in this way:

> . . . We suffer from hardening of the categories. Our mental filing system, filled with arid, unrelated facts, becomes rigid and inflexible. Further, the movement from concrete to abstract learning requires . . . a concern with the higher mental processes. Instead of accepting and learning what the book *says,* students must analyze what the author meant, compare and contrast it with their own experiences —synthesize, evaluate, apply.

Jacques Barzun (1969) in urging an emphasis on thinking in education explains the process of thinking in this very concrete way. "Thinking is doing to a fact or an idea what we do to beefsteak when we distribute its parts throughout our body. We are presumably stronger and better for it, readier for attack and defense, as well as more competent to assimilate more of the same protein without strain."

So it is that the thinking skills are being stressed by educators in all fields and we are being told repeatedly that our present students, who are facing the vicissitudes of a changing, uncertain world, cannot rely on the accumulated experience of mankind; nor will it do them any good to ignore situations, shrink from decisions or retreat in confusion. We as teachers in general know full well that we should be teaching children to *think,* that we should be providing practice to develop *thinking skills* higher than those involved in memorization. We as *reading* teachers know that communication is the best medium for developing thinking skills and that reading content is the richest and most rewarding of all the communication media to use for this purpose. Reading content reposes in a bed of details not present in mass communication media, and these details offer stepping stones to the reader in aiding him to go over, beyond and above what the

mere words may say. Teachers of reading truly have the best medium in the world to use as a vehicle in developing the higher intellectual processes. As yet, however, possibilities of doing this have not been adequately explored. We do not have clear and concise concepts of the different faces of comprehension which deal with the higher mental processes, nor do we have adequate procedures to serve us in providing practice on these specific processes in connection with reading content.

Needs for More Emphasis on Higher Mental Processes in Reading

Several needs must be met if we are really to implement the thinking skills objective of this emerging period. Some of these needs will be enumerated.

More Research Is Needed

It is regretted that more research is not being conducted in regard to the development of the thinking skills in connection with reading content. We are going all out in research on decoding, the disadvantaged, perception, etc. These are important areas for investigation but the thinking processes in reading are also important. It is discouraging to find that during the last few years comprehension has dropped to a new low in terms of number of studies reported.

As an example of reduced current research in this area we might refer to the latest summaries of reading research appearing in the March, 1969 *Journal of Educational Research* and the February, 1969 *Reading Research Quarterly.* In the *Quarterly,* Robinson, *et al.* (1969) reported 374 researches, only two of which had to do with "interpretation" which term of course connoted comprehension. In the *Journal,* Harris, *et al.* (1969) summarize only three studies dealing with comprehension out of a total of 194. Hence, the proportion of the number of studies reported on comprehension is pitifully small in comparison with that dealing with other topics.

Comprehension is the very heart of the reading act. There is no use of reading unless one understands the meanings. Could it be that investigators think that comprehension has already been researched to its limits? That there is very little new to be explored in this area? If so, I, personally, cannot agree with them. With the strong present movement in education toward the development of inquiry, questioning, reasoning, and evaluating we in the field of reading have an entirely new horizon opened up to us. We must find out how better to use the content of reading in developing ability to think in depth. An exciting frontier beckons to those who would like to ascertain which of the higher mental processes best lend themselves to development in reading, and what procedures are most effective in developing these processes with different students at all levels.

Need for Improved Techniques in Stimulating Depth Reading

Teachers' questions are probably used more than any other technique in attempts to develop comprehension.

What kind of questions are teachers asking? A study by Guszak (1969) reported in the *Journal of Educational Research* provides some insight that helps to answer this question. Guszak visited and recorded teachers' questions on assigned reading in second, fourth and sixth grade classrooms. He concluded: 1) that literal questions were most frequently asked across grade levels, 2) that more incorrect answers to questions were accepted as correct by teachers in the fourth and sixth grade than in the second, and 3) that the dominant pattern of interaction at all grade levels was a teacher's question followed by a single congruent response.

According to this study plus our own common knowledge, teachers of reading generally are asking *literal* comprehension questions and devoting little or often no attention to discussion. Under this condition how can we expect to develop use of the higher thinking processes in connection with reading content?

Needs of Children in Understanding Reading

A third need for greater emphasis on depth in reading is found in results of studies showing that children are not doing well in grasping meanings in reading.

I will refer to one of the latest and most comprehensive investigations in regard to this matter. Bormuth (1968) conducted a study designed to ascertain students' ability to comprehend at different levels—primary, intermediate, junior high, and high school levels. In his conclusion he makes these statements.

> For many years reading experts and educators in general have maintained that the ultimate objective of reading instruction was to enable the child to understand what he read and not just to enable him to call the words on the page. And they have argued that this is the objective upon which we should expend our major efforts, since it is only through the child's use of these skills that he is able to acquire much of the knowledge he will need throughout his life. On the whole, this argument seems well reasoned.
>
> But when we examine how well this goal is being accomplished we find a rather discouraging situation. Children are not able to read their instructional materials well enough to gain much information from them until they reach high school. Even in high school a large proportion of the materials remain essentially incomprehensible to a large proportion of the students. Furthermore, the apparently improved ability of the high school student may, in fact, have resulted merely because the less able students, the students who were unable to read well enough to learn the content of

their instruction, have failed in school, dropped out, and are no longer present to pull down the average performance to its true level.

A more detailed analysis of children's comprehension skills showed that in the fourth grade a great many of the children were unable to exhibit comprehension of even the simplest structures by which language signals information.

In discussing his study, Bormuth says further:

. . . An analysis of the materials used to teach comprehension skills and of the curriculum guides and textbooks which instruct the teacher in how to teach the skills tends to suggest instead that there is no clear concept of what skills are to be taught. Furthermore, the teaching procedures described are described only in the vaguest terms.

In the final analysis, we cannot, at present, definitely reject or disapprove procedures for teaching reading comprehension, but we must voice grave doubts about their efficacy. And we can definitely say that they do not produce sufficient results to enable children to profit from much of their reading.

I have now indicated some of the urgent needs in developing thinking skills in reading. Comprehension is a complex process, and its faces are multiple and divergent. Research on reading in depth is much too scant; the thinking skills involved are not as specifically delineated as we would like to have them; effective methodology in this area is limited. With these thoughts in mind I shall devote the remainder of this article to an attempt to sort out and label the thinking skills in the language of teachers, and to give constructive suggestions for developing these skills in the classroom.

Recognizing Many Faces of Comprehension

First we must realize that reading instruction had no comprehension face at all until about fifty years ago. The corpus of reading instruction up until 1915 to 1925 was that of teaching word recognition. When a child had learned to pronounce the words in reading, the teaching objective had been met.

Then rather suddenly a change took place. Standardized tests were developed. In order to use these tests in reading it was now necessary to ask questions on content rather than having children read orally. They did so poorly in answering questions that everyone became excited about teaching them to get the thought, and the term "comprehension" came into our reading vocabulary for the first time. We have used this terminology indiscriminately ever since and in my opinion this omnibus term of "comprehension" has stood in the way of developing true depth in reading which makes use of the many different thinking processes. In general comprehension has meant to most people literal comprehension—giving back what the book says.

With the emergence of the present new period in reading instruction under the general educational influence of placing emphasis on the thinking skills, comprehension which first stuck its head above the surface in the 1920's seems to have developed many faces, at least vocabulary-wise and it appears to be revolving around so fast that all of the faces are blurred and merging and overlapping, and the features of none are clear-cut or distinct. We hear of literal comprehension, factual reading, close reading, inferences, interpretation, critical reading, creative reading, etc., etc. Comprehension has indeed become a many splendored, many-faced thing.

It is good that we have advanced beyond our first concept of comprehension. Many people at present, however, seem to be taking just one step in extending their concept of this process. They recognize only two faces of comprehension. They teach the literal comprehension face in which the child gives back what the book says. Then they make some effort to recognize a second face which they call "inferences." This term is altogether too broad. There are many different kinds of inferences that make use of different thinking skills. This inference face should be broken down into other faces.

By the way, I would like to say a word about the shibboleth of using the *wh* words *who, what, why, when* as a sure-fire means of giving practice on inferences or any other aspect of depth reading. Answers to all of these questions usually are given in the text and require only literal comprehension. Developing the thinking processes in reading isn't so easy that we can get results by using a trick so simple as this.

I have spoken of people who recognize only the two faces of comprehension which they call "literal comprehension" and "inferences." Others, and probably a larger group, recognize two faces only which they call "literal comprehension" and "critical reading." This phrase "critical reading" has come to be a sort of a catch slogan. Many are using this term about as indiscriminately as the broad term of "comprehension" has been used in the past. Critical reading is used very generally to include all of the thinking skills.

If we are to break down these big "lump-sum" concepts into a variety of thinking processes in order to distribute practice over different ones of them, we need to know what the thinking skills are. Some people have analyzed the thinking processes into separate skills and listed them. Here is one such list according to Bloom (1956):

1. *Memory*: The pupil recalls or recognizes information.
2. *Translation*: The pupil changes information into a different symbolic form or language.
3. *Interpretation*: The pupil discovers rela-

tionships between facts, generalizations, definitions, values, and skills.
4. *Application*: The pupil solves a lifelike problem that requires the identification of the issue and the selection and use of appropriate generalizations and skills.
5. *Analysis*: The pupil solves a problem through his conscious knowledge of the parts and forms of thinking.
6. *Synthesis*: The pupil solves a problem that requires original, creative thinking.
7. *Evaluation*: The pupil makes a judgment of good or bad, or right or wrong, according to designated standards.

I know of a situation in which teachers are given this list and told to ask questions in each of these categories in their reading lessons. The list has the advantage of presenting a diversity of skills to be developed. The teachers tell me, however, that they can't remember this long list; that they can't clearly distinguish between some of the categories; that they can't think of questions for some of them; and that some of the items are rarely, perhaps never applicable to the reading that the children are doing.

I am giving this example to indicate that a long list of higher mental processes does not seem to be very helpful to teachers in providing practice on depth skills in reading. In the interest of attempting to offer some practical, down-to-earth assistance to the classroom teacher I would like to suggest some models for reference in conducting meaning-getting discussion of reading content. The four models or categories of skills which I shall suggest are broad enough to include all of the thinking skills usually listed by psychologists, each category covering a cluster of these skills; the categories are clearly differentiated one from the other; they are applicable to most any selection in any book; and teachers can easily grasp and apply them. These four categories are 1) literal comprehension, 2) interpretation, 3) critical reading, and 4) creative reading. Many teachers with whom I have been working have used these models in formulating questions and making statements designed to stimulate discussion which would give practice on a planned variety of thinking skills rather than just asking questions hit or miss which may give practice on one or two thinking skills over and over again at the neglect of the others.

Literal Comprehension

The first category is labeled "literal comprehension," the term which I have mentioned several times before. This category does not include the *thinking* skills. Teachers do not need special help on this. I include it, however, as a contrast to the other categories which I shall describe and because after all it does have a place in meaning gathering.

I like to define literal comprehension as the skill of getting the primary, direct literal meaning of a word, idea, or sentence in context. There is no depth in this kind of reading. It is the lowest rung in the meaning-getting ladder, yet it is the one on which teachers of the past have given the most practice, and to which most still are devoting the preponderance of their comprehensive efforts. A teacher gives practice in literal comprehension when she asks, "With what was Johnny playing?" and the pupil answers, "With his red fire engine," these are the exact words given in the book. Giving this answer requires no thinking. Such a question simply demands the pupil to recall from memory what the book says, simply asks him to repeat parrot-like the words that are in the book.

Throughout the elementary grades and high school, practice in literal comprehension dominates practice in the meaning-getting skills because the following techniques are so widely used: 1) fact questions based directly on the text, 2) true-false statements, 3) completion sentences, 4) multiple-choice exercises. These objective techniques used in standard-ized tests, informal tests, discussions, and assignments give practice in literal comprehension but they do little or nothing to develop the ability to use the thinking skills in obtaining deeper meanings.

Interpretation

Interpretation is the label for a very usable category of thinking skills which should be emphasized in reading. This term could be used in a sense broad enough to cover all of the thinking skills. But teachers of reading need something more definitive; they need categories which are sharply differentiated from one another. If the whole set of thinking skills were included under the term of "interpretation" or "inferences," some of the most distinctive and desirable skills would probably become smothered and obscured.

In general, it may be said that interpretation probes for greater depth than literal comprehension. It is concerned with supplying meanings not directly stated in the text.

For example, in a third grade class the children were reading a ship story. Among other things there was a sentence saying, "The captain swung himself up on to the roof of the cabin." The teacher asked, "Where did the captain swing himself?" This was a literal comprehension question. Instead she might have used a question which would have given the children a chance to think. She might have said, "Can you give a reason why he went up on the roof?" or, "The sentence says he swung himself up on the roof. Can you tell just how he got up there?"

This is a very simple example. As children progress through the grades and secondary school, text becomes more complex and opportunities for interpretation experiences may increase rapidly if teachers of all subjects are watching for chances to stimulate their students in the use of their thinking skills.

Interpretation involves a cluster of several different kinds of thinking skills, such as: 1) supplying additional information by "reading between the lines," 2) making generalizations, 3) reasoning cause and effect, 4) anticipating endings, 5) making comparisons, 6) sensing motives, 7) discovering relationships.

These are important skills that the teacher should have in mind in teaching students to read in depth. He should raise the level of understanding far above literal comprehension, guiding it and directing it into interpretation of deeper meanings.

Critical Reading

A third cluster of thinking skills is involved in critical reading, skills that are over, above, and apart from those in interpretation as I see it. The critical reading skill category is the one most direly in need of development in American life at the present time, and I deplore the fact that many are using the term as a general heading under which to classify all of the thinking skills ever used by human beings. Critical reading in my opinion should be singled out for its own area of development and for practice on its own specific thinking skills.

Critical reading is the third level in the hierarchy of reading-for-meaning skills. According to my thinking it includes literal comprehension and interpretation as defined above, but it goes further than either of these in that the reader *evaluates, passes personal judgment on the quality, the value, the accuracy,* and *the truthfulness* of what is read. These skills should not be included under interpretation. They belong specifically to critical reading.

The distinction indicated above is appropriate in terms of the meaning of the word *critical,* an adjective derived from the noun *critic* which in turn has as one of its foreign sources the Greek word *krinein* meaning "to judge, discern."

One dictionary definition of critical is "exercising or involving careful judgment; exact; nicely judicious as a critical examination." Another dictionary defines critical as "to judge with severity."

Critic is defined as "one who expresses a reasoned opinion . . . on any matter . . . involving a judgment of its value, truth or righteousness . . . ." Criticism is defined as "A critical observation or judgment"; and criticize is defined thus, "To examine and judge as a critic."

According to the established meaning of the word then, critical reading would seem to be the kind of reading in which the reader gives his personal reaction to the text, passes his personal judgment upon it.

Critical thinking and critical reading can be cultivated in very young children. For example, Susan and other first graders were reading a story in their primers about a dog riding downhill in a cart. The accompanying picture showed the dog riding down the steep hill all by himself in the cart. A girl standing at the top of the hill had evidently given the cart a push. Susan blurted out, "This is foolish. A dog wouldn't sit in a cart and ride downhill like this. He'd jump out. My dog won't even sit in a cart and let me pull him around." Susan was doing critical reading. She was evaluating in terms of personal experience.

Throughout the elementary grades, students giving such evidences of critical thinking and reading should be warmly commended and other students encouraged to do likewise.

In later grades planned experience in critical reading may be provided, for example, developing with the class criteria in regard to the author's background, position, experience with the subject, prejudices; holding panel discussions, supported by reference to readings, etc. Evaluating ads, news items, editorials, cartoons, etc., in terms of propaganda is important. There is a very fertile field for critical reading at the higher levels.

Creative Reading

The term "creative reading" is frequently used in as broad a sense as "inferences," "critical reading" and other current popular terms which many have fallen into the habit of employing as one label to cover all thought processes in reading. Creative reading accompanies and grows out of literal comprehension, interpretation or critical reading but it is different from any one of these. As is the case with these other kinds of reading, how is the teacher going to stimulate or encourage this thing called creative reading if she doesn't know what it is?

Creativity is a pretty involved subject with roots deep down in psychology. An adequate discussion of the creative art is quite complicated. It is a fascinating subject though and if some of you would like to read more about it I have listed some good references. I recommend that you delve into these (Knell, 1965; Stauffer, 1969; Torrance, 1969; Vinacke, 1952).

As a starting point, however, I would like to describe creative reading in such very simple terms that a teacher can immediately see the difference between this kind of reading and the other kinds that I have mentioned. First by way of contrast we should consider that in literal comprehension the student tries to get the direct meaning of the author who wrote the text; in interpretation he tries to supply meanings to complete the author's text; in critical reading he evaluates, passes judgment on the author's text. In creative reading, however, the individual leaves the author's text and goes out on his own beyond the author's text to seek out or express new ideas, to gain additional insights, to find the answer to a question or the solution to a lifelike problem. (Incidentally, I include problem-solving in creative reading because in processing this mental activity the individual goes beyond the text to think toward a solution creatively.)

Creative reading in its higher form starts with a question or an inquiry which arises in the mind of the reader, personally, and is usually carried forward with high motivation, often a sense of urgency. We cannot expect this higher type of creative reading to happen in the classroom very often unless the teacher does something to develop it. Since inquiry is the starting point of creative reading, the teacher may ask questions which cause children to go beyond direct implications gathered from the text, at least calling for creative thinking, and she can encourage children, themselves, to ask questions. Once she develops the process of inquiry within children themselves, concerning reading content, creative reading is apt to follow, and when it does follow it should be praised warmly.

Summary

I have now tried to describe four different faces of comprehension which together include all of the thinking processes listed by psychologists, and to offer them as models to assist teachers in differentiating between the various kinds of reading, thus resulting in an increased possibility at least of providing children experiences in the use of the many different thinking skills in reading.

Here is one short and extremely simple example of how a teacher might give a class experience in using thinking skills involved in all four categories that I have discussed.

The children were reading a story about a little girl named Ruth who was left at home to take care of her younger brother while her mother went away somewhere. The youngster wanted a cooky to eat. The cooky jar was kept on the basement steps. Ruth opened the door to the basement and stepped down to get a cooky. At that moment little brother slammed the door shut. It had a snaplock so Ruth was locked in the basement when she was supposed to be upstairs taking care of little brother. She began to puzzle over her predicament. Finally she asked little brother to take the receiver off the phone and say "16 Wood Street" over and over again. This he did. The operator hearing a child's voice repeating this address suspected trouble and sent a policeman to the address and he let Ruth out of the basement.

Now for the four different types of meaning questions:

Literal comprehension: "What did little brother want to eat?"

Interpretation: "Why was the cooky jar kept on the basement steps?"

Critical reading: "Did mother do the right thing in leaving the children alone?"

Creative thinking: "How would you have solved this problem?"

Some printed materials are very helpful in giving practice in thinking in reading, and this is good. The development of the many different thinking processes in reading, however, depends to a large extent upon the teacher who knows and recognizes these different processes. Thinking is a personal matter. It varies with different groups and different individuals within groups. The best guarantee for development of the thinking skills is an informed, understanding teacher of reading to guide and encourage students to invent questions as well as to answer them; to reflect, infer and predict; to string together beads of information in arriving at generalizations; to aid independence in thinking; to foster creativity; to nourish values; and to refine sensitivities. The major re-

sponsibility rests with the teacher during her daily interactions with her students.

References

Barzun, J., quoted from Russell, J. E. *Change and Challenge in American Education*. Boston: Houghton Mifflin, 1969. P. 103.

Bloom, B. S. (ed.) *Taxonomy of educational objectives*. New York: David McKay, 1956. Pp. 186-87.

Bormuth, J. R. The effectiveness of current procedures for teaching reading comprehension. Paper presented at Fifty-Eighth Annual Meeting of the National Council of Teachers of English, Milwaukee, November 29, 1968.

Dale, E. Things to Come. *The Newsletter*, 1969, *34*, 3.

Guszak, J. J. Teacher questioning and reading. In T. Harris, et al. *The Journal of Educational Research*, 1969, *62*, 306.

Harris, T., Otto, W., and Barrett, T. Summary and review of investigations relating to reading, July 1, 1967 to June 30, 1968. *The Journal of Educational Research*, 1969, *62*, 306.

Knell, G. F. *The art and science of creativity*. New York: Holt, Rinehart and Winston, Inc., 1965.

Robinson, Helen M., Weintraub, S., and Smith, Helen. Summary of investigations related to reading, July 1, 1967 to June 30, 1968. *Reading Research Quarterly*, 1969, *4* (2), 193-94.

Stauffer, R. G. *Teaching Reading as a Thinking Process*. New York: Harper & Row, 1969.

Torrance, P. E. Developing creative readers. In R. Stauffer (Comp.) Dimensions of critical reading. *Proceedings of the Annual Education and Reading Conferences, 1963 and 1964*. Newark, Del.: University of Delaware, 1964.

Vinacke, W. E. *The Psychology of Thinking*. New York: McGraw-Hill, 1952.

Module Competencies

There are two purposes reflected in the competencies specified for this module. The first purpose is to help you develop an understanding of the complexities that have surrounded the concept of comprehension in reading. It is, moreover, to provide you with a classification of comprehension outcomes that can serve as a framework as you begin to assess children's needs in the area of comprehension. The second purpose is to help you learn how to apply this classification system in planning activities and designing materials which will contribute to children's growth in comprehension. In the postassessment for this module, you will have the opportunity to demonstrate both your understanding of a specific taxonomy of comprehension outcomes and your ability to apply this taxonomy in planning activities which focus on increasing children's comprehension ability.

Instructional Activities

The taxonomy of comprehension outcomes that is used in this module is presented and explained in activity 2 (competency 1). In activity 3, the relationship between teachers' questions and the comprehension achieved by children is discussed. Following this discussion, you are given the opportunity to analyze the questions which one teacher developed through the use of the taxonomy presented in activity 2 (competency 1). Activities 4 and 5 focus on an analysis of the types of comprehension questions which are suggested for use in the teachers' guides of reading series (competency 3). The discussion and exercise presented in activity 6 are directed toward helping you learn to plan for the sequential development of comprehension outcomes (competency 2). The difficulties that can be encountered in using commercial materials designed to increase comprehension ability are discussed and illustrated in activity 7 (competency 3). Examples of the types of comprehension exercises that can be developed by teachers are shown in activity 8 (competency 3). The plan presented in activity 9 provides you with a framework for developing comprehension lessons to be used with children (competency 2). In activity 10 you are asked to develop comprehension lessons and use them with children, and to assess the effectiveness of those lessons (competency 2). Observing teachers as they work with children in the area of comprehension, suggested in activity 11, will provide you with an opportunity to analyze the ways in which a variety of teaching strategies and materials can be used (competency 3). In activity 12 you are encouraged to design other activities which you feel will enable you to achieve the module competencies.

Competencies

1. Identify comprehension outcomes presented in the Barrett Taxonomy of the Cognitive and Affective Dimensions of Reading Comprehension.

2. Use the Barrett taxonomy as the basis for planning developmental lessons in comprehension.

3. Use commercial and teacher-prepared materials designed to increase children's ability to read for a wide range of comprehension outcomes.

Instructional Activities

Select from the following learning experiences those which you feel will enable you to achieve the competencies stated for this module:

Activity 1

Attend a seminar for orientation to this module.

Activity 2

Different types of information may be derived from reading the same material: for example, one may read for details, to find the main idea, to draw an inference, etc. Since these types of information represent *outcomes* of the comprehension process,[2] they will be referred to as *comprehension outcomes* in this module.

Comprehension outcomes are defined and classified in a variety of ways by writers in the field of reading. The system of classification introduced in this module is the Taxonomy of the Cognitive and Affective Dimensions of Reading Comprehension developed by Thomas C. Barrett. This taxonomy will be referred to in subsequent modules in order to provide a consistent framework for you in your development of comprehension activities. The five categories of the taxonomy are organized on the basis of difficulty—the fifth category representing the most difficult. Within each category is a series of tasks which teachers can apply in helping children increase their ability to comprehend what they read.

In his discussion of Barrett's taxonomy, Clymer suggests two ways in which it can be used: first, as a basis for developing purposes and questions for guiding children's reading; and second, as a tool in analyzing the questions presented in reading materials in order to determine the types of comprehension outcomes that are being emphasized. In using the taxonomy in either of these ways, a knowledge of the reading selections upon which the questions are based is essential in determining the relative difficulty of the questions. Questions that may appear to belong in the in-

---

2. George D. Spache, *Toward Better Reading* (Champaign, Ill.: Garrard Publishing Company, 1963), p. 62.

ferential category, for example, may actually belong in the literal category if the answers are stated in the reading selection.[3]

In addition to discussing the uses of the taxonomy, Clymer also points out that there is one important factor that the taxonomy cannot take into account:

> . . . the taxonomy cannot take into account the background which the reader brings to the comprehension tasks. Background must in many cases be a deciding factor in the type or level of comprehension required by the question. The type of comprehension demanded and the difficulty of the task is a product of (a) the selection, (b) the questions, and (c) the reader's background. The taxonomy in its usual application can take only the first two into account.[4]

Read the Barrett taxonomy, which follows, using these three questions as your purposes for reading:

1. Do you agree with the ordering of the levels in terms of difficulty?
2. What tasks are required in the Appreciation category that make it more difficult than the preceding categories?
3. In which categories might the nature of the reader's background affect the difficulty of the questions?

The Barrett Taxonomy

Cognitive and Affective Dimensions of Reading Comprehension

1.0 *Literal Comprehension.* Literal comprehension focuses on ideas and information which are *explicitly* stated in the selection. Purposes for reading and teacher's questions designed to elicit responses at this level may range from simple to complex. A simple task in literal comprehension may be the recognition or recall of a single fact or incident. A more complex task might be the recognition or recall

Thomas C. Barrett, "The Barrett Taxonomy of the Cognitive and Affective Dimensions of Reading Comprehension," in *Innovation and Change in Reading Instruction,* ed. Helen M. Robinson (Sixty-seventh Yearbook of the National Society for the Study of Education, pt. 2 [Chicago: The National Society for the Study of Education, 1968]), pp. 19-23. Reprinted by permission of Thomas C. Barrett and The National Society for the Study of Education.

3. Theodore Clymer, "What is 'Reading'?: Some Current Concepts," in *Innovation and Change in Reading Instruction,* ed. Helen M. Robinson (Sixty-seventh Yearbook of the National Society for the Study of Education, pt. 2 [Chicago: The National Society for the Study of Education, 1968]), p. 17.
4. Ibid., p. 19.

of a series of facts or the sequencing of incidents in a reading selection. Purposes and questions at this level may have the following characteristics.

1.1 *Recognition* requires the student to locate or identify ideas or information *explicitly* stated in the reading selection itself or in exercises which use the explicit ideas and information presented in the reading selection. Recognition tasks are:

  1.11 *Recognition of Details.* The student is required to locate or identify facts such as the names of characters, the time of the story, or the place of the story.

  1.12 *Recognition of Main Ideas.* The student is asked to locate or identify an explicit statement in or from a selection which is a main idea of a paragraph or a larger portion of the selection.

  1.13 *Recognition of a Sequence.* The student is required to locate or identify the order of incidents or actions explicitly stated in the selection.

  1.14 *Recognition of Comparison.* The student is requested to locate or identify likenesses and differences in characters, times, and places that are explicitly stated in the selection.

  1.15 *Recognition of Cause and Effect Relationships.* The student in this instance may be required to locate or identify the explicitly stated reasons for certain happenings or actions in the selection.

  1.16 *Recognition of Character Traits.* The student is required to identify or locate explicit statements about a character which help to point up the type of person he is.

1.2 *Recall* requires the student to produce from memory ideas and information *explicitly* stated in the reading selection. Recall tasks are:

  1.21 *Recall of Details.* The student is

asked to produce from memory facts such as the names of characters, the time of the story, or the place of the story.

  1.22 *Recall of Main Ideas.* The student is required to state a main idea of a paragraph or a larger portion of the selection from memory, when the main idea is explicitly stated in the selection.

  1.23 *Recall of a Sequence.* The student is asked to provide from memory the order of incidents or actions explicitly stated in the selection.

  1.24 *Recall of Comparisons.* The student is required to call up from memory the likenesses and differences in characters, times, and places that are explicitly stated in the selection.

  1.25 *Recall of Cause and Effect Relationships.* The student is requested to produce from memory explicitly stated reasons for certain happenings or actions in the selection.

  1.26 *Recall of Character Traits.* The student is asked to call up from memory explicit statements about characters which illustrate the type of persons they are.

2.0 *Reorganization.* Reorganization requires the student to analyze, synthesize, and/or organize ideas or information explicitly stated in the selection. To produce the desired thought product, the reader may utilize the statements of the author verbatim or he may paraphrase or translate the author's statements. Reorganization tasks are:

2.1 *Classifying.* In this instance the student is required to place people, things, places, and/or events into categories.

2.2 *Outlining.* The student is requested to organize the selection into outline form using direct statements or paraphrased statements from the selection.

2.3 *Summarizing.* The student is asked to condense the selection using direct or paraphrased statements from the selection.

2.4 *Synthesizing.* In this instance, the student is requested to consolidate explicit ideas or information from more than one source.

3.0 *Inferential Comprehension.* Inferential comprehension is demonstrated by the student when he uses the ideas and information explicitly stated in the selection, his intuition, and his personal experience as a basis for conjectures and hypotheses. Inferences drawn by the student may be either convergent or divergent in nature and the student may or may not be asked to verbalize the rationale underlying his inferences. In general, then, inferential comprehension is stimulated by purposes for reading and teachers' questions which demand thinking and imagination that go beyond the printed page.

3.1 *Inferring Supporting Details.* In this instance, the student is asked to conjecture about additional facts the author might have included in the selection which would have made it more informative, interesting, or appealing.

3.2 *Inferring Main Ideas.* The student is required to provide the main idea, general significance, theme, or moral which is not explicitly stated in the selection.

3.3 *Inferring Sequence.* The student, in this case, may be requested to conjecture as to what action or incident might have taken place between two explicitly stated actions or incidents, or he may be asked to hypothesize about what would happen next if the selection had not ended as it did but had been extended.

3.4 *Inferring Comparisons.* The student is required to infer likenesses and differences in characters, times, or places. Such inferential comparisons revolve around ideas such as: "here and there," "then and now," "he and he," "he and she," and "she and she."

3.5 *Inferring Cause and Effect Relationships.* The student is required to hypothesize about the motivations of charac-

ters and their interactions with time and place. He may also be required to conjecture as to what caused the author to include certain ideas, words, characterizations, and actions in his writing.

3.6 *Inferring Character Traits.* In this case, the student is asked to hypothesize about the nature of characters on the basis of explicit clues presented in the selection.

3.7 *Predicting Outcomes.* The student is requested to read an initial portion of the selections and on the basis of this reading he is required to conjecture about the outcome of the selection.

3.8 *Interpreting Figurative Language.* The student, in this instance, is asked to infer literal meanings from the author's figurative use of language.

4.0 *Evaluation.* Purposes for reading and teacher's questions, in this instance, require responses by the student which indicate that he has made an evaluative judgment by comparing ideas presented in the selection with external criteria provided by the teacher, other authorities, or other written sources, or with internal criteria provided by the reader's experiences, knowledge, or values. In essence evaluation deals with judgment and focuses on qualities of accuracy, acceptability, desirability, worth, or probability of occurrence. Evaluative thinking may be demonstrated by asking the student to make the following judgments.

4.1 *Judgments of Reality or Fantasy.* Could this really happen? Such a question calls for a judgment by the reader based on his experience.

4.2 *Judgments of Fact or Opinion.* Does the author provide adequate support for his conclusions? Is the author attempting to sway your thinking? Questions of this type require the student to analyze and evaluate the writing on the basis of the knowledge he has on the subject as well as to analyze and evaluate the intent of the author.

4.3 *Judgments of Adequacy and Validity.* Is the information presented here in keeping with what you have read on the subject in other sources? Questions of this nature call for the reader to compare written sources of information, with an eye toward agreement and disagreement or completeness and incompleteness.

4.4 *Judgments of Appropriateness.* What part of the story best describes the main character? Such a question requires the reader to make a judgment about the relative adequacy of different parts of the selection to answer the question.

4.5 *Judgments of Worth, Desirability and Acceptability.* Was the character right or wrong in what he did? Was his behavior good or bad? Questions of this nature call for judgments based on the reader's moral code or his value system.

5.0 *Appreciation.* Appreciation involves all the previously cited cognitive dimensions of reading, for it deals with the psychological and aesthetic impact of the selection on the reader. Appreciation calls for the student to be emotionally and aesthetically sensitive to the work and to have a reaction to the worth of its psychological and artistic elements. Appreciation includes both the knowledge of and the emotional response to literary techniques, forms, styles, and structures.

5.1 *Emotional Response to the Content.* The student is required to verbalize his feelings about the selection in terms of interest, excitement, boredom, fear, hate, amusement, etc. It is concerned with the emotional impact of the total work on the reader.

5.2 *Identification with Characters or Incidents.* Teachers' questions of this nature will elicit responses from the reader which demonstrate his sensitivity to, sympathy for, and empathy with characters and happenings portrayed by the author.

5.3 *Reactions to the Author's Use of Language.* In this instance, the student is required to respond to the author's craftsmanship in terms of the semantic dimensions of the selection, namely, connotations and denotations of words.

5.4 *Imagery.* In this instance, the reader is required to verbalize his feelings with regard to the author's artistic ability to paint word pictures which cause the reader to visualize, smell, taste, hear, or feel.

Activity 3

As Smith points out in the article which introduces this module, teachers use questioning probably more than any other technique in their efforts to help children increase their ability in comprehension.[5] It is important, then, to consider the relationship between teachers' questions and the comprehension achieved by children. Spache and Spache summarize significant aspects of this relationship:

> . . . It appears that what the reader retains while reading reflects such influences as: (1) his purpose in reading or what he intends to retain; (2) the instructions he is given before reading, which may lead him to find only the precise answers to specific questions or to secure a broader comprehension if the questions are more general. Comprehension is affected even more,

5. Smith, "The Many Faces," p. 251.

however, by the pattern of questions the child learns to anticipate. He learns to read with only those types of thinking that the teacher's questions demand. Since teachers' questions appear to be limited in type and depth, children's thinking (or comprehension) tends to be superficial and stereotyped, and lack critical thinking.[6]

Viewing oral questions as the major thinking stimulus of the teacher in working with children in reading, Guszak conducted an investigation designed to gather data concerning the kinds of questions teachers use to stimulate comprehension.[7] Teachers and pupils in randomly selected second-, fourth-, and sixth-grade classes in one city were the subjects of the study. Each reading group in four classes at each of the three grade levels was observed and recorded over a three-day period. The recordings were then transcribed and analyzed.

Guszak found that two types of literal comprehension questions (those asking for the recall or recognition of information) accounted for 70.4 percent of all of the questioning activity recorded. The second most frequently asked questions were those requiring evaluation (15.3 percent). Questions requiring explanation (7.2 percent) and conjecture (6.5 percent) were the third most frequently asked. Almost no questions (.6 percent) asking children to translate words, ideas, or pictures into different symbolic form were asked.

In comparing grade levels, Guszak found that the percentage of literal questions decreased as the grade level increased. The data also indicated that the teachers of the second and fourth grades asked nearly three times as many questions as did the teachers of the sixth grades.

In a study which also focused on teaching reading-thinking skills, Bartolome examined and categorized the questions asked by teachers in relation to their objectives for primary reading classes.[8] Six teachers from each of the first, second, and third grades in one school system were randomly selected as subjects for the study from a group of fifty-eight teachers who had expressed a willingness to participate. Each teacher was observed six times.

The data collected by Bartolome indicated that 47.54 percent of the questions recorded were those requiring pupils to use memory skills in locating and recalling information from the materials they had read. Questions requiring pupils to analyze what they were reading were the next

6. George D. Spache and Evelyn B. Spache, *Reading in the Elementary School*, 3d ed. (Boston: Allyn & Bacon, 1973), p. 542.
7. Frank J. Guszak, "Teachers' Questions and Levels of Reading Comprehension," in *The Evaluation of Children's Reading Achievement*, Perspectives in Reading, No. 8, ed. Thomas C. Barrett (Newark, Del.: International Reading Association, 1967), pp. 97-109.
8. Paz I. Bartolome, "Teachers' Objectives and Questions in Primary Reading," *The Reading Teacher* 23 (October 1969):27-33.

most frequently asked (25.94 percent). Rarely asked were questions requiring application (2.29 percent) or evaluation (2.25 percent).

Bartolome's second purpose in this study was to classify the objectives teachers expected to accomplish in their reading lessons, and to compare these categories of objectives with the categories of questions asked by the teachers. Bartolome reported that classifying the teachers' objectives presented problems because the objectives were often expressed in vague, general terms. The results of the comparison of the teachers' objectives with the questions they asked indicated that the frequencies of teachers' questions and objectives belonging to each category differed. Objectives frequently stated by the teachers involved analysis and application. The questions frequently asked required memory. On the basis of these findings, Bartolome concluded that while there is general agreement regarding the need to develop thinking skills among students, the accomplishment of this goal is insignificant.

The results of the Guszak and Bartolome studies make apparent that it is essential for teachers to define their objectives for reading comprehension in terms of specific outcomes that reflect different levels of thinking, and that they then ask questions which will stimulate children to read for comprehension outcomes at these levels. Only as teachers analyze both their obectives and the questions they ask, can children be helped to develop the ability to read beyond the level of literal comprehension.

The Barrett taxonomy (activity 2) can provide a useful framework for the development of questions to stimulate children's thinking skills in reading. Teachers, by using this framework in the analyzing of reading selections, can develop questions at a range of levels to be used for setting overall purposes for reading, for guiding children's reading as they progress through the selection, and for stimulating discussion following the reading of the selection. The following story, "Needing a Friend" (fig. 5.1), was used by one teacher in applying the Barrett taxonomy for the development of comprehension questions for part of the reading program. Read the story "Needing a Friend" (fig. 5.1) and then read the questions that were developed for this selection. Use the following questions as a guide in analyzing the questions and the selection on which they were based.

1. Do the questions listed in each category appear to be appropriate for that category?
2. As you read the questions and the selection, can you think of other questions that could be written?
3. Can you identify questions the difficulty of which would be affected by the reader's background?

Note: It is not being suggested here that questions can be written in all categories for every reading selection. The content of reading selections varies in terms of the types of questions that are appropriate.

Application of the Barrett Taxonomy

"Needing a Friend"

1.0 *Literal Comprehension*:
  1.1 *Recognition*
    1.11 Find the sentence that tells who Pedro is.
    1.12 Find the sentences on page 17 that tell what Tina and the girl in the blue dress both need.
    1.13 Number these sentences in the order in which they happen in the story:
      _____ The girl in the blue dress talks to Tina.
      _____ Carla asks Tina what she is looking at out the window.
      _____ Pedro meets two boys.
      _____ Tina and the girl in the blue dress decide to be friends.
      _____ Tina runs out of the house crying.
    1.14 Look at the pictures of Tina on pages 13 and 17. What differences can you see in the way Tina looks?
    1.15 Find the sentence on page 16 that tells why the girl in the blue dress sits by the window all day.
    1.16 Not appropriate in this story.
  1.2 *Recall*
    1.21 Who are the main characters in this story?
    1.22 Why are Tina and the girl in the blue dress happy they met?
    1.23 How do Tina and the girl in the blue dress become friends?
    1.24 How are Tina and her new friend alike?
    1.25 Why does the girl in the blue dress have no one to play with before she meets Tina?
    1.26 Not appropriate in this story.
2.0 *Reorganization*:
  2.1 Put each word under the proper heading:

Pedro	dress	friends	Tina
city	downstairs	window	Carla
house		wheelchair	
People	*Places*	*Things*	

  2.2 Not appropriate in this story.
  2.3 What was this story about?
  2.4 Pedro says that the big city is a good place for his Dad to find work. Where could we look to find out what kind of job his father might find if he lived in our city?
3.0 *Inferential Comprehension*:
  3.1 What else could the author have told us about Tina and her family?
  3.2 What can we learn from this story?
  3.3 If the story hadn't ended here, what do you think would have happened to Tina and her new friend?
  3.4 How do you think Tina's feelings about the city change from the time she first comes to the city to live to the time she meets the girl in the blue dress?
  3.5 Why do you think Pedro meets some friends before Tina does?
  3.6 What kind of girl do you think Tina's new friend is?
  3.7 Read pages 12-14. What do you think will happen next?
  3.8 What does Tina mean when she calls the girl downstairs "stuck-up"?
4.0 *Evaluation*:
  4.1 Could this be a true story?
  4.2 Not appropriate in this story.
  4.3 How many of you have ever seen a person in a wheelchair or have read a book about a person who couldn't walk? The girl in the blue dress says that she can't go out because she can't walk. From

FIGURE 5.1.

Needing a Friend

Tina stood looking out the window.
"WHY did we have to come to this place?"
she asked her brother Pedro.

"You know why as well as I do,"
said Pedro. "This is a big city. It's
a good place for Dad to find work."

"But I don't LIKE it here,"
said Tina, starting to cry. "There's
no one to play with. The only girl
around is that stuck-up one who lives
downstairs. She never comes out. All
SHE ever does is sit at her window."

"Well, WE'LL never make friends
just standing at THIS window,"
said Pedro. "I'm going out!"

12

Pedro ran out the door, and Tina
looked out of the window again.

"He isn't going to make any friends,"
she told herself as she watched him
from the window.

But soon, two boys ran up to Pedro.
The three boys talked a little. Then,
they all walked down the street.

13

From John M. Franco et al., *I Build, Belong, and Believe*, American Book Company (New York: Litton Educational Publishing, Inc, 1970), pp. 12-17. Reprinted by permission of the publisher.

FIGURE 5.1. Continued.

Tina nodded.

"Is that why you're crying?" asked the girl.

Tina nodded again, but she stopped crying.

"What are you looking at?" asked Tina's sister Carla, coming into the room.

"Nothing!" said Tina.

"You've been looking out that window for days now," said Carla. "Why don't you go out and try to make friends?"

"I can't," said Tina, starting to cry again. "Things aren't the same here."

Then, still crying, Tina ran out of the house and down to the street.

"What's the matter?" someone asked.

Tina looked up. A girl in a blue <u>dress</u> was at a window just <u>above</u> her. It was the girl Tina'd told Pedro about.

"You're new here, aren't you?" asked the girl.

14

"Why don't you come in and talk to me?" asked the girl in the blue dress.

"Why don't you come out?" asked Tina.

"I can't," said the girl. "Come on in."

So, Tina walked back up the steps and into the girl's house. The girl in the blue dress was still sitting at the window.

"What's the matter with you?" asked Tina. "Why are you just sitting there like that?"

"I can't walk," said the girl.

"That's why I have no one to play with."

"I'll play with you if you want," said Tina, sitting down beside the girl.

"But I can't go out," said the girl.

"That's OK," said Tina. "We can still be friends. We can play in here."

"I'm glad you've come here to live," said the girl. "I need a friend."

"Me, too," said Tina. "Me, too."

16

what you have seen or read, do you agree that all people in wheelchairs can't go out? Why? Why not?

4.4 What part of the story best tells how Tina felt about the city?

4.5 Should Pedro have gone outside without Tina?

5.0 *Appreciation:*

5.1 What parts of the story were most interesting to you?

5.2 How did you feel when Tina was crying because she had no friends?

5.3 Why do you think the we'll and this are in capital letters in this sentence: " 'Well, WE'LL never make friends just standing at THIS window', said Pedro"?

5.4 How does the author let you know that the girl in the blue dress is lonely and wants to have a friend?

Activity 4

One source of materials and activities for the development of comprehension ability is the group of selections that make up the book(s) provided for each level in a reading series. The teachers' guide that accompanies each book typically provides questions to be used for establishing purposes for silent reading, and for guiding discussion during and after the reading of the selection.

The next story, "Who Hates Billy Wong?" (fig. 5.2), is taken from a reading series published by the American Book Company, and is reprinted as it appears in the Teacher's Annotated Edition (the questions in the overprint do not appear in the pupils' book). Following the story is the section from the Teacher's Guide which details the story presentation and outlines questions to be used in developing comprehension of the story.

As Clymer points out in his discussion of Barrett's taxonomy (activity 2),[9] one way of using the taxonomy is as a tool in analyzing the questions presented in reading materials. The results of such analyses will indicate the types of comprehension outcomes being emphasized. If the teacher finds that certain outcomes are being emphasized to the exclusion of others in the materials he is using, he can then devise questions of his own to correct the imbalance.

Read "Who Hates Billy Wong?" and the material that follows. When you have finished, analyze both the story and the questions using the Barrett taxonomy. Use the following questions as a guide:

1. How many categories of the taxonomy are reflected in the questions asked?

2. Are some categories emphasized much more than others, or do the questions seem relatively evenly distributed?

You may find it helpful to use the format shown on page 163 as you analyze the story and the questions.

9. Clymer, "What is 'Reading'?"

Activity 5

Select several books at different levels from each of two reading series. Analyze the selections and the questions presented for use with them in the teachers' guides using the Barrett taxonomy. Focus your analysis on collecting data that will enable you to respond to the following questions:

1. Do the questions presented in each series reflect the entire range of outcomes of the Barrett taxonomy? If not, do the questions in one series more fully reflect the range of outcomes than do the questions in the other series?
2. If the questions in either or both series represent the full range of outcomes, are certain categories of outcomes emphasized more than others?
3. If certain categories of outcomes are emphasized more than others, does this appear to be caused by the content of the selections? That is, does the nature of the content limit the types of questions that can be asked?
4. Do you find differences in the types of comprehension outcomes that are being emphasized from level to level in either or both series?

Activity 6

The categories of comprehension outcomes presented in the Barrett taxonomy are arranged in a hierarchy of difficulty. In her discussion of the development of comprehension ability, Helen K. Smith suggests that it is also important to provide opportunities for sequential growth *within* each comprehension outcome. Smith explains this point of view and gives examples which illustrate it:

> . . . Begun in a simple manner in the primary grades, each skill in comprehension becomes increasingly complex and more refined and subtle as mastery of reading takes place. . . .
>
> . . . Just as there appears to be a hierarchy of the different skills, there also appears to be sequential growth within each skill.
>
> A primary child, for example, is asked to note one or two details at a time concerning such things as the color of the girl's dress or the size of the dog; by the time a student has finished high school, he should be able to select pertinent details which will aid him in achieving broad purposes in reading. . . .
>
> Children in the first grade learn to tell how story boys and girls are like each other and how they are different. In the middle and upper grades many uses are made of the ability to make comparisons and contrasts: the way people lived in two or more countries or times, weather at different times of the year; and the endings of two or more stories.[10]

10. Helen K. Smith, "Sequence in Comprehension," in *Sequential Development of Reading Abilities*, ed. Helen M. Robinson (Chicago: University of Chicago Press, 1960), pp. 53-54.

FIGURE 5.2.

What is the boy in the picture writing? ("Nobody likes Billy Wong.") Who do you think the boy is? (Encourage speculation.)

Why do you think he's writing that nobody likes Billy Wong? (Encourage speculation. Maybe because he doesn't like Billy Wong.)

Who Hates Billy Wong?

NOBODY LIKES BILLY WONG, he wrote.

He turned and looked around. No one had seen him. He ran down the dark street, turned the corner, and stopped at another wall. *What does Billy feel is bad about himself? (There is nothing he can do better than anyone else.)*

NOBODY LIKES BILLY WONG, he wrote. He *anyone else.)* looked around again. Someone was coming at the far end of the street. He turned back the way he had come, ran past the first sign and on to his house.

Why do you think the boy didn't want anyone to see what he was doing? (He didn't want anyone to know who wrote "Nobody Likes Billy Wong.")

3

When he opened the door, his mother was standing there. "Billy Wong! Where have you been?" she asked. "It's way past your bedtime!"

"I had to go out for a while, Ma," he said.

"Well, I did it," Billy told himself as he got into bed. "I feel better already." Then he turned over and went to sleep.

Everyone in the Wong family could do something really well. Billy's brother, Jim, was first in his class. All *his* marks were A's. His other brother, Jack, played the horn so well that everyone called him *great.* And Billy's sister, who was only six, was reading books all the time. And they were books that Billy couldn't even read too well himself!

It was the same with all of his cousins, too.

Every one of them could do *something* better than anyone else. Everyone but Billy. How does Billy feel about his family? (proud, sad, and envious that he isn't as good as others)

His marks were fair in school, and he got by in just about everything. But there really wasn't anything he did better than anyone else, and in a family like his, that was real bad!

What does Billy think about most of his ideas? (They are dumb.)

4

99

100

"Who Hates Billy Wong?" From John M. Franco et al., Teachers' Edition, *I Can, Compete, and Care,* American Book Company (New York: Litton Educational Publishing Inc, 1970), pp. 99-106. Reprinted by permission of the publisher.

Billy was very sorry for himself. He'd thought and thought for a long time, and he'd made up his mind that the only thing left to be was the <u>dumbest</u>, or the meanest, or the most hated Wong in the world. "Being the most hated would be the best," he told himself. "I don't think too many kids try for *that!*"

If you were going to pretend to be mean or dumb, which would be harder for you to pretend to be? Tell why? (Accept all reasonable answers.)

Billy thought about it again when he woke up the next morning. His plan still sounded good, so he felt better as he dressed and went in to breakfast. But he was so busy thinking about being the most hated kid, that he almost <u>burned the toast.</u> After breakfast, Billy ran outside.

Why don't more children try to be hated? (To be hated you must do bad things. Doing bad things brings punishment, lack of privileges and causes all kinds of problems; most people really want to be liked.)

"Say, Billy! Who's mad at you?" yelled his cousin Lee.

"Don't know," said Billy, "most anyone, I guess." Lee and Billy were in the same class.

They were also very good friends.

"Well, *Lee* saw it," Billy told himself as he ran down the street. "But I'm still not sure it's really going to work."

How do you think Billy hopes his plan will turn out? (He thinks when the other kids see the sign they'll believe he is the most hated boy in the world.)

5

101

What is Billy doing? (fixing a skate) How do you think he learned how to fix skates? (Encourage discussion of how he might have learned.) At the corner, Billy saw little Molly West. She was crying, and holding a broken roller skate in her hands. Billy stopped to fix the skate. Then, he showed Molly how to put it on.

How do you think Molly feels toward Billy? (She likes him.)

6

102

Developing Comprehension Ability   159

FIGURE 5.2. Continued.

Walking on, Billy passed some girls jumping rope. He hoped they'd say, "Who hates Billy Wong? Everybody! Who likes Billy Wong? Nobody!" But they never even saw him!

Everywhere Billy went, it was the same. Nothing had changed. If the other kids *had* seen the signs, they weren't saying so.

Outside the Second Hand Store, Billy pulled an old clock out of a box of trash. He sat down and started fiddling with it. "I'm not even good at being hated," Billy told himself. "It was a dumb idea anyway. Most of my ideas are pretty dumb, I guess."

Billy was so busy with the old clock that he didn't even see his Aunt Alice coming down the street. Her arms were full of big bags.

"Hello, Billy," she said. "Will you help me with these, please? My wagon is broken."

"Sure, Aunt Alice," Billy said, putting down the clock and taking one of the bags.

When they got to Aunt Alice's house, Billy fixed the shopping wagon.

How did Billy feel after seeing the girls? (disappointed and sad because he wasn't noticed nor was his sign noticed)

What does Billy like to do? (fix things)

How is Billy making out in his attempt to be the meanest, most hated Wong? (not very well; he does too many nice things)

7

"Thank you," said Aunt Alice. "By the way, Billy, tell your mother that I got a letter from Aunt Betty. She writes about all the children and the fine things they're doing. My, but they're all so smart!"

Billy waved and started to the door. "That's all I need," he thought, "hearing about all those smart little kids of Aunt Betty's."

Billy went to the Second Hand Store. Mr. Robinson was standing out in front.

"Did you fix this clock, Billy?" asked Mr. Robinson.

"It wasn't really broken," Billy said. "There was just one part that had slipped a little."

"Well, thank you very much," said Mr. Robinson. "Can I pay you something for fixing it?"

"Oh, no! No, thank you," said Billy. "I *like* doing stuff like that."

The rest of the morning passed without anything special happening. Then after lunch, Billy went out to play with Lee.

How did Billy feel hearing of his cousins? (He just felt worse; more ashamed about his own lack of accomplishments.)

How does Billy change his sign? (Now it says "Billy Wong is a great mechanic.")

8

104

103

"Sure!" said Lee. "All I can do is *school* stuff, nothing special, like you. You can fix *anything*. Everybody knows that!" *How does Lee feel about Billy? (admires him for his ability to fix things)*

That night, Billy did a lot of thinking, "I have to go out for a while," he told his mother.

Billy ran down the street to the first sign he'd made the night before. He looked all around to be sure no one was watching. Then, he scratched out the old words and wrote:

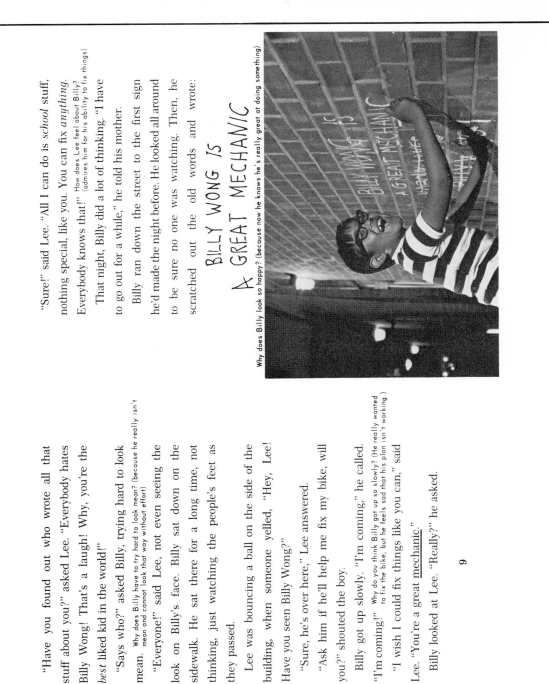

BILLY WONG IS A GREAT MECHANIC

Why does Billy look so happy? (because now he knows he's really great at doing something)

"Have you found out who wrote all that stuff about you?" asked Lee. "Everybody hates Billy Wong! That's a laugh! Why, you're the *best* liked kid in the world!"

"Says who?" asked Billy, trying hard to look mean. *Why does Billy have to try hard to look mean? (because he really isn't mean and cannot look that way without effort)*

"Everyone!" said Lee, not even seeing the look on Billy's face. Billy sat down on the sidewalk. He sat there for a long time, not thinking, just watching the people's feet as they passed.

Lee was bouncing a ball on the side of the building, when someone yelled, "Hey, Lee! Have you seen Billy Wong?"

"Sure, he's over here," Lee answered.

"Ask him if he'll help me fix my bike, will you?" shouted the boy.

Billy got up slowly. "I'm coming," he called.

"I'm coming!" *Why do you think Billy got up so slowly? (He really wanted to fix the bike, but he feels sad that his plan isn't working.)*

"I wish I could fix things like you can," said Lee. "You're a great mechanic."

Billy looked at Lee. "Really?" he asked.

9

FIGURE 5.3.
From John M. Franco
et al., Teachers' Edition,
*I Can, Compete, and
Care,* American Book
Company (New York:
Litton Educational Pub-
lishing, Inc., 1970), pp.
47-49. Reprinted by per-
mission of the publisher.

SELECTION PRESENTATION

You may wish to use the following motivational activity before asking the children to read the story.

Have the children take turns pantomiming something they do well or wish they could do well.

Let the child performing indicate by shaking his head "yes" for something he does well and "no" for something he wishes he could do well. Then children in their seats must guess what the action is.

Direct the class's attention to the story title and the picture on page 3. Ask the questions provided in the overprint. Then introduce the story.

Today's story is about Billy Wong who has a plan that will make people think of him as the very best. His plan to get others to notice him will surprise you and what happens to Billy is something you will learn when you read the story.

Present the following General Purpose Question to the pupils and ask them to keep this question in mind as they read the story.

How does Billy's feeling about himself change?

SILENT READING

Have pupils read silently to answer the Specific Purpose Questions in the overprint. After pupils have answered each question, use questions like the following to check story comprehension.

1. See page 3 of the overprint for the Specific Purpose Question.
   a. *What made Billy feel better?* (He wrote the signs on the wall and no one saw him do it.)
   b. *What could Billy's brother Jim do well?* (get good grades in school)
   c. *What could his brother Jack do best?* (played a great horn)
   d. *What made Billy's six year old sister so good?* (She could read well.)
2. See page 5 of the overprint for the Specific Purpose Question.
   a. *What was it that not too many kids try to be?* (most hated)
   b. *What is Billy's plan?* (to be the most hated kid)
   c. *Who is Lee?* (Billy's cousin and friend)
   d. *What did Billy do for Molly that really hurt his chance of being the most hated kid?* (helped her with her skates)
3. See page 7 of the overprint for the Specific Purpose Question.
   a. *How is Billy helpful to his Aunt Alice?* (carried her groceries and fixed her wagon)
   b. *How did Billy help Mr. Robinson?* (fixed his clock for him)
4. See page 8 of the overprint for the Specific Purpose Question.
   a. *Why does Lee laugh at the sign?* (The signs are stupid because Billy is the best liked kid.)
   b. *How does the boy get his bike fixed?* (Billy fixes it.)
   c. *What did Billy learn about himself that everybody already knew?* (that he was the best at fixing things and best at helping others)

ORAL READING

Read the part that tells:

1. *what Billy was doing at the wall.* (p. 3)
2. *what the Wong family could do.* (p. 4, para. 4-6)
3. *what Billy had made up his mind to do.* (p. 5, para. 1)
4. *what Cousin Lee asked Billy.* (p. 5, para. 4)
5. *what happened outside the Secondhand Store.* (p. 7, para. 3)
6. *what happened after lunch.* (p. 9)
7. *what Billy did that night.* (p. 10, para. 3)

Analysis of Comprehension Questions

Barrett Taxonomy Categories	Number of Questions from "Who Hates Billy Wong?"
1.0 Literal Comprehension	
1.1 Recognition	
1.2 Recall	
2.0 Reorganization	
3.0 Inferential Comprehension	
4.0 Evaluation	
5.0 Appreciation	

FIGURE 5.4.

Sequence in Reading for a Comprehension Outcome
Main Idea

Each of the exercises listed below represents one way in which children can be asked to read for main idea, or for main idea and details. As a group, the exercises represent a sequence in terms of difficulty. Number the exercises in the order in which you would present them to children who are learning to read for main idea (use 1 to indicate the least difficult and 6 to indicate the most difficult). Since the length and reading level of the selections to be read can affect the relative difficulty of the exercises, assume that the selections to be read for these exercises are of the same length (several paragraphs) and are at the same reading level.

_____ A. Underline the sentence that states the main idea of the selection.

_____ B. Read the statements that follow the selection. Write *M* next to the statement that gives the main idea. Write *C* next to the statements that are correct according to the selection. Write *I* next to the statements that are incorrect according to the selection. Write *N* next to the statements that are not included in the selection.

_____ C. Read the statements that follow the selection. Write *M* next to the statement that gives the main idea.

_____ D. Read the statements that follow the selection. Write *M* next to the statement that gives the main idea. Write *C* next to the statements that are correct according to the selection. Write *I* next to the statements that are incorrect according to the selection.

_____ E. Write the main idea of the selection in your own words.

_____ F. Underline the sentence in each paragraph that gives the main idea of the paragraph.

Answer Key:
D-4, E-6, F-1.
A-2, B-5, C-3.

In concluding her discussion, Smith suggests three implications for the teaching of comprehension:

. . . First, the pupil needs much experience at every grade level in mastering and using all comprehension skills. Second, because there are so many kinds of comprehension skills, students should be taught how to formulate their purposes in reading and how to read for these different purposes. Third, the teacher's well-formulated questions requiring thoughtful, penetrating answers before an assignment is given and during discussion period are strong determiners of the breadth and depth of comprehension achieved.[11]

Complete the activity presented in figure 5.4 in order to further your understanding of sequential development within specific comprehension

11. Ibid., p. 56.

outcomes. Respond to the following questions after you have completed the exercise:

1. Do you agree with the sequence presented in the answer key?
2. If you disagree with the sequence presented in the answer key, in what order would you place the activities?
3. How do your responses compare with those of others who have completed the exercise?

Activity 7

The sequence of books provided in a reading series was identified in activity 4 as one source of material for use in the development of comprehension ability. Two additional sources are (1) the workbooks that accompany the books in a reading series, and (2) sets of workbooks that focus on specific reading skills (e.g., comprehension) and are designed to supplement the material presented in reading series. Exercises in both types of workbooks are usually intended for use by children independently.

Several difficulties become apparent when one examines the materials which have been developed to help children learn to read for specific comprehension outcomes:

1. Often the comprehension outcomes are not defined or are defined very vaguely (this is particularly true in the case of such higher level outcomes as inference, generalization, and conclusion).
2. Within materials in which more specific definitions of outcomes are presented, it is possible to find that the definition of an outcome used in one set of materials differs from the definition used in another set of materials.
3. Often there is no indication that the exercises in a particular book have been developed sequentially.
4. Frequently there is no attempt to indicate to children the purpose of the activity, or the comprehension outcome for which they are to read.
5. The exercises are typically designed to provide *practice* in reading for a specific outcome rather than as an *introduction* to reading for that outcome (a child must be *introduced* to the concept of "main idea" before he can *practice* reading for main ideas).

Examples of exercises that illustrate these difficulties are presented in figures 5.5, 5.6, and 5.7. The exercise shown in figure 5.5 focuses on reading for generalizations. Notice that a *generalization* is defined as a *general conclusion*. Does this definition give you a clear idea of what the writer means

FIGURE 5.5.
"Making Generalizations": From Nila Banton Smith, *Be A Better Reader Book II*, Third Edition (Englewood Cliffs, N. J.: Prentice-Hall, © 1969) page 136. Reprinted by permission of the publisher.

MAKING GENERALIZATIONS

Many paragraphs contain a series of related facts about one subject. Sometimes you need to remember each of these separate facts. At other times all you need to do is to get a general idea of what the several facts imply when taken together. The general conclusion which you draw from several facts is called a *generalization*.

See if you can make a generalization after reading the facts in each paragraph below. The first generalization has been written for you.

1. Perhaps you think pilots and stewardesses are the only type of workers employed by an airline. If you should visit an airport you would see ticket agents, secretaries, typists, and bookkeepers—all at work on the airline's business. Then there are the highly skilled mechanics who keep the planes in good flying condition. Cargo handlers take care of the mail-boxes, express, and baggage. A superintendent works with the pilot of each plane to plan his route and altitude. Radio operators direct take-offs and landings.

What generalization can you make about the employees of an airline? *Many different workers are employed by an airline.*

2. Corn is grown from southern Canada throughout the United States and Mexico. In South America, corn is found from the northern part of the continent to Argentina. Corn grows in Europe from the central part of that continent to the northern part of Africa. It is raised in the southeastern part of Asia. And cornfields are found also in the southeastern part of Africa.

What is your generalization in regard to places where corn is grown? _____

3. New England has no iron or coal mines. It has no oil wells or natural gas. There are many hills and mountains in New England. Large areas of level soil such as farmers have in the Midwest are lacking in New England. The soil is poor in most places. The glaciers of early times pushed away the rich topsoil leaving a layer of gravel and sand. In many places only bare rocks were left after the glacier passed over the land. The people of New England are very prosperous, however, because of the manufacturing which they do.

What is your generalization concerning the natural resources of New England? _____

4. In oceans you find large animals such as whales and porpoises. There are many different kinds of fish. Snails, clams, lobsters, crabs, and eels live in the sea. These animals are large enough so that a person can see them with the naked eye. But there are also hundreds of animals in the sea that can not be seen without a microscope. Oceans are filled with plants as well as animals. There are seaweeds of many different kinds. And there are hundreds of tiny plants too small to be seen unless we use a microscope.

What generalization would you make about things that live in the sea? _____

5. Some seeds are scattered by the wind. The white head of the dandelion is made up of seeds with a parachute attached to each one. Some seeds have wings which help them to "fly" through the air. Seeds of the maple, ash, thistle, and milkweed have wings. Water also helps to scatter seeds. The seeds of grass, the sycamore, and the bitter pecan are light enough to float in water. They fall into streams and are carried along with them. Some seeds stick to animals and plants and are carried from place to place in this way. Some plants scatter their own seeds. When their seed pods are ripe they burst open with such force that their seeds are scattered for quite a distance.

What generalization can you make in regard to the ways in which seeds travel? _____

by *generalization?* It is important to note, also, that in some reading materials *generalization* and *conclusion* are treated as separate comprehension outcomes.

Reading in order to draw a conclusion is the focus of the exercise shown in figure 5.6. How is the comprehension outcome *conclusion* defined? Is the definition precise enough so that you understand the way the term *conclusion* is being used here? Notice that while the exercise

DRAWING CONCLUSIONS ABOUT DIAMONDS

Sometimes you can make a decision about something based on what you read about it. This is called **drawing a conclusion**.

FIGURE 5.6. "Drawing Conclusions About Diamonds." From Sandra M. Brown, *Increasing Comprehension,* D in the *MCP Skillbooster Series* (Cleveland, Ohio: Modern Curriculum Press, 1975), p. 15. Reprinted by permission of the publisher.

For example, if you are going out and someone tells you it's raining, you will probably draw the conclusion that you had better wear your raincoat.

Read the paragraphs below. Then, in the list under each paragraph, put a check next to the conclusion that is the better one to draw from what you have read.

1.   Did you know that there was once a diamond that weighed over a pound (0.4 kilograms)? The largest diamond ever found, it was cut into smaller stones. But the biggest piece is still the largest cut diamond in the world.

_____ a. Most cut diamonds weigh less than a pound (0.4 kilograms).

_____ b. Most cut diamonds weigh more than a pound (0.4 kilograms).

2.   The giant diamond was found in South Africa, one of the few places in the world where diamonds have been discovered. Russia, India, and South America have important diamond fields, too. The United States has only one diamond mine, and it is in Arkansas.

_____ a. Diamonds are found almost anywhere.

_____ b. Diamonds are rare.

3.   Diamonds are not used only to make beautiful jewelry. Because the diamond is the hardest natural material known to man, it can be used to cut and grind other materials. This makes diamonds one of the most useful and valuable stones in the world.

_____ a. Diamonds have many uses.

_____ b. The only important use of diamonds is in making jewelry.

MAKING INFERENCES — 15

---

focuses on *drawing conclusions,* it is labeled as an exercise on *making inferences* at the bottom of the page. In many reading materials, *conclusion* and *inference* are treated as separate outcomes.

The exercise shown in figure 5.7 is taken from one booklet in a sequentially developed series of booklets designed for use in grades two through twelve. The teacher's manual indicates that the questions which follow each reading selection are based on stated facts, implications, or

FIGURE 5.7.
From William A. McCall
and Lelah Mae Crabbs,
*Standard Test Lessons in
Reading, Book B* (New
York: Teachers College
Press, Columbia Univer-
sity, 1961), p. 43. Re-
printed by permission of
the publisher.

It was the last half of the ninth inning. The score stood 2 to 1 in favor of the Yankees. The Dodgers, then the "beloved bums" of Brooklyn, were at bat. There were two out and two men on base. Bill Bevans of the Yankees was on the mound. A few more successful pitches and he would enter baseball's hall of fame for having pitched the first no-hitter in the history of the World Series.

Lavagetto, who had been longest with the Dodgers, was sent in as a pinch hitter. Rubbing dirt on his hands, this player who was nearly a has-been strode to the plate, struck viciously at the first pitch, and missed. New York fans yelled for joy, and Brooklyn was in breathless suspense. Lavagetto swung again, connected, and the ball soared over the head of the farthest outfielder.

As the Dodgers did a victory dance, the Yankees' pitcher trudged off the field with bowed head and tears in his eyes.

1. This is a story of which sport?   (a) tennis   (b) golf   (c) baseball   (d) football
2. At the beginning of the last half of the ninth inning, the score was   (a) 2 to 1   (b) 2 to 2   (c) 3 to 1   (d) 3 to 2
3. Who won this game?   (a) Yankees   (b) Bill Bevans   (c) New York   (d) Brooklyn
4. The Yankees were   (a) disappointed   (b) disagreeable   (c) triumphant   (d) joyful
5. The New York fans   (a) yelled for joy   (b) shed tears   (c) bowed their heads   (d) moaned
6. What did the victors do?   (a) wept   (b) danced   (c) shouted   (d) yelled for joy
7. When the game ended, who trudged sadly off the field?   (a) Bill Bevans   (b) Lavagetto   (c) an outfielder   (d) a Dodger
8. The Yankees' first pitch was for them a (a) failure (b) poor try (c) success (d) miss
9. Who rubbed dirt on his hands?   The   (a) baseman   (b) shortstop   (c) center fielder   (d) batter

No. right	0	1	2	3	4	5	6	7	8	9
G score	3.2	3.3	3.5	3.7	4.0	4.5	5.0	5.6	6.2	7.1

general reasoning.[12] Notice that no attempt is made to indicate to students what the purposes for reading are in terms of specific comprehension outcomes. As you read the questions following the selection, can you determine which questions are based on stated facts, which on implications, and which on general reasoning?

Not all of the difficulties that were pointed out in the exercises in figures 5.5-5.7 are consistently evident in all materials. The exercises shown in figures 5.8, 5.9, and 5.10, for example, illustrate sequential development in helping children read for main ideas and details. The exercises in figures 5.8 and 5.9 appear at the beginning of the comprehension workbook from which they are taken. Notice that an explanation of each comprehension outcome is included. After children are given several opportunities to read for main ideas and details in separate exercises, they move to the type of exercise shown in figure 5.10 in which they read the same material for both main idea and supporting details. Additional exercises of the type shown in figure 5.10 are then provided in this workbook.

The analyses of the materials that have been presented here make it apparent that it is essential for teachers to exercise caution in selecting and using comprehension materials. The following guidelines are suggested as an aid to the use of the variety of materials available for providing optimal learning experiences for children:

1. It is important that the teacher have his own clear, precise definitions of the comprehension outcomes for which he wants children to read.
2. In selecting supplementary materials, it is necessary to search for exercises that define outcomes in ways that are consistent with the definitions the children are accustomed to using.
3. It is often necessary to consider an exercise in terms of what children are asked to do, rather than in terms of the label given the exercise. If what the children are asked to do appears to fit the teacher's objective, while the way in which the exercise is labeled (inference, conclusion, etc.) does not, the exercise can be used by replacing the inappropriate label with one the children will recognize.
4. It is not always necessary to reject material just because comprehension outcomes are defined in vague or confusing terms. If exercises appear to be appropriate, the teacher can rewrite existing definitions to increase their clarity and to make them consistent with the definitions he has been using with the children.

12. William A. McCall and Lelah Mae Crabbs, *Teacher's Manual and Answer Key for McCall-Crabbs Standard Test Lessons in Reading,* 3d ed. (New York: Teachers College, Columbia University, 1961).

5. It is essential that the materials that are selected are appropriate sequentially in terms of the children's experience. Children should not be expected to complete an exercise in reading for a specific comprehension outcome independently at a level of difficulty that is beyond what they have experienced.

6. In all material that is used, the reasons for reading should be made clear to the children. If an exercise does not include pur-

FIGURE 5.8.
"That's the Idea!" From Sandra M. Brown, *Increasing Comprehension*, D in the *MCP Skillbooster Series* (Cleveland, Ohio: Modern Curriculum Press, 1975), p. 6. Reprinted by permission of the publisher.

THATS THE IDEA!

The **main idea** is the most important thing the writer says about a topic.

Read the paragraphs below. Under each paragraph put a check next to the main idea of the paragraph.

1.   Everything seemed to go wrong that morning. When Sid got out of bed, he tripped over his slippers. Then, he pulled a button off his new shirt. Next, he spilled orange juice all over the kitchen floor. It was just one of those mornings.

_____ a. The slippers were in Sid's way.

_____ b. Sid would have to clean up the orange juice.

_____ c. That morning several things went wrong.

2.   Have you ever listened to how different people laugh? My uncle has a loud, deep laugh. He opens his mouth wide to let it out. My little brother giggles a lot. He puts his hand in front of his mouth as if to hold the giggle back. My sister's laugh is high. It starts, then it stops, and then it starts again. Everyone laughs in a different way. I wonder how I sound when I laugh.

_____ a. A loud laugh is better than a giggle.

_____ b. People can't hear how they sound when they laugh.

_____ c. Everyone laughs in a different way.

poses for reading, the teacher can write an introduction to the exercise which will identify the purposes for the children.

Examine sets of materials designed to help children learn to read for specific comprehension outcomes. Which of the difficulties identified in this activity do you find? In which materials do you find that attempts have been made to overcome one or more of these difficulties?

DETAILS, DETAILS

A **detail** is one small piece of information. Details help you understand the main idea.

The main idea of the paragraph below is that Tammy is a good athlete. Read the paragraph. Then, under the paragraph, put a check next to each detail that shows that Tammy is a good athlete.

Tammy lives next door to me. I've known her all my life. The thing that impresses me most about her is what a good athlete she is. Tammy is in my gym class. When we play basketball in gym, the team that Tammy is on almost always wins. She's also the best baseball player in the class. Our school day ends at three o'clock. Every day after school Tammy runs home. It's over a mile, but she runs all the way without stopping. She says she does it to get in shape for the track team. Track season starts in April. Naturally Tammy is the star of the track team. She's even a good horseback rider. Last year she won two blue ribbons for horseback riding at the county fair.

_____ 1. When we play basketball in gym, the team that Tammy is on almost always wins.

_____ 2. She's also the best baseball player in the class.

_____ 3. I've known her all my life.

_____ 4. Every day after school Tammy runs home. It's over a mile, but she runs all the way without stopping.

_____ 5. Our school day ends at three o'clock.

_____ 6. Naturally Tammy is the star of the track team.

_____ 7. The track season starts in April.

_____ 8. She's even a good horseback rider.

_____ 9. Tammy is in my gym class.

_____ 10. Last year she won two blue ribbons for horseback riding at the county fair.

FIGURE 5.9. "Details, Details." From Sandra M. Brown, *Increasing Comprehension,* D in the *MCP Skillbooster Series* (Cleveland, Ohio: Modern Curriculum Press, 1975), p. 7. Reprinted by permission of the publisher.

FIGURE 5.10.
"That's Hockey!" From
Sandra M. Brown,
Increasing Comprehension, D in the *MCP
Skillbooster Series*
(Cleveland, Ohio: Modern Curriculum Press,
1975), pp. 42-43. Reprinted by permission of
the publisher.

THAT'S HOCKEY!

As you know, the main idea is the most important thing a writer has to say about a topic. You also know that the writer uses details to support the main idea.

The topic of the following article is ice hockey. Read the article carefully, paying attention to the main idea and the details. Then follow the directions on page 43.

There are few sports that are as exciting and fast moving as ice hockey. Playing this thrill-a-minute game takes great skill and courage. Each player must be an expert ice skater in order to help his team win. The object of the game is for each team to try to hit the puck, a small disk made of hard rubber, into the other team's net, or goal cage. Each time a team hits the puck into the other team's net, it scores a point. The team that scores the most points wins the game.

The players hit the puck with long L-shaped sticks. In professional hockey the puck is sometimes hit so hard that it travels across the ice faster than one hundred miles (160 kilometers) an hour. The players skate after the puck at top speed, crashing into walls and one another. Sometimes the game leads to fighting. The players swing their sticks and throw punches at one another. Because the game is so rough and action packed, the players wear special protective equipment to cut down the number of injuries.

Fast and exciting action — that's hockey!

42 — RECOGNIZING THE MAIN IDEA AND SUPPORTING DETAILS

The following is a list of materials which may be available for examination in your college library or instructional materials center:

Boning, Richard A. *Specific Skills Series.* New York: Barnell Loft, 1962-73.
Gates, Arthur I., and Peardon, Celeste C. *Gates-Peardon Reading Exercises.* rev. ed. New York: Teachers College Press, 1965.
Guiler, W. S.; Coleman, J. H.; and Jungeblatt, A. *Reading for Meaning.* Books 4-12. Philadelphia: Lippincott, 1955-65.

In the box below put a check next to the sentence that tells the main idea of the article "That's Hockey!" on page 42.

1. What is the most important thing the writer has to say about hockey?

    ____ a. The players wear protective equipment.

    ____ b. The puck sometimes travels faster than one hundred miles (160 kilometers) an hour.

    ____ c. Hockey is an exciting and fast-moving sport.

In the list below put a check next to each detail that supports the main idea.

2. ____ a. Players skate at top speed.

    ____ b. The players carry long L-shaped sticks.

    ____ c. The puck sometimes travels faster than one hundred miles (160 kilometers) an hour.

    ____ d. The players crash into walls and one another.

    ____ e. The puck is made of hard rubber.

    ____ f. Each goal is worth one point.

    ____ g. Sometimes fights break out during the game.

RECOGNIZING THE MAIN IDEA AND SUPPORTING DETAILS — 43

Johnson, Eleanor M., ed. *New Diagnostic Reading Workbooks.* Columbus, Ohio: Charles E. Merrill Publishing Company.

McCall, W. A., and Crabbs, L. M. *Standard Test Lessons in Reading.* rev. ed. New York: Teachers College Press, 1961.

Merrill Skilltexts. Columbus, Ohio: Charles E. Merrill Publishing Company.

New Reading Skill Builder Series. Pleasantville, N. Y.: Reader's Digest Services, 1966-73.

Parker, Don H. *SRA Reading Laboratories.* Chicago: Science Research Associates, Pt. 1, 1961; Pt. 2, 1960.

Reading for Understanding. Chicago: Science Research Associates, 1963.

Sanford, Adrian B., et al. *Reading Comprehension.* Macmillan Reading Spectrum. rev. ed. New York: Macmillan Publishing Company, 1973.

Stone, Clarence R., and Grover, Charles C., et al. *New Practice Readers.* New York: Webster Division of McGraw-Hill Book Co., 1962.

Activity 8

Two sources of materials for the development of comprehension ability were presented through activity 4 and activity 7. In addition to using these sources, many teachers design their own activities and materials. In developing their own activities, teachers can focus on the specific comprehension needs of the children with whom they are working, and can also avoid the difficulties, such as those identified in activity 7, that are often encountered in using commercial materials.

The following exercises (figs. 5.11, 5.12) are illustrative of the types of activities that can be developed by teachers. The exercises shown here are taken from a series of exercises which one teacher developed using a newspaper column that was familiar to the children in her class.

Read the exercises using the following questions as a guide:

1. In what ways do the exercises provide for sequential growth in comprehension ability?
2. In what categories of the Barrett taxonomy (other than the ones included in the exercises) could questions be written for these reading selections?

The activities that follow provide additional examples of the types of exercises that teachers can develop to help children increase their ability to read for a range of comprehension outcomes.

Identifying Emotional Reactions
Grades one, two, three, and four

After a story has been read, the children may complete sentences by selecting words which pertain to each character's reaction. The exercise may be duplicated or written on the board.

Example: a. John felt _____.
(happy, sad, angry)
b. Mary felt _____.
(proud, embarrassed, sad)[13]

---

13. Selma E. Herr, *Learning Activities for Reading*, 2d ed. (Dubuque, Iowa: Wm. C. Brown Company Publishers, 1970), p. 54.

Interpreting Behavior of Characters

Grades two, three, four, five, and six

After reading a story, the children answer questions similar to the examples given below.

Example: a. Why do you think Mary wanted to wait for Jane?
     b. Why did Mary have so many friends?[14]

Identifying Self with Character

Grades four, five, and six

Questions similar to those listed below are asked about a story in the reader. These may be duplicated or written on the chalkboard.

Example: a. If you had been in Jane's place, what would you have done?
     b. If you had seen the bear, what would you have done?[15]

Outlining

Make a simple outline form from oaktag to accompany a short selection. On the oaktag, print specific phrases needed to complete the outline. The outline phrases and frame may be kept in a large envelope. A smaller envelope containing an answer key may be attached. Students read the story, construct the outline and check their work.

Students may be given a list of words and an outline. They are to organize the words and fill in the blanks in the outline.

Example:

cabbage	dress	I. Clothing	III. Pets
hat	shirt	A.	A.
dog	rabbit	B.	B.
bird	corn	C.	C. [16]
string beans		II. Food	
		A.	
		B.	
		C.	

Fact or Opinion

To gain proficiency in distinguishing between fact and opinion, the pupils might do the following:

Study news reports and editorials to determine the essential differences in the two types of writing.

Indicate which of a series of statements express facts only and then rewrite those that are not purely factual so that they do not express an opinion.

Delete from paragraphs or longer selections statements that are not entirely factual.[17]

---

14. Ibid.
15. Ibid.
16. Evelyn B. Spache, *Reading Activities for Child Involvement* (Boston: Allyn & Bacon, 1972), pp. 216-18.
17. Martha Dallmann, Roger L. Rouch, Lynette Y. C. Chang, and John J. DeBoer, *The Teaching of Reading*, 4th ed. (New York: Holt, Rinehart and Winston, 1974), p. 196.

ASK ANDY

What Are Sponges?

*Andy sends a complete, 20-volume set of the "World
Book Encyclopedia to Mary Jo Mallon, age 13, of
Portland, Oregon, for her question: Does a sponge
really live?*

Most sponges are marine animals which spend
their lives squatting on the floor of some warmish sea.
They look for all the world like chubby lettuces and
small round shrubs. Ususally there are a lot of them together and you could easily mistake them for an un-

derwater vegetable gar-
den. Some are drabbish
grey, some are rosy red,
yellow, orange, violet or
even black.

There are some 3,000
spongy members of the
animal phylum Porifera,
ranging in size from a fraction of an inch to six feet.
There are trumpet-shaped sponges, basket-shaped, fin-
ger-shaped and dome-shaped sponges. All have tough,
leathery skins stretched tight over cushiony layers of
fleshy tissue. All have skins riddled with tiny pores,
which is why the name of their phylum means the pore
bearers.

Water, bearing oxygen and scraps of foods, passes
into the body of a sponge where it circulates through
a network of connecting canals. In the center of the
fleshy tissue we find the skeleton of the sponge, which
is also riddled with tubes. The skeleton which supports
the soft body tissues may be made of hard, glassy material, soft, rubbery material or a mixture of both, depending on the kind of sponge.

The bathtub sponge is a dome-shaped fellow who
enjoys life in warm surroundings, such as the Medi-
terranean Sea. Its skeleton is made entirely of soft,
rather elastic spongin—though this cannot be seen while
the animal is alive. Other spongin sponges are found
off the coast of Florida and in the warm waters of the
Gulf of Mexico.

*Send your questions to Ask Andy in care of The Times-Union.
Be sure to give name, age, and address.*

What Are Sponges?

For your answer write *M* in front of the statement that tells the main idea of the selection.

_____ 1. Sponges must live in warm surroundings.
_____ 2. All sponges have skins riddled with tiny pores.
_____ 3. Sponges are marine animals found on the floors of warm seas.
_____ 4. There are many different types of sponges.

For your answer write *C* (correct), *I* (incorrect), or *N* (not included).

_____ 1. The skeleton of the sponge surrounds the fleshy tissue.
_____ 2. Porifera means pore bearers.
_____ 3. The skins of sponges are used for leather.
_____ 4. Sponges eat plants and other small marine animals.
_____ 5. Sponges generally live in groups.
_____ 6. The skeleton of a sponge is either hard and glossy or soft and rubbery.

Make a partial outline of the selection by writing in the proper spaces the numbers of seven of the items listed in the left-hand column.

1. material the skeleton is made of
2. color
3. kinds of food eaten
4. layers of fleshly tissue
5. shape
6. inhabit warm seas
7. tough skins
8. length of life
9. size

  I. Ways in which all sponges are alike
    A.   B.   C.
 II. Ways in which sponges may differ
    A.   B.   C.   D.

FIGURE 5.12.
From the "Ask Andy"
series (July/August
1962). Copyright Los
Angeles Times. Reprinted
with permission.

ASK ANDY

What Stars Are Made Of

Andy sends a complete, 20-volume set of the "World Book Encyclopedia" to Joyce Hunt, age 10, of Rochester for her question: What are the stars made of?

Compared with a blazing star, our wonderful world is a frozen lump. But both the star and the earth are made from about 100 different types of atoms.

On earth, the temperature is so low that atoms of iron, tin and other substances reach their frozen state  and become solid. Water particles are cool enough to be in a liquid state. But the earth is warm enough to keep a blanket of air made from atoms in a gaseous state.

No star is cool enough for any of its atoms to form solids or even liquids. If we dropped an iron poker into the sun, it would melt and turn to gassy vapor in a moment. If we wrapped the sun in a sheet of ice 12 feet thick, the ice would turn to gaseous water vapor in less than a minute. All stars, then, are made entirely from seething gases.

On the cool earth, hydrogen is one of the rarest elements. But in a seething star, hydrogen is the most plentiful. In fact, hydrogen is the fuel which a star uses to keep its nuclear furnace going. And this hydrogen is exactly like the small traces of hydrogen we find here on the earth.

The star we know most about is our sun and it is an average-sized star made of average star materials. Most of it is hydrogen gas, but there are traces of other elements, just like those we find on our solid world. In the gases of the sun there are traces of iron and carbon and more than 60 other elements we find on earth.

A star, we are told, begins life as a cloud of hydrogen gas. The atoms of hydrogen are the simplest of all atoms, having just one proton in the nucleus and one orbiting electron. As the star grows older, some of these hydrogen atoms team up to form larger atoms of helium and other elements. The older stars have had time to form a few metals. But all the elements present in a star are in gaseous form.

Send your questions to Ask Andy in care of The Times-Union. Be sure to give name, age, and address.

What Stars Are Made Of

For your answer write *M* in front of the statement which tells the main idea of the selection, *S* in front of the *two* statements which are subordinate details, and *I* in front of the *two* statements which are incorrect.

_____ 1. When it is first formed, each star contains only hydrogen gas.
_____ 2. Our sun is much smaller than most other stars.
_____ 3. Helium is one of the most common elements on the earth.
_____ 4. Stars are composed of gases containing many of the elements which are found on earth.
_____ 5. As a star grows older, the hydrogen gas it contains is replaced by helium.
_____ 6. The sun is about 100 times as hot as our earth.
_____ 7. Stars are made from many different types of atoms just as the earth is.

For your answer write *C* (correct), *I* (incorrect), or *N* (not included).

_____ 1. Compared with other stars, our sun is not unusual.
_____ 2. There is approximately the same amount of hydrogen on the earth as there is in a star.
_____ 3. There are traces of iron and carbon in the gases of most stars.
_____ 4. Helium is composed of more complex atoms than is hydrogen.
_____ 5. Stars contain more hydrogen than any other element.
_____ 6. Stars are made of more different types of atoms than the earth is.
_____ 7. The temperature is the same on all stars.

Activity 9

The following lesson plan illustrates a procedure for helping children develop the ability to read for a variety of comprehension outcomes. The plan was designed for use with the story "Kareem of the Crop" which is reprinted here (fig. 5.13). Read both the lesson plan and the story. Use the following questions as a guide in reading the lesson plan:

1. What attempt is made in the prereading discussion (introduction) to relate the story to the interests of the children?
2. Note that new vocabulary words are introduced before the story is read. How does the context of each sentence help the children derive the meaning of the underlined word?
3. The children are given two overall purposes for reading the story before they begin. When are these purposes discussed?
4. After the purposes for reading have been discussed, additional questions are asked to stimulate children's thinking. Which of the categories in the Barrett taxonomy are reflected in these questions?

Lesson Plan
Comprehension

Grade Level: Sixth

I. Behavioral Objectives
   A. The students will be able to draw inferences about the main character based on information presented in the article.
   B. The students will be able to interpret the author's use of figurative language.
   C. The students will be able to draw inferences about the motivations of the main character.
   D. The students will be able to evaluate the author's qualifications for writing the article.
   E. The students will be able to identify correctly the main idea and details of the article by completing a written exercise.

II. Procedure
   A. Introduction
      Does anyone here play basketball or go to basketball games? (Place a picture of Kareem on the board). Does anyone recognize the name Kareem Abdul-Jabbar (write the name under the picture)? This is a picture of Kareem. Read the title of the story. What does it mean when we say that someone is the "cream of the crop"? Why does the author say "Kareem of the Crop"?
   B. Development
      1. Before we read let's go over some words that might be new to you (Have these sentences on the board.)

Herman L. Masin

FIGURE 5.13.
From Herman L. Masin, "Kareem of the Crop," in *Scholastic* (December 1971). © 1971 by Scholastic Magazines, Inc. Reprinted by permission of the publisher.

Kareem of the Crop

Some people remember the Alamo. A few remember the Maine. Others remember Mama. I remember Lew Alcindor,* and this is what I've said about him over the years:

At St. Jude's grade school, New York City, 1961: "13-year-old Lew Alcindor will be the next Wilt Chamberlain."

At Power Memorial High School, New York City, 1963: "Alcindor is the greatest high school player I've ever seen. He can't miss making All-American."

At UCLA, 1965: "The Bruins are going to win three straight championships. Alcindor makes them unbeatable."

Upon joining the pros, 1969: "Alcindor is going to be the most dominating force in the NBA. He's going to be greater than Russell or Chamberlain—or anyone else who ever played the game."

What was so smart about all that? Didn't *everyone* see his greatness? No. Everyone knew he had ability. But many experts nit-picked. Kareem was "too skinny." Or "too weak." Or "not a good enough shooter." All I saw was his terrific size, agility, quickness, smartness, good hands, and willingness to work. I never was surer of an athlete in my life.

43

It was a little scary. Watching him grow taller every year, stronger, surer of himself. And finally putting it all together—becoming the most overpowering player in history. Sparking an expansion team to the world championship.

That was in 1970-71. The big fellow started 1971-72 with a new name—Kareem Abdul-Jabbar. But he had the same old act—destroying opponents. What can you do about a 7′2″ "monster" who can out-rebound anyone, out-score anyone, out-shot block anyone? Only one thing—pray. That's what the rest of the NBA is doing. But it isn't going to help. With Kareem at center, the Bucks are unbeatable.

No one who knew Kareem back in grade school is surprised to find him sitting on top of the world. Though he hails from the sidewalks of New York, he was no ghetto kid. His parents weren't rich, but they gave him all a boy could ask for—love, comforts, ideals, and ambition. They also gave him height. (His mother is 5′10″ and his father 6′4″.)

By the time Kareem turned 11, he was already as tall as his dad. He was just learning how to play basketball. But, except for his height, he didn't show much promise. He didn't have the coordination to go with his size.

At St. Jude's grade school, he sprouted up to 6′7″. And it was there that he came to the attention of Jack Donohue, basketball coach at nearby Power Memorial High School. The coach gave Kareem a scholarship to Power. By the end of his freshman year, he had shot up to 6′10″, and Coach Donohue knew that he had something special.

44

*Lew Alcindor changed his name to Kareem Abdul-Jabbar in 1971.

FIGURE 5.13.
Continued.

In most ways Donohue was the perfect coach for Kareem. He treated him exactly the same as anyone else, never as a star. He taught Kareem the whole game, not just shooting, and he taught him to do *everything* the right way.

And so Kareem became the perfect player. He had no bad habits. He was completely unselfish. And, for all his talent, he always played a *team* game. He played not to score points or to look good, but to *win*.

Though Coach Donohue developed Kareem into the greatest high school player of all time, he never quite understood how touchy Kareem was about his height and color. And he also built a fence around him. No one on the outside—no writer or coach—was allowed to talk to him. It saved Kareem some headaches, but it also cut him off from the adult world.

On the court, the Donohue-Jabbar team was a complete success. In his four years at Power Memorial, Kareem sparked the team to a 95-6 record, including a 71-game winning streak. The big fellow set a city scoring record and led Power to three straight Catholic school crowns.

Kareem also starred in the classroom. From grade school through high school, he never let his average fall below 90, which made him an "A" student.

Practically every college in America offered him a scholarship. Kareem chose the University of California at Los Angeles (UCLA). Poor Kareem. Everything went wrong right from the start. UCLA also built a fence around him. No interviews, little contact with the outside world.

It was a lonely life for the big fellow. And he never did get to enjoy college. In fact he soon moved to an apartment off campus. He played his jazz records, read a great deal, and had few dates. Every summer he made a beeline for New York, **45** where he served as a recreation director in ghetto housing projects.

Though he led a lonely life, Kareem at least was his own man. Proud of being black, he spoke freely and often bitterly on social issues. But always from the heart.

As at Power Memorial, the unhappy student was a smash hit on the court. UCLA lost only two games in Kareem's career. They became the first team in history to win three straight national crowns.

Kareem also made history by being picked "most valuable player" three times. He also became the first player since Jerry Lucas to make All-American every year.

Shortly afterward, Kareem made another bit of history. He became the first athlete to sign a contract for a million dollars. It started out with the two rival pro leagues offering him everything—including the kitchen sink—to sign with them. Kareem then showed his class. Instead of playing one off against the other, he made them submit bids. He would sign with the team that made the largest offer. The New York Nets offered him an even million. The Bucks offered $1,400,000. True to his word, Kareem chose the Bucks. Then the Nets came back with a second offer—$3,250,000! Kareem refused to consider it.

And so the tall, quiet man became an instant millionaire. But he was a bargain at that price. He made the Bucks a winner right off the bat.

The young millionaire still doesn't whistle while he works. He still is tough to interview, and he can be sullen and tactless. But everyone now accepts him for what he is, an unusually honest, sensitive, and moody person, a man who always speaks straight from the shoulder.

47 And, oh yes, the world's greatest basketball player.

a. Many people don't like the word "ghetto" because it makes some people think that everyone who lives in that neighborhood would rather live someplace else.

b. Because he lacked coordination, his movements were awkward and clumsy.

c. When we say things that offend others, we are being tactless.

d. Jack was in a disagreeable and sullen mood because he had just been told that he could not go to the baseball game.

2. The author of this story has watched Kareem from the time he was in grade school. Let's read the story to find out:

a. What does the author think of Kareem as a basketball player? What does he say that tells you this?

b. What does the author think of Kareem as a person? What does he say that tells you this?

Have these questions writen on the board so that the children can refer to them as they read.

3. After the students have read the story silently, have them discuss the answers to the questions that were given as purposes for reading.

4. Sometimes authors use words in ways that are different from the ways in which they are usually used. Find the sentence on story page 44 where the author calls Kareem a 7'2" 'monster'." What do you think he means? Discuss in the same way:

story page 45—"built a fence around him"
story page 45—"saved Kareem some headaches"
story page 45—"made a beeline for New York"
story page 47—"offering him everything—including the kitchen sink"

story page 47—"still doesn't whistle while he works"

5. On story page 45 the author states that Kareem was touchy about his height and color when he was in high school. What things might Kareem have done to give the writer the impression he was touchy? What might have made Kareem feel touchy? How do you think you might have felt if you had been in Kareem's place?

6. On story page 47 the author says that Kareem can be sullen and tactless. What might cause him to say this? Why might Kareem be this way?

7. Why might Kareem have changed his name?

8. Why do you think Kareem went back to New York every summer?

Developing Comprehension Ability

C. Conclusion

Why do you think this author was asked to write about Kareem Abdul-Jabbar? Do you think he knew enough about Kareem to write the story? Why? Why not? If someone else had written the story, how might parts of it have been different?

Now that we have read the story, let's continue our work with main ideas and details using these sentences about Kareem. The children will complete the following written exercise independently.

Write <u>M</u> in front of the statement which tells the main idea of the selection, <u>S</u> in front of the three statements which are subordinate details, and <u>I</u> in front of the two statements which are incorrect.

_____1. Kareem was picked "most valuable player" three times in his career.

_____2. The happiest years of Kareem's life were those he spent at UCLA.

_____3. Every summer during his years at college, Kareem worked as a recreation director in ghetto housing projects.

_____4. Kareem is a sensitive but moody person, and a great basketball player.

_____5. Before he changed his name to Kareem Abdul-Jabbar, he was known as Wilt Chamberlain.

_____6. During high school Kareem was touchy about his height and color.

Write <u>C</u> (correct), <u>I</u> (incorrect), or <u>N</u> (not included).

_____1. Kareem is an honest person who kept his word even when he was offered $3,250,000, or more than twice as much as he had agreed to.

_____2. Kareem came from a very sad home life where his parents did not love or care for him.

_____3. All the other players in the NBA were jealous of Kareem.

_____4. Kareem is concerned not only with his basketball career, but also with social issues and trying to help others.

_____5. Kareem changed his name in 1971 because people always made fun of his former name.

_____6. Kareem became a show-off on the basketball court and only tried to make a name for himself.

III. Evaluation

A. The student's ability to respond to the questions, and to support his answers, indicates achievement of obectives A, B, C, and D.

B. The student's ability to complete correctly the written exercise indicates achievement of objective E.

Activity 10

Develop one or more comprehension lessons for use with a group of children or peers. Analyze the material to be read using the Barrett taxonomy, and select those outcomes that seem most appropriate to focus upon in terms of the content of the material. It is not always necessary to select several outcomes to emphasize in each comprehension activity; you may decide, on the basis of your diagnosis of children's needs, to focus on only one or two comprehension outcomes in an activity.

If you use the activities with a group of children, be certain that the material you select is at the appropriate reading level. Be certain also that the level of difficulty of the questions you develop is appropriate in terms of the children's previous experience in reading for the outcome(s) you select. Assess the effectiveness of the activities in terms of the children's success in achieving the objectives. The following references are good sources of ideas:

Dallmann, Martha; Rouch, Roger L.; Chang, Lynette Y. C.; and DeBoer, John J. *The Teaching of Reading*. 4th ed. Chap. 6B, "Developing Comprehension." New York: Holt, Rinehart and Winston, 1974.

Herr, Selma E. *Learning Activities for Reading*. 2d ed. Dubuque, Iowa: Wm. C. Brown Company Publishers, 1970.

Russell, David H., and Karp, Etta E. *Reading Aids Through the Grades*. Second revised edition by Anne Marie Mueser. Sec. 4, "Advanced Reading Skills." New York: Teachers College Press, Columbia University, 1975.

Smith, James A. *Creative Teaching of Reading in the Elementary School*. 2d ed. Chap. 7, "The Creative Teaching of Reading in the Intermediate Grades." Boston: Allyn & Bacon, 1975.

Smith, Nila Banton. *Reading Instruction for Today's Children*. Chap. 22, "Practice and Maintenance Activities in Getting Meanings." Englewood Cliffs, N. J.: Prentice-Hall, 1963.

Spache, Evelyn B. *Reading Activities for Child Involvement*. Chap. 8, "Comprehension and Interpretation Skills." Boston: Allyn & Bacon, 1972.

Activity 11

Observe one or more lessons designed to develop children's ability to comprehend what they read. Use the following questions as a guide:

1. Which comprehension outcomes are the focus of the lesson?
2. Do the teacher's questions provide opportunities for children to respond at levels beyond that of literal comprehension?
3. Is the lesson being used as an *introduction* to reading for a specific outcome, or as *practice* in reading for that outcome?
4. What evidence is there that the children know which comprehension outcomes they are reading for?

Activity 12

Design activities of your own which you feel will enable you to achieve the competencies stated for this module.

Preassessment and Postassessment

A. Knowledge Level
   1. Read the story "The Mists of Change," by Charlotte Epstein, which is reprinted here. After you have read the story, complete the matching exercise which follows it. In this exercise you are asked to match questions based on the story with categories of comprehension outcomes from the Barrett taxonomy. *Criterion for successful performance:*

   Each question is correctly matched with the corresponding category from the Barrett taxonomy.[18]

B. Performance Level
   1. Planning the Lesson
      a) Select two comprehension outcomes from two different categories of the Barrett taxonomy. For each outcome develop a plan for
         (1) a lesson for the introduction of the outcome and,
         (2) a lesson for the further (sequential) development of the outcome.

         For both (1) and (2) design a written exercise to be used as part of the lesson.
      b) Criteria for successful performance:
         (1) the objectives are stated in terms of pupil behavior;
         (2) the instructional procedures are developed in ways that are appropriate for the comprehension outcomes being taught;
         (3) the written exercises are appropriate for the comprehension outcomes selected;
         (4) the procedures for the evaluation of pupil achievement are identified.
   2. Teaching the Lesson
      a) Arrange to teach the lessons to a group of children who are reading at the same instructional level.
         Arrange to

18. The Answer Key for the matching exercise is located at the end of the Preassessment and Postassessment section of this module.

The Mists of Change

Charlotte Epstein

FIGURE 5.14. Charlotte Epstein, "The Mists of Change" (Philadelphia, Pa.: 1976). Reprinted by permission of the author.

Lucy was delighted when she was hired as supervisor in the machine shop. Her experience as a drill press operator in her uncle's small business had given her a chance to become very skillful on the drill press, and she was able to demonstrate to Mr. Fallon, the foreman, that she could turn out parts to the most exact specifications.

Her uncle had been skeptical about her chances: not only was she a girl, but she had quit school without talking with the guidance counselor about problems she might encounter in the job market.

"Do you mean to tell me," her uncle asked, "that they're putting you in charge of a department of men?"

"That's right! Isn't it wonderful?"

The job was hers, and she couldn't wait to get started.

On Monday, there she was in the plant, half an hour before the first man showed up. She waited in Mr. Fallon's office until he came and led her into a corner of the shop. "Here is where you'll work," he said. He introduced her to the four men already engaged in preparing their machines for the day's work.

"As I told you on Friday, we have government contracts. There's plenty of work here for a long time—if you do the job."

"Oh, I'll do it," Lucy said eagerly. "I've been working for this day for a long time."

"Yeah, Okay. Well, there's nothing much to do for a while—until they get started. Just feel your way—no pressure."

"Thank you, Mr. Fallon."

As the day went on, Lucy saw men come in with blueprints and discuss materials and specifications with the machine operators, who asked questions and then went to work. Nobody seemed to notice her, except for an occasional curt nod. When she joined two people poring over a blueprint, the look she got almost congealed her blood, and she backed off.

About eleven o'clock she turned into the mesh gate behind which parts were kept in neat little bins, and she began to look into each bin, fingering and identifying the parts. Several times men came to the gate and asked for a part, and she was able to locate it and hand it out immediately. At one point, one of the machinists called to her, "Would you mind grabbing a broom and sweeping up some of these filings? I almost tripped."

Tears came to her eyes, but she got the broom and swept the floor. When the quitting bell rang, she walked slowly out of the plant and home, saying nothing even when her uncle greeted her and asked how things had gone.

She had been working for several days when she began to know why her uncle had worked for so many years to complete the high school apprenticeship program and join the union. She knew that she had been easily fooled by Fallon. Her experience in her uncle's shop had not prepared her for all the things that could happen once she left his protection.

FIGURE 5.14.
Continued.

On Friday, she saw another woman come on the floor of the plant and stand talking with Mr. Fallon. Lucy saw her being led to another group of machines and left there, looking as uncomfortable as Lucy knew she must have looked on her first day.

At lunchtime, Lucy made a beeline for the other woman and suggested they have lunch together. The new "supervisor" was Amy, and Lucy lost no time in telling her that Fallon was a liar, that he hired women as "supervisors" to fulfill the letter of the government contract that said there was to be no discrimination in hiring. But they were no more supervisors than they were plant managers!

But Amy needed the job desperately. She had a sick mother and a young brother to support and no prospect of any other kind of job. She had the rent to pay and food to buy; she had to stay on the job.

Lucy felt even more depressed. She was not coming back to work on Monday. She was lucky that she had a comfortable home and a family that could take care of her for a little while longer. She was determined, however, that when she went back to school, she would bring up this experience and try to find ways of preventing employers from evading the law.

Matching Exercise

Each of the questions in the column on the left is based on the story "The Mists of Change." Each of the items in the column on the right identifies one category of comprehension outcomes in the Barrett taxonomy. In the blank in front of each question place the letter preceding the category that the question represents. Use each letter only once.

Questions		Categories	
_____ 1.	What else could the author have told us about Lucy's quitting school?	A. 1.21	Recall of Details
_____ 2.	What did Lucy tell Amy was the real reason they had been hired?	B. 1.26	Recall of Character Traits
_____ 3.	What made Lucy begin to know why her uncle had worked so hard to complete the high school apprenticeship program?	C. 3.1	Inferring Supporting Details
		D. 3.2	Inferring Main Ideas
		E. 3.4	Inferring Comparisons
_____ 4.	What was Mr. Fallon's attitude toward the women who worked for him?	F. 3.5	Inferring Cause and Effect Relationships
		G. 3.6	Inferring Character Traits
_____ 5.	What part of the story best describes why Amy needed this job?	H. 4.1	Judgments of Reality or Fantasy
		I. 4.3	Judgments of Adequacy and Validity

_____ 6.	What did Lucy learn from working in the machine shop?	J.	4.4	Judgments of Appropriateness
_____ 7.	How would you have felt about working for Mr. Fallon if you had been Lucy?	K.	4.5	Judgments of Worth, Desirability and Acceptability
_____ 8.	Should Amy have stayed with the job even though she knew that Mr. Fallon was a liar?	L.	5.1	Emotional Response to the Content
_____ 9.	Could the experience Lucy and Amy had with Mr. Fallon really happen?	M.	5.2	Identification with Characters or Incidents
_____10.	How did your feelings change as you read different parts of the story?	N.	5.3	Reactions to the Author's Use of Language

(1) have the instructor or cooperating teacher observe the lessons or

(2) tape the lessons.

b) Criteria for successful performance:

(1) there is evidence that the pupils have achieved the objectives;

(2) the student has demonstrated the ability to adapt his teaching procedures, as necessary, in response to pupil needs during the lesson.

3. Evaluating the Lesson

a) After the lessons have been taught, write an evaluation of each one. Respond to the following questions in your evaluations.

(1) Did the pupils achieve the objectives? Support your answer with specific evidence.

(2) If there were pupils who did not achieve the objectives, can you identify the experiences they still need in order to reach those objectives?

(3) Are there elements of the lesson that you would approach differently if you were to teach the lesson again?

b) Follow one of these procedures:

(1) If the instructor has observed the lessons, schedule a conference to discuss the plans and lessons.

(2) If the cooperating teacher has observed the lessons, ask for written evaluations and then schedule a conference with the instructor to discuss the plans, the lessons, and the cooperating teacher's evaluations.

(3) If the lessons have been taped, schedule a conference with the instructor to discuss the plans and the taped lessons.

References

Bond, Guy L., and Wagner, Eva Bond. *Teaching the Child to Read.* 4th ed. Chap. 9, "Basic Comprehension Abilities"; chap. 10, "Diversified Comprehension Abilities." New York: Macmillan Company, 1966.

Bush, Clifford L., and Huebner, Mildred H. *Strategies for Reading in the Elementary School.* Chap. 5, "Comprehension: Basic Factors." New York: Macmillan Company, 1970.

Dallmann, Martha; Rouch, Roger L.; Chang, Lynette Y. C.; and DeBoer, John J. *The Teaching of Reading.* 4th ed. Chap. 6A, "Comprehension"; chap. 6B, "Developing Comprehension." New York: Holt, Rinehart and Winston, 1974.

Durkin, Dolores. *Teaching Them to Read.* 2d ed. Chap. 14, "Teaching Comprehension Skills." Boston: Allyn & Bacon, 1974.

Harris, Albert J., and Sipay, Edward R. *Effective Teaching of Reading.* 2d ed. Chap. 11, "Developing Comprehension in Reading." New York: David McKay Company, 1971.

————. *How to Increase Reading Ability.* 6th ed. Chap. 16, "Improving Reading Comprehension, 1"; chap. 17, "Improving Reading Comprehension, 2." New York: David McKay Company, 1975.

Herr, Selma E. *Learning Activities for Reading.* 2d ed. Dubuque, Iowa: Wm. C. Brown Company Publishers, 1970.

Kottmeyer, William. *Decoding and Meaning.* Chap. 7, "Comprehension." New York: McGraw-Hill Company, 1974.

May, Frank B. *To Help Children Read.* Module 6, "Developing Children's Reading Comprehension and Thinking Skills." Columbus, Ohio: Charles E. Merrill Publishing Company, 1973.

Otto, Wayne; Chester, Robert; McNeil, John; and Myers, Shirley. *Focused Reading Instruction.*
Chap. 9, "Objective for Comprehension." Reading, Mass.: Addison-Wesley Publishing Company, 1974.

Russell, David H., and Karp, Etta E. *Reading Aids Through the Grades.* Second revised edition by Anne Marie Mueser. Sec. 4, "Advanced Reading Skills." New York: Teachers College Press, Columbia University, 1975.

Smith, James A. *Creative Teaching of Reading in the Elementary School.* 2d ed. Chap. 7, "The Creative Teaching of Reading in the Intermediate Grades." Boston: Allyn & Bacon, 1975.

Smith, Nila Banton. *Reading Instruction for Today's Children.* Chap. 9, "Getting Meanings from Reading"; chap. 22, "Practice and Maintenance Activities in Getting Meanings." Englewood Cliffs, N. J.: Prentice-Hall, 1963.

Spache, Evelyn B. *Reading Activities for Child Involvement.* Chap. 8, "Comprehension and Interpretation Skills." Boston: Allyn & Bacon, 1972.

Spache, George D., and Spache, Evelyn B. *Reading in the Elementary School.* 4th ed. Chap. 13, "Developing Comprehension and Critical Reading Skills." Boston: Allyn & Bacon, 1977.

Stauffer, Russell G. *Teaching Reading as a Thinking Process.* Chap. 2, "Group Directed Reading-Thinking Activities." Pp. 50-55. New York: Harper & Row, Publishers, 1969.

Tinker, Miles A., and McCullough, Constance M. *Teaching Elementary Reading.* 3d ed. Chap. 9, "Comprehension and Interpretation"; chap. 10, "Comprehension and Study Skills." New York: Appleton-Century-Crofts, 1968.

Walcutt, Charles C.; Lamport, Joan; and McCracken, Glenn. *Teaching Reading.* Chap. 20, " 'Comprehension Skills' are Thinking Skills." New York: Macmillan Company, 1974.

Wallen, Carl J. *Competency in Teaching Reading.* Sec. 2, "comprehension skills." Chicago: Science Research Associates, 1972.

Zintz, Miles V. *The Reading Process: The Teacher and the Learner.* 2d ed. Chap. 11, "Comprehension Skills"; chap. 13, "Developing Critical Reading Abilities." Dubuque, Iowa: Wm. C. Brown Company Publishers, 1975.

6

Planning Directed Reading Lessons

Overview

During the period from 1918 to 1925, reading instruction underwent a dramatic shift in emphasis from oral to silent reading. Prior to this time, oral reading had been the predominant method of instruction. The major impetus for the shift to silent reading was the emergence of research evidence indicating the advantages of silent reading over oral reading in both speed and comprehension.[1]

Smith suggests that the shift to silent reading procedures resulted in the widespread development of teachers' manuals to accompany basal readers:

> Emphasis upon the new silent reading procedures was responsible for bringing teachers' manuals into general use during this period. Every author of new reading textbooks furnished generous instructions for the use of his material. Furthermore, authors of texts which had appeared during the preceding period without detailed instructions now came forth with manuals emphasizing silent reading and suggesting procedures in silent reading to be used with their literary readers.[2]

In the years since this period of shift in reading instruction, authors of reading series have continued to provide manuals or guides with their materials, although the procedures suggested in these guides have long since ceased to reflect the earlier exaggerated emphasis on silent reading.

1. Nila Banton Smith, *American Reading Instruction* (Newark, Del.: International Reading Association, 1965), p. 160.
2. Ibid., p. 169.

While differences exist among series in the content and presentation of a procedure for teaching reading selections, certain basic elements are common to most series. The combination of these elements in a specific sequence is frequently referred to as the procedure for a Directed Reading Lesson or a Directed Reading Activity. This sequence will be identified in this module as the procedure for a Directed Reading Lesson (DRL).

Because the Directed Reading Lesson appears to have originated in the teachers' manuals of basal reading series, it is most often thought of in connection with this type of material. The position taken here is that the DRL should not be viewed as a procedure to be used *solely* with basal reading material, but rather as a framework for planning guided reading experiences that is applicable to a variety of materials: basal material, non-basal material (children's news magazines, newspapers, etc.), and content field material (the use of this procedure for teaching children to read content field material is discussed in Module 8: "Reading in the Content Fields"). The use of the DRL as a framework that can be used in planning a variety of types of reading experiences for children is the focus in this module.

The module is introduced through Helen F. O'Leary's article, "Preserve the Basic Reading Program."[3] O'Leary introduces her discussion by suggesting that the steps that are essential in teaching basic reading material correspond to the steps that are necessary in planning for any teaching situation. She then identifies these steps and provides specific suggestions for their development. Use the following questions as a guide as you read O'Leary's article:

1. What are the steps that comprise what O'Leary considers to be an effective teaching procedure?
2. What contributions does O'Leary suggest can be made by children to the development of specific lessons?
3. What reading experiences, in addition to those in basic reading, does O'Leary identify as essential components of a comprehensive reading program?

3. Helen F. O'Leary, "Preserve the Basic Reading Program," *Education* (September 1963), pp. 12-16.

Preserve the Basic Reading Program

Helen F. O'Leary

So many adverse criticisms and so many provocative questions are being voiced about the limitations, the regimentation, the lock-step tendencies, and the alleged monotony of the basic reading program technique that a comprehensive review of its possibilities and an evaluation of its recommended procedures deserve to be presented and evaluated.

Moreover, despite the introduction of many versions of individualized reading instruction plans which tend to displace and discourage the use of basic reader series, and despite the increasing use of multi-level reading kits, this basic reading series program still continues to maintain its status as the most widely used and the most popularly known equipment for one important part of an effective reading program—namely, the developmental phase wherein sequential aspects of reading growth are analyzed, recognized, planned for, and carefully paced through a series of graded readers arranged in levels of reading difficulty.

Obviously, teaching materials are enriched or impoverished by those who administer them, and a teaching tool without a good teacher becomes a weak and barren instrument. Therefore, it is my opinion that in the hands of a competent and imaginative teacher the basic reading series can contribute most effectively to the so-called developmental phase of the reading program.

In fact, the features which comprise the essential steps in the teaching procedure of a basic reading series correspond to the principal steps in an effective lesson plan for any type of subject-matter presentation.

What are these steps which are common both to a basic reading setup and a good lesson plan?

Readiness for Reading

INTRODUCTION OF VOCABULARY

First, there is readiness or preparation for reading. In this vital introductory program the teacher sets the stage with the introduction of all necessary vocabulary, development of concepts, establishment of reading purpose, and building of adequate background. In this part of the reading plan the richness or paucity of the teacher's skill becomes the potent and deciding factor.

Since reading lessons form such a major part of a day's work, oftentimes dull routine and take-it-for-granted attitudes characterize stilted reading lessons which become meaningless, uninspiring, and nonproductive. But imagine the contrast when a teacher realizes and utilizes countless ways for introducing words!

For the teacher who possesses knowledge, ingenuity, and skill in presentation of vocabulary a reading lesson gets off to a stimulating and interesting start:

1. Using *concrete objects* which are readily available, such as a darning needle, an abacus, a compass, an avocado, a jigsaw puzzle.
2. Showing *pictures* to depict native cos-

From Helen F. O'Leary, "Preserve the Basic Reading Program" in *Education* (September 1963), pp. 12-16. Reprinted from the September, 1963 issue of *Education*. Copyright, 1967, by The Bobbs-Merrill Company, Inc., Indianapolis, Indiana.

tumes, a seashore, a horizon, types of animals, colors, types of homes.

3. Running *filmstrips* to develop concepts of irrigation, conservation, the solar system, the making of honey, etc.

4. Utilizing *moving pictures* to give enough information about sheep shearing, wheat farming, lumbering, the meat packing industry, a rodeo, and other activities not a part of the community scene.

5. Telling *stories* to exemplify the meaning of greatness, poverty, humility, heroism, or some other abstract quality.

6. Taking *field trips* to have direct contact with such areas as an airport, paper-making, samples of erosion, kinds of trees, moss, a silo, a state capitol.

7. Holding *conversations* to build gradually such appreciations and understandings as the work of pilots, postmen, or scientists or conversing to gauge the scope of knowledge possessed by the class.

8. Arranging *display tables* to present objects and symbols characteristic of any central theme of a unit of stories such as pioneer life, inventors, reference books.

9. Analyzing by *structural analysis* to discover how words have been built, such as *discouragement, unhappy, mislaid,* or *refreshment.*

10. Relating *word histories* which reveal how words originated such as *boycott, bonfire, fallout.*

11. Illustrating by diagramming words which lend themselves to this technique such as a *perpendicular line,* a *cataract,* a *plateau.*

12. Suggesting by *clues* which encourage students to guess or analyze the mysterious word which can be concealed until a successful solution is reached—words like *cotton, cellophane, brick, petrified wood, memento.*

13. Displaying *a series of three or four pictures* which suggest one common adjective such as *enthusiastic, anxious, young,* or *daring* .

Naturally such preparation for vocabulary presentation cannot represent any spur-of-the-moment preparation. However, neither is it a mammoth undertaking, for it is almost a point of view about the importance of this step that matters. A teacher who is aware of varieties of techniques in word presentation will know how to combine methods, motivate challenging word reviews, prepare classes interestingly for vocabularly tests, and in general add spark and vitality to a lesson.

This mode of word introduction truly represents a far cry from the too-common method in which a teacher puts a word on the board in one context situation, acquaints the children with the fact that this is the new word, and admonishes them to remember it. Such a teacher, who may be pressuring to get to the reading book, will need time to be converted comfortably to this point of view about word presentation, but she will soon recognize that more challenging learning situations are paying dividends.

BUILDING BACKGROUND

Building background, the second part of the preparation for reading, is, of course, very closely related to the previous task of vocabulary development. This phase also imposes tremendous responsibility upon the teacher, who must appraise the environment in which the children live, the first-hand and vicarious experiences they have had, and the background required for full comprehension of the story.

For example, children who live in a dairy-farm community contribute rather than require knowledge about such a farm. However, these same children might associate an erroneous concept with the elevator in the big city or evince absolute ignorance concerning the "dumb waiter" in the apartment block or the escalator in the department store. A class in

Pennsylvania can be a resource expert about mining and greatly supplement a teacher's knowledge.

Definitely the teacher must realize that many children in the class are experts and resource persons in various areas. It should be her privilege and pleasure not only to discover the stamp collector, the expert fisherman, the skillful golfer, the clever dressmaker, and the budding cook, but also to arrange situations for children to reveal their expertness. Rarely will the child forget the teacher who arranged for him to have a "red-letter" day, and fortunate is the class led by a teacher who releases all channels of learning whether from pupils or teacher.

ESTABLISHING A PURPOSE

Establishing a purpose for reading the story is the last step in preparation for reading. Allowing a reader to have some question that needs to be answered is a stimulus to thoughtful and intelligent inquiry.

Thus, this first major part of the plan preparation consists of presentation of vocabulary, building of necessary background, and establishment of reading purpose.

Interpreting the Story

The second major step, interpreting the story, concerns itself with the actual reading and takes in both silent and oral aspects, with silent reading always preceding oral reading.

In the primary grades silent reading takes the form of so-called "guided reading" in which the teacher with pertinent questions motivates the silent reading of a short section which may be a paragraph or a page. The answers to these questions and the resultant discussion aid considerably in developing fuller comprehension and preparing for later interpretative reading.

For children with limited reading skill guided reading is a most valuable aid, for questions asked by the teacher often clear up misconceptions, errors in pronunciation, and stir up waning interest. Then comes the oral reading, which in the beginning stages of reading growth should merit careful supervision and evaluation.

Teachers in primary grades should establish criteria for good reading and guard against their students' becoming accustomed to poor reading. Good oral reading, for instance, should simulate a child's normal conversational tone and pace. Any artificial speech inflection, a marked difference in pace between reading and speaking, difficulties in word perception, and signs of uneasiness and fidgeting should be recognized as symptoms of reading difficulty.

At this stage in the reading plan teachers should improvise reasons for rereading such as, "Mary, how would you read that page?" or "Remember, Father was a little puzzled about what was happening. Can you read that page so that you will sound like Father?" Or, reassign the same lesson for dramatization or audience reading for another day. Let a pair of children try to reread the entire story to each other without a mistake.

In the intermediate grade levels the lesson either in parts or in entirety is read silently without the direct guidance of the teacher but always in response to a definite pre-established purpose or purposes. This is followed by a discussion directed by the teacher's questions, which again aids comprehension, tests for reactions and inferences, and stimulates interest. Oral reading at intermediate grade levels occurs only when specific purposes can be established and can be justified.

In some stories only vocabulary may be stressed—for example words which express action or denote color. In other stories sequential elements may be emphasized. In still other selections parts of the stories may be reread in order to answer specific questions, and in exciting and interesting stories rereading or dramatization may be suggested.

Thus, in the second major phase of the plan, silent and oral reading characterize the activities.

Development of Word Analysis

In the third major phase comes the area most often neglected but vitally needed, the development of word analysis skills. Actually, the stories have been selected, written, and arranged to provide a frame of reference, as background of understanding for the presentation of these skills. And it is in this part of the basic reading series that the teacher realizes that reading is a sequential skill, for one glance at the index of skills, listed in the basic reader, reveals the vast number of separate abilities which the good reader must possess.

In this stage of the plan the teacher's manual is most helpful in supplying specific sentences, word lists, questions, and seatwork necessary to promote proficiency and to provide variety. The workbooks, also, are specifically geared to supplement the lesson.

However, even though these workbooks are regarded as independent activities, they are independent only in the final analysis. Enough help and direction should be presented in an actual reading period so that when children are on their own, these activities can be performed with a high degree of accuracy and assurance. Moreover, they should be corrected carefully and thoroughly in another reading period with each child having an opportunity to evaluate and inspect his own results.

Thus, the third phase of the basic reading plan, the teaching of word analysis, is an essential step requiring an extensive knowledge on the part of the teacher.

Extension of Interests

The final phase of the basic reading program, referred to as the extension of interests or related enrichment activities, can prove to be very enjoyable, but again it often represents one aspect of the plan which is entirely omitted.

What prompts a teacher to minimize this phase of the program? First of all, many teachers do not see the relation between these activities and the teaching of reading. However, the enrichment offered by suggesting stories to be read either by the teacher to the children, or by the children independently, the rhythmic activities which emphasize the tone of the story, the suggested art activities, the records, films, and filmstrips all strongly indicate that a basic reading program does not have to be a stilted monotonous routine. The program will be as alive as the teacher who directs it.

In this phase of the program reading really joins hands with the other aspects of the language arts—poetry, choral reading, storytelling, independent reading suggestions, vocabulary illustration, outlines through scenes in a mural, original stories, and other enrichment activities.

Oftentimes a teacher can even in a three-group situation turn these activities into entire class activities. The storytelling, the independent reading, the poetry activities, the rhythmic interpretations can furnish life to the daily language lessons. However, the teacher must not favor any one group but must introduce a book by some reference such as the following:

"Jim's group enjoyed the story about *Red Flame*."

"This story of *Black Beauty* is a story about a horse that children have enjoyed. I'll read you the introductory chapter, and then I'll put it on the library table."

"Mary's group has finished its unit on pioneer stories. Let's imagine what activities children had then and let us compare them with your activities."

"Who are our modern pioneers?"

With a superior group a teacher can read from the manual the suggested activities and let each member of the group choose one for class or group presentation.

Conclusion

In this review of the typical plan in the basic reading series it becomes quite evident that there are ample opportunities for originality, ingenuity, variety, and imagination for the teacher who utilizes all phases of the basic series program.

Moreover, instead of disregarding entirely the philosophy behind individualized or personal selection plans for reading, the resourceful teacher incorporates these ideas into a strong recreational or free reading program, another important phase of the total reading program. With the further addition of a functional reading phase, an effective reading program is being planned for and utilized to develop readers for all purposes.

Module Competencies

One purpose of this module is to help you develop an understanding of the sequence involved in the procedure for teaching a Directed Reading Lesson. A second purpose is to help you develop the ability to use this procedure in two ways: (1) as a framework for integrating sequential instruction in the skills included in basal reading series, and (2) as a framework for planning experiences in reading a variety of nonbasal material. These purposes are reflected in the competencies which identify the specific skills you will develop as you work with the activities included in this module.

Instructional Activities

The components of the procedure for teaching a Directed Reading Lesson are identified in activity 2 (competency 1). The application of this procedure using material in a basal reading series is also presented in this activity. In activity 3 you are encouraged to observe teachers' use of basal reading material, and to identify the components of a Directed Reading Lesson as they occur (competency 2). The focus in activity 4 is your use of the DRL procedure with basal reading material (competency 2). The use of the DRL procedure with nonbasal reading material is illustrated in activity 5 (competency 3). In activity 6 you are encouraged to observe lessons in which nonbasal reading material is being used (competency 3). Your use of the DRL procedure with nonbasal material is the focus of activity 7 (competency 3). It is suggested in activity 8 that you design activities of your own which you feel will enable you to achieve the competencies stated for this module.

1. Identify the procedure for teaching a Directed Reading Lesson (DRL).
2. Plan and teach a DRL using a selection from a basal reading series.
3. Plan and teach a DRL using material from a source other than a basal reading series.

Select from the following learning experiences those which you feel will enable you to achieve the competencies stated for this module:

Activity 1

Attend a seminar for orientation to this module.

Activity 2

In her article, O'Leary discusses the components of the procedure that is referred to in this module as the Directed Reading Lesson (DRL). The following outline identifies these components and the sequence in which they occur in the DRL. Included in each section of the outline are questions that can serve as guides as you analyze material for the purpose of planning Directed Reading Lessons.

Procedure for a Directed Reading Lesson

1. Developing Readiness for Reading[4]
   a. Development of Concepts and Background
      1) How can the children be stimulated to read the material?
      2) What experiences have the children had that relate to the selection?
      3) What experiences can be provided to help the children develop the background they will need to understand the selection?
      4) What concepts will the children need to develop in order to read the selection? How can these concepts be developed?

---

4. O'Leary provides specific suggestions for ways of doing this on pages 194-96 of "Preserve the Basic Reading Program."

    b. Introduction of Vocabulary
        1) Which unfamiliar words will need to be introduced? What phonic or structural analysis skills can be used with the children in analyzing these words? In what contexts can the words be presented to provide help in developing word meanings?
        2) Which unfamiliar words will not need to be introduced because the children will be able to analyze them independently using context and previously learned phonic and structural analysis skills?
2. Setting the Purposes for Reading
    a. What purposes for reading will be set by the teacher? (If the material is to be read in sections, purposes will need to be set for each section.)[5]
    b. In what ways can the children's thinking be stimulated so that they set their own purposes for reading?
3. Silent Reading of the Selection
4. Discussing the Selection
    a. As the purposes that were set for reading are discussed, what information can be gained regarding the children's ability to read for specific comprehension outcomes?
    b. What additional questions can be asked that will stimulate children to expand their thoughts and feelings regarding the concepts, generalizations, and relationships they have encountered in the material read?
5. Rereading the Selection
    a. Are there purposes, other than the original purposes for reading, for which it would be worthwhile to reread part or all of the selection silently?
    b. Are there purposes, other than the original purposes for reading, for which it would be worthwhile to reread part of all of the selection orally?
6. Developing and Refining Essential Skills
    a. What word recognition and/or comprehension skills will be introduced in this lesson?
    b. What opportunities will be provided for children to apply new skills or previously learned skills?
7. Carrying Out Related Activities
    a. What activities will provide children with opportunities to use and extend what they have read?

---

5. As suggested in Module 5: "Developing Comprehension Ability," the Barrett taxonomy can be useful in helping teachers develop questions that will guide children in reading for different types and levels of comprehension outcomes.

b. How can children be provided with the opportunity to suggest related activities?

c. How will the related activities be organized and carried out?

As suggested in the "Overview" section of the module, the elements which comprise the DRL are typically found in the teachers' guides which accompany basal reading series. The objective in preparing teachers' guides for basal readers is to help the teacher make the most effective use of the material in developing the skills the series is designed to teach. Used with basal material, the DRL becomes a framework for integrating sequential instruction in the skills of phonic analysis, structural analysis, and comprehension.

Over the years, however, teachers' guides for basal readers have been the subject of extensive criticism. The following have been among the more frequently voiced criticisms: (1) the guides do not provide a sufficient number of suggestions, or suggestions that are specific enough, to be of real value in the use of the material, (2) the guides provide so many suggestions and procedures in such great detail that the teacher would be severely hampered in his use of the material if he were to attempt to follow all the suggestions, and (3) the guides do not contain procedures and activities that make provision for the development of children's critical and creative thinking. While one or more of these criticisms may be valid with regard to a specific series at a given time, the major difficulty with teachers' guides appears to lie in the ways in which teachers regard and use them. In the first place, guides are not written for specific groups of children (a reading group in Mr. Rinella's fourth-grade class at the Duckrey School in Philadelphia, for example); it is the *teacher's* responsibility to adapt suggested procedures and activities to meet the needs of the children with whom he is working. In the second place, the teachers' guide is just that, a *guide*; it is intended to be used flexibly, not rigidly. It is interesting, in connection with this point, to note the more frequent use today of the term *guide*, rather than of the earlier term *manual* which implies a prescribed set of procedures to be followed inflexibly.

It is the point of view in this module that the procedures for Directed Reading Lessons presented in teachers' guides, when used flexibly and adapted to the needs of specific children, provide an effective framework for integrating the teaching of skills presented in basal reading series. The following lesson plan illustrates the application of the procedure for teaching a DRL using basal reader material. Following the lesson plan are the selection for which the plan was developed and the suggestions for teaching the selection provided in the teachers' guide which accompanies the reader. Use the following questions as a guide in examining the plan, the selection, and the teachers' guide material:

1. Can you identify the steps included in the procedure for teaching a DRL in the plan?
2. Compare the teachers' guide material with the lesson plan in order to identify the ways in which the suggestions have been adapted for this group of children.
   a) in the introduction of vocabulary how does the teacher make use of previously learned word recognition skills?
   b) which categories of the Barrett taxonomy are reflected in the questions suggested in the teachers' guide? Why do you think the teacher included additional questions in his plan?
   c) look at the steps included in the plan for decoding activities 2 and 3. Can you identify the steps included in McCullough's Inductive Approach to Word Analysis (presented in Module 3: "Developing Phonic Analysis Skills")? In what way(s) do the procedures included in the lesson plan provide more guidance for the teacher as he works with the children than do the suggestions in the teachers' guide?

Lesson Plan
Directed Reading Lesson with a Basal Reading Selection

Grade Level: Second

I. Objectives

   A. The students will be able to use previously learned word recognition skills to identify new vocabulary.
   B. The students will be able to answer questions that require:
      1. inferring main idea.
      2. identifying with characters or incidents.
      3. recognizing details.
      4. making judgments of reality or fantasy.
   C. The students will be able to pronounce words ending in the graphemic base <u>ame.</u>
   D. The students will be able to pronounce words ending in the letter <u>m</u> followed by the <u>e</u>-marker.
   E. The students will be able to dictate and illustrate individual stories telling how they learned to do something.

II. Procedure

   A. Introduction
      Can anyone here whistle? How did you learn to whistle? Why do people like to whistle? Let's read the poem on the board. This poem is about a boy named Pete who wants to whistle.

B. Development
1. I am Pete
    I am Pete.
    I am five.
    I am too little to <u>shave.</u>
    I guess I am too little to <u>whistle,</u> too.
    I cannot do it.
    All that comes out is "<u>Wh</u>."
    One time when I jumped up and down
    a whistle <u>came</u> out.
    Will a <u>jump</u> make me whistle now?

    a. When the children come to the word *shave,* ask what sound the letter <u>a</u> will have when there is an <u>e</u>-marker. Discuss the meaning of the word "shave."
    b. Refer the students to the word *whistle* for the /w/ sound.
    c. The word *came* has an <u>e</u>-marker, so what sound will the letter <u>a</u> have?
    d. The word *jump* may have to be given. Ask the students if they can find the word *jump* anywhere else in the poem. How does the <u>ed</u> ending change the meaning of the word?

2. Our story today is about Pete and how he tries to learn to whistle. In the poem Pete wonders if jumping will make him whistle. Do you think it will? How do you think Pete can learn how to whistle? Write their suggestions on the board. Now read the story to yourselves to see if Pete learns to whistle using any of your ideas.

3. After silent reading of the story discuss how Pete did learn to whistle and why he said "Wh-wh-wh!"

4. How do you think Pete felt when Jen and Ken wouldn't teach him to whistle? Has anything like this ever happened to you?

5. Look at the picture on story page 123. How can you tell that Pete's dad is whistling?

6. Read the sentences on story page 124 that tell what happened when Pete was holding the can of shaving cream. Have a student read the sentences orally.

7. Do you think that Pete could really have learned to whistle this way? Why? Why not?
   Developing Reading Skills

8. Omit Decoding Activity 1: unnecessary for this class.

9. Decoding Activity 2
    a. Distribute worksheets (teachers' guide page 191).
    b. Look at the first word on the paper. This word was in our poem today. Who can remember this word? Yes, *came* (write the word on the board). Who can pronounce the

word under *came*? Write the word on the board. Who can use the word in a sentence? Use the same procedure with the remainder of the words. What is the same about all the words? Ask one child to underline the <u>ame</u> base in each word. Now when we see a word that ends in <u>ame</u>, what will we know about the way the ending of the word sounds?

c. Ask a child to read the paragraph. What do you think about these surprises? Would you like to get a box like this? Let's look at the questions under the heading <u>Tell the Answer</u>. Read the questions silently, and when you have finished make up a story that will tell the answer to one of the questions. After the students have had time to think of a story ask them to give their answers (stories) to the group.

10. Decoding Activity 3

a. Put the following words on the board: *swim,time, came, am.*

b. Let's say the words on the board. What sound do you hear that is the same in all the words? Where do you hear that sound in each of the words? (at the end of the word). Let's say the first word and make sure we are right: swi<u>m</u>. Underline the letter <u>m</u>. Say the next word: ti<u>m</u>e. Underline the letter <u>m</u> and the <u>e</u>-marker. Continue in the same way with the other words.

c. Do all the endings of these words look like? (no). Right, some end with the letter <u>m</u> and some end with the letter <u>m</u> and the <u>e</u>-marker. We also said that all the words ended with the /m/ sound.

d. Who can make up a rule that tells us how the end of a word will sound if the word ends with the letter <u>m</u> or with the letter <u>m</u> and the <u>e</u>-marker? (When we see a word that ends with the letter <u>m</u> or with the letter <u>m</u> and the <u>e</u>-marker we know that the word will end with the /m/ sound.)

e. Let's look at the sentences on the board.

   I think the best meat to eat is <u>ham</u>.
   A <u>lime</u> looks like a green lemon.
   The boy named <u>Jim</u> is my friend.

   Who can read the first sentence? How did you know how to say the word *ham*? Discuss the meaning of the word using the sentence as a clue. Continue with the other two sentences. Have the students repeat the rule again.

C. Conclusion

Related Activities

1. Read the story *Whistle for Willie* and have the students compare it with "Pete Wants to Whistle."
2. Have each child dictate a story that tells how he learned to do something. The students can then illustrate their stories.
3. Collect the stories and bind them together to form one book, *How We Learned To Do Things.* Put the book in the library corner where other children can read it.

III. Evaluation

A. If the students are able to identify the new vocabulary using word recognition skills, they have fulfilled objective A.
B. If the students are able to answer questions that require inferring main idea, identifying with characters or incidents, recognizing details, and making judgments of reality or fantasy, they have fulfilled objective B.
C. If the students are able to pronounce the given words that end in the graphemic base ame, they have fulfilled objective C.
D. If the students are able to pronounce words ending in the letter m and words ending in the letter m followed by the e-marker, they have fulfilled objective D.
E. If the students are able to dictate and illustrate individual stories telling how they learned to do something, they have fulfilled objective E.

Activity 3

Observe one or more lessons involving the use of basal reader material. Ask the teachers whose lessons you are going to observe for the teachers' guides pertaining to the selections that are going to be taught. Read the appropriate section of the teachers' guide before you observe each lesson. Use the following questions as a guide for your observations:

1. Are the steps in the procedure for teaching a Directed Reading Lesson included in the lesson?
2. Compare the teachers' guide material with the lesson being taught. Is the teacher adapting the procedures suggested in the guide?
3. If adaptations of the suggested procedures are evident, can you determine why the teacher finds them appropriate for this particular group of children?

Check the accuracy of your responses to the guide questions by discussing them with the teacher following each observation.

PETE WANTS TO WHISTLE

Pages 121-125

NEW WORDS

Basic	Enrichment
whistle	wh
jump	
shave	
came	
whistled	

DECODING SKILLS

Elements Introduced	Word Examples
Correspondence /hw/wh	whistle
Graphemic base ame	came

Element Reviewed	
Correspondence /m/m (in final position)	came

TEACHING THE SELECTION

STORY SUMMARY

Pete asks both Jen and Ken to help him learn to whistle. They are busy playing. Dad, who is shaving, tries to show him how, but Pete can't do it. As Pete plays with the shaving cream can, he accidentally squirts some shaving cream on his face and mouth. When he tries to blow the shaving cream off, he produces a whistle.

SPECIFIC OBJECTIVES

Inferential comprehension
  Making comparisons

Understanding of language
  Dictating to the teacher an original story
  Observing as the teacher puts his oral language into writing
Creativity development
  Predicting from limited information

PREPARATION FOR READING

Introducing the Vocabulary

Write on the chalkboard or on a chart the following sentences:

I Am Pete

I am Pete.
I am five.
I am too little to shave.
I guess I am too little to whistle, too.
I cannot do it.
All that comes out is "Wh."
One time when I jumped up and down
a whistle came out.
Will a jump make me whistle now?

Help the children to use their decoding skills to read the sentences. Point out the e-marker pattern a—e in the words shave and came. Some children will be able to read the word jump. The children may need to have some of the underlined words read for them.

After the sentences have been read, ask the children to reread each of the underlined words.

Leads to Motivation

Ask the children to discuss whether jumping could make Pete whistle. Let them suggest ways that Pete might learn to whistle.

READING THE STORY

Purposes for Reading

Have the children locate the story by referring to the Contents page.

Ask the children to read the story to themselves to find out how Pete did learn to whistle. Some children may need help to identify the word whistled.

Pete Wants to Whistle

Pete said, "I want to whistle,
but I can't.
Will you help me?"

"Not now," said Jen.
"I want to jump."

"All you do is jump," said Pete.
"You jump all the time!"

121

Pete said, "Help me, Ken.
I want to whistle, but I can't."

"I can't help you now," said Ken.
"I'm playing ball."

"You play all the time!"
said Pete.
"Who will help me?"

Ken said, "Ask Dad.
He can whistle."

122

FIGURE 6.1. Continued.

Activity 4

Identify a group of children who are reading at the same level in a basal reading series. Using the book in which they are currently reading, plan and teach a DRL. As you plan the DRL, determine what adaptations of the teachers' guide material you will have to make in order to meet the needs of the children with whom you will be working.

"Wh-wh-wh!" said Pete.
"Wh-wh-wh!"

He looked up and said, "I whistled!
I whistled, Dad."

"Yes, you did," said Dad.
"That was a good whistle."

"I went wh-wh-wh," said Pete,
"and the whistle came out."

DISCUSSION OF PURPOSES

Let the children tell how Pete did learn to whistle. Ask them to make the "wh-wh-wh" sound as Pete did. Let them decide why Pete was blowing when the sound came out.

Review with the children the reasons Jen and Ken would not help Pete learn to whistle. Discuss Pete's feelings toward them. Compare these episodes with problems which the children may have experienced with brothers and sisters.

RELATED LANGUAGE ACTIVITIES

Read to the children Whistle for Willie by Ezra Jack Keats. Help the pupils to compare it with "Pete Wants to Whistle."

Ask the children to come one at a time to dictate a story which will be written down by the teacher. Suggest that they dictate stories telling how they learned to do something. As each child dictates and watches, write the words of his story for him on a sheet of paper which can be placed in the book he is making about himself. Use the child's own wording—do not simplify the sentences. The child may wish to illustrate the story with his own drawings.

Allow the children to read the stories to one another in a sharing session.

DEVELOPING READING SKILLS

DECODING ACTIVITY 1

Specific Objective

Phonemic analysis: Associating the sounds /hw/ or /w/ with the letters wh and w

NOTE: In some regions of our country, speakers do not emit the puff of air, and words beginning with the letters wh are spoken with the initial sound /w/. In such regions, the children should not be asked to make the /hw/wh association. They should be permitted to respond with the sound /w/ when they see the letters wh, but they may be made aware of the fact that some people use the sound /hw/ in such cases.

Write on the chalkboard these two word groups:

walk	were	where	when
was	work	whistle	what
went	way	why	

You may find it helpful to use the form shown in figure 6.2 as a guide in planning your DRL. You may find it useful, also, to refer to the questions included in each section of the outline for a Directed Reading Lesson presented in activity 2.

Planning Directed Reading Lessons

FIGURE 6.1. Continued.

Ask the children to read aloud the words in each group. Then elicit the generalization that all of the words in the first group begin with the letter w and that all of the words in the second group begin with the letters wh.

Ask each child to hold the palm of one hand an inch or two away from his lips. Have the children read one word from each column and feel the puff of air when the word beginning with the sound /hw/ is read. As they continue to say a word from each column, they should be able to feel a puff of air hit the palm of the hand for each word beginning with the letters wh.

Write the following decodable words on the chalkboard:

whip	whee	whack
wham	white	whine
	wheat	

Give the children some time to study the words and decode them. Then ask volunteers to come to the chalkboard to find and read:

1. something you say when you are having a great time. whee
2. something that is used in making flour. wheat
3. a sound you make when you hit water with a flat board. whack
4. something a dog does when it is unhappy. whine
5. a word you use to mean "hit hard." wham
6. something a lion tamer uses to make the lions do what he wants. whip
7. the name of a color. white

Ask the children to read the words on the chalkboard and hold their palms so that they can feel the puff of air which comes at the beginning of each word.

DECODING ACTIVITY 2

Specific Objective

Structural analysis: Learning about graphemic base ame

Distribute to the children copies of the following worksheet. Help the children decode the words listed at the top of the page. Then ask a child to read aloud the paragraph following the word lists.

| came | lame | tame | same | name | game |

Five boys and girls were playing at Ken's house. A big box came. In it were five surprises for the boys and girls. The surprises were

  a tame duck
  a lame dog
  a parrot with a funny name
  a good game
  the same game

Read the words Tell the Answer for the children. Let them read the questions silently and be ready to tell the answer to one of them. (The children are to create whatever stories they wish, to answer the questions.)

Tell the Answer

1. What was the parrot's name? Where did it get that name?
2. What made the dog lame?
3. Who made the duck tame?
4. What was the name of the game? What did the children do with two games that were the same?

DECODING ACTIVITY 3

Specific Objective

Phonemic analysis: Associating the sound /m/ with the letter m in final position and in the spelling patterns a_e and i_e

Write on the chalkboard the words swim, time, came, am.

Ask the children to read the words and tell how they are alike. (The final consonant sound is the same.) Then ask the children to notice whether the words all look alike at the end. Since they do not, generalize with the children that the final consonant sound may be represented by letter m, but if the letter occurs in an e-marker spelling pattern, letter e appears at the end of the word.

Write the following known words on the chalkboard:

| hat | Jill | like |

After each word has been read by the children, erase the final letter or digraph and substitute letters m or me to make a new word:

| ham | Jim | lime |

Activity 5

The procedure for teaching a Directed Reading Lesson can be used as a framework for planning guided experiences in reading a variety of material other than that included in basal reading series. The following lesson plan illustrates the application of this procedure using a selection from a children's magazine. This selection (fig. 6.3), "Picking Locks and Cracking Safes for Honest Money!" follows the lesson plan. Read the lesson plan and the selection on which it was based using the following questions as a guide:

Ask the children to read each new word and use it in a sentence.

Write the following word pairs on the chalkboard. (All of the words are decodable.)

beat—beam   trick—trim   dig—dim
save—same   whip—whim   fake—fame

Ask the children to find and point to a word which:

1. tells what lace is used for. trim
2. means to hit many times. beat
3. means to keep. save
4. means not bright. dim
5. means not real. fake
6. is the name of something that can make a cracking noise. whip

---

| SKILLS HANDBOOK |

ADJUSTING TO INDIVIDUAL NEEDS

DECODING ACTIVITY

Specific Objective

Phonemic analysis: Decoding words with final consonant sounds

Distribute copies of the following worksheet. Ask the children to read the sentences to themselves and write the correct word in each blank. When the children have completed the exercise, have the sentences read orally.

1. That little girl does not ___seem___ to know where she is.
          seem   seed
2. Pete lost ___his___ whistle in the park.
    him   his

3. Dad___gave___Pete something he wanted.
    game   gave
4. It is ___time___ to get up now.
    time   tide
5. The fox ate a duck and a ___hen___ .
      hem   hen
6. "Pete and James will be on my ___team___," said Ken.   tear   team
7. You will have to pay a ___dime___ for the ride.   dive   dime
8. We ate some ___cake___ when we got home.
      cake   came

COMPREHENSION ACTIVITY

Specific Objective

Literal comprehension: Recalling sequence of events

Distribute copies of the following worksheet. Ask the children to read the sentences by groups and then to number the sentences to show which event happened first, second, third and (once) fourth. They may refer to the story if they need help in recalling the sequence of events.

2	Pete said, "All you do is jump."
1	Pete asked Jen to help him whistle.
3	Pete asked Ken to help him whistle.
3	Dad said, "Do what I am doing."
2	Pete asked Dad to help him whistle.
1	Pete went to find Dad.
2	Something came out of the can.
4	Pete whistled.
1	Pete wanted to shave.
3	Pete went, "Wh-wh-wh."

---

1. Can you identify the steps included in the procedure for teaching a Directed Reading Lesson?[6]
2. How are the children encouraged to set their own purposes for reading?
3. Which categories of the Barrett taxonomy are reflected in the questions that are set as purposes for reading and in the additional discussion questions?
4. What has the teacher used as a basis for planning the related activities included in the Conclusion section of the lesson plan?

6. The Developing and Refining Essential Skills step is not included because new skills are introduced to the children sequentially in the basal reading series they are using. The children are, of course, applying word recognition and comprehension skills as they read and discuss the selection.

Planning Directed Reading Lessons   211

FIGURE 6.2.

Guide for Planning a Directed Reading Lesson

I. Developing Readiness for Reading

    A. Development of Concepts and Background

_____

_____

_____

_____

    B. Introduction of Vocabulary

_____

_____

_____

_____

II. Setting Purposes for Reading

    A. Purposes for Reading the Selection as a Whole

_____

_____

_____

_____

    B. Purposes for Reading the Selection in Parts

_____

_____

_____

_____

III. Silent Reading of the Selection

    A. Pages (for entire selection if it is to be read as a whole)

    _____

    B. Pages (for each section if the story is to be read in parts)

    _____

    _____

    _____

    _____

IV. Discussing the Selection

    A. Purpose questions

    _____

    B. Extended discussion questions

    _____

    _____

    _____

    _____

V. Rereading the Selection

    A. Purposes for rereading part or all of the selection silently

    _____

    _____

    _____

    _____

FIGURE 6.2.
Continued.

B. Purposes for rereading part or all of the selection orally

_____

_____

_____

_____

VI. Developing and Refining Essential Skills

A. Skills to be Introduced

_____

_____

_____

_____

B. Application of Skills

_____

_____

_____

_____

VII. Carrying Out Related Activities

A. Activities

_____

_____

_____

B. Organization of the Activities

_____

_____

_____

_____

Lesson Plan
Directed Reading Lesson with Nonbasal Material

Grade Level: Sixth

I. Objectives

    A. The students will be able to use word recognition skills and sentence context to identify new vocabulary (e.g., analyze the compound word "locksmith").

    B. The students will be able to answer questions that require the recall of cause and effect relationships.

    C. The students will be able to answer questions that require:
        1. inferring details.
        2. inferring cause and effect relationships.
        3. inferring comparisons.

    D. The students will be able to locate information concerning locksmiths and compare it with information located by others.

II. Procedure

    A. Introduction

    If you were digging in your yard and found a locked treasure chest how would you get it open? The lock is made of gold so you wouldn't want to break it off. What could you do? If no one comes up with the idea, suggest calling a locksmith. Today we are going to read about how a person learns to be a locksmith, and about the kinds of work locksmiths do.

    B. Development
        1. Before we start, let's look at these sentences on the board. The underlined words are words you will find in the story.

           When the locksmith begins learning his trade he is an apprentice for a few years.

Large factories use electronic locks so that at closing time one switch will lock all the doors.

The city issues a license for each locksmith; without this permission the locksmith is not allowed to practice his trade.

2. Now let's look at the word *locksmith*. What two words do you see in the word *locksmith*? What do you call a word that takes its meaning from two different words? (compound word). Look up the word *smith* in the dictionary (a worker in metals). Does that definition of *smith* fit with what we think a locksmith does? What other compound word contains the word *smith*? (blacksmith).

3. What questions about locksmiths might the article help us answer? Write their questions on the board. Add these questions if they are not given by the students:
   a. What are some of the advantages and disadvantages of being a locksmith?
   b. Why can learning how to become a locksmith be a problem? Let's read to find out which questions the article will help us answer.

4. After silent reading of the article discuss the purposes for reading.

5. Additional discussion questions:
   a. Why might an apprentice slow down a locksmith's work?
   b. Why might locksmith's sons not want to be locksmiths?
   c. Roger tells the story of how honest his father was in returning the jewels. Can you think of similar situations in which a locksmith might find himself?

C. Conclusion
1. Which of our questions about locksmiths were we unable to answer after reading the article? What could we do to try to find this information? Add the following suggestions if they are not included in the students' responses:
   a. Write to the Associated Locksmiths of America.
   b. Read books about locksmiths.
   c. Locate articles dealing with locksmiths in books about careers and trades.
   d. Have a locksmith come in and talk about his work.
   e. Ask the school guidance counselor if he has any information about locksmiths.
2. When the students have gathered their information, have each group present what it has found. Have the students compare their information and check for any inconsistencies.

Picking Locks & Cracking Safes
For Honest Money!

FIGURE 6.3.
"Picking Locks and Cracking Safes for Honest Money!" in *Scholastic Scope* 9 (November 1968), pp. 20-21. Reprinted by permission of the publisher.

Break into a place with the police standing there? Get paid for cracking a safe? It's all part of the job for a locksmith.

"Of course, it's not always an emergency like that," says Joe Inga, 23. "Often the work is putting in new locks, or opening them when keys are lost. But even then, it's a challenge. When you go out on a call, you never know just what the problem will be."

Joe works in a small, busy shop. He has always been interested in mechanics. But until three years ago, he hadn't thought about being a locksmith.

He was working as a handyman in a hospital, when one of the hospital's locksmiths left. Joe was asked if he wanted the job. It was a good chance to learn a skilled trade, while getting his regular salary. So he became an apprentice.

He stayed at the hospital a year, then got his present job. He was still an apprentice until January, when he finished two years of training. Then he got a license and joined the Locksmith Association. The Association helps locksmiths keep up with what is new in the trade.

"Most people don't know much about locks," Joe says. "When someone wants a new lock, the locksmith must be able to say what kind of lock is best for that situation."

Locksmithing used to be a trade passed on from father to son. But more locksmiths are needed today. And their sons do not always want to enter the trade.

Roger Schillizzi is one who did. At 20, he is a skilled locksmith in his father's shop.

"I started working after school when I was 14—cleaning up and fitting keys. Today I have my own truck, and I do almost everything. I make a lot of night calls.

"Sometimes you have problems. One night, a woman wanted new locks on the doors. She wanted to keep her husband out. As I was changing the last lock, her husband appeared. They started fighting, and I started to go. But the woman said, "You were hired to change the locks." Well, I was scared, but I finished the job.

"But most people are grateful when I help them. Especially girls who lose their keys. They're locked out in the middle of the night. When I pick the lock, they make me feel as if I've done a great thing."

Roger adds that a locksmith must be honest. "Once my father and I opened some safes. A man had died, and the bank was checking his belongings. We found thousands of dollars in the safe. The bank people took it. After they left, Dad found some jewelry inside. The bank people wouldn't have known about it— if Dad hadn't told them what had happened."

In large shops, locksmiths often do one kind of work. One may be an expert on safes. Another on electronic locks. A skilled cabinet maker may put locks on fine furniture.

FIGURE 6.3.
Continued.

There are also locksmith jobs outside shops. Large industries, hospitals, and schools often have their own locksmiths, who look after the locks in several buildings.

The money is good. In a shop, a locksmith may earn from $5,000 to $40,000 a year. Those who work in industries or schools earn from $500 to $650 a month.

Training can be a problem, though. Locksmiths have to pay apprentices the minimum wage. Teaching an apprentice slows down the locksmith's work, and the money he can earn. So many locksmiths won't take apprentices. When they do, they want to be sure the new man has the ability, and the drive to keep learning. Then it will be worth the time and money.

Some cities have locksmith training programs. The Locksmith Association is trying to set up training schools in more cities around the country.

Are you interested in becoming a locksmith? You can write to the Associated Locksmiths of America, 767 Lexington Ave., New York, N.Y. 10021. They will tell you someone to contact in your area. Or they will send you information about training schools.

III. Evaluation

A. If the students are able to identify new vocabulary by using word recognition skills and sentence context, they have fulfilled objective A.

B. If the students are able to answer questions dealing with the recall of cause and effect relationships, they have fulfilled objective B.

C. If the students are able to answer questions that require inferring details, inferring cause and effect relationships, and inferring comparisons, they have fulfilled objective C.

D. If the students are able to locate information concerning locksmiths and compare it with information located by others, they have fulfilled objective D.

Activity 6

Observe one or more lessons involving the use of reading material other than basal or other textbook material. Use the following questions as a guide for each of your observations:

1. Are the steps in the DRL procedure included in the lesson?

2. In what ways does the teacher relate the material to the experiences of the children?

3. Which categories of the Barrett taxonomy are reflected in the questions that are set as purposes for reading and in the additional discussion questions? Can you identify questions in other categories of the taxonomy that would be appropriate for the material being used?
4. What activities are provided to help the children use and extend what they have read? Can you identify additional activities that would provide meaningful experiences for the children?

Activity 7

Plan and teach a Directed Reading Lesson using reading material other than basal or other textbook material. Be certain that the material you select is at the appropriate reading level for the group of children you will be teaching.

Both the questions included in each section of the outline for a Directed Reading Lesson (activity 2), and the format for planning a DRL (see activity 4), can serve as guides in planning this DRL.

Activity 8

Design activities of your own which you feel will enable you to achieve the competencies stated for this module.

Preassessment and Postassessment

A. Knowledge Level
   1. Identify and briefly describe, in sequence, the steps involved in the procedure for teaching a DRL.
      Criteria for successful performance:
      a) the sequence of steps corresponds to the sequence in the Procedure for a Directed Reading Lesson as presented in activity 2;
      b) each step in the sequence is accurately described.

B. Performance Level
   1. Planning the Lesson
      a) Identify a group of children who are reading at the same level in a basal reading series and develop a plan for teaching a DRL using a selection from the book in which they are reading. Adapt the teachers' guide material, as needed, in order to make the DRL appropriate for the children you will be teaching.

b) Criteria for successful performance:
   (1) the objectives state the desired behavior;
   (2) the instructional procedure for teaching a Directed Reading Lesson (activity 2) is identifiable and in the correct sequence;
   (3) the instructional procedures include appropriate adaptations of the teachers' guide material;
   (4) the procedures for the evaluation of pupil achievement are identified.
c) Identify a group of children who are reading at the same level and develop a plan for teaching a DRL using material other than basal or other textbook material.
d) Criteria for successful performance:
   (1) the objectives state the desired behavior;
   (2) the instructional procedure for teaching a Directed Reading Lesson (activity 2) is identifiable and in the correct sequence;
   (3) the procedures for the evaluation of pupil achievement are identified.

2. Teaching the Lesson
   a) Arrange to teach the lessons to groups of children. Arrange to
      (1) have the instructor or cooperating teacher observe the lessons or
      (2) tape the lessons.
   b) Criteria for successful performance:
      (1) there is evidence that the pupils have achieved the objectives;
      (2) the student has demonstrated the ability to adapt his teaching procedures, as necessary, in response to pupil needs during the lesson.

3. Evaluating the Lesson
   a) After the lessons have been taught, write an evaluation of each one. Respond to the following questions in your evaluations:
      (1) Did the pupils achieve the objectives? Support your answer with specific evidence.
      (2) If there were pupils who did not achieve the objectives, can you identify the experiences they need now in order to reach the objectives?
      (3) Are there elements of the lessons that you would approach differently if you were to teach those lessons again?

b) Follow one of these procedures:
  (1) If the instructor has observed the lessons, schedule a conference to discuss both plans and lessons.
  (2) If the cooperating teacher has observed the lessons, ask for written evaluations and then schedule a conference with the instructor to discuss the plans, the lessons, and the cooperating teacher's evaluations.
  (3) If the lessons have been taped, schedule a conference with the instructor to discuss the plans and the taped lessons.

References

Bond, Guy L., and Wagner, Eva Bond. *Teaching the Child to Read.* 4th ed. Chap. 7, "Teaching a Lesson in a Unit." New York: Macmillan Company, 1966.

Bush, Clifford, L., and Huebner, Mildred H. *Strategies for Reading in the Elementary School.* Chap. 11, "Program Planning." New York: Macmillan Company, 1970.

Harris, Albert J., and Sipay, Edward R. *Effective Teaching of Reading.* 2d ed. Chap. 3, "Beginning to Read." New York: David McKay Company, 1971.

Russell, David H. *Children Learn to Read.* 2d ed. Chap. 5, "Overview of the Whole Reading Program: Methods and Materials." Waltham, Mass.: Blaisdell Publishing Company, 1961.

Spache, George D., and Spache, Evelyn B. *Reading in the Elementary School.* 4th ed. Chap. 2, "Using the Basal Reader Approach." Boston: Allyn & Bacon, 1977.

Stauffer, Russell G. *Teaching Reading as a Thinking Process.* Chap. 2, "Group Directed Reading-Thinking Activities"; chap. 3, "Directed Reading-Thinking Activity Illustrations." New York: Harper & Row, Publishers, 1969.

Tinker, Miles A., and McCullough, Constance M. *Teaching Elementary Reading.* 3d ed. Chap. 23, "Recommended Practices in Fourth, Fifth, and Sixth Grades: Diagnosis and Basal Instruction." New York: Appleton-Century-Crofts, 1968.

Zintz, Miles V. *The Reading Process: The Teacher and the Learner.* 2d ed. Chap. 5, "Organizing the Classroom Reading Program." Dubuque, Iowa: Wm. C. Brown Company Publishers, 1975.

7

Adjusting Instruction to Individual Differences

Overview

Perhaps no other matter of concern in reading instruction has received such continuous attention as that having to do with meeting the needs of individual learners through adjustments in materials and procedures. Although the need to provide for individual differences has been recognized for some time, the rate at which new techniques for adjusting instruction have been developed has accelerated in recent years. As Smith traces the history of reading instruction in the United States, she notes the beginnings of concern for the needs of individuals:

> In the preceding chapter we noted that a beginning had been made in the recommendation of ability grouping in reading, the use of diagnostic tests, and remedial work—all as a means of meeting individual differences. The number of teachers' manuals and courses of study, however, which made such recommendations prior to 1925 was exceedingly limited. Since that date practically every publication of either of these types has devoted considerable space to a discussion of these topics, some of them giving an entire chapter to the subject of individual needs.[1]

This concern for the adjustment of instruction to the needs of individuals has resulted, in recent years, in experimentation with a variety of organizational plans, the refinement of instruments for diagnosing children's needs, and the development of a wide range of materials which focus on helping children progress at their own rates in mastering specific skills. The ways in which certain current approaches to reading instruction

---

1. Nila Banton Smith, *American Reading Instruction* (Newark, Del.: International Reading Association, 1965), p. 239.

are identified clearly reflect concern for the individual: individualized reading, individually prescribed instruction, programmed instruction. Regardless of the label attached to an approach, however, every reading program today attempts to provide for adjustments to individual learners in a variety of ways.

A discussion, by Harry W. Sartain, of patterns of organization for reading instruction, is presented as an introduction to the complex area of adjusting instruction to individual differences. This discussion, "Specific Patterns of Current Interest," is a section of Sartain's "Organizational Patterns of Schools and Classrooms for Reading Instruction."[2] Sartain describes the essential features of ten organizational plans. He identifies, for each plan, those aspects which are viewed as strengths and those which are viewed as limitations. In addition, he cites the results of research efforts through which attempts have been made to determine the effectiveness of these organizational plans. As you read Sartain's discussion, use the following questions as your purposes for reading:

1. What is the rationale of each plan?
2. How is each plan implemented by the teacher?
3. What strengths and limitations are associated with each plan?
4. What conclusions can be drawn regarding the effectiveness of each plan on the basis of research findings?

Specific Patterns of Current Interest

Harry W. Sartain

The effects of innovation and change in organizational patterns of American schools have been under examination for a long time. However, in spite of its obvious shortcomings, an innovation of more than a century ago, the graded school, still may be found side by side with the newest innovations of the atomic era. Many plans, old or new, are characterized by

From Harry W. Sartain, "Organizational Patterns of Schools and Classrooms for Reading Instruction," in *Innovation and Change in Reading Instruction,* ed. Helen M. Robinson (Sixty-seventh Yearbook of the National Society for the Study of Education, pt. 2 [Chicago: The National Society for the Study of Education, 1968]), pp. 213-32. Reprinted by permission of Harry W. Sartain and The National Society for the Study of Education.

2. Harry W. Sartain, "Organizational Patterns of Schools and Classrooms for Reading Instruction," in *Innovation and Change in Reading Instruction,* ed. Helen M. Robinson (Sixty-seventh Yearbook of the National Society for the Study of Education, pt. 2 [Chicago: The National Society for the Study of Education, 1968]), pp. 213-32.

more than one of the general features described in the preceding paragraphs. The better-known plans are discussed in the following pages.

Intraclass Grouping Within the Self-Contained Classroom

The self-contained classroom, found only at the elementary level, has one inherent weakness for which it is much criticized—it requires all things of each teacher, thereby failing to capitalize on his special capabilities. At the same time, it can be rated positively on almost every other criterion for good organization listed in the first section of this chapter. Because he handles all or most curricular fields, a competent elementary teacher can provide systematic structure, intercorrelations, variety in learning experiences, and a consistent work load. Because he teaches the same children all day, he can maintain an entirely flexible schedule, come to understand each child well enough to appreciate his uniqueness and to offer a supportive relationship, help the child build an adequate self-image, and maintain and utilize comprehensive individual records.

If he groups the children appropriately within the room, the professionally well-prepared teacher is able to make effective general and diagnostic appraisals, adapt the curriculum to each member of the class, offer needed corrective instruction, and provide the guidance that each child should have in strengthening his reading skills in relation to every school subject. By grouping, he can make the most efficient use of his own time. He can also provide adequately for pupil interaction. Such interaction within groups is helpful in refining comprehension abilities. According to Stauffer, ". . . It is here—in the reading-thinking situation directed by a wise teacher—that pupils can acquire the attitudes of honest thinking, so that later in life they will always desire to be enlightened and informed, rather than blind and unreasoning. . ."[1]

At least eight types of grouping have been described: ability, achievement, special needs, interest, research, social, tutorial, and invitational.[2] For this discussion, they are reclassified into three general types: reading-power groups, skills-refinement groups, and reading-activity groups.

The *reading-power group* may be described as the developmental or the basal instruction group. The child is assigned to it because he can recognize approximately 95 percent of the vocabulary in instructional materials at a given level without assistance and he can perceive the literal meanings of 60 to 75 percent (depending on the difficulty) of the ideas. After instruction, he can recognize practically all of the vocabulary and comprehend most of the literal ideas as well as the more subtle meanings that require interpretive thinking. Grouping can be based on performance on specially prepared tests.[3] The type of informal inventory offered by Betts is also a suitable tool for initially dividing children into small power groups.[4] The number of groups will vary according to the capability of the teacher and the diversity within the body of students, but rarely will the traditional three-group plan be adequate.

Usually, it is recommended that primary power groups meet twice and intermediate power groups meet once daily for some phase of their work. Incidentally, individual and small-group instruction should not be restricted to the self-contained classroom. It should be provided for elementary and secondary pupils regardless of the organizational pattern.

Since children progress at different rates, several may be expected to move from one power group to another each year. One investigator found that these changes occurred more often in the early part of the term, when teachers were becoming acquainted with their pupils; it was implied that more changes should have been made, but evidence was not supplied to support this view.[5]

For years, writers have asserted that grouping for reading instruction must be kept flexible.[6] Wilt says, "In grouping for teaching reading, flexibility is probably the major condition."[7] However, the classroom teacher sees no logic in moving an individual pupil into a power group for which his vocabulary and comprehension background are not suitable. Such a practice almost certainly would result in arrested progress; the child would be either inadequately challenged or overwhelmed. But, while the organized, systematic introduction of new skills and vocabulary can be provided in developmental power groups, there are occasions for setting up ". . . small reading groups in which neither age nor ability level are the major determiners but rather 'Who can profit from the experience.'"[8] This means the formation of *skills-refinement groups* and *reading-activity groups.*

Although a half-dozen children may have approximately the same general reading power, each may lead or lag behind others in learning some specific skills, such as recognizing certain prefixes, adapting rate to purpose, reading to detect propaganda, or using a particular reference book. Regardless of their power-group membership, all children who are ready for extra help with a specific skill, whether the help is needed for acceleration or as corrective reteaching, may be brought together for additional small-group instruction. Such a skills-refinement group should meet for ten to twenty minutes once, twice, or as many times as necessary. After this group work has served its purpose, a new skills-refinement group may be formed to include those children who need help with another skill.

Frequently during the year, children may be regrouped on the basis of their own preferences for such experiences as sharing their independent reading, participating in choral reading, working on unit projects, or dramatizing stories read. Membership in these *activity groups* is flexible and temporary, as in the skills-refinement groups. In such groups, children may read extensively in dozens of books and become fluent readers by applying skills that have been introduced systematically in power groups.

Although space permits the description of only the simplest types of grouping, the writer recommends that skillful teachers vary their arrangements for group and individual reading to permit work in language experience, topical reading, and other instructional units.[9] The teacher who fails to provide organizational flexibility in one form or another is failing to follow a practice which is in accord with the best thought of today.

Because its success depends entirely on the capability and industry of the individual teacher, the self-contained classroom is slowly giving way to other plans. It is recommended, however, that school administrators be extremely cautious and not adopt a less adequate form of organization merely for the sake of change. Where self-contained classrooms are continued, teachers can be substantially aided by additional staff—special instructors for art, music, physical education, and so on. Also, an increased number of specialized consultants can help teachers learn diagnostic-corrective techniques and can keep them informed of new materials and curriculum improvements.

Departmentalization

Because teachers are prepared as subject specialists, departmentalization at the senior-high-school level has not been seriously challenged except by occasional moves toward eliminating departmental organization while retaining its major feature—teacher specialization. Recently, team teaching has been advocated as a means of lowering departmental walls and increasing teacher co-operation.[10]

Many junior high schools have adopted core and block plans, wherein developmental reading is taught by a teacher who has the class for at least two hours for work in social studies and the language arts. Such innovative modifications of departmentalization substantially increase opportunities of the competent teacher to relate reading instruction to content study and, at the same time, to provide increased classroom diagnostic and corrective assistance. Some of the research comparing fully departmentalized and core programs has been equivocal, but other studies suggest increased progress in reading through core organization.[11]

Elementary-school departmentalization, which advanced and then sharply declined earlier in this century, has attracted renewed attention during the movement of the sixties toward a content-centered curriculum. It has the obvious advantage of permitting full use of the teachers' special capabilities, and, in these days of teacher shortage, administrators have observed that it gives children a better chance of avoiding placement with a weak teacher all day. It has, however, all of the shortcomings previously ascribed to multiple-teacher plans, and most teachers in such situations apparently feel that each group is with them too short a time to permit instructional grouping within the room.[12] The hourly movement of pupils from one room to another makes it practically impossible for teachers to become intimately familiar with each child or to deal effectively with the personal problems that may affect his reading growth.

Although a 1954 study of semidepartmentalized sixth grades relates improved progress in reading to departmentalization[13] and a recent study suggests that some teachers are more effective in one or two fields than in all fields,[14] most careful experiments have failed to demonstrate that full departmentalization offers advantages for reading instruction. Investigations by Otto,[15] Rouse,[16] Jackson,[17] and Spivak[18] have indicated that pupils in departmentalized programs do no better and sometimes not so well as pupils in self-contained rooms. Recently the school system of Montgomery County, Maryland, undertook an experiment with departmentalization in fourth, fifth, and sixth grades. Although many pupils reported they had more stimulating learning activities in certain departmentalized courses, test results did not show superior achievement. In fact, the pupils in self-contained classrooms as a rule scored higher in reading and in arithmetic than did those in departmentalized classes; pupils in the lower I.Q. range (75-89) achieved better in all subjects in self-contained rooms.[19]

The Joplin Interclass Grouping Plan

This plan, sometimes called redeployment, cross-class, or interclass grouping, requires that teachers of several classes follow identical daily schedules. During the reading period, children are assigned to different rooms according to general reading level, and, at the beginning of each succeeding hour, they may be reassigned to rooms according to general achievement in other subjects. Balow has shown that this redeployment into presumably homogeneous sections reduces the range of pupils' specific-skills differences very little,[20] but Austin and Morrison found "most teachers equated a reduction in range of ability with homogeneity. The result was they usually had all children reading from the same page of the same book. . ."[21]

Under this plan, interclass grouping may embrace all the weaknesses of so-called homogeneous sectioning plus those of departmentalization (in fact, departmentalization without teacher specialization). Although it recognizes that a pupil's capabilities may not be the same in different subjects, it does not recognize, unless it also includes grouping within classes, that an individual child's various skills in reading may be developed at entirely different levels. In schools where redeployment does include within-class grouping for diagnostic and differentiated instruction, the hourly change of classes seems to be an impediment to the teacher's success in relating reading to other areas of the curriculum.

Although interclass grouping without intraclass grouping is only a half-measure in providing adequately for individual differences, even this plan may represent a slight improvement over whole-class teaching at a single level. A few studies have shown it to produce better results.[22] More experiments have shown interclass grouping to have no significant effect[23] or to have a negative effect on pupil achievement at some or all levels of ability.[24] The inconsistency of experimental results suggests that the administrative plan is not as crucial as the action taken by the teacher. After finding very small differences in results yielded by an experiment comparing crossclass grouping with individualized and intraclass grouping, Ramsey concluded, "Given the good teacher other factors in teaching reading tend to pale to insignificance."[25]

The Dual Progress Plan

The dual-progress plan, developed by Stoddard for the elementary school, combines some of the features of the earlier semidepartmentalized platoon system, the Joplin plan, and the secondary-level core curriculum.[26] During one-half of the day, the children are heterogeneously sectioned in a graded manner while they are instructed in the language arts and social studies by one teacher and take physical education from another. During the other half-day they are sectioned by achievement levels in each subject, as under the Joplin plan, to study mathematics, science, music, and art with different subject specialists.

While this plan gives the children at least two consecutive hours to get to know each other and to receive individualized guidance, it still incorporates many of the shortcomings of other multiple-teacher and homogeneous grouping plans. Heathers reported that, after two years of an experiment involving Grades III-VIII, pupil achievements under the plan showed no definite superiority except that the ablest pupils appeared to have advanced more rapidly in mathematics and science. Pupils appeared to like the plan, but teachers' opinions were divided. Their criticisms focused on difficulties encountered in getting to know pupils well, in teaching low-ability groups adequately, and in dealing with emotional and conduct problems.[27] The plan has been adopted by relatively few school systems.

Co-operative Teaching (Team Teaching)

Anderson, who has participated actively in the development of team teaching, describes the team and the co-operative teaching situation as follows:

A teaching team is a group of several teachers (usually three to six) with joint responsibility for planning, executing, and evaluating an educational program for a specified number of children, which is usually 25 to 30 times the number of teachers in the team. At the elementary level, the team may include pupils of the same age or grade level or of adjoining age or grade levels. In general, each teacher in an elementary team teaches all subjects taught in her grade and works at one time or another with every child in the group. Each teacher might, however, have special competency and interest in a curriculum area, so that the total team would include a number of specialists (e.g., one in science-mathematics, one in language arts, one in social studies, one in the creative arts), each capable of taking leadership for the planning and perhaps for a major share of the teaching in his area.

However, because all teachers are involved in the total instructional program, there would not be departmentalization in the usual sense.[28]

At the secondary level, teams may be formed either within subject fields or across subject lines. Both elementary and secondary teams usually have a leader who co-ordinates planning and an aid or "team mother" who is employed to do clerical and other nonprofessional work.

Among the major advantages given for co-operative teaching is its provision for altering group sizes for different types of instruction. In a team of six or seven teachers, two may offer reading instruction to very large groups while the others work with smaller groups on advanced or corrective lessons. Team meetings are held, usually once a week, to discuss pupil progress, to plan groupings, and to determine each teacher's responsibilities for future lessons.

Teachers of the large groups in elementary schools mention two serious problems: (a) maintaining class control and (b) finding an appreciable number of assignments which can be studied as appropriately at one level with fifty to one hundred children as in small differentiated groups. If groups are too large or change teachers too often, it is extremely difficult to make diagnostic observations and to provide sympathetic personal support for any except those who stand out strongly as being either very advanced or in great difficulty.

Team organization gives inexperienced teachers an excellent opportunity to learn from capable, experienced persons. This advantage occasionally is partly neutralized by personality conflicts, but even so, some professional growth accrues through team meetings. When teachers having different academic majors or minors are assigned to a team, each can function as a valuable resource person for a different aspect of curriculum planning. However, if this specialization results in one person's teaching all classes in his favorite field, cooperative teaching will become nothing more than departmentalization.

Although numerous schools have adopted the co-operative teaching plan, little objective evaluative evidence on its results has been published. Probably the lack of evidence is attributable to the great difficulty involved in equating all factors in experimental and control situations. One reviewer of the limited research states, "The reports offer assurance that team teaching does at least as well as conventional plans with respect to outcomes measured by standardized tests."[29] A recent study comparing progress of primary and intermediate team classes with the progress of pupils in self-contained classes favored the latter during the first year of the study but found teamed classes gaining more during the second year.[30]

Co-operative teaching in elementary schools is to be highly recommended if the grouping permits a child to remain with one teacher a large part of the day and if team and class sizes are kept small enough to permit the teachers to become thoroughly familiar with each child's personal and academic characteristics. If, however, teams consist of more than three or four teachers and if they function as in departmentalization, all the weaknesses of older multiple-teacher plans may be evident, and the differentiation of instruction will be seriously limited.

Individualized Reading

Although numerous variations are being utilized today, individualized reading is usually considered to be a procedure in which each child chooses a book he wants to read from a large selection and is given needed instruction in individual conferences with his teacher each week. The child progresses at his own rate; little assistance is provided outside the conference. Detailed discussion of individualized reading have been presented by Veatch and others.[31]

Because individualized reading requires differentiation only within the classroom, it can be undertaken regardless of the school's overall organization. Programs of individualized reading provide for abundant independent study but sometimes have been criticized for their failure to provide enough directed work to insure that all pupils learn skills in the most meaningful sequences. Research has shown some teachers to be successful with individualized reading[32] and others to be very unsuccessful.[33] In a careful analysis of the procedure, Robinson pointed out that teachers who adopt individualized reading should have exceptional knowledge of the skills program, should be excellent diagnosticians, and should be thoroughly familiar with the hundreds of basal and trade books that children may read.[34]

Two of the first-grade studies sponsored by the Office of Education during 1964-65 dealt with special adaptations of individualized reading. In one, children were given a concentrated preliminary series of lessons on word analysis, and then both word-analysis and sight-vocabulary lessons were taught individually, in small and large groups, and in pupil-team activities during the months when children were reading from books individually. Many new books and extra in-service work for teachers were provided.[35] It is not surprising that this vigorously instituted combination program of group and individualized instruction produced better results than were produced by a standard basal program having few of the extra embellishments.

The second experiment compared progress of the pupils using the same basal readers (a) in an individual-conference program and (b) in a small-group program. Except that attitudes in individualized classes were more favorable to reading and high-readiness pupils in grouped classes achieved higher test scores

than their counterparts, few differences were noted.[36]

Few experiments in individualized reading have been carefully controlled with respect to instructional time, instructional materials, and teacher capability. But, on the basis of available evidence, it can be concluded that some teachers, especially the more enthusiastic and experienced ones, can teach individualized reading successfully. Many children, especially the more capable ones, make adequate progress in individualized reading programs. The less capable students are less likely to progress satisfactorily in an individualized situation because they are not able to work independently for long periods of time.[37]

In some situations, the personal conference between the student and teacher seems to have great motivational value for the child; this is not invariably true, perhaps because of the lack of teacher-pupil rapport. Most children read more books in a program of individualized self-selection with conferences than in a basal program with supplementary books, unless the teachers of the basal program make a special effort to promote extension reading. The additional amount of individualized reading practice does not always result in proportionately greater attainment of skills—perhaps because not every teacher can give enough help during the short conferences.[38]

Individualized reading has reawakened teachers to the fact that children should read far beyond basal books. Basal materials can serve to introduce reading skills systematically, but these skills must be practiced in many other books if the child is to become a fluent reader. The best features of individualized reading can be combined with basal-group reading by completing basal books early in the year and continuing with individualized reading, by doing group reading in the morning and individualized reading in the afternoon, by following several days of group work with several days of individualized extension reading, or by including both in broad language-arts units on a specific literary theme.

Individually Prescribed Instruction

A program of individually prescribed instruction has been demonstrated since 1964 in the suburban Oakleaf School by the staff members of the Baldwin-Whitehall schools and the Learning Research and Development Center of the University of Pittsburgh under a grant from the Office of Education. Non-graded courses in reading, mathematics, and science are planned in carefully developed sequences of numbered lessons spanning the first six years of school. These lessons, which may be in programed form or taken from books and workbooks, are filed on shelves and on library carts in a materials center that connects several rooms. Lessons may call for use of tapes, recordings, library books, packets of materials for first-hand experiences, or for a face-to-face reading session with the teacher.

On four mornings of the week, the child looks in his personal folder to find the lesson assignments that his teacher has prescribed for him for the half-day given to individually prescribed instruction. (At present, children study other subjects in regular graded-room situations the other half-day.) He locates the required lesson sheets, goes to his desk or to a special audio-visual station, and proceeds to study independently, making the written or oral responses that are called for at each step. He works at his own rate, signaling the teacher for help when needed. Items responded to are scored, objective items by the pupil or an aide and subjective items by the teacher. Then the teacher studies the results to decide what the next lesson should be and prescribes it for the following day. Although some lessons call for group work, each pupil progresses quite independently. Readiness, achievement, and di-agnostic tests are used frequently to determine whether the child has mastered the work at one stage and is ready to move to the next. A lesson may be skipped if a readiness test shows that the child has already learned it incidentally.

During one half-day a week, the pupils meet in ordinary whole-class groups for "seminar" sessions. Sometimes these sessions may be broken into smaller group meetings. In the seminar session, the pupils share experiences, ask questions about work in progress, or listen to and observe the teacher's presentations of concepts and processes that cannot be learned readily from planned written material.

Children and parents seem to like the program. The lack of unfair competition and pressures and the feeling of continuous success and progress are probable reasons for the school's better-than-average attendance record. Test results indicate that the range of achievement in classes is approximately that found in situations in which teachers divide children into several instructional groups. Although general achievement averages are about the same as in other schools, children score higher on tests of specific knowledge which teachers in other situations might overlook because of the pressures of time or inadequate preparation.[39]

Because of its emphasis on personal involvement in learning and on individualized work, this plan fulfils more of the previously listed organizational criteria than do most traditional procedures. It may be criticized for pupil interaction in small groups and for the the somewhat limited opportunities it offers for lack of adequately differentiated work on the fifth day—work which seems out of step with that of other days. Teacher aids are provided, and, once the prodigious task of curriculum development has been completed (with expert outside help), the teacher has a marvelous fund of resources to make teaching effective. This feature may, however, present problems; it may tend to make teaching so mechanical and the teacher so dependent on the content programers that he may be led to forfeit his prerogative of making intelligent decisions about instructional approaches that should be used with children having different types of backgrounds and perceptual capabilities.

Pupil-Team Study

Durrell has urged that pupils be paired to lead each other in certain practice experiences.[40] Reading activities for pairs might involve word analysis and recognition, shared oral reading, storytelling, dictionary use, and checking workbooks. Experimental results in one situation in which pupil-team study was utilized for a year showed over-all average achievement (compared with the prior year's achievement) to be six months higher in Grade VI, four months higher in Grade V, but higher only in spelling in Grade IV. An instrument for rating teacher practices showed that classroom adjustments to individual differences had improved "one hundred percent," with the most effective application of the team-study technique being in reading.[41] Psychological research cautions that children in teams must exchange roles, because the one in the pupil role learns and retains substantially more than the one in the teacher role.[42]

If experiences are appropriately selected, planned, and supervised, pupil-team study can be recommended as a classroom procedure in keeping with the criteria for effective organization.

Non-graded Classes

Within the non-graded organization, children of either a narrow or a wide age-span are assigned to classrooms with little regard for academic capability and are guided at their own rates (individually or in small, flexible groups) through planned learning sequences of several years' duration. (In some places, homogeneous sectioning is erroneously called non-grading.) The age span in a non-graded class may be one year or several, but the mixing of several age levels has been shown to have academic value,[43] and such mixing permits pleasant adjustment within a wide range of differences in social growth. In primary and intermediate units, non-grading often is employed only for reading and arithmetic, the other subjects being taught at a single broad level.

Some children may take more or fewer years than the average to complete a given non-graded block of learnings, but progress is differentiated and continuous, with no artificial end-of-the-year promotions and no forced repetition of hastily covered work. When a child responds to a challenge to make progress beyond his own current level of achievement instead of being obliged to compete with classmates having different capabilities, it is believed that he will acquire a wholesome feeling of success instead of the feelings of defeat or smugness that often result from being judged on the basis of uniform expectations.

One-third of the school systems responding to a National Education Association survey in 1965 reported that they were trying some form of non-grading.[44] Detailed explanations of these procedures at both elementary[45] and secondary levels[46] are available.

Research on non-grading like most research on organization, has produced conflicting results. Carbone found progress to be significantly greater in graded schools.[47] Hopkins found that reading achievement was not significantly different in graded and non-graded schools but that teachers of non-graded classes, on the whole, expressed more satisfaction.[48] Skapski[49] and Ingram[50] both concluded that non-graded primary classes made significantly greater gains than ability-grouped classes. In a matched-pairs experiment continuing for three years, Hillson found that non-graded classes scored significantly higher than graded classes (at .01) on standard reading tests.[51] Uncertainties about the researchers' interpretation of non-grading make it inadvisable to mention additional studies which appear to favor this type of organization.

The non-graded plan is to be recommended because it proposes to make differentiated progress the rule rather than the exception. Administrators must be cautioned, however, that, in order to prevent misunderstandings and a haphazard development of concepts, it is important that non-graded curriculum sequences, achievement-marking systems, pupil records, and progress-reporting procedures should be carefully planned to reflect the philosophy of individualization. In instances in which preparation for the change has not been adequate, the result has been (a) confusion, (b) a continuation of the same old rigid practices under a new name, or (c) the introduction of some new form of lock-step arrangement.

Continuous Progress Plan

The continuous-progress plan represents a refinement of non-grading that has been developed in a few university laboratory schools. As instituted in the Falk School (located on the campus of the University of Pittsburgh),[52] it features a combination of organizational innovations—non-grading, multi-age heterogeneous sectioning, and modified team teaching—a combination which has been recommended by some authorities.[53] Elementary-school classes are designated as "primary," "midgroup," and "intermediate," each embracing an age range of at least two years but more often of three or four years. Within any room, children usually are divided into four to seven power groups for reading and into three to six groups for other fields of study to accommodate an I.Q. range sometimes from 80 to 180. Children of various ages participate in the group that offers intellectual challenge, and they make friends in the room with those at compatible stages of physical and social development.

A team usually consists of no more than two homeroom teachers and the special teachers in art, music, and physical education who have the children part of the time. The two homeroom teachers belonging to the team plan class schedules that are almost identical. Together they discuss the progress of the twenty-five children in each room and determine at which instructional levels there may be too few children in either room to make a small working group. Then they arrange for these pupils to exchange rooms at certain times of the day to fit into groups in the other room. Once a week the two team teachers meet, sometimes with student teachers and special teachers, to discuss the progress of groups and individuals. Through this meeting, the homeroom teacher is kept informed about his "exchange" pupils. Teachers also do general planning together and schedule occasional field trips, audiovisual experiences, and auditorium activities in which all fifty children participate.

Homeroom teachers get to know children and their learning traits very well because most pupils stay in a room two years, the older ones leaving and younger ones moving in each term. A few remain longer, and others may leave after a shorter period. When any child has progressed beyond the top group in his team and is mature enough to fit socially with younger children in the next higher team section, he is moved. This occurs fairly frequently, preferably during the year rather than at the end of the term.

Because of teacher specialization involved at the junior-high-school level and the very small size of the enrollment at that level in the

Falk School, it is not possible to provide as much schedule flexibility as at the elementary level. However, within three class sections in each field there are usually between six and eighteen small groups for differentiated instruction.

The continuous-progress plan at Falk School differs from most non-graded plans especially with respect to the structure of its curriculum. In each broad field, there are several planned sequences of basic learnings, each sequence developing some concept or set of related concepts and skills. These streams of educational outcomes are divided into sequential "develoblocks" of increasing difficulty. The several develoblocks at the same level for the different conceptual streams in any one field of study are called an "incline." In any field, there may be between ten and twenty inclines in the continuum of growth from kindergarten through junior high school. The teaching unit planned for each develoblock in the content fields indicates expected outcomes and experiences and lists readings at four general levels—minimal, basal (which may be further differentiated), horizontal enrichment (study in depth of the same topic), and vertical enrichment (study at the level of the next higher incline in the sequence). These "levels" broaden to provide for the entire range of capability in a class. Reading-skills units include both introductory basal reading and extensive individual reading. Consequently, great quantities of books of different literary types and varied content must be made available.

Many of these books are shelved in individual study carrels provided for all pupils in intermediate rooms and for the more mature children in midgroup rooms. When children are not working with the teacher in a small group at the instruction table in a corner of the room, they may study and write independently in their carrels, or they may go to an alcove to work in pairs or as a committee on unit activities.

This organization was developed gradually over a period of several years. Therefore, it has not been possible to arrange an objective "before-and-after" evaluation. The range of scores on standard achievement tests is wide enough to suggest that even the brightest children are challenged. An individual test of sight vocabulary in reading, given in the spring of 1965 and again in the spring of 1966, showed that the brightest pupils in their first year beyond kindergarten were able to recognize more than five thousand words and third-year pupils nearly ten thousand words.

After the first year of multi-age grouping, teachers were asked to list the pupils whose social and academic adjustment had been especially aided by the plan; most teachers listed between 10 and 30 percent of their children.

Because its whole purpose is to focus attention on individuals in a structured but flexible manner, this plan fulfills most of the organizational criteria. Its chief disadvantage is that it requires highly competent, dedicated teachers. These are in short supply. Perhaps such intellectually challenging plans will attract more persons of outstanding capability into the teaching profession.

1. Russell G. Stauffer, "The Role of Group Instruction in Reading," *Elementary English*, XLI (March, 1964), 231.
2. Josephine T. Benson, "Grouping for Individual Differences," *Individualizing Reading Instruction*, ed. Donald L. Cleland and Elaine C. Vilscek (Report of the Twentieth Annual Conference on Reading [Pittsburgh: University of Pittsburgh Press, 1964]), pp. 123-29.
3. George D. Spache, *Diagnostic Reading Scales* (Monterey: California Test Bureau, 1963).
4. Emmett A. Betts, *Handbook on Corrective Reading for the American Adventure Series* (Chicago: Wheeler Publishing Co., 1956); additional suggestions by Lester E. Wheeler and Edwin H.

Smith, "A Modification of the Informal Reading Inventory," *Elementary English,* XXXIV (April, 1957), 224-26; similar instruments provided by Nila Banton Smith, *Graded Selections for Informal Reading Diagnosis, Grades 1 through 3* [1959] and *Grades 4 through 6* [1963] (New York: New York University Press); also Mary C. Austin, Clifford L. Bush, and Mildred H. Huebner, *Reading Evaluation* (New York: Ronald Press Co., 1961), pp. 235-46.

5. Patrick J. Groff, "A Survey of Basal Reading Grouping Practices," *Reading Teacher, XV* (January, 1962), 232-35.

6. Robert E. Martin, "The Teacher's First Step: Discovering and Planning for Individual Needs in Reading," *Reading Teacher,* X (December, 1956), 77-81.

7. Miriam E. Wilt, "Grouping for Reading or for Reading Instruction?" *Educational Leadership,* XXIV (February, 1967), 451.

8. Ibid.

9. Arthur W. Heilman, *Principles and Practices of Teaching Reading* (Columbus, Ohio: Charles E. Merrill Books, Inc., 1961), pp. 273-82; David H. Russell, *Children Learn To Read* (Boston: Ginn & Co., 1961), pp. 409-51; Bond and Wagner, *op. cit.,* pp. 116-27; Paul McKee with William K. Durr, *Reading, A Program of Instruction for the Elementary School* (New York: Houghton Mifflin Co., 1966), pp. 197-200.

10. Carl H. Peterson, *Effective Team Teaching: The Easton Area High School Program* (West Nyack, N.Y.: Parker Publishing Co., 1966).

11. William A. Reiner, *A Third Report on the Evaluation of Pupil Growth in the Core Program of Two Academic High Schools 1953-1954* (New York: City Board of Education, 1955); Arthur C. Kelly and Robert E. Beatty, "Here's Proof that Core Program Students Learn Basic Skills," *School Executive,* LXXII (February, 1953), 54-55.

12. Margaret Rouse, "A Comparison of Curriculum Practices in Departmental and Nondepartmental Schools," *Elementary School Journal,* XLVII (September, 1946), 34-43.

13. Charles T. Hosley, "Learning Outcomes of 6th Grade Pupils under Alternate Grade Organization Patterns" (unpublished Ph.D. thesis, Stanford University, 1954), quoted by Harold G. Shane and J. Z. Polychrones, *Encyclopedia of Educational Research,* ed. Chester W. Harris (New York: Macmillan Co., 1960), p. 426.

14. Goldberg and Passow, *op. cit.,* p. 28.

15. Summarized by Koury, *op. cit.,* pp. 3-4.

16. Rouse, *op. cit.*

17. Joseph Jackson, "The Effect of Classroom Organization and Guidance upon the Personality Adjustment and Academic Growth of Students," *Journal of Genetic Psychology,* LXXXIII (September, 1953), 159-70.

18. Monroe L. Spivak, "Effectiveness of Departmental and Self-Contained Seventh and Eighth Grade Classrooms," *School Review,* LXIV (December, 1956), 391-96.

19. Fred M. King, "A Corner on Research," *Curriculum Leadership* (Minnesota Association for Supervision and Curriculum Development), III (October, 1965), 28-29; also summarized in "Instructor News Front," *Instructor,* LXXV (September, 1965), 2.

20. Balow, *op. cit.*

21. Mary C. Austin and Coleman Morrison, *The First R* (New York: Macmillan Co., 1963), p. 73.

22. Donald C. Cushenbery, "The Intergrade Plan of Grouping for Reading Instruction as Used in the Public Schools of Joplin, Missouri" (unpublished Ph.D. dissertation, University of Missouri, 1964); Elmer F. Morgan, Jr., and G. R. Stucker, "The Joplin Plan of Reading vs. a Traditional Method," *Journal of Educational Psychology,* LI (April, 1960), 69-73; Donald M. Green and Hazel W. Riley, "Intraclass Grouping for Reading Instruction in the Middle Grades," *Journal of Experimental Education,* XXXI (March, 1963), 273-78.

23. William F. Morehouse, "Interclass Grouping for Reading Instruction," *Elementary School Journal,* LIV (February, 1964), 280-86; Wallace Ramsey, "An Evaluation of a Joplin Plan of Grouping for Reading Instruction," *Journal of Educational Research,* LV (August, 1962), 567-72; Roy M. Carson and Jack M. Thompson, "The Joplin Plan and Traditional Reading Groups," *Elementary School Journal,* LXV (October, 1964), 75-77; William F. Koontz, "A Study of Achievement as a Function of Homogeneous Grouping," *Journal of Experimental Education,* XXX (December, 1961), 249-53.

24. David H. Russell, "Inter-class Grouping for Reading Instruction in the Intermediate Grades," *Journal of Educational Research,* XXXIX (February, 1946), 462-70; William R. Powell, "The Joplin Plan: An Evaluation," *Elementary School Journal,* LXIV (April, 1964), 387-92.

25. Wallace Ramsey, "An Evaluation of Three Methods of Teaching Sixth Grade Reading," in *Challenge and Experiment in Reading,* ed. J. Allen

Figurel (International Reading Association Conference Proceedings, Vol. VIII, 1962), p. 153.

26. George D. Stoddard, *The Dual Progress Plan* (Evanston, Ill.: Harper & Row, 1961).

27. Glen Heathers, "Dual Progress Plan," *Educational Leadership*, XVIII (November, 1960), 89-91.

28. Robert H. Anderson, "Organizing Groups for Instruction," chap. xiii in *Individualizing Instruction, op. cit.*, p. 257.

29. Glen Heathers, "Research on Team Teaching," in *Team Teaching*, ed. Judson T. Shaplin and Henry F. Olds, Jr. (Evanston, Ill.: Harper & Row, 1964); and "Research on Implementing and Evaluating Co-operative Teaching," *National Elementary Principal*, XLIV (January, 1965), 27-33.

30. Philip Lambert et al., "A Comparison of Pupil Achievement in Team and Self-Contained Organizations," *Journal of Experimental Education*, XXXIII (Spring, 1965), 217-24, as summarized by Helen Robinson et al., *Reading Research Quarterly*, I (Winter, 1965), 69, 104.

31. Jeanette Veatch, *Individualizing Your Reading Program* (New York: G. P. Putnam's Sons, 1959).

32. Rodney H. Johnson, "Individualized and Basal Primary Reading Programs," *Elementary English*, XLII (December, 1965), 902-4, 915.

33. Alton L. Safford, "Evaluation of an Individualized Reading Program," *Reading Teacher*, XIII (April, 1960), 266-70.

34. Helen M. Robinson, "News and Comment—Individualized Reading," *Elementary School Journal*, LX (May, 1960), 411-20.

35. Doris U. Spencer, "Individualized First Grade Reading versus a Basal Reader Program in Rural Communities," *Reading Teacher*, XIX (May, 1966), 595-600.

36. James B. Macdonald, Theodore L. Harris, and John S. Mann, "Individual versus Group Instruction in First Grade Reading," *Reading Teacher*, XIX (May, 1966), 643-46, 652.

37. Adapted from Harry W. Sartain, "Individualized Reading," in *Recent Developments in Reading*, ed. H. Alan Robinson ("Supplementary Educational Monographs," No. 95 [Chicago: University of Chicago Press, 1965]), p. 85; and Sartain, *The Place of Individalized Reading in a Well-Planned Program*, ("Contributions in Reading," No. 28 [Boston: Ginn & Co., 1964]).

38. Ibid.

39. John O. Bolvin and C. Mauritz Lindvall, "One Approach to the Problem of Individual Differences" ("Learning Research and Development Working Paper," No. 8 [Pittsburgh: School of Education, University of Pittsburgh, 1966]); also Lindvall and Bolvin, "Programed Instruction in the Schools: An Application of Programing Principles in Individually Prescribed Instruction," chap. viii in *Programed Instruction*, ed. Phil C. Lange (Sixty-sixth Yearbook of the National Society for the Study of Education, pt. 2 [Chicago: Distributed by the University of Chicago Press, 1967]).

40. Donald Durrell, "Implementing and Evaluating Pupil Team Learning Plans," *Journal of Educational Sociology*, XXXIV (April, 1961), 360-65; and "Pupil Team Learning," *Instructor*, LXXIV (February, 1965), 5.

41. Ibid.

42. Kent E. Meyers et al., "Learning and Reinforcement in Student Pairs," *Journal of Educational Psychology*, LVI (April, 1965), 67-72.

43. Walter Rehwaldt and Warren W. Hamilton, "An Analysis of Some Effects of Interage and Intergrade Grouping in an Elementary School" (mimeographed; Torrance, Calif.: Unified School District, 1965).

44. "Nongraded School Organization," *National Education Association Research Bulletin*, XLIII (October, 1965), 93-95.

45. John I. Goodlad and Robert H. Anderson, *The Nongraded Elementary School* (rev. ed.; New York: Harcourt, Brace and World, Inc., 1963); Lillian Glogau and Murray Fessel, *The Nongraded Primary School: A Case Study* (West Nyack, N.Y.: Parker Publishing Co., 1967).

46. B. Frank Brown, *The Nongraded High School*. Englewood Cliffs, N.J.: Prentice-Hall, Inc., 1963.

47. Robert F. Carbone, "The Non-Graded School: An Appraisal," *Administrators Notebook* (Midwest Administration Center, University of Chicago), X (September, 1961).

48. Kenneth D. Hopkins, O. A. Oldridge, and Malcom L. Williamson, "An Empirical Comparison of Pupil Achievement and Other Variables in Graded and Ungraded Classes," *American Educational Research Journal*, II (November, 1965), 207-15.

49. Mary Skapski, "Ungraded Primary Reading Program: An Objective Evaluation," *Elementary School Journal*, LXI (October, 1960), 41-45.

50. Vivien Ingram, "Flint Evaluates Its Primary Cycle," *Elementary School Journal*, LXI (November, 1960), 76-80.

51. Maurie Hillson et al., "A Controlled Experiment

Evaluating the Effects of Non-Graded Organization on Pupil Achievement," *Journal of Educational Research*, LVII (July-August, 1964), 548-50.

52. Harry W. Sartain and the Falk School Faculty, *The Continuous Progress Plan at Falk School* (mimeographed; Pittsburgh: School of Education, University of Pittsburgh, 1966).

53. Robert W. Anderson, "Some Types of Cooperative Teaching in Current Use," *National Elementary Principal*, XLIV (January, 1965), 22-26.

Module Competencies

The overall purpose in this module is to help you develop the ability to plan and implement a reading program which meets the needs of individual learners. This overall purpose is reflected in the specific competencies identified for the module. The first competency focuses on administering and interpreting an informal reading inventory as a means of determining the appropriate level of reading instruction for each child. The development of your understanding of the similarities and differences among approaches to grouping for reading instruction is the focus of the second competency. The objective reflected in the third competency is that of helping you develop the ability to plan a variety of independent activities for children as part of a total reading program.

Instructional Activities

In activity 2 you are encouraged to extend your knowledge of approaches to grouping for reading instruction by reading about organizational patterns other than those discussed in the article which introduces the module (competency 2). The procedures for constructing, administering, scoring, and interpreting an individual informal reading inventory are presented in activity 3 (competency 1). The development of your ability to administer an informal reading inventory and interpret the results is the focus of activity 4 (competency 1). In activity 5 you are encouraged to collect information concerning the ways in which teachers organize and implement their reading programs (competency 2). Examples of independent reading activities that can be developed for children are presented in activity 6 (competency 3). In activity 7 you are provided with the opportunity, on the basis of your comparison of grouping approaches, to plan a reading program which you feel will meet the needs of a specific group of children (competency 2). In activity 8 you are encouraged to design other activities which you feel will help you develop the module competencies.

Competencies

1. Administer and interpret an individual informal reading inventory.
2. Compare and contrast approaches to grouping.
3. Design independent activities which will enable children to use the reading skills they are learning.

Instructional Activities

Select from the following learning experiences those which you feel will enable you to achieve the competencies stated for this module:

Activity 1

Attend a seminar for orientation to this module.

Activity 2

In the discussion which introduces this module, Sartain describes ten approaches to grouping for reading instruction. Read one or more of the following references in which additional grouping plans are described. Use the following questions as your purposes for such reading:

1. What is the rationale of each plan?
2. How is each plan implemented by the teacher?
3. What strengths and limitations are identified for each plan?

Dallmann, Martha; Rouch, Roger L.; Chang, Lynette Y. C.; and DeBoer, John J. *The Teaching of Reading.* 4th ed. Chap. 13, "Adapting Instruction to the Needs of the Learner." New York: Holt, Rinehart and Winston, 1974.

May, Frank B. *To Help Children Read.* Module 9, "Organizing and Managing Your Reading Program." Columbus, Ohio: Charles E. Merrill Publishing Company, 1973.

Smith, Nila Banton. *Reading Instruction for Today's Children.* Chap. 6, "Grouping Plans Take on New Forms." Englewood Cliffs, N. J.: Prentice-Hall, 1963.

Wallen, Carl J. *Competency in Teaching Reading.* Chap. 19, "Grouping for Instruction." Chicago: Science Research Associates, 1972.

You may find it helpful to use table 7.1 to summarize the essential features of the grouping plans described in the references, as well as of those described by Sartain.

Table 7.1
Summary of Essential Features of Selected Grouping Plans

Grouping Plan	Major Characteristics			
	Rationale	Teacher's Role	Strengths	Limitations

Activity 3

The focal point both of the Sartain article which introduced the module, and of activity 2, is the variety of ways in which teachers adjust instruction to individual differences through grouping. In order to group children for reading instruction, the teacher must determine for each child the reading level at which he can derive the maximum benefit from instruction. Because of the limitations involved in using standardized test results as a basis for grouping, many teachers use a diagnostic instrument called the *informal reading inventory* or *IRI* to determine children's reading levels. The IRI is administered by the teacher to each child individually. The child is asked to read, both orally and silently, selected passages from material at increasing levels of difficulty, and to respond at each level to comprehension questions derived from the material. On the basis of the child's performance, the teacher determines the reading level at which to begin instruction.

Through the use of the informal reading inventory, the teacher is able to determine three levels for each child: (1) the independent level, (2) the instructional level, and (3) the frustration level. Some variation exists among the sets of criteria that have been proposed for use in defining these levels. The criteria used in this module are those suggested by Johnson and Kress in *Informal Reading Inventories*.[3]

Independent Level   A child's independent level is the highest level at which he can read easily and effectively without assistance. He makes almost no errors in word recognition and demonstrates accurate comprehension of the material. When he is reading at his independent level, the child appears comfortable and relaxed; he exhibits no signs of strain or tension. Johnson and Kress define the independent level in terms of the following criteria.

Criteria for the Independent Level

Word Recognition: 99% accuracy
Comprehension: 90% accuracy (average of scores from oral and silent reading selections)

Accompanying Behaviors

Clear Indication of	*No Indication of*
Oral reading with appropriate expression	Lip movement
Observing punctuation accurately	Head movement
	Finger pointing

3. Marjorie Seddon Johnson and Roy A. Kress, *Informal Reading Inventories*, in the *Reading Aids Series*, ed. Ira E. Aaron (Newark, Del.: International Reading Association, 1965).

| Reading more rapidly silently than orally | Vocalization Anxiety[4] |

Instructional Level A child's instructional level is the highest level at which he can read with only slight difficulty in word recognition and with relatively accurate comprehension. When he is reading at this level, the child is still comfortable and exhibits no signs of tension. It is in material at this level that the child can progress satisfactorily *with instruction from the teacher.* When the child's instructional level has been determined, he can be placed in a reading group with others whose instructional level is the same. Johnson and Kress use the following criteria to define the instructional level.

Criteria for the Instructional Level
Word Recognition: 95% accuracy
Comprehension: 75% accuracy (average of scores from oral and silent reading selections)

Accompanying Behaviors

Clear Indication of	*No Indication of*
Oral reading with appropriate expression	Lip movement
Observing punctuation accurately	Head movement
Reading more rapidly silently than orally	Finger pointing
	Vocalization
	Anxiety[5]

Frustration Level A child's frustration level is the lowest level at which he experiences more than slight difficulty in word recognition and demonstrates only minimal comprehension of the material he is reading. When the child is attempting to cope with material at his frustration level, he becomes obviously uncomfortable, and exhibits signs of strain, tension, and anxiety. When he determines that a child has reached his frustration level, the teacher ends the informal reading inventory. Johnson and Kress define the frustration level in terms of the following criteria.

Criteria for the Frustration Level
Word Recognition: 90% accuracy
Comprehension: 50% accuracy (average of scores from oral and silent reading selections)

4. Ibid., p. 6.
5. Ibid., p. 8.

(May indicate one or more)
Tone of voice too loud or soft
Word-by-word oral reading
Lack of expression in oral reading
Failure to observe punctuation accurately
Finger pointing
Lip movement
Head movement
Requesting help frequently
Showing signs of fatigue[6]

Constructing the Informal Reading Inventory

The selection of a set of reading materials that is graded in difficulty is the initial step in developing an informal reading inventory. Since the purpose in administering the inventory is to determine the level at which the child should begin receiving instruction, the inventory should be developed from those materials which the teacher will be using in his reading program. By using an inventory developed from the materials of the reading program, the teacher can assess the level at which the child can progress most effectively in the materials he will be encountering.

The procedures that have been proposed for the development of informal reading inventories vary somewhat. The following procedures are suggested here:

1. From each level of the material, preprimer through sixth, select two passages (one to be read orally and one to be read silently).
   a) the passages should be taken from material far enough along in each book so that it is not merely a review of vocabulary from the previous level. Zintz suggests taking the passages from the end of the first third of the book.[7]
   b) the passages selected at each level should be sequential, so that the child is presented with continuous material to read.
   c) at the beginning levels, select passages of 50-100 words. The length of the passages can be increased gradually to 200-300 words at the upper levels.
2. For each passage selected, develop a series of comprehension questions.
   a) Opinions differ with regard to the types of questions that should be used. Johnson and Kress suggest that for each pas-

6. Ibid., p. 10.
7. Miles V. Zintz, *The Reading Process: The Teacher and the Learner*, 2d ed. (Dubuque, Iowa: Wm. C. Brown Company Publishers, 1975), p. 77.

sage questions be written in the following categories: under-standing of vocabulary, recalling of factual information, and drawing of inferences.[8] In the selection of passages to be used for the inventory, these categories should be kept in mind so that the material selected is appropriate for the development of these types of questions.

b) the number of questions for each passage will vary according to length and content. It is important to remember, however, that the number of questions should be sufficient to insure an adequate sampling of the child's comprehension and a score which accurately reflects his ability to cope with the material. If only five questions are asked, for example, an error on one question results in a score of 80 percent. If ten questions are asked, the resulting score could reflect more accurately the child's ability to comprehend the material.

Administering the Informal Reading Inventory

Once the inventory has been developed, the teacher must decide at what level to begin administering it to each child. One way of determining this is to consult records of the child's reading progress during the previous year. The information on these records should indicate the level at which the child was reading at the end of the school year. It is suggested that the inventory be started one level below the reading level indicated on the records so that the child begins the inventory at a level at which he can read with ease.

The inventory should be administered in a setting that is comfortable for the child and is as free of distractions as possible. The purpose of the inventory should be explained to the child so that he understands that he is not taking a test, but is rather helping the teacher determine the book that will be best for him. The child should also know that he will begin with material that will be easy for him to read, and then progress to more difficult material.

When the teacher and the child are ready to begin the inventory, this procedure is followed:

1. The child is given the first passage from the level that has been selected to begin the inventory.
2. The teacher prepares the child for reading by providing him with an orientation to the material and a purpose for reading it.
3. The child reads the passage orally (he may read directly from the book or from a copy of the material).

8. Johnson and Kress, *Informal Reading Inventories,* p. 33.

4. While the child reads, the teacher records, on his copy of the material, the child's errors (the symbols used to record the errors will be presented in the next section of this activity). If the child hesitates for a period of five seconds in pronouncing a word, the word should be pronounced for him. It is helpful to tape-record the oral reading sections of the inventory so that the accuracy in recording errors can be checked at a later time.

5. Following the oral reading, the teacher asks the child the comprehension questions for that passage and records the child's responses. It is important to record the child's actual response, rather than merely to indicate whether or not it is correct. This provides the teacher with specific information concerning the nature of the child's comprehension difficulties.

6. The child is then given the second passage from the same level, and the teacher provides a purpose for reading it. The child then reads the material silently. As the child reads, the teacher observes him and records such behaviors as lip movement, vocalization, and any indications that the child is feeling tense or anxious.

7. When the child has completed the silent reading passage, the teacher asks the comprehension questions and records the child's answers. The final comprehension score is an average of the child's comprehension scores for the oral and silent reading selections at each level.

8. The preceding steps are repeated at each successive level of difficulty of the inventory until the child's frustration level is identified. If the teacher is uncertain as to whether the child has reached his frustration level, e.g., he scores at the criterion level for either word recognition or comprehension (but not both), he can proceed to the next level of the inventory in order to be certain that the frustration level has been reached.

Scoring the Informal Reading Inventory

Variations exist among the sets of symbols used to record the oral reading sections of informal reading inventories. The symbols to be used in this module are presented in table 7.2.

In figure 7.1 is an example of one child's oral reading errors marked according to the symbols shown in table 7.2. Also included in figure 7.1 are the child's responses to the comprehension questions for the passage. Finally, the child's word recognition and comprehension scores are indicated.

It is generally agreed that errors are counted according to the following guidelines:

1. Mispronunciations of difficult proper names are not counted as errors.

FIGURE 7.1.
The oral reading selection, "An Airplane Trip," and the comprehension questions, are taken from the *Pupil Placement Tests*, Grade 2 Marking Booklet, Oral Reading Selection, by Hollander and Reisman which accompany the *Houghton Mifflin Reading Program.* Copyright © 1970. Houghton Mifflin Company. Reprinted by permission.

An Airplane Trip

Janet and Jim looked out the airplane window. Far below them the trees and houses looked so small that they seemed to be toys.

A little ~~while later~~ *will land*, Janet said, "Everything's getting gray now. I can't see the ground any more."

Suddenly there was a flash of light and a very loud noise.

"What was that?" cried Jim.

"Thunder," answered Father. "We're in a storm now."

The plane started to bounce up and down.

"Oh, Father," said Janet, "we're ~~falling~~ *flying* down." And she began to cry.

"We're not ~~falling~~ *flying*. We're ~~going higher~~ *gone here*," said Father.

Soon the plane stopped *it below* ~~bouncing~~. The sun ~~became~~ *become* bright again and the children could see blue sky outside the window. Jim said, "Look at all ~~those~~ *things* dark ~~clouds~~ *clothes* down there. We got out of the storm by going over it."

Comprehension Questions

(M) 1. What was the exciting thing that happened on the trip? . . .
(*The plane got into a thunderstorm.*)
a storm came up.

(F) 2. How did the plane get out of the thunderstorm? . . .
(*by going higher and flying over it*)
from going up top; over it

(S) 3. What did Janet notice just before the loud noise and the flash of light?
. . .
(*that she couldn't see the ground any longer* or *that everything had become gray outside*)
It was thundering.

(F) 4. What did the houses and trees look like from the plane? . . .
(*toys*)
toys

(F) 5. Who was traveling with Janet and Jim? . . .
   (*Father*)

   their father

(I) 6. Why did Janet think the plane was falling? . . .
   (*It started bouncing up and down.*)

   'cause it was getting ready to land

(I) 7. How did Janet feel when the plane was bouncing up and down? . . .
   (*afraid, frightened, scared*)

   sad, and she was crying

(I) 8. How did Father know they were in a thunderstorm? . . .
   (*by the flash of light and the loud noise*)

   There was a loud noise

(V) 9. What does *ground* mean in this story? . . .
   (*the earth where we live*)

   It's getting ready to land

(F) 10. How did Jim know they had flown above the storm? . . .
   (*He could see a lot of dark clouds beneath the plane.*)

   Father told them.

(F) Factual   (I) Inference   (M) Main Idea   (S) Sequence   (V) Vocabulary

Uncorrected substitutions	*10*	*Word Recognition Score
Insertions	*1*	*84* % accuracy
Omissions	___	**Comprehension Score
Repetitions	*8*	*60* % accuracy
Words pronounced by teacher	*3*	
Total errors	*22*	

*To compute the percentage of accuracy in word recognition: Count the number of errors and divide this total by the number of words in the selection. Subtract this quotient from 100. The remainder is the percentage of accuracy.

**To compute the percentage of accuracy in comprehension: Count the number of errors and divide this total by the number of questions asked. Subtract this quotient from 100. The remainder is the percentage of accuracy. Average the percentage of accuracy scores for the oral and silent reading comprehension to obtain a final comprehension score for each level.

Table 7.2
Symbols for Recording Oral Reading Errors

Oral Reading at Sight		Silent Reading	
Key	Behavior noted	Key	Behavior noted
HM-	head movement	LM-	lip movement
FP-	finger pointing	HM-	head movement
↑↓	rising or falling inflection	FP-	finger pointing
		SV-	sub-vocalization
was-	repetition	V-	vocalization
saw / ~~was~~	substitution	(was)	examiner help given
saw ✓ / ~~was~~	self-correction		
~~was~~	omission		
the/man	pause (one/per second)		
w x w	word by word		
big / the ∧ man	insertion		
(was)	examiner help given		

Source: From Marjorie Seddon Johnson and Roy A. Kress, *Informal Reading Inventories* (Newark, Del.: International Reading Association, 1965), p. 36. Reprinted by permission of Marjorie Seddon Johnson, Roy A. Kress, and the International Reading Association.

2. Omission of a phrase of several words is counted as only one error.
3. Insertion of a phrase of several words is counted as only one error.
4. Self-corrected substitutions are not counted as errors.
5. The substitution of one word for another is counted as an error each time it occurs. If the child substitutes the same word, e.g., *horse* for *house* twice, it is counted as two errors.

Critical questions have been raised recently concerning the practice of counting *every* error in computing the word recognition score on informal reading inventories. These questions derive, in part, from work being done in the area of *miscue* research. The contention of those working in this area is that the *nature* of the child's errors must be analyzed; merely counting the *number* of errors can result in inaccurate judgments regarding the child's reading ability. Yetta Goodman summarizes this position:

Research for the last ten years on reading miscues continuously reaffirms the conclusion that when a reader's errors are simply counted and this quantitative information is used for placement, the reader may be encouraged to read material which is either too simple or too difficult for him. Reader's miscues must be *evaluated* based on the degree to which the miscue disrupts the meaning of the written material.[9]

A miscue is defined as "any observed response (OR) which differs from the expected response (ER) to the text."[10] Goodman gives the following example of miscues that do not cause a loss of meaning in the material read:

to lie   *this*

... for him in there like that.[11]

The type of analysis of oral reading errors being proposed by writers in the area of miscue research has particularly significant implications for teachers working with children whose oral language reflects any of the dialects[12] typically not found in reading materials. Goodman and Buck discuss the importance of considering dialect differences in determining which oral reading responses can be considered *expected*:

> Early in our research we became aware that the expected response in oral reading is not an exact single response but a range of responses which depends on variability among the subjects in their oral language. Dialect differences must certainly be considered in judging whether a particular response (OR) is within the expected range. But even within dialects, considerable variation must be expected. In our area, for example, *roof* and *root* have two common pronunciations. Both are to be expected. At one point we discovered that *with'm* was the most likely response to both printed phrases: *with them* and *with him* for all readers, all races, and all classes.[13]

The findings resulting from miscue research suggest how vitally important it is for teachers to develop a thorough understanding of the dialect or dialects spoken by the children they teach. Only with this understanding can teachers accurately determine which responses can be considered *expected* in oral reading and accurately identify the child's reading level

---

9. Yetta M. Goodman, "Reading diagnosis—qualitative or quantitative?," *The Reading Teacher* 26 (October 1972):32.
10. Kenneth S. Goodman and Catherine Buck, "Dialect barriers to reading comprehension revisited," *The Reading Teacher* 27 (October 1973):7.
11. Yetta M. Goodman, "Reading Diagnosis," p. 34.
12. A dialect is a pattern of speech which is used and understood by members of a subgroup within a large speech community. A dialect is a complete, adequate system of language and is simply a variant of a more widespread speech system or of the language of the country. Nebraska Curriculum Development Center, *A Curriculum for English: Language Explorations for the Elementary Grades* (Lincoln, Neb.: University of Nebraska Press, 1966), pp. 7, 163.
13. Kenneth S. Goodman and Catherine Buck, "Dialect barriers," p. 7.

by not considering as significant those responses that reflect the dialect of the reader.

Much of the work that has been done in analyzing dialects has been done by linguists interested in studying a variety of English known as black dialect or black English. For this reason, the following examples of black dialect are presented to indicate the kind of knowledge that is needed by teachers working with children who speak black dialect. This in no way implies, however, that *only* teachers working with children who speak black dialect need to make a conscious effort to understand thoroughly the oral language of the children they teach. It is the responsibility of *every* teacher to develop a knowledge of the dialect variations that exist in his classroom, and to use this knowledge in making judgments about children's reading ability. Seymour identifies the following features of black English:

The forms of Black English that are most likely to confuse the teacher are grammatical. While expressions in Black English vary from one part of the country to another, the examples below are typical of black speech in most places.

		Standard English	Black English
1.	Verb Usage		
	Present tense	He runs.	He run.
	Present progressive	He is running.	He run.
	Past tense, irreg. verb	He took it.	He taken it.
	Past perf., irreg. verb	He has taken it.	He have took it.
	Future	I will do it, or	I'm a do it.
		I am going to do it.	
	Present habitual	He is (always, usually) doing it.	He be doing it.
	Past habitual	He (always) used to do it.	He been doing it.
2.	Negation	I don't have any.	I don't got none.
		He hasn't walked.	He ain't walked.
3.	Question	How did he fix that?	How he fix that?
	Indirect Question	I asked if he fixed that.	I asked (aksed) did he fix that.
4.	Treatment of Subject	My brother is here.	My brother, he here.
5.	Noun plural	those books	them book
		men	mens
6.	Pronouns	We have to go.	Us got to go.
7.	Possessive	Jim's hat	Jim hat
		The hallway of Jim's family's building	Jim and them hallway[14]

footnote
14. Dorothy Seymour, "Black English in the Classroom," *Today's Education* 62 (February 1973):63-64.

Summarizing and Interpreting the Results of the Informal Reading Inventory

The results of the informal reading inventory provide the teacher with two types of information. The level at which to begin instruction is one type. In addition, the teacher will have information concerning the types of word recognition and comprehension errors the child has made. On the basis of this information, the teacher can plan specific activities to help the child in the areas in which he is experiencing difficulty.

Teachers typically find it useful to summarize the information obtained from each child's informal reading inventory. The form shown in figure 7.2 is an example of one way of bringing together this information. When a form has been completed for each child, groups of those children who are reading at the same instructional levels can be made up. The summarized information can also be used as a basis for forming temporary skill groups with children who are encountering the same word recognition or comprehension difficulties.

While the focus in this activity has been the informal reading inventory that has been developed by the teacher, there are two additional sources of informal reading inventories: (1) inventories that accompany basal reading series, and (2) published inventories that are not associated with any specific set of materials. If the basal material that the teacher is going to use for reading instruction includes an informal reading inventory, it is unnecessary for the teacher to develop his own inventory based on the same material. Using a published inventory that is not associated with a set of materials can present a serious problem, however. The results of such an inventory tell the teacher *only* how well children function in that material; they may not be an accurate indication of how well children will function in the materials to be used in the classroom reading program. If the inventory and reading program materials are dissimilar, errors can result in the reading level placement of children.

Examine several of the published informal reading inventories (enumerated below) which may be located in your college library or instructional materials center. Use the following questions as a guide in examining those inventories:

1. What differences do you find among the inventories in the sections that are included (e.g., do all the inventories provide a section for silent reading as well as for oral reading)?
2. What differences are there in the symbols that are used to record oral reading errors?
3. What differences are there in the types of comprehension questions that are asked?
4. What differences are there in the criteria used to define independent, instructional, and frustration levels?

Adjusting Instruction to Individual Differences

FIGURE 7.2.

Summary of the Informal Reading Inventory Results

Name *Keith*

Book Levels	Word Recognition	Comprehension
Primer	*100* % accuracy	*90* % accuracy
First Reader	*96* % accuracy	*80* % accuracy
Grade Two	*90* % accuracy	*70* % accuracy
Grade Three	*84* % accuracy	*30* % accuracy
	____ % accuracy	____ % accuracy
	____ % accuracy	____ % accuracy
	____ % accuracy	____ % accuracy

Independent Level *Primer*

Instructional Level *First Reader*

Frustration Level *Grade Two*

Types of Word Recognition Errors	*Types of Comprehension Errors*
Repetitions	*Inference*
Substitutions	*Main Idea*
	Vocabulary

Comments

There were some finger pointing and head movement which increased as Keith reached his frustration level. He needs work with punctuation.

Informal Reading Inventories

Botel, Morton. *The Botel Reading Placement Test.* Chicago: Follett Publishing Company, 1961.

Silvaroli, Nicholas. *Classroom Reading Inventory,* 3d ed. Dubuque, Iowa: Wm. C. Brown Company Publishers, 1976.

Smith, Nila Banton, and Harris, Anna. *Graded Selections for Informal Reading Diagnosis: Grades 1 Through 3.* New York: New York University Press, 1959.

————. *Graded Selections for Informal Reading Diagnosis: Grades 4 Through 6.* New York: New York University Press, 1963.

Spache, George D. *The Diagnostic Reading Scales.* New York: McGraw-Hill Book Company, 1963.

Sucher, Floyd, and Allred, Ruel A. *Sucher-Allred Reading Placement Inventory.* Oklahoma City: The Economy Company, 1973.

Activity 4

Administer an informal reading inventory to one or two children following the procedures identified in activity 3. Use an informal reading inventory that you have developed or one that accompanies a basal reading series. Tape each inventory so that you can check your accuracy in recording oral reading errors and responses to comprehension questions. Score each inventory and summarize the results in the way shown in the Summary of the Informal Reading Inventory Results (figure 7.2, activity 3).

Interpret the results of each inventory using the following questions as a guide:

1. What are the child's independent, instructional, and frustration levels?
2. What word recognition and/or comprehension problems can you identify?

Activity 5

When the teacher has determined the instructional levels of the children in his class, he is ready to form instructional groups, each of which will be composed of children who are reading at the same level. It is essential that the teacher view this initial grouping as flexible; it is to be expected that some children will move from one group to another in accordance with their progress and specific needs, therefore no group assignment should be viewed as permanent.

Once initial grouping has been achieved, the teacher can begin to organize his reading instruction on a daily and weekly basis. The overall aspects of the teacher's reading program will be determined by the organizational pattern being used in his school or at his grade level. Depending on the pattern, he may either plan independently or work with other teachers in planning the program. In either case, specific plans must be made for those aspects of the program for which each teacher is responsible.

In figure 7.3 is shown a sample weekly plan for three groups at a fourth-grade level. It is important to note that while the plan consists primarily of the teacher working with small groups, opportunities for the children to work individually are also provided. As Sartain points out, both small group and individual instruction should be part of every reading program, regardless of the overall organizational pattern being used.[15]

Just as he must view the composition of reading groups as flexible, so the teacher must view his basic plan as one which can be altered, if changes are indicated, in response to the needs of individuals. The potential value for effective instruction inherent in systematic planning will be lost if the basic plan is not seen as flexible. Any plan that is followed rigidly, regardless of the need for change, can severely impede the progress of the children for whom it was developed.

Request interviews with several teachers in the school in which you are working. Use the following questions as a basis for collecting data regarding the ways in which the teachers organize their reading programs:

1. What overall organizational pattern is being used (intraclass grouping, team teaching, nongraded, etc.)?
2. If the children are grouped, what information was used as a basis for forming the groups?
3. What number of reading groups is seen as manageable within a single classroom?
4. How does the teacher provide in his planning for working both with groups and with individuals?
5. On what basis does the teacher move children from one group to another?
6. What types of independent activities are provided for children in the reading program?

Observing the implementation of the reading programs in the classrooms of the teachers you have interviewed will provide you with another means of collecting information regarding the questions identified here. Compare the results of your interviews and observations with the results obtained by others who have completed this activity.

Activity 6

The successful implementation of the classroom reading program is highly dependent upon the types of activities provided for children to

---

15. Sartain, "Organizational Patterns," p. 216.

Low Group	Middle Group	High Group

Whole class: Directions and assignments are given to each group each day (10 min.)

MONDAY

Low Group	Middle Group	High Group
T Preparation, guided silent reading and discussion	Silent reading (Preparation on preceding Friday) Related workbook	Independent reading (entire period)
Related workbook	T Discuss story, check workbooks, oral rereading	

Whole class: Reading and discussing weekly newspapers

TUESDAY

Low Group	Middle Group	High Group
Related skills: practice exercises in word analysis, word games	T Related skills Preparation for new story	Silent reading of new story
Independent reading	Silent reading, new story	T Discussion, oral rereading, related skills

Whole class: Independent reading period, teacher circulates and has individual conferences or works with a group that has a special need in common

WEDNESDAY

Low Group	Middle Group	High Group
T Check workbooks, Oral rereading and discussion, preparation for new story	Related workbook If finish early, independent reading	Workbook not correlated with reader, discuss answers with group chairman
Silent reading, new story	T Check workbooks Discussion and Oral rereading of story	Silent reading of new story

Whole class: Word analysis, syllabication, dictionary guide to pronunciation

THURSDAY

Low Group	Middle Group	High Group
Related workbook	With group chairman, plan and rehearse dramatization of story	T Discussion of story, oral rereading, related skills

FIGURE 7.3.
A three-group plan for the fourth grade. Copyright © 1971 by David McKay Company, Inc. From the book *Effective Teaching of Reading* (second edition) by Albert J. Harris and Edward R. Sipay, published by David McKay Co., Inc. Reprinted by permission of the publishers.

FIGURE 7.3. Continued.	T Check workbooks, discussion and oral rereading	Independent reading	Research reading on special topics

Whole class: Independent reading period, teacher circulates and has individual conferences or works with a group that has a special need in common

FRIDAY

Whole class: Independent recreational or research reading, teacher circulates and has individual conferences
Afternoon: book club meeting, audience reading, dramatization, oral reports.

complete independently. As the teacher moves from group to group and from individual to individual during the reading period, those children with whom he is not working need to be engaged in meaningful learning experiences that can be completed without direct assistance from the teacher.

There is a wide range of materials and activities that can be considered for use in planning independent work that children will find both profitable and enjoyable. The following criteria can serve as guidelines for the teacher as he plans independent work for groups and individuals:

1. The activities should provide for the reinforcement of previously taught skills.
2. The purpose of each activity should be clear to the children.
3. The directions should be clearly written so that the children know exactly what to do in order to complete the activities.
4. The activities should be interesting so that the children's attention is maintained.
5. Activities in which children are encouraged to respond creatively should be provided as often as possible.
6. The activities should provide for self-correction whenever this is appropriate.
7. Each child should encounter a variety of activities in his independent work.

Both commercial and teacher-developed activities and materials can be used to provide meaningful independent work for children. Examples of both types of materials and activities in specific skill areas were presented in the modules dealing with phonic analysis, structural analysis, and comprehension. The focus in this activity is a discussion of additional ways of organizing and presenting independent activities.

Many teachers find that workbook material can be used most effectively to individualize instruction when it is organized in the form of reading skill kits. When material is organized in this way, each child can be directed to those activities which meet his specific needs. Teachers can develop skill kits by following this procedure, as discussed by Spache and Russell and Karp:

1. Separate workbooks containing different types of skill exercises into single pages (two copies of each workbook should be obtained so that both the odd- and even-numbered pages can be used).
2. Organize the skill exercises according to skill areas and subareas (e.g., comprehension: reading for main ideas, details, inferences, etc.).
3. Within each skill area and subarea, arrange the exercises sequentially.
4. Label the exercises clearly so that they can be identified easily by the children.
5. Rewrite the directions on the exercises, if necessary, to eliminate any difficulties the children might encounter in completing them independently.
6. Provide an answer key with the exercises in order to make them self-correcting.
7. Mount the exercises or place them in individual acetate folders.
8. Arrange the exercises in boxes according to skill areas.[16]

When the reading skill kits are completed, the teacher has a wide range of material available to use in meeting the specific needs of individuals. Teachers usually find that once the procedures for using the kits are explained, children (even in the primary grades) experience no difficulty in working with them independently.

Recent interest in the concepts of "open education" and "activity-centered" classrooms has encouraged many teachers to develop one or more "learning" or "activity" centers within their classrooms. Approaches to developing such centers and their use with children vary from teacher to teacher, but the objective remains the same: providing a variety of meaningful learning experiences that can be carried out by children independently.

In their discussion of reading learning centers, Thompson and Merritt describe a reading center as a place in the classroom where children en-

---

16. David H. Russell and Etta E. Karp, *Reading Aids Through the Grades*. Second Revised Edition by Anne Marie Mueser (New York: Teachers College Press, Columbia University, 1975); Evelyn B. Spache, *Reading Activities for Child Involvement* (Boston: Allyn & Bacon, 1972).

gage in a variety of reading activities, such as practicing skills, locating information, and reading for pleasure.[17] They suggest the following as examples of the types of activities that can be included in a reading center:

Prepare a picture dictionary using magazine pictures to illustrate selected words.
What's the opposite? Write opposites for a given word list.
Rebus stories. Write a rebus story using a selection from your basal.
Present a panel discussion and develop two sides of an issue.
Prepare a puppet show writing your own dialogue for a favorite story.
Pretend you are sending a telegram to a friend about an exciting book you have read.
Present an illustrated talk on a historical book you have read.
Make a cartoon book.
Haiku.
Travelogues.
Make an unusual bulletin board.[18]

Thompson and Merritt stress the importance of developing and posting a time schedule, so that each child knows when he may use the center. The number of children who can effectively use the center at one time will depend on the size of the center and the number of activities involved.[19]

In addition to the kinds of activities suggested by Thompson and Merritt, many teachers develop "activity" or "task" cards for use in learning centers. Each card focuses on one skill exercise or activity that the child can complete independently. Sets of activity cards can be developed to meet children's needs and interests in a wide range of areas. Figure 7.4 provides two examples of activity cards developed for a classroom learning center.

Activity 7

The data presented in table 7.3 represent a summary of the information collected by one sixth-grade teacher as a basis for organizing his reading program. In addition to the results of the informal reading inventories he has administered, the teacher also has intelligence test results and percentile rankings from the standardized reading test taken by the children toward the end of the previous school year. Analyze the data presented in table 7.3 and respond to the following questions on the basis of your analysis:

17. Richard A. Thompson and King Merritt, Jr., "Turn on to a reading center," *The Reading Teacher* 28 (January 1975):385.
18. Ibid., p. 386.
19. Ibid.

FIGURE 7.4.

Activity Card
Comprehension

Read the story and then answer the questions.

Eric and Edward are in the same fourth-grade class. Eric is always in a bad mood and he likes to start fights. No one ever plays with Eric at recess because he gets into trouble. One day Eric asked Edward to play ball with him. All the other children told Edward not to play with Eric. Edward told Eric that he would not play with him. Eric was very sad.

1. Would you have done the same thing that Edward did?
2. What else could Edward have done?
3. What do you think Eric did next?
4. How would you have felt if you were Eric?
5. Has anything like this ever happened to you?
6. Why do you think Eric started fights?

Talk about your answers with someone else who has completed this activity card.

Activity Card
Suffixes

Add one of the following suffixes to each italicized word to have the story make sense:

er   ness   est   ly

Samantha is the *fast*_____ runner in the whole school. One day Miss Richardson, Samantha's *teach*___, announced that there would be a big race on Monday. Samantha was sure that she could win. She practiced all day Saturday. On Monday Samantha ran with such *sure*_____ that all the children watching felt that she would *certain*_____ win. By working hard Samantha did win the big race.

Check your answers with the answer key on the back of this card.

Table 7.3
Distribution of Estimated Reading Levels, Intelligence Test Scores, and Reading Test Percentile Rankings for Twenty-One Sixth-Grade Children

	September '76	March '76	May '76	September '76
Name	Age	I.Q.	Standardized Reading Test: Percentile Rank	Estimated Instruction Level
1. Angela	11	134	90th	6
2. Stacey	11	116	25th	4
3. Susan	11	134	99th	6
4. Karen	11	135	85th	6
5. Michele	11	119	50th	5
6. Renee	11	absent	65th	6
7. Paula	11	137	65th	5
8. Lisa	11	116	30th	5
9. Erik	11	114	absent	4
10. Mark	11	112	60th	5
11. Harold	11	absent	75th	6
12. Ronald	11	123	75th	6
13. Curtis	11	106	65th	6
14. Anthony	12	91	70th	5
15. Kevin	10	134	90th	6
16. Robert	11	113	30th	4
17. Herbert	11	104	40th	4
18. Jaison	10	127	65th	5
19. Michael	11	107	20th	4
20. Thomas	11	105	30th	4
21. Jon	11	146	95th	6

1. Which of the organizational plans you have examined would you use with this group of children? What are your reasons for selecting this plan?
2. Using the plan you have selected, how many instructional groups would you form? Which children would you place in each group?
3. What additional information about the children would you find helpful in organizing the reading program for this class?

Develop a weekly plan for working with these children, basing it on the organizational pattern you have selected and the instructional groups you have formed. Compare your choice of organizational pattern and weekly plan with others who have completed this activity. Can you understand the reasons given by others for selecting a different pattern? Do others appear to understand the reasons for your selection?

Activity 8

Design activities of your own which you feel will enable you to achieve the competencies stated for this module.

Preassessment and Postassessment

A. Knowledge Level
1. Compare and contrast three approaches to grouping. Include the following dimensions in your discussion of each approach: (a) assumptions or rationale of the approach, (b) procedures for implementing the approach, (c) strengths and limitations of the approach.
   Criteria for successful performance:
   a) the dimensions of each approach are accurately identified;
   b) the similarities and differences among approaches are clearly specified.
B. Performance Level
1. Select two children and administer an informal reading inventory to each one. Develop your own selections using a basal reading series or use a published inventory which accompanies a basal reading series. Determine the following reading levels for each child: (a) independent, (b) instructional, (c) frustration. Arrange a conference with the instructor to discuss the results of the informal reading inventories.
   Criteria for successful performance:
   The three reading levels are correctly identified for each child in terms of percentage of accuracy in both word recognition and comprehension.
2. Design for each child two independent reading activities that are appropriate for his instructional reading level and for meeting specific needs identified through the informal reading inventory.
   Criteria for successful performance:
   a) the objectives state the desired behavior;
   b) the activities are appropriate for each child's instructional level and are clearly based on the information obtained from the informal reading inventory;

Adjusting Instruction to Individual Differences

c) following the use of the activities there is evidence that the pupils were able to complete the activities successfully.

References

Baratz, Joan C., and Shuy, Roger W. *Teaching Black Children to Read.* Washington, D.C.: Center for Applied Linguistics, 1969.

Bond, Guy L., and Wagner, Eva Bond. *Teaching the Child to Read.* 4th ed. Chap. 16, "Adjusting to Individual Needs." New York: Macmillan Company, 1966.

Bush, Clifford L., and Huebner, Mildred H. *Strategies for Reading in the Elementary School.* Chap. 10, "Organization of the Reading Program." New York: Macmillan Company, 1970.

Cullinan, Bernice E., ed. *Black Dialects and Reading.* Urbana, Ill.: National Council of Teachers of English, 1974.

Dallmann, Martha; Rouch, Roger L.; Chang, Lynette Y. C.; and DeBoer, John J. *The Teaching of Reading.* 4th ed. Chap. 12, "Classroom Diagnosis of Reading Ability"; chap. 13, "Adapting Instruction to the Needs of the Learner." New York: Holt, Rinehart and Winston, 1974.

Durkin, Dolores. *Teaching Them to Read.* 2d ed. Chap. 3, "Organizing for Instruction." Boston: Allyn & Bacon, 1974.

Goodman, Kenneth S., and Buck, Catherine. "Dialect barriers to reading comprehension revisited." *The Reading Teacher* 27 (October 1973):6-12.

Goodman, Yetta M. "Reading diagnosis—qualitative or quantitative." *The Reading Teacher* 26 (October 1972):32-37.

Harris, Albert J., and Sipay, Edward R. *Effective Teaching of Reading.* 2d ed. Chap. 7, "Providing for Individual and Group Needs." New York: David McKay Company, 1971.

———. *How to Increase Reading Ability.* 6th ed. Chap. 5, "Meeting Individual Needs in Reading"; chap. 6, "Efficient Reading Instruction in Groups." New York: David McKay Company, 1975.

Herr, Selma E. *Learning Activities for Reading.* 2d ed. Dubuque, Iowa: Wm. C. Brown Company Publishers, 1970.

Johnson, Marjorie Seddon, and Kress, Roy A. *Informal Reading Inventories.* In the *Reading Aids Series,* edited by Ira E. Aaron. Newark, Del.: International Reading Association, 1965.

May, Frank B. *To Help Children Read.* Module 5, "Assessing the Reading Levels and Problems of Your Pupils"; module 9, "Organizing and Managing Your Reading Program." Columbus, Ohio: Charles E. Merrill Publishing Company, 1973.

Nebraska Curriculum Development Center. *A Curriculum for English: Language Explorations for the Elementary Grades.* Lincoln: University of Nebraska Press, 1966.

Otto, Wayne; Chester, Robert; McNeil, John; and Myers, Shirley. *Focused Reading Instruction.* Chap. 11, "Organizing Learning Situations for Individual Differences." Reading, Mass.: Addison-Wesley Publishing Company, 1974.

Russell, David H. *Children Learn to Read.* 2d ed. Chap. 15, "Providing for Individual Differences in Reading Abilities." Waltham, Mass.: Blaisdell Publishing Company, 1961.

Russell, David H., and Karp, Etta E. *Reading Aids Through the Grades.* Second Revised Edition by Anne Marie Mueser. New York: Teachers College Press, Columbia University, 1975.

Seymour, Dorothy Z. "Black English in the Classroom." *Today's Education* 62 (February 1973):63-64.

Smith, Nila Banton. *Reading Instruction for Today's Children.* Chap. 6, "Grouping Plans Take on New Forms." Englewood Cliffs, N. J.: Prentice-Hall, 1963.

Smith, Nila Banton, and Harris, Anna. *Graded Selections for Informal Reading Diagnosis.* New York: New York University Press, 1963.

Spache, Evelyn B. *Reading Activities for Child Involvement.* Boston: Allyn & Bacon, 1972.

Spache, George D., and Spache, Evelyn B. *Reading in the Elementary School.* 4th ed. Chap. 14, "Approaches to Classroom Management." Boston: Allyn & Bacon, 1977.

Tinker, Miles A., and McCullough, Constance M. *Teaching Elementary Reading.* 3d ed. Chap. 18, "Organization and Administration of the Reading Program." New York: Appleton-Century-Crofts, 1968.

Veatch, Jeannette. *Reading in the Elementary School.* Chap. 5, "The Independent Work Period"; chap. 7, "Grouping." New York: Ronald Press Company, 1966.

Wallen, Carl J. *Competency in Teaching Reading.* Chap. 19, "grouping for instruction." Chicago: Science Research Associates, 1972.

Zintz, Miles V. *The Reading Process: The Teacher and the Learner.* 2d ed. Chap. 4, "The Informal Reading Inventory"; chap. 5, "Organizing the Classroom Reading Program." Dubuque, Iowa: Wm. C. Brown Company Publishers, 1975.

8

Reading in the Content Fields

Overview

As children move through the primary grades and into the intermediate grades, their school achievement steadily becomes more closely related to their ability to read materials in the content fields of science, social studies, mathematics, and literature. Huus summarizes the factors that have contributed to the current need for instruction that will enable children to meet the demands of content reading:

> . . . beginning in the middle grades, pupils today are faced with a sharp increase in the number of texts and supplementary books they are expected to read, and, by the time college is reached, the reading-study load becomes extremely demanding. The pressure for academic excellence, the attention to greater depth in learning, the increase in the amount and availability of materials, and changes in the curriculum have accentuated the current need to improve reading-study skills.[1]

While reading educators consider it essential to provide instruction in content field reading, they consider it equally essential that this instruction not be viewed as separate from other aspects of the reading program. Rupley identifies this position in his review of the literature in content reading:

> In general, the previously cited reading authorities agree that the teaching of reading in the content area is too important to be deferred until a stu-

---

1. Helen Huus, "Innovations in Reading Instruction: At Later Levels," in *Innovation and Change in Reading Instruction,* ed. Helen M. Robinson, (Sixty-seventh Yearbook of the National Society for the Study of Education, pt. 2 [Chicago: The National Society for the Study of Education, 1968]), p. 138.

dent is in the secondary grades. They also indicate that the teaching of reading should not be dichotomized into teaching reading during one period and
teaching a subject or content during other periods. The teaching of reading
should be an ongoing activity throughout the school day; when social
studies, math, science, or language arts is being taught, reading should be
taught as well![2]

The focus in this module reflects the position identified by Rupley.
While attention is directed specifically toward instruction which will enable children to meet the demands of content reading, this instruction is
viewed as an integral component of the total reading curriculum.

The module is introduced through two articles that deal with content
field reading: "Developing Reading Competencies Through Social Studies
and Literature," by I. E. Aaron,[3] and "Developing Reading Competencies
Through Mathematics and Science," by Henry A. Bamman.[4] In his article,
Aaron identifies ten competencies which he views as essential for the
effective reading of material in social studies and literature. In addition to
identifying the competencies, Aaron discusses the role of the teacher in
helping children develop them. Bamman begins his discussion by identifying factors that contribute to the difficulty children have in reading science
and mathematics material. He then discusses the ways in which teachers
can help children develop the competencies which they need in order to
read effectively in science and mathematics. Use the following questions
as your purposes for reading these articles:

1. What specialized competencies are necessary for effective reading in
    social studies, literature, mathematics, and science?
2. What are the responsibilities of the teacher, as viewed by Aaron and
    Bamman, in helping children develop these specialized competencies?

2. William H. Rupley, "Content Reading in the Elementary Grades," *Language
    Arts* 52 (September 1975):804.
3. I. E. Aaron, "Developing Reading Competencies Through Social Studies and
    Literature," in *Reading as an Intellectual Activity,* ed. J. Allen Figurel (Newark,
    Del.: International Reading Association, 1963), pp. 107-10.
4. Henry A. Bamman, "Developing Reading Competencies Through Mathematics
    and Science," in *Reading as an Intellectual Activity,* ed. J. Allen Figurel (Newark,
    Del.: International Reading Association, 1963), pp. 110-12.

Developing Reading Competencies Through Social Studies and Literature

I. E. Aaron

Reading in social studies and literature involves more than a mastery of basal reading skills. To be sure, the fundamental skills and abilities are necessary for all reading, but each content area demands additional competencies. These competencies grow out of and are peculiar to the subject matter involved.

Reading materials in the social studies and literature are wide and varied. In the social studies, they include textbooks, encyclopedias, newspapers, magazines, biography, fiction with authentic settings, and appropriate reference books. In literature, the pupil reads such materials as literary anthologies, supplementary and enrichment readers, a variety of library books, magazines, reference materials, collections of poems, and short stories.

One of the major problems teachers encounter is helping children to select materials suited to their reading levels. Teachers cannot depend upon one textbook for all pupils in the social studies or in literature. They know that up to one fourth of a typical class at fourth-grade level or above cannot read text or other material written on a difficulty level in keeping with the grade in which they are placed. Before teachers can do much about teaching the specialized skills, they must make certain that the materials are not too difficult.

The remainder of this paper will be devoted to a discussion of some selected specialized reading competencies necessary for effective reading in social studies and literature. Most of the competencies selected for discussion apply to both subject areas. In the discussion that follows the assumption will be made that the pupils being taught the reading skills in social studies and literature are being taught them in materials they *can* read.

Mastering the Special Vocabulary

In reading history, children encounter such words as *citizen, democracy, republic,* and *settlement.* They turn to a selection in geography and meet such words as *island, continent, latitude,* and a host of names of places, many of them difficult to pronounce. They encounter words such as *poem, novel, article,* and *prologue* in literature.

Teachers in social studies and literature are responsible for teaching these special vocabularies. Leaving the development to chance will not get the job done. The teachers must first identify the special vocabulary important enough to be taught. They must next set up situations that will assure the students' learning of the vocabulary, and, finally, they must check to make certain it has been learned.

Building Adequate Concept Background

Even though the children recognize the individual words in a paragraph or longer selection, they sometimes are unable to interpret them as the writer intended. The concept load

From I. E. Aaron, "Developing Reading Competencies Through Social Studies and Literature," in *Reading as an Intellectual Activity*, ed. J. Allen Figurel (Newark, Del.: International Reading Association, 1963), pp. 107-10. Reprinted by permission of I. E. Aaron and the International Reading Association.

in the social studies and in literature presents problems for some students. We get *from* the printed page in proportion to what we take *to* the printed page. The reader who has the best background, other factors being equal, will get the most from his reading.

The alert teacher of literature or social studies anticipates meaning problems the reader is likely to encounter and helps him to build the background needed for adequate understanding.

Reading the Specialized Materials

Reading a factual discussion about the life of Edgar Allan Poe is quite different from reading one of his poems. Getting the meaning from a book-length novel differs from understanding and enjoying a short story. Reading a geography text and a fable involves some reading skills that are similar, but reading in each type of material also brings into use skills peculiar to that particular kind of reading matter. Purposes for reading each would also differ, thus bringing into play different reading competencies.

Teachers in social studies and in literature have obligations to teach the students how to read their subject matter. The English teacher in the junior high or high school, for example, needs to help the student to understand what is involved in reading a play. Here the reader sets the stage in his own mind. The teacher may ask a good reader to read a poem aloud while the class members listen to the rhythm. Or a symbolic poem may be discussed first from the standpoint of literal meaning and then from the symbolic viewpoint. A civics teacher may suggest a survey, question, read, recall, and reread approach to the text. If there are any best ways of reading the materials, the teacher must teach them to the children.

Among the specialized materials of each subject are the various reference aids in that particular content area. Some of these are common to more than one subject-matter area, while others are limited in their usefulness to one subject field only. Mastering the use of these reference aids leads the child into independence in his reading and studying. Pupils should be taught how to use map and illustrations lists, the card catalogue, encyclopedias, books such as *The World Almanac,* the *Readers' Guide,* biographical dictionaries, the atlas, and any other special reference aids available for their use. Commercial materials for helping the teacher to develop the use of reference materials are now available at most grade levels. However, much of the teacher's instruction in the use of reference aids will come along with actual experience in the use of these aids.

Drawing Conclusions and Getting Implied Meanings

Getting the literally stated facts is only a part of the job of reading. The good reader in the social studies and in literature can draw intelligent conclusions from the facts, and he can read between the lines. He brings his own experiences with him to the printed page and gets accurate meanings beyond those stated in the selection. The good reader thinks as he reads. He "feels" with the characters in a story and can recognize the relationships between characters.

The pupil reads in terms of the questions he is asked by the teacher. If the questions are strictly factual and involve no real thinking, the pupil will learn to read for facts—and do very little real thinking in which he uses the facts. On the other hand, if the teacher asks questions involving thought along with the facts, the children will think as they read.

When children have been reading to answer factual questions only, they often appear lost if confronted with questions demanding thought. A gradual process must be followed in leading them toward competency in this area.

Reading Critically

Children sometimes develop the impression that "it's true because it's in print." Such children may grow up to be gullible adults. In a democracy it is extremely important that citizens learn to evaluate that which they read. Reading critically is an instructional goal as early as the first grade. This lays the foundation for critical reading in the social studies and in literature.

Events occurring without plan in the classroom offer some opportunities for developing the ability to read critically, but planned instruction is also necessary. When children discover conflicting statements in different books, or in the same book, and call these to the teacher's attention, a natural situation exists for furthering this all-important ability. However, the questions teachers ask are again important in determining how children read. Lead children into evaluating what they read, and they are likely to continue it into adult life.

The good reader makes use of his experience background to evaluate what he reads. He distinguishes the real from the make-believe and separates fact from opinion. He does not question for the sake of questioning, but he questions in order to be accurate in the information he obtains.

Understanding Time Sequence and the Relationship of Cause and Effect

So much in comprehending the full significance of history depends upon an accurate concept of time and the cause and effect relationship between events. This competency is also important in literature. The time line is a useful technique for charting events in time. This ordering of events in terms of their occurrence aids in understanding the relationship between cause and effect.

Establishing cause and effect relationships goes beyond *who, when, what,* and *where. How* and *why* are involved. The teacher's questions will often determine whether the child considers the *how* and the *why.*[1]

Reading Maps and Globes

Children need to know what maps and globes are and how they are made. Among the many understandings they must develop are the special terms associated with maps and globes (*latitude, longitude, equator,* and the like), the purpose of the grid system, the purpose of a North and South pole, distortions caused by attempting to portray the earth's surface on the flat surface of the map, the legend, the symbols used, and the meaning of the various colors used.

An incidental approach will not get the job done adequately. Lessons should be planned to teach each of these skills, and once competency in map and globe reading is developed, the stage must be set periodically for use of this competency.

Reading and Enjoying Poetry

Children of all ages need to know how to read poetry and to enjoy it. Some classrooms have not given enough time to poetry and, hence, some children do not enjoy it. By selecting interesting and appropriate poems, the teacher can lead even the most reluctant pupil toward appreciation and enjoyment of verse. Children like poems with a strong beat of rhythm and with meanings they can easily grasp. Humorous poems may serve as a starting point for the child or the adolescent who thinks he does not like poetry. The teacher needs a file of poems handy so he can use the appropriate poem at any time.

Interpreting Figurative Language

In the intermediate grades, children encounter more and more instances of words carrying figurative rather than strictly literal meaning. Figures of speech are used both in social studies and in literature. Children often meet metaphor, simile, hyperbole, and personification. They need to recognize these for what they are, to understand their figurative meanings, and to appreciate their value in written and oral expression.

Learning to Enjoy Reading

Enjoying reading, though not a skill, is one of the most important factors in reading. Children may read well from a skills standpoint and still not read unless they are forced to do so.

We must teach reading skills in such a manner that enjoyment of reading is not sacrificed.

Parent and teacher interest in reading govern in large part the development of the child's interest and enjoyment in reading. If parents and teachers enjoy books, children are more likely to enjoy them. The teacher who dislikes reading is not likely to do much toward developing permanent reading interests in others.

In both social studies and literature, reading offers adventure, challenge, information, and enjoyment to the child. We, as teachers, are obligated to help children to get the most from their reading by helping them to develop fully all of the special competencies needed in these two important content areas.

1. Mildred A. Dawson and Henry A. Bamman, *Fundamentals of Basic Reading Instruction.* Second Edition. New York: David McKay Company, Inc., 1963, p. 271.

Developing Reading Competencies Through Mathematics and Science

Henry A. Bamman

Children and youth in all levels of American schools are being encouraged today to include in their programs of study an increasing emphasis upon science and mathematics. This emphasis has arisen partially because of the strong public interest engendered by modern nuclear discoveries and space developments and partially because of the shortage of personnel for positions in science and mathematics. We have made great strides in developing modern curricula for these two important areas; however, teachers everywhere are increasingly concerned with the lack of reading competencies of young people in both science and mathematics. Despite a strengthening of

programs for developing basic reading skills, observable in most schools of our nation, we have made little progress in training teachers to teach specific reading skills for the content areas.

There are several reasons why reading in science and mathematics is more difficult than the reading in which the child normally en-

From Henry A. Bamman, "Developing Reading Competencies Through Mathematics and Science," in *Reading As An Intellectual Activity,* ed. J. Allen Figurel. (Newark, Del.: International Reading Association, 1963), pp. 110-12. Reprinted by permission of Henry A. Bamman and the International Reading Association.

gages during the first three or four years of his school life. The materials which we use for the teaching of fundamental skills is usually narrative in nature, and the young reader becomes accustomed to description, plot, characterizations, and definite patterns of sentence and paragraph construction. Let us examine some of the reasons why reading for the content areas, such as science and mathematics, is difficult for our students.

1. Ideas are frequently more complex, and there is little control over the *number of concepts* introduced on a page or within a chapter of science or mathematics.
2. The vocabulary is specific to the content area. Very often technical terms are encountered in a specific context and those same terms may not be repeated.
3. In both science and mathematics, the reader is required to relate his previous experience and knowledge to the reading task at hand; concepts are developed on an ascending scale of difficulty.
4. Wide reading, particularly in science, is often demanded from a variety of sources—sources in which the readability may vary dramatically.
5. Inter- and intrarelationships in mathematics and science are numerous and complex. Relationships must be recognized by the reader if he is to understand what he reads.
6. The reader is required to read critically; despite the fact that science and mathematics are regarded as "exact" sciences, the reader must judge the pertinence, authenticity, and value of much of what he reads in these areas.
7. A mastery of study skills (use of graphs, tables and charts; use of reference materials; and the use of textbooks) is essential for efficient reading in these content areas.
8. Finally, a wide variety of materials of different levels of reading difficulty is difficult

to obtain for both science and mathematics, particularly in the latter area.

Determining the Difficulties

It would be both foolish and impractical to point out the difficulties of reading in content areas unless we could suggest means of improving the instruction in our classrooms. A beginning may be made by assessing the difficulties which our students have in either of the areas of science or mathematics.

Early in the school year the teacher should take inventory of the study and reading skills of the students, as well as ascertain the various students' backgrounds in the content areas. Standardized tests, informal tests and checklists, and discussions may reveal what students' reading and study habits are, what vocabulary has already been developed, and which areas of the curriculum have particular appeal. Further, the teacher should observe the reading of his students in the textbook and watch for obvious signs of difficulties in word attack skills, vocabulary, comprehension skills, and study skills.

Students who are suspected of having difficulty with basic skills should receive additional instruction during the regular reading period; it is not impractical to suggest that much of that instruction should be given through the use of science and mathematics books, rather than the regular developmental reading books. For students in junior and senior high schools, the *Be A Better Reader*[1] texts provide excellent practice materials for developing skills in reading in science and mathematics.

Developing Vocabulary

The vocabulary of science and mathematics is often much more specific, more descriptive, than vocabulary found in other content areas. However, the greatest difficulty in learning such specific terminology seems to lie in the inability of many students to apply a term to a process, a classification, or a broad concept. Many words need special attention, since they take on new and different meanings when used in science or mathematics. For instance, the words *product, rate, base, interest, root,* and *literal* are mathematics terms which have different connotations in other areas. Too often writers of textbooks introduce technical vocabulary under the assumption that the simpler phases of the subject have already been mastered by students. Teachers may make these same assumptions, and the responsibility of introducing technical terms and relating them to processes or classifications is definitely a major task for the classroom teacher.

An example of one means of developing vocabulary in science and mathematics, using knowledge of structural analysis, is derived from the Greek and Latin terms for *one.* The Greek *mono* in biology is found in *mono*cotyledon; chemistry, *mono*mer; physics, *mono*chromatic; and in mathematics, *mono*mial. The Latin equivalent, *uni* may be *uni*valve in biology; chemistry, *uni*valent; physics, *uni*ts; and in mathematics, *uni*on. The use of prefixes, suffixes, and root forms may be one of the richest sources of word knowledge in these content areas.

Reading for Comprehension

An integral part of reading for science and mathematics is the interpretation of problems, preceded by precise, methodical reading. The student must learn that almost every word is crucial to complete understanding of a problem or a process. Recognizing all the words, applying their specific meanings to the problem at hand, and sensing the relationships among the several conditions which are presented by the problem are prerequisites to actual problem-solving.

Careful questioning by the teacher may determine which students are grasping main ideas and essential details; some students are incapable of seeing relationships among the main ideas and need careful guidance in determining the main ideas and their supporting details. Students benefit from opportunities to restate main ideas in their own words and to state essential sequences of ideas. Listening and speaking become an integral part of good reading when the teacher involves the student in stating clearly and succinctly the ideas that have been encountered in reading.

Too often students are requested to work problems or perform experiments before they have carefully read them; efficient problem-solving is dependent upon deliberate, careful reading. The following suggestions will help:

1. Read the problem carefully,
2. Reread it and determine what it is about (main ideas),
3. What are the conditions (details)?
4. What, exactly, are you asked to find? Do?
5. What is the order in which the conditions of the problem should be used?
6. What processes are required?
7. What is a reasonable answer?
8. Perform the necessary steps, compare with the estimate, and reread the problem if the answer seems unreasonable.

Rate of Reading

So many of our students have been made aware of the necessity for reading rapidly. The amount of reading to be done in each day's work is increasing with each generation, and the availability of a wide variety of supplementary materials for each content area has emphasized the necessity for selecting wisely, skimming, and reading intensively. The student who reads science and mathematics must be prepared to make adjustments to the basic materials, both in terms of his speed of reading and his purpose for reading the material.

Reading in these content areas is often slow, deliberate reading. Skimming is seldom applicable as a skill, except in searching for related ideas. Directions must be read and reread, with attention directed toward the sequence of those directions and exactly what is demanded by each. Fortunately, many of the concepts of science and mathematics are both observable and demonstrable; many of the ideas are precise and easy to relate to laws and principles.

Making Assignments

Certainly the idea of making a good assignment is not unique in science and mathematics. So much of what a student learns from day to day is dependent upon *how* a teacher assigns the work to be done. As it has been stated, there is a definite scale of difficulty in the curriculum of mathematics and science. Each new concept is built on previously developed concepts. Our students frequently do not establish essential relationships; they work from day to day, with little awareness of the effect of previous learning upon today's understanding of new ideas.

A major role of the teacher is to help students relate what *is* to be learned to what *has* been learned. Assignments in textbooks and related materials should include a careful statement of relationships, a review of what has been learned, and predictions of what is to be accomplished through further reading.

Mapping out a textbook or a chapter for a student is like preparing carefully for a trip. Hours of wasted energy and backtracking may be obviated by a carefully stated assignment, in which both students and teacher are involved.

Use of Diversified Materials and Activities

Classroom teachers are certainly aware that our textbooks are not appropriate for all of the students in a class. This problem is compounded at higher levels of education, particularly in the junior and senior high schools, where the use of a single text is prevalent in science and mathematics classes, and where the range of reading abilities of the students may range all the way from third-reader level to the level of a mature adult.

Fortunately, the unit or project plan of teaching makes possible the diversity of materials, both in terms of interests and reading abilities of the students. A textbook is less essential when a broad unit is developed. However, in mathematics we are constantly confronted with the problem of a single textbook and virtually no supplementary reading materials. As a result, we must diversify the activities in terms of the abilities of the students. Oral reading of problems, discussions of problems, and numerous teaching aids are necessary if we are to involve all students in solving the problem at hand. Recent developments in materials for the teaching of mathematics have incorporated the use of multisensory approaches to learning.

Summary

Teachers and students in science and mathematics classes are involved in two vital processes: the development of knowledge of specific content, and the development of skills for lifelong acquisition of knowledge.

1. Nila Banton Smith, *Be A Better Reader,* Books I-VI. Englewood Cliffs, N. J.: Prentice-Hall, Inc., 1959.

Module Competencies

One purpose in this module is to help you develop an understanding of the skills needed by children for effective reading of content field material. A second purpose is to provide you with a means of estimating the difficulty of textbook material so that you can determine its appropriateness for specific groups of children. The third purpose is to help you plan for content field teaching in ways that provide for individual differences in reading ability. These purposes are reflected in the module competencis which specify the skills and understandings you will need as you work with children in helping them meet the demands of content field reading.

Instructional Activities

In activity 2 the areas in which instruction must be provided for reading in content fields are identified (competencies 1 and 2). You are encouraged in this activity to analyze specific textbook material in order to identify the instruction children would need to be able to read it effectively. Estimating the difficulty level of content field material through the use of a readability formula and the cloze test procedure is the focus in activity 3 (competency 3). A procedure for teaching content field reading is presented and illustrated in activity 4 (competency 3). In activity 5 you are encouraged to teach a lesson using the procedure identified in activity 4, (competency 3). Adjusting the use of material for children reading at different levels is the focus in activity 6 (competency 3). The classroom observations suggested in activity 7 can provide you with information concerning the ways in which teachers help children learn to read content field material (competency 3). Examples of activities and materials designed to help children learn and apply study skills are provided in activity 8 (competency 2). It is suggested in this activity that you plan and teach a sequence of lessons involving study skills (competency 4). Through the classroom observations suggested in activity 9 you can gain a variety of techniques for teaching the study skills (competency 4). In activity 10 you are encouraged to design activities of your own which you feel will enable you to develop competence in teaching content field reading.

Competencies

1. Identify skills in the categories of vocabulary, organization, and comprehension that are necessary for effective reading in the content fields.
2. Identify study skills that are necessary for effective reading in the content fields.

3. Develop plans for teaching lessons in content field reading that provide for individual differences in reading ability.
4. Develop plans for teaching study skills.

Instructional Activities

Select from the following learning experiences those which you feel will enable you to achieve the competencies stated for this module:

Activity 1

Attend a seminar for orientation to this module.

Activity 2

Textbooks and teaching materials reflect differences in the identification and classification of skills associated with reading in the content fields. Regardless of the way in which the skills are presented, there is general agreement that direct instruction must be provided in the following areas in each of the content fields in order to enable children to meet the demands of content reading:

1. *Vocabulary*: instruction in (1) the vocabulary that is unique to each field, and (2) the vocabulary with specialized meanings, i.e., words whose meanings are different when they are used in specific fields (*charge* in science; *belt* in social studies).
2. *Organization*: instruction in recognizing the different patterns of organization found in content material (the organization of a short story in contrast to the organization of mathematics material).
3. *Comprehension*: instruction in reading for those comprehension outcomes that are essential to understanding the material in different fields (e.g., determining cause and effect relationships in social studies; interpreting figurative language in literature).
4. *Study Skills*: instruction in (1) locating, evaluating, organizing, and presenting information, and (2) interpreting maps, globes, graphs, charts, tables, diagrams, symbols, and pictures.

The first step in planning for reading instruction in the content fields is analysis of the material to be read in order to identify the specific demands it presents. Select one textbook in each of two content fields, and in each text choose a section for analysis. Respond to the following questions in your analysis of the material from each textbook:

1. What specialized vocabulary is included in the material?
2. How is the material organized? What aspects of the material are helpful in understanding the organization (e.g., headings, sub-headings)?
3. What are the major comprehension outcomes for which the material should be read?
4. What maps, graphic, or tabular material will need to be interpreted?

You may find it useful to summarize the results of your analyses using table 8.1.

Activity 3

For effective content reading it is essential that children be given material that is at their independent or instructional reading level. Selecting material that is appropriate involves determining the *readability* of the material being considered. Carrillo defines readability as "the relation of the level of the printed material to the reading ability of the students."[5] The readability of material is affected by legibility, vocabulary, sentence structure, and clarity of presentation.

A major problem encountered by teachers in the use of textbooks in content fields is that textbooks are frequently written at grade levels that are higher than the grade levels designated for their use by publishers. For this reason, it is necessary that teachers assess the readability of textbooks and determine their appropriateness for use with specific children.

Concern for determining the difficulty of printed material has resulted in the development of several readability formulas. The following formulas are frequently used: Edgar Dale and Jeanne Chall,[6] Rudolph Flesch,[7] Irving Lorge,[8] and George Spache.[9] A readability formula that can be easily and quickly applied has been developed by Edward Fry.[10] The directions for applying Fry's formula and the graph that is used for estimating readability are shown in figure 8.1.

5. Lawrence W. Carrillo, *Teaching Reading: A Handbook* (New York: St. Martin's Press, 1976), p. 107.
6. Edgar Dale and Jeanne S. Chall, "A Formula for Predicting Readability," *Educational Research Bulletin* 27 (January 1948):11-20.
7. Rudolph F. Flesch, *Marks of Readable Style: A Study of Adult Education* (New York: Teachers College Press, Columbia University, 1943).
8. Irving Lorge, "Predicting Readability," *Teachers College Record* 45 (March 1944):404-19.
9. George Spache, "A New Readability Formula for Primary-Grade Reading Materials," *Elementary School Journal* 53 (March 1953): 410-13.
10. Edward Fry, "A Readability Formula That Saves Time," *Journal of Reading* 11 (April 1968):577.

Table 8.1
Analysis of Content Field Textbooks

Textbook Analyzed	Vocabulary	Organization	Comprehension Outcomes	Maps, Graphic or Tabular Material
Name of text				
Publisher				
Pages Analyzed				
Grade Level				
Content Field				
Name of Text				
Publisher				
Pages Analyzed				
Grade Level				
Content Field				

FIGURE 8.1.

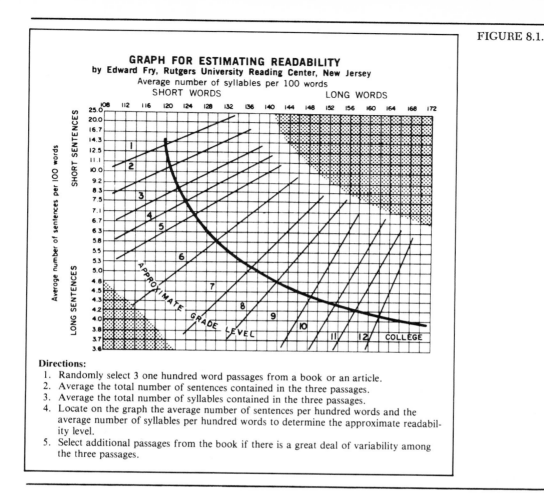

GRAPH FOR ESTIMATING READABILITY
by Edward Fry, Rutgers University Reading Center, New Jersey
Average number of syllables per 100 words

Directions:

1. Randomly select 3 one hundred word passages from a book or an article.
2. Average the total number of sentences contained in the three passages.
3. Average the total number of syllables contained in the three passages.
4. Locate on the graph the average number of sentences per hundred words and the average number of syllables per hundred words to determine the approximate readability level.
5. Select additional passages from the book if there is a great deal of variability among the three passages.

An additional approach to determining readability is the use of the *cloze* procedure. The cloze procedure involves the reader in filling in words deleted from a passage, through the use of context. The extent to which the reader can accurately supply the missing words is an indication of how well he has comprehended the material.[11] The steps involved in constructing, administering, and scoring a cloze test are as follows:

1. Select a passage from the textbook you want to evaluate. The passage should contain at least 250 words.
2. Mark every fifth word in the passage for deletion.

11. Miles V. Zintz, *The Reading Process: The Teacher and the Learner*, 2d ed. (Dubuque, Iowa: Wm. C. Brown Company Publishers, 1975), pp. 292-93.

Reading in the Content Fields

3. Type the material substituting a blank (underline) for each of the marked words. The inserted underlines should be of the same length.
4. Administer the test by asking the children to read the material and to fill in the blanks with the words they think were deleted.
5. Determine for each child the percentage of correct answers. Only the exact words from the original material are counted as correct.

In interpreting the results of cloze tests, Zintz suggests using the following criteria for determining reading levels.[12]

Score	Level
40% or below correct	Frustration
40%-50% correct	Instructional
above 50% correct	Independent

Figure 8.2 presents an example of a cloze test, with instructions for completing it.

Select two content field textbooks currently being used by the children with whom you are working. Analyze the appropriateness of the material in each book by completing the following activities:

1. Apply the readability formula developed by Fry (fig. 8.1) to one of the textbooks.
    a. Does the readability level which results from your application of the formula differ from the level designated by the publisher?
    b. Compare the readability level with the instructional reading levels of the children in the class. For how many of the children is the textbook material suitable?
2. Construct and administer a cloze test based on the second textbook you selected. For how many of the children is the material at the instructional reading level?

Activity 4

The overall framework for teaching reading in content fields includes essentially the same elements as those found in the Directed Reading Lesson. The following outline provides a review of this procedure with special attention to areas of particular concern in content field reading.

Procedure for Teaching Content Field Reading
1. Developing Readiness for Reading
    a. Building background necessary for understanding the material.
    b. Introducing new vocabulary and concepts.

12. Ibid., p. 294.

Instructions

At the bottom of this page is a sample of a new kind of test. Each of these tests is made by copying a few paragraphs from a book. Every fifth word was left out of the paragraphs, and blank spaces were put where the words were taken out.

Your job will be to guess what word was left out of each space and to write that word in that space.

It will help you in taking the test if you remember these things:

1. Write only one word in each blank.
2. Try to fill every blank. Don't be afraid to guess.
3. You may skip hard blanks and come back to them when you have finished.
4. Wrong spelling will not count against you if we can tell what word you meant.
5. Most of the blanks can be answered with ordinary words but a few will be

numbers like .... 3,427 or $12 or 1954
contractions like .... can't or weren't
abbreviations like .... Mrs. or U.S.A.
parts of hyphenated words like .... self- in the word self-made

FIGURE 8.2.
Cloze test. From John R. Bormuth, "Literacy in the Classroom," in *Help for the Reading Teacher: New Directions in Research*, edited by William D. Page (Urbana, Ill.: ERIC Clearinghouse on Reading and Communication Skills and the National Conference on Research in English, 1975), p. 70. Reprinted with permission of the author.

Sample Test

Below is a sample of one of these tests. Fill each blank with the word you think was taken out. You may check your paper when you finish it by looking at the answers which are written upside down at the bottom of the page. Write neatly.

The Beaver

Indians call beavers the "little men of the woods." But they _____ really so very little. _____ beavers grow to be _____ or four feet long _____ weigh from 30 to _____ pounds. These "little men _____ the woods" are busy _____ of the time. That _____ why we sometimes say, "_____ busy as a beaver." _____ know how to build _____ that can hold water. use their two front _____ to do some of _____ work. Cutting down a _____ with their four sharp-_____ teeth is easy. A _____ can cut down a _____ four inches thick in _____ 15 minutes.

Answers: 1. aren't 2. Most 3. three 4. and 5. Most 6. of 7. most 8. is 9. as 10. Beavers 11. dams 12. They 13. paws 14. their 15. tree 16. pointed 17. beaver 18. tree 19. about

c. Identifying those aspects of the material that indicate the way in which it is organized (e.g., headings, subheadings, boldface type, summaries; use of maps, graphs, charts).

2. Setting Purposes for Reading.
   a. Purposes set by the teacher.
   b. Purposes set by the children.
3. Silent Reading of the Material.
4. Discussing the Material Read.
   a. Discussion of purposes for reading.
   b. Discussion of additional concepts and generalizations; interpretation of maps or graphic and tabular materials.
5. Rereading the Material.
   a. Oral rereading for specific purposes, if appropriate.
   b. Silent rereading for specific purposes, if appropriate.
6. Applying the Information Gained.
   a. Reorganizing, summarizing, or synthesizing the information for a specific purpose.
   b. Presenting the information in the form of a map, chart, graph, table, model, diorama, etc.

The following lesson plan illustrates the application of this procedure in a social studies lesson. The material on which the lesson is based follows the plan. Read both the lesson plan and the material, using these questions as a guide:

1. Can you identify the steps outlined in the Procedure for Teaching Content Field Reading?
2. The Barrett taxonomy was used in developing the questions given as purposes for reading and rereading, and in developing the additional discussion questions. Which categories of the taxonomy are reflected in these questions?
3. How do the questions that are asked about the maps and the graph help the children use the information presented in them?
4. In what other ways could the information gained in this lesson be applied?

Lesson Plan
Reading a Social Studies Textbook

Grade Level: Sixth

I. Objectives
   A. The students will be able to explain the influence Japan's environment has on its people.

B. The students will be able to tell how the Japanese have adapted to their environment.

C. The students will be able to read and interpret the maps and the graph included in the material.

D. The students will be able to infer the effects that living on an island have had on the Japanese.

II. Procedure

A. Introduction

If there was a volcano in the school yard, and it could erupt at any time, how would that change our lives? If mountains covered most of the land in Philadelphia, how would it make a difference in the way we live? If we lived on an island would it make any difference in what we ate or where we could go? The people in Japan face all three of these conditions every day. Today we will read about how the Japanese have adapted to their land.

B. Development

1. There will be some words unfamiliar to you in this section. Look at each of the following sentences on the board and see if you can tell the meaning of the underlined words using the rest of the sentence as a clue.

   a) The tidal wave washed most of the seacoast village into the sea.

   b) The high winds of the typhoon destroyed the entire city.

   c) By double cropping his land, a farmer can plant two different crops, in the same season, one after the other.

2. What aids are given in figure 8.3 to help you gather information on Japan's environment? What information does the map on page 293 give? How does the information given in the two maps on page 294 differ? How do you know what information you can find on the graph? What kind of information can you find in the map on page 295?

3. How many sections are there to read on these pages? Where does the second section begin? What does the heading "Abundance" tell you about what you can expect to read in this section? When you read that section, what information will you be looking for?

4. Knowing what information you are looking for will help you read these pages. These purposes for reading are on the board:

   a) What are some of the environmental factors in Japan that would influence the lives of the people living there?

b) What are some of the resources that the Japanese have used to their great advantage?

Now let's add the question you have raised:

c) What do the Japanese have an abundance of?

5. After the students have read the pages, discuss the purposes for reading. Have the students also discuss the relationship between the answers for "b" and "c".

6. After discussing the purposes for reading, discuss the following questions:

a) What effect do you think living on an island has had on the Japanese?

b) The Japanese do an intensive amount of farming. What are the advantages and disadvantages of this great amount of farming?

c) Using the map on page 293, name the continents that surround Japan. How does the size of Japan compare with the size of the United States?

d) Look at the population density map on page 294. Have the students answer the questions under the map. Why do you think the most densely populated areas are located around these cities?

e) Look at the ocean current map on page 294. Answer the questions under the map. How does the Japan Current help the farming in Japan?

f) Answer the questions located beside the map on page 295.

g) Using the graph on page 294, answer the questions under the graph.

7. When we think of people in other countries, many times we think they eat food that is very different from our own food. Skim pages 294 and 295 and see how many foods you can find that the Japanese people eat. After skimming, discuss the types of foods they found. Which of these food are also foods that we eat? Are there any foods that the Japanese eat that we don't eat? Why do you think they eat seaweed?

C. Conclusion

What other sources could we use to see how the environment influences life in Japan? Where could we find these sources? Why would we want to use more than one source? If we find information that conflicts with other information we have found, what can we do to find the correct information?

During the following days, the students will read about Japan's environment from additional sources found in the room and in the library. At the end of the week the students will discuss and compare their findings in order to identify any conflicting information.

III. Evaluation
  A. If the students are able to answer the questions posed as purposes for reading, they have fulfilled objectives 1 and 2.
  B. If the students are able to answer correctly the questions requiring reading of the maps and the graph, they have fulfilled objective 3.
  C. If the students are able to answer question 6(a), then they have fulfilled objective 4.

Activity 5

Using the procedure outlined in activity 4, plan a lesson involving reading in one of the content fields. If you are going to teach the lesson to children be certain that the material you select is at their instructional reading level.

You may find it helpful to refer to the following questions as you plan your lesson.

1. What background should be developed?
2. What concepts and vocabulary should be introduced?
3. How is the material organized? What aspects of the organization should be discussed before the material is read?
4. Which comprehension outcomes of the Barrett taxonomy are appropriate as purposes for reading?
5. How can the children be helped to set additional purposes of their own for reading the material?
6. Which comprehension outcomes of the Barrett taxonomy are appropriate for further discussion?
7. Are there maps and/or graphic and tabular materials that will need to be interpreted?
8. Will oral or silent rereading be appropriate? What will be the purposes for rereading?
9. In what ways will the information gained from reading the material be applied?

Activity 6

Since the children in any classroom will be reading at a range of levels, the teacher's planning for the content fields must include adjusting instruction so that each child can participate at his own instructional read-

FIGURE 8.3.
"Japan—The Island
Chain" from *Culture in
Transition* (*World of
Mankind Series*) by
Hane, Hantula, Mysli-
wiec, and Yohe. Copy-
right © 1973 by Follett
Publishing Company.
Used by permission of
the publisher.

Japan—The Island Chain

Stormy seas isolate Japan. Volcanos, earthquakes, tidal waves, and typhoons batter the land. Mountains crowd the small islands, leaving only one-fifth of the land for homes and farms. And the world's sixth largest population squeezes into this fraction of the country.

You might expect a rugged environment like this to provide only poverty and disaster for its people. But the Japanese have created a prosperous life from their surroundings. It is hard to judge which has the stronger influence in Japan, the people or the natural environment.

From early times the environment has shaped the Japanese way of life. Nature is often cruel in Japan, but it is also very beautiful. The power of nature has always stirred feelings of love and respect in the Japanese. Japan is an island nation, separated from its neighbors. Until recently, this isolation allowed Japan to choose when to open its doors and when to close them to outsiders. Japan was often left alone for long periods to develop under the influence of its own environment.

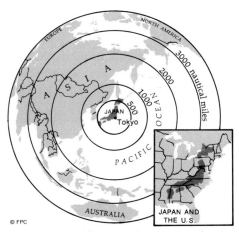

How do the United States and Japan compare in the extent of their land areas?

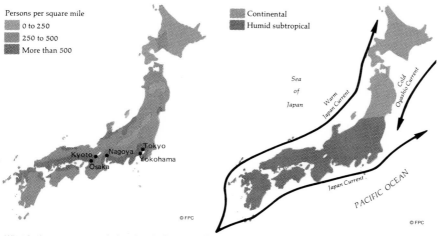

Persons per square mile
- 0 to 250
- 250 to 500
- More than 500

Continental
Humid subtropical

Sea of Japan

Warm Japan Current

Cold Oyashio Current

Japan Current

PACIFIC OCEAN

© FPC

© FPC

What is the average population density for most of Japan? What cities are located in the most densely populated regions?

The Japan Current is a warm ocean current. The Oyashio Current is a cold ocean current. How do these currents affect the Japanese people?

Abundance

The Japanese have prospered by making excellent use of their most important resource—water. Most farmland in the United States receives between 20 and 40 inches of precipitation yearly. But in Japan many areas get more than twice that much yearly rainfall. All this moisture, plus a warm ocean current, gives Japan a long, mild growing season. The ideal crop for this kind of climate is rice. Japan's rice crop is so large that a surplus is produced each year.

The long growing season also makes double cropping possible. In this process farmers put their land to more than one use. A farmer may plant a fast-growing rice in May. After he harvests it in August, he uses the same land to plant vegetables or sugar beets. Meanwhile, on another part of his farm, a slow-growing rice is ripening. When this rice is harvested in late October, it is replaced by wheat. And even before this wheat is harvested in May, it is tied into bundles to let the sun reach to-

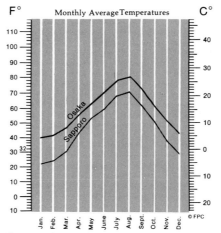

Monthly Average Temperatures

F°   C°

Osaka
Sapporo

Jan. Feb. Mar. Apr. May June July Aug. Sept. Oct. Nov. Dec.

© FPC

Compare the monthly average temperatures for Osaka and Sapporo. How would you account for the temperature differences between these two Japanese cities?

matoes or melons planted beneath! As a result of this kind of intensive farming, Japan produces more per acre of farmed land than any other nation in the world.

FIGURE 8.3.
Continued.

295

Sapporo •Kushiro
Hokkaido
•Hakodate
Tsugaru Strait
Sea
of
Japan
Akita •
Niigata• •Sendai
Kanazawa•
h
H o n s u
Lake
Biwa
Kyoto Tokyo
Yokohama
Korea Strait Kobe• Mt. Fuji
Kitakyushu• Hiroshima Osaka• Nara• (12,398)
Inland Sea •Nagoya
Kochi
Nagasaki• Shikoku PACIFIC
Kyushu OCEAN
© FPC

Miles
0 100 200 300 400
0 200 400 600
Kilometers

What are the names of the four main islands of Japan? Which of these is the largest? Find the least densely populated region of Honshu on the population density map. Use the map on this page to tell why fewer people live there. How do the Japanese people use this region?

In the mountains heavy rainfall creates many lakes and streams. The streams are mostly short, swift, and shallow. They are an excellent source of electric power. The rains also encourage the growth of lush forests. Besides providing wood and paper products, the forests provide recreation. The Japanese enjoy hiking and camping in these scenic areas. In northern Japan, where the precipitation comes in the form of snow, ski resorts draw tourists from all over the world.

Finally, the ocean waters around Japan are a major resource. Fish make up a large part of the Japanese diet. The yearly catch is large enough to supply the whole nation, with a surplus left for export. The shallow coastal waters provide seaweed, which the Japanese eat as a vegetable, and oysters, which are raised for the pearls they produce.

What are some advantages and disadvantages of having no borders with other countries? What countries do you think first had contact with Japan?

What are some problems that intensive farming might cause? What part would you expect fertilizers to play in Japanese agriculture? Why?

How does the natural environment in Japan differ from the area in which you live? If you were Japanese, what feelings do you think you would have about the mountains? The sea? Do you feel that in Japan the environment has a greater effect on the people than the people have on the environment? Explain.

ing level. Providing children with a variety of materials, at different levels, in which they can find information relating to the same topic is the most effective means of insuring successful participation by all the children. This range of materials can include textbooks, reference books, newspapers, trade books, pictures, graphic and tabular materials, and audiovisual materials.

While every effort should be made to provide material at a range of levels in content reading, occasionally the teacher may decide that a portion of one textbook should be read by all the children. This decision may be made owing to the unavailability of additional material, or because the textbook provides the most relevant or accurate information concerning a specific topic or subtopic. In either case, adjustments will have to be made so that the material can be used effectively by children reading at different levels. This can be accomplished by differentiating the purposes for reading according to levels of reading ability. For example, those children for whom the material will be relatively difficult can read for such literal comprehension outcomes as recognition of details or of a sequence; children for whom the material will present few difficulties can read to infer cause and effect relationships; and children who will be able to read the material easily can read for the purpose of judging adequacy or validity. If the purposes are differentiated according to reading ability in this way, each child will be able to experience success in achieving his specific purposes for reading.

The following is an example of the way in which one teacher differentiated the purposes for teaching a section of a science text (fig. 8.4) according to the reading levels of the children in her class.

Purposes for Reading "How Are Beavers Dependent on One Another?"

Group A: Literal Comprehension
How do beavers warn each other that danger is near?
What are beaver homes called?
Where do beavers store food for the winter?
What food do they store for the winter?
For how long do young beavers stay with their parents?
How do beavers help each other?

Group B: Inferential Comprehension
Of what kinds of danger might beavers warn each other?
What do you think the beavers do when they are warned of danger?
Why do you think only one family lives in each beaver lodge?
Why do you think the young beavers leave their parents after two years?
What is the main idea of this selection?

FIGURE 8.4.
From Herbert A. Smith,
Milo K. Blecha, and
Herbert Pless, Teachers'
Edition, *Modern
Science*, Level Five
(River Forest, Ill.: Laid-
law Brothers, 1974), pp.
77-78. Reprinted by
permission of *Laidlaw
Brothers*, A Division of
Doubleday & Company,
Inc.

3. How Are Beavers Dependent on One Another?

The engineers. If you have ever seen a beaver colony, you would say that beavers are the engineers of the animal world. They build dams which are very strong. Look at the beaver colony in the picture. Observe the dam which the beavers built. Where do you think they got the wood to build the dam? The building of such a dam would take many beavers working together several years.

Notice that the beavers' home is nearly in the middle of the stream. If there is only a small stream to begin with, the beavers must build

a dam so that the water will back up. The water will then surround each of the homes. How do you think this would help to protect them from their enemies?

Beavers are expert woodsmen. They use their razor-sharp teeth and strong jaws in cutting down trees. The beavers gnaw the branches and the main trunk of a fallen tree into desired lengths. Then they float or drag these branches to the place where they are building. The branches are woven together. This makes the dam or house stronger. After the branches are in place, the cracks between branches are filled with stones and mud.

Observe the tail of the beaver in the picture. It may remind you of the end of a canoe paddle. When danger is near, the beavers warn others by slapping their tails on the water. Their tails are also used as rudders when they swim. On land beavers sometimes use their tails to help balance themselves.

The lodges. Beaver homes are called *lodges*. Usually only one family lives in each lodge. However, there may be many lodges in a community. In the picture you see that the floor of the lodge is several inches above the water level. Are both of the entrances to the lodge below the water level? Why do you think they are this way?

Near the entrances into the lodge, the beavers store large amounts of food for the winter. The stored food is usually the twigs and bark from willow, birch, and poplar trees.

Think for Yourself

Why do you think beavers have two entrances to their lodges?

Family units. Beavers remain with the same mates throughout their lives. A pair of beavers has from two to six baby beavers, called kittens, each year. The young kittens remain with their parents for two years. Then they leave. Each chooses a mate of its own. Each pair then begins building a lodge.

Probably beavers are not as dependent upon other beavers as much as honeybees are dependent upon other honeybees. However, beavers work together to build dams and lodges. Their family units are examples of social animals working together.

Group C: Evaluation

The author states that beavers probably do not depend upon one another as much as honeybees depend upon each other. Compare the information in this selection with the information on honeybees in the selection you have already read. Do you agree with the author's statement about beavers and honeybees? Why? Why not?

Compare the information in this selection with information from the other sources you have used to learn about beavers. Do you find any disagreements in the information presented? If you do, how can you find out which information is correct?

Select a content field textbook that is being used by the children with whom you are working. Plan a lesson that involves using a section of the textbook with a group of children whose reading abilities reflect two or more levels. Include in your plan a set of purposes for reading that is appropriate for the range of levels you have identified. After you have taught the lesson, evaluate its effectiveness in terms of each child's achievement of his specific purposes for reading.

Activity 7

Observe one or more lessons involving reading in the content fields. Use the following questions as a guide for your observations:

1. Is the material being used at the instructional reading level of all the children participating in the lesson?
2. If the children's reading abilities reflect two or more levels, are adjustments being made which make it possible for each child to participate at his own reading level?
3. Does the lesson follow the procedure for teaching reading in content fields that is outlined in activity 4?

Activity 8

In order to read and interpret content field material effectively, children need to develop a set of skills usually referred to as *study skills*. In their introductory articles, Aaron and Bamman have given examples of these essential skills, and stressed the importance of providing instruction in their development. The following outline identifies and classifies the study skills considered essential for content field reading.

Outline of Study Skills

1. Locating Information
   a. Using libraries effectively.
   b. Knowing which references to use for specific purposes.
   c. Locating information in references using key words, indexes, and cross references.
   d. Locating information in textbooks using the table of contents, index, glossary, and appendix.
   e. Locating information in magazines and newspapers.
2. Evaluating Information
   a. Judging the relevancy of material.
   b. Differentiating between important and unimportant facts.
   c. Distinguishing fact from opinion.
   d. Judging the relative accuracy of conflicting statements.
   e. Determining whether conclusions or generalizations are warranted.
3. Organizing Information
   a. Taking notes.
   b. Classifying information using charts or tables.
   c. Summarizing information from one or more sources.
   d. Outlining material of increasing length and complexity.
4. Presenting Information
   a. Preparing written reports.
   b. Preparing oral reports.

    c. Preparing maps, graphs, charts, or tables for use in presenting information.

5. Interpreting Maps and Globes
    a. Using key and map symbols.
    b. Understanding scales, directions, and use of color distinctions.
    c. Understanding the kinds of information provided by maps (political, economic, scientific).
    d. Constructing maps.

6. Interpreting Symbolic Language and Graphic and Tabular Material
    a. Understanding the symbols used in different content fields.
    b. Interpreting and constructing different types of graphs.
    c. Interpreting and constructing charts and diagrams.
    d. Interpreting and constructing tables.

In order to make their work in the development of the study skills meaningful to children, it is important that instruction in these skills be related to the work being carried on in each of the content fields. When the study skills are taught as children find that they need them to complete specific projects and activities, the usefulness of these skills becomes apparent to them. Once the skills have been introduced in this context, practice activities can be provided for individuals and groups who demonstrate a need for additional work with one or more of the skills.

Activities and exercises for the development of the study skills can be found in three types of material: (1) basal reading material, (2) content field textbooks, and (3) workbooks that are designed specifically to provide for the development of content reading skills. It is as essential for the study skills as it is for skills in other areas of the reading program that instruction provide for sequential development. For this reason, it is important that the teacher select activities and materials that are appropriate in terms of the level of skill development of the children who will use them. This is particularly necessary when the children are going to complete the activities independently. The exercises shown in figures 8.5, 8.6, 8.7, and 8.8 are examples of the kinds of activities that provide for the development of study skills. As you read each exercise, try to determine whether it is designed to (1) introduce the skill, or (2) provide for the further development of the skill after it has been introduced.

The following workbooks and kits are sources of activities for the sequential development of study skills:

Graph and Picture Study Skills Kit. Chicago: Science Research Associates, Inc.
Herber, Harold L. *Go: Reading in the Content Areas.* New York: Scholastic Book Services, 1974.
Learning to Use the Library. Columbus, Ohio: Xerox Education Publications.
Map and Globe Skills Kit. Chicago: Science Research Associates, Inc.

FIGURE 8.5.
Introducing the
Encyclopedia. From
Sandra M. Brown, *Using
References,* D in the
MCP Skillbooster Series
(Cleveland, Ohio:
Modern Curriculum
Press, 1975), p. 8.
Reprinted by permission
of the publisher.

A CIRCLE OF LEARNING

An **encyclopedia** is one of the most important references that you can use.

Read the article below. Then read and follow the directions that come after the article.

The English word *encyclopedia* is made up of three Greek words. These words are *en,* meaning "in," *kyklos,* meaning "circle," and *paideia,* meaning "education." *Encyclopedia* first meant a general, well-rounded education. Now it usually means a set of reference books that contain information about many different subjects. This kind of encyclopedia is called a general encyclopedia.

A good general encyclopedia gives accurate, up-to-date information about places, persons, events, and things. It gives this information in easy-to-understand language. Its subjects are arranged in a way that makes them easy to find. Usually the subjects are arranged in alphabetical order, from *A* to *Z*.

An encyclopedia contains knowledge about almost every subject. Because of this, an encyclopedia usually has several volumes, or separate books. The subjects in each volume are arranged according to a part of the alphabet. For example, all the articles about subjects that begin with the letters *J* and *K* may be in one book.

Below are six unfinished sentences. These sentences have blank spaces in them. Finish the sentences by writing the correct words in the blanks. Base your answers on what you read in the article.

1. The word *encyclopedia* first meant a well-rounded _____.

2. A general encyclopedia contains information about many different _____.

3. A good encyclopedia gives accurate information about _____, _____, _____, and _____.

4. The subjects are usually arranged in _____ order.

5. An encyclopedia usually has several _____.

6. The subjects in each volume of an encyclopedia are arranged according to a _____ of the alphabet.

8 — INTRODUCING THE ENCYCLOPEDIA

Map Skills for Today. Columbus, Ohio: Xerox Education Publications.
Organizing and Reporting Skills Kit. Chicago: Science Research Associates.
Smith, Nila Banton. *Be a Better Reader: Foundations.* Englewood Cliffs, N. J.: Prentice-Hall, 1968.
Study Skills for Information Retrieval Series. Boston: Allyn & Bacon, 1970.
Study Skills Library. New York: Educational Developmental Laboratories.
Table and Graph Skills. Columbus, Ohio: Xerox Education Publications.
Thirty Lessons in Outlining. Newton, Mass.: Curriculum Associates.

WHICH ONE SHOULD I USE

What reference you use depends on what kind of information you need. You may want to look back at pages 6 through 12 before working this exercise.

FIGURE 8.6. Using the Proper Reference. From Sandra M. Brown, *Using References,* D in the *MCP Skillbooster Series* (Cleveland, Ohio: Modern Curriculum Press, 1975), p. 13. Reprinted by permission of the publisher.

Look carefully at each topic in the list below. Will you find the topic in **a. an atlas, b. an encyclopedia, c. an almanac, d. a dictionary,** or **e. a textbook**? Decide which reference you would use to find each topic. Write the letter of the reference (**a, b, c, d,** or **e**) on the line next to the numeral.

_____ 1. the respelling of the word *avocado*

_____ 2. winner of last year's baseball World Series

_____ 3. nuclear energy

_____ 4. location of the city of Minneapolis on a map

_____ 5. the heading of a chapter on proper diet

_____ 6. the parts of speech of the word *sign*

_____ 7. the living habits of a robin

_____ 8. the magazine that sells, or circulates, the most copies in the United States

_____ 9. map showing the provinces on the boundaries of Ontario

_____ 10. a special word in a glossary

_____ 11. the meaning or meanings of the word *delight*

_____ 12. an article on the subject of medicine

USING THE PROPER REFERENCE — 13

Activities and materials developed by the teacher can also be used to help children develop and apply study skills in a variety of contexts. The following are examples of activities that teachers find effective:

Locating Information

Prepare a worksheet asking questions that can be answered by referring to the table of contents of a given book. For example, here are some

FIGURE 8.7.
Making a Living in
Mexico. Pages 112-14
from *Be a Better Reader
Foundations B* by Nila
Banton Smith © 1968 by
Prentice-Hall, Inc., En-
glewood Cliffs, N. J.
Reprinted by permission.

MAKING A LIVING IN MEXICO

Pancho lived on a high plateau where there was little rain. His people had to make a living by making pottery, weaving straw hats and baskets, and raising turkeys. People living in other parts of Mexico make their living in other ways. These three maps and the article on page 114 will give you much information about Mexico. They will tell you other ways in which the Mexicans earn their living. The maps will also tell you why people do different kinds of work in different parts of Mexico.

Chiefly Plains Chiefly Plateaus Chiefly Hills Chiefly Mountains

MAP 1

TROPIC OF CANCER

Yearly Rainfall in Inches
Under 10   10 to 20   20 to 40   40 to 80   Over 80

MAP 2

TROPIC OF CANCER

C — Copper   S — Silver
G — Gold   CO — Coal
L — Lead   PE — Petroleum

MAP 3

Reading Causes and Effects from Maps

The ways in which people make their living usually depend upon the country itself. Kinds of work done vary with climate, rainfall, and the different types of land. Kinds of work also depend upon forests, mineral resources, available water, and many other things. Most of these things are shown on maps. If you know how to read different kinds of maps, you can learn much information from them. It is just as important for you to know how to read maps as it is for you to know how to read books.

From reading the maps, you will now have a chance to gather much information about how Mexican people earn a living.

Above you will see three maps of Mexico. Map Number 1 is a physical map showing mountains, plateaus, and plains. Map No. 2 shows where there is light rainfall, medium rainfall, and heavy rainfall. Map No. 3 shows where there are natural resources of gold, silver, lead, copper, coal, and oil. Study these maps as you answer the questions which follow.

112   BE A BETTER READER

1. Look at Map No. 1. Does the high central plateau make up the largest part of

Mexico? _____

2. Next look at this plateau in Map No. 2, the rainfall map. (a) Is the rainfall light or heavy in the entire northern part of this

plateau? _____ (b) Do you expect many people in this section to be farmers?

_____

3. Look at Map No. 3. (a) Is there any gold, silver, copper, lead, or coal in this

plateau? _____ (b) What kind of work would you expect people who live on

the plateau to do for a living? _____

4. Look at the rainfall map again. (a) Does more rain fall in the southern part of

the plateau? _____ (b) Would you expect that plants would grow well there?

_____ (c) Do you think many people might be engaged in farming there?

_____

5. Now in Map No. 1, look at the range of mountains that border on the plateau in the west. (a) According to the rainfall map are these mountains in the northern

part mostly in a dry area? _____
(b) Look at Map No. 3. Might mining be

done in these mountains? _____

6. Note the small plains along the western coast that receive rainfall. (a) Would you think any crops might be grown there?

_____ (b) Since this is a warm country like our southern states, what do you think the most important crop in this

part might be? _____

7. Now find the eastern mountains and coastal plain on Map No. 1. (a) Look at Map No. 2. Do the eastern side of these mountains and the coastal plain receive more rain than the northwest coast?

_____ (b) Do you think trees could be grown on the lower slopes of these moun-

tains? _____ (c) If so, have you any

idea what kind they might be? _____

8. (a) Would you suspect that grass for grazing might grow on the lower slopes of

these mountains? _____ (b) If so, how might some people make their living

in this area? _____

9. Look at Map No. 3. (a) Is there a clue that tells you another way people on

the east coast make a living? _____

(b) How do they make a living? _____

_____

10. Look at the plains in the south as shown in Map No. 1. (a) Referring to Map No. 2, do these plains receive a good

rainfall? _____ (b) Would you

FOUNDATIONS B   113

FIGURE 8.7.
Continued.

expect the climate to be cold or tropical?

_____ (c) Would this be a good or a

poor place for growing crops? _____

(d) How would most people in this section

make their living? _____

_____

_____

_____

11. From working with the maps, you know that the eastern and southern plains of Mexico are in a moist, hot section with a year-long tropical climate. (a) Do you think there would be many plantations

here? _____ If so, what kind?

_____

_____

_____

questions which can be answered from the table of contents in *All About Great Medical Discoveries,* by David Diety (Random House, 1960).

1. How many chapters are there in *All About Great Medical Discoveries?*
2. If you wanted to read why doctors wash their hands often, you would turn to page_____ .
3. A chapter about vitamins begins on page_____ .
4. The name of one chapter mentions two kinds of animals. It begins on page_____ .
5. Page 26 is the first page in a chapter called_____ .
6. Page 111 is in a chapter called_____ .
7. The chapter about polio begins on page_____ .
8. "The Murderous Germs" is a chapter with_____ pages.[13]

Give the student a book with an index, or a worksheet that reproduces a portion of a book's index. For example:

Airplanes
    Advantages of air travel   112-114
    Construction of   110
    Definition   103
    Disadvantages of air travel   115
    Early experiments with   104
    How brought to earth   110-112
    How controlled in the air   108

13. David H. Russell and Etta E. Karp, *Reading Aids Through the Grades.* Second Revised Edition by Anne Marie Mueser (New York: Teachers College Press, Columbia University, 1975), p. 249.

FIGURE 8.8.

Reading Graphs. Pages 138-39 from *Be a Better Reader Foundations B* by Nila Banton Smith © 1968 by Prentice-Hall, Inc., Englewood Cliffs, N. J. Reprinted by permission.

READING GRAPHS

Everyone should know how to read and understand a graph. Graphs are found everywhere—in newspapers, magazines, and history, geography, social studies, and science books.

A graph shows at a glance how certain numbers are related. A graph is a *picture* which describes number relations. Graphs often tell a story better than a table of numbers.

There are many kinds of graphs. We shall examine three kinds that are widely used.

1. Every graph has a title. Sometimes it is below the graph, sometimes above. Always read this title first to find out what it is that the graph is showing.

2. In many graphs there is a vertical line at the left side and a horizontal base line at the bottom of the graph. Each of these lines represents something that has to do with the subject named in the title. Read to find what each of these lines represents.

3. Study the graph carefully and get all of the information that you can from it.

READING DIFFERENT GRAPHS*

READING A HORIZONTAL BAR GRAPH

In this type of graph the things to be compared are shown in bars running from left to right across the graph. The graph below is a horizontal bar graph.

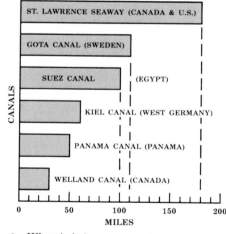

LENGTHS OF FAMOUS CANALS

1. What is being compared in this graph?

_____

2. About how many miles long is the Suez

Canal? _____

The Welland Canal? _____

3. About how many miles long is the St.

Lawrence Seaway? _____

The Gota Canal? _____

4. About how many times as long as the Panama Canal is the Suez Canal?

_____

5. How does the St. Lawrence Seaway compare in length with the Panama

Canal? _____

_____

READING A VERTICAL BAR GRAPH

In this kind of graph the bars run up and down from the base line instead of across the page. When a bar graph is used to show how quantities are related to different times, we generally draw vertical bars instead of horizontal bars.

* These graphs were prepared especially for this book by William L. Schaaf.

138 BE A BETTER READER

FIGURE 8.8.
Continued.

SHIP TRAFFIC THROUGH THE PANAMA CANAL

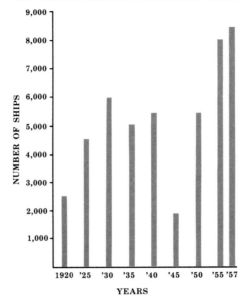

1. What is being compared in this graph?

_____

_____

2. What number unit is being used in

making these comparisons? _____

3. About how many times as many ships passed through the Panama Canal in

1935 as in 1920? _____

4. Would you agree that from 1945 to 1955 the yearly number of ships passing through the canal had increased about

four times? _____

5. Did the amount of shipping tend to increase or decrease from 1945 to 1957?

_____

READING A BROKEN-LINE GRAPH

The graph below is called a broken-line graph, and, like the vertical bar graph, it is used to show changes in quantity or number over periods of time.

FOREIGN SHIPPING THROUGH
UNITED STATES PORTS

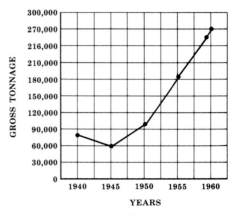

1. What is being compared in this graph?

_____

_____

2. During what years? _____

3. How much tonnage was shipped to the

United States in 1960? _____

4. What is the difference in the amount of tonnage during the 15 years from 1945

to 1960? _____

5. The tonnage in 1955 was nearly how

many times as great as in 1950? _____

_____

Then ask to what pages one should turn to find the answer for each of the following questions.

1. How does one steer a plane?
2. How many people can fly in a 747 jumbo jet?
3. Who invented the airplane?
4. How does one land a plane?
5. Can you ship a dog by air?
6. What are some of the problems of air travel?
7. How do modern planes differ from early ones?
8. What is an airplane?[14]

Organizing Information

Give the student a selection to read and an envelope containing a cut-up outline of the selection. (Before cutting, mount the outline on oaktag for durability.) The task for the student is to assemble the outline correctly. This is easier than copying the pieces of an outline, because the student can arrange and rearrange them until they look right. This is an excellent technique for teaching outlining skills before asking the student to make an outline on his own.[15]

After a student can assemble an outline of a reading selection, the next step is to complete an outline of a selection. Provide some major headings and some of the other items. The student should be able to fill in the missing parts before you expect him to construct a total outline from scratch.[16]

Using Information

After the exact information needed has been located, skill in utilizing it can be acquired through activities such as the following:

1. Having the pupils judge whether a statement is reliable by considering who wrote it or in what book it appeared.
2. Giving pupils practice in deciding which of a series of statements are relevant to their problem.
3. Providing opportunity for the pupils to give a talk or write a paper on information they have gathered.
4. Giving the pupils opportunity to explain to others what they learned, by putting on puppet shows or making friezes or "movies."

14. Ibid., p. 250.
15. Ibid., p. 240.
16. Ibid.

5. Giving the pupils an opportunity to compare facts read in an encyclopedia with their own experiences.
6. Having pupils compare the information on a given subject gained from one encyclopedia with that on the same topic in another encyclopedia.[17]

Using Maps

A group of children make a map of their neighborhood, community or school. Discussion should be held concerning scale and symbols. Let the children decide on a scale and appropriate symbols to use, and draw the map accordingly. Practice may be given in locating streets, buildings, parks, rivers, and distances from one location to another.[18]

A good way to practice map skills is to plan a trip the child would like to take. By studying road maps, he marks his exact route. In order to learn to read and interpret maps and graphs, children must be trained to develop this type of reading skill. They must be taught map scales and symbols in order to interpret the information accurately.[19]

Maps, brochures, and pamphlets may be glued inside folders, along with questions pertaining to them.

For example:
1. Find Tallahassee on the map.
2. How far is it from Jacksonville, Florida to Charleston, South Carolina?
3. Name the states through which the Mississippi River flows.[20]

Plan and teach a sequence of lessons involving one of the study skills to a group of children or peers. If you are going to teach the lessons to children, determine where they are in relation to the skill you have selected by answering the following questions:

1. Has the skill been introduced to the children?
2. At what levels of difficulty have the children applied the skill?
3. What levels of difficulty in applying the skill are appropriate for your sequence of lessons?

The following references are good sources of ideas for developing activities and materials:

Dallmann, Martha; Rouch, Roger L.; Chang, Lynette Y. C.; and DeBoer, John J. *The Teaching of Reading.* 4th ed. Chap. 8B, "Developing Skill in Lo-

17. Martha Dallmann, Roger L. Rouch, Lynette Y. C. Chang, and John J. DeBoer, *The Teaching of Reading*, 4th ed. (New York: Holt, Rinehart and Winston, 1974), pp. 273-74.
18. Evelyn B. Spache, *Reading Activities for Child Involvement.* (Boston: Allyn & Bacon, 1972), p. 177.
19. Ibid., p. 179.
20. Ibid.

cating Information and in Using It." New York: Holt, Rinehart and Winston, 1974.

Herr, Selma E. *Learning Activities for Reading.* 2d ed. Dubuque, Iowa: Wm. C. Brown Company Publishers, 1970.

Russell, David H., and Karp, Etta E. *Reading Aids Through the Grades.* Second Revised Edition by Anne Marie Mueser. Sec. 4, "Advanced Reading Skills." New York: Teachers College Press, Columbia University, 1975.

Smith, Nila Banton. *Reading Instruction for Today's Children.* Chap. 23, "Practice and Maintenance Activities for Use in Developing Study Skills in Content Areas." Englewood Cliffs, N. J.: Prentice-Hall, 1963.

Spache, Evelyn B. *Reading Activities for Child Involvement.* Chap. 6, "Location Skills"; chap. 7, "Content Reading Skills." Boston: Allyn & Bacon, 1972.

Activity 9

Observe one or more study skills lessons. Use the following questions as a guide for your observations:

1. Is the skill being introduced?
2. If the skill is not being introduced, can you tell at what levels of difficulty the children have previously worked with the skill?
3. Is the skill being developed in relation to work the children are currently doing in one of the content fields?
4. What opportunities are provided for the children to apply the skill they are learning?

Activity 10

Design activities of your own which you feel will enable you to achieve the competencies stated for this module.

Preassessment and Postassessment

A. Knowledge Level
   1. Select two of the content fields that have been discussed in this module. Identify two skills in each of the following categories (vocabulary, organization, and comprehension) that are necessary for effective reading in each content field selected.
   Criteria for successful performance:
      a) the skills are accurately identified with the categories of vocabulary, organization, and comprehension;
      b) the skills are accurately identified with the content fields selected.

2. Select three categories of study skills and identify two specific skills in each category.
   Criteria for successful performance:
   a) the categories of study skills are accurately identified;
   b) the specific skills are accurately identified with the categories selected.

B. Performance Level
1. Planning the Lesson
   a) Identify a group of children who are reading at more than one instructional level. Develop a plan for teaching a lesson involving reading in one content field that provides for these differences in reading levels. Follow the procedure outlined in activity 4 in planning your lesson.
   b) Criteria for successful performance:
      (1) the objectives state the desired behavior;
      (2) the instructional procedure outlined in activity 4 is identifiable and in the correct sequence;
      (3) the instructional procedures clearly provide for adjustments to different reading levels in ways that are appropriate for the material being used, and for the reading levels identified;
      (4) the procedures for the evaluation of pupil achievement are identified.
   c) Identify a group of children who are reading at the same instructional level. Develop plans for teaching two sequential lessons that focus on the development of one study skill.
   d) Criteria for successful performance:
      (1) the objectives state the desired behavior;
      (2) the instructional procedures are developed in ways that are appropriate for the study skill selected;
      (3) the procedures for the evaluation of pupil achievement are identified.
2. Teaching the Lesson
   a) Arrange to teach the lessons to groups of children. Arrange to
      (1) have the instructor or cooperating teacher observe the lessons or
      (2) tape the lessons.
   b) Criteria for successful performance:
      (1) there is evidence that the pupils have achieved the objectives;
      (2) the student has demonstrated the ability to adapt his

teaching procedures, as necessary, in response to pupil needs during the lesson.

3. Evaluating the Lesson

    a) After the lessons have been taught, write an evaluation of each one. Respond to the following questions in your evaluations.

        (1) Did the pupils achieve the objectives? Support your answer with specific evidence.

        (2) If there were pupils who did not achieve the objectives, can you identify the experiences they still need in order to reach the objectives?

        (3) Are there elements of the lessons that you would approach differently if you were to teach the lessons again?

    b) Follow one of these procedures:

        (1) If the instructor has observed the lessons, schedule a conference to discuss both plans and lessons.

        (2) If the cooperating teacher has observed the lessons, ask for written evaluations and then schedule a conference with the instructor to discuss the plans, the lessons and the cooperating teacher's evaluations.

        (3) If the lessons have been taped, schedule a conference with the instructor to discuss the plans and the taped lessons.

References

Bond, Guy L., and Wagner, Eva Bond. *Teaching the Child to Read.* 4th ed. Chap. 11, "Basic Study Skills"; chap. 13, "Reading Content-Subject Materials." New York: Macmillan Company, 1966.

Bush, Clifford L., and Huebner, Mildred H. *Strategies for Reading in the Elementary School.* Chap. 6, "Comprehension: Skills." New York: Macmillan Company, 1970.

Dallmann, Martha; Rouch, Roger L.; Chang, Lynette Y. C.; and DeBoer, John J. *The Teaching of Reading.* 4th ed. Chap. 8A, "Locating Information and Using It"; chap. 8B, "Developing Skill in Locating Information and in Using it"; chap. 10, "Reading in the Content Areas." New York: Holt, Rinehart and Winston, 1974.

Durkin, Dolores. *Teaching Them to Read.* 2d ed. Chap. 15, "Content Subjects and Study Skills." Boston: Allyn & Bacon, 1974.

Harris, Albert J., and Sipay, Edward R. *Effective Teaching of Reading.* 2d ed. Chap. 12, "Developing Efficiency in Functional Reading." New York: David McKay Company, 1971.

Heilman, Arthur W. *Principles and Practices of Teaching Reading.* 3d ed. Chap. 13, "Developing and Expanding Concepts"; chap. 14, "Teaching Reading-Study Skills." Columbus, Ohio: Charles E. Merrill Publishing Company, 1972.

Herr, Selma E. *Learning Activities for Reading.* 2d ed. Dubuque, Iowa: Wm. C. Brown Company Publishers, 1970.

May, Frank B. *To Help Children Read.* Module 4,

"Helping Children Read for Information and Pleasure." Columbus, Ohio: Charles E. Merrill Publishing Company, 1973.

Otto, Wayne; Chester, Robert; McNeil, John; and Myers, Shirley. *Focused Reading Instruction*. Chap. 8, "Objectives for study skills." Reading, Mass.: Addision-Wesley Publishing Company, 1974.

Russell, David H. *Children Learn to Read*. 2d ed. Chap. 11, "The Program in Work-Type Reading and Study Skills." Waltham, Mass.: Blaisdell Publishing Company, 1961.

Russell, David H., and Karp, Etta E. *Reading Aids Through the Grades*. Second Revised Edition by Anne Marie Mueser. Sec. 4, "Advanced Reading Skills." New York: Teachers College Press, Columbia University, 1975.

Smith, Nila Banton. *Reading Instruction for Today's Children*. Chap. 10, "Study Skills in Reading Content Subjects"; chap. 23, "Practice and Maintenance Activities for Use in Developing Study Skills in Content Areas." Englewood Cliffs, N. J.: Prentice-Hall, 1963.

Spache, Evelyn B. *Reading Activities for Child Involvement*. Chap. 6, "Location Skills"; chap. 7, "Content Reading Skills." Boston: Allyn & Bacon, 1972.

Spache, George D., and Spache, Evelyn B. *Reading in the Elementary School*. 4th ed. Chap. 9, "The Combined Program for Intermediate Grades." Boston: Allyn & Bacon, 1977.

Tinker, Miles A., and McCullough, Constance M. *Teaching Elementary Reading*. 3d ed. Chap. 13, "Reading in the Content Fields"; chap. 24, "Recommended Practices in Fourth, Fifth, and Sixth Grades: Reading in the Content Fields and Personal Reading Activities." New York: Appleton-Century-Crofts, 1968.

Veatch, Jeannette. *Reading in the Elementary School*. Chap. 10, "Reading at the More Advanced Levels." New York: Ronald Press Company, 1966.

Walcutt, Charles C.; Lamport, Joan; and McCracken, Glenn. *Teaching Reading*. Chap. 25, "Elementary Techniques for the Content Areas." New York: Macmillan Company, 1974.

Zintz, Miles V. *The Reading Process: The Teacher and the Learner*. 2d ed. Chap. 12, "Study Skills." Dubuque, Iowa: Wm. C. Brown Company Publishers, 1975.

Evaluating Growth in Reading Ability

Overview

The process of evaluating children's progress toward reaching the objectives of the reading program is essential to providing effective instruction. Without current, accurate information regarding each child's status in relation to specific skills and abilities, it is impossible to design learning experiences that will meet the needs of individual learners and insure their continued progress. Two points of emphasis emerge as critical if evaluation is to be effective: (1) it must be a continuous process; it cannot be an activity that takes place only at stated intervals throughout the year, and (2) it must involve the collection of a variety of types of data using a range of techniques and instruments.

Both points of emphasis identified here are developed in the article through which this module is introduced, "Evaluation: What Is It? Who Does It? When Should It Be Done?," by Margaret Ammons.[1] Ammons begins by placing evaluation within the framework of the overall instructional process. She then clarifies the concept as she contrasts the definition of evaluation with the definitions of terms with which "evaluation" is sometimes used interchangeably. Ammons follows this clarification with an identification of the specific characteristics of evaluation and with illustrations of selected techniques. She concludes her discussion by recommending the steps to be taken in developing a comprehensive evaluation program. In order to develop an understanding of the concept of evalua-

---

1. Margaret Ammons, "Evaluation: What Is It? Who Does It? When Should It Be Done?," in *The Evaluation of Children's Reading Achievement,* Perspectives in Reading, no. 8, ed. Thomas C. Barrett (Newark, Del.: International Reading Association, 1967), pp. 1-12.

tion and the factors associated with it, read Ammons's article using the following questions as your purposes for reading:

1. How does the author differentiate *evaluation* and the concepts of *testing/measurement* and *grading?*
2. What are the characteristics of evaluation identified by Ammons?
3. What categories of evaluation are identified and described?

Evaluation: What Is It? Who Does It? When Should It Be Done?

Margaret Ammons
University of Wisconsin

Before discussing what evaluation is, it may be helpful to make an assertion regarding current education and the relation of evaluation to it. In the final portion of the paper, this point is raised again.

The assertion states that in today's school there is determinism, i.e., individuals are classified early in their school careers and tend to retain that classification throughout their years of schooling. Evaluation, properly employed, can reduce this determinism.

Analysis of Evaluation

Historically, four classes of activity have been associated with curriculum development: 1) identification and formulation of educational objectives, 2) selection of learning activities, 3) organization of learning activities, and 4) evaluation. By definition these four activities are closely related, mutually dependent. Therefore, in order to discuss evaluation it is necessary to construct a context by defining objectives and activities and describing their relation to each other and to evaluation.

The specific topics which comprise the remainder of this paper, are as follows: 1) definition of terms, 2) characteristics of evaluation contrasted with such activities as testing, 3) identification of techniques, 4) individuals responsible for evaluation, and 5) some recommendations for a total evaluation program.

Definition of Key Terms

As stated earlier, the major activities in curriculum development and improvement focus on objectives, learning activities, and evaluation. For purposes of clarity the following definitions are used throughout the discussion.

Educational Objectives. Educational objectives are statements of purpose which contain a description of possible and desirable student behavior and an indication of appropriate content. Important at this point is the recognition that behavior, as it is used here, is much more inclusive than those behaviors which are

From Margaret Ammons, "Evaluation: What Is It? Who Does It? When Should It Be Done?" in *The Evaluation of Children's Reading Achievement,* Perspectives in Reading, no. 8, ed. Thomas C. Barrett (Newark, Del.: International Reading Association, 1967), pp. 1-12. Reprinted by permission of Margaret Ammons and the International Reading Association.

observable. One useful illustration of possible student behaviors can be found in two volumes, *Taxonomy of Educational Objectives—Handbook I: The Cognitive Domain* (1) and *Taxonomy of Educational Objectives—Handbook II: The Affective Domain* (3). Within the cognitive domain the following behaviors are included: knowledge of specifics, comprehension, and application. The affective domain considers five different behaviors: receiving, responding, valuing organization, and characterization by a value or value concept.

In the case of both the cognitive and affective domains the behaviors are said to be listed in the order of increasing complexity. Thus, knowledge of specifics is the simplest behavior, and evaluation is the most complex. Similarly in the affective domain receiving is the simplest with characterizations being most complex.

In either domain, content is conceived of as much broader than material found in a book. The intent of the term content is to indicate ideas—written or spoken, an object, a person, and the like.

The function of such objectives is to give guidance to teachers in the selection of learning activities and in the selection of evaluation techniques.

To summarize, an educational objective is a statement of purpose which describes possible and desirable student behavior which serve to give guidance to teachers in the selection of learning activities and evaluation techniques.

Learning Activities. Learning activities are those situations which are created by teachers and learners which allow learners to exhibit the behaviors described in an objective or objectives. There are many sources of criteria for judging activities. One set is by Goodlad in the 1959 ASCD Yearbook, *Learning and the Teacher* (1). In passing, it should be noted that any activity can and should be designed so that individual learners may be given the opportunity to work toward different objectives.

Evaluation. Evaluation in this context is defined as the description of student progress toward educational objectives. The description is to be used in making and reviewing decisions about individual students and their program. Technically, the word derives from Latin to mean to extract the value from. Since objectives describe desirable student behavior, or valued student behavior, the relation between objectives and evaluation can be seen. Further, as learning activities are to be designed to offer learners opportunities to engage in the behavior described in the objective, the cycle from objectives to activities to evaluation back to objectives, and the mutual dependency of all three can be seen.

Evaluation Contrasted to Other Activities

Perhaps because educators have not been careful in using terms—for example, there is a doctoral dissertation on the definitions of curriculum—the term evaluation is understood on occasion to mean testing, measurement, and grading. This section attempts to clarify the differences among these terms.

Testing and Measurement. The major distinction to be made between evaluation and testing and/or measurement is a relation to educational objectives. While tests or other measures, for example, height and weight, may in fact relate specifically to objectives adopted by a teacher or a school system, this is not necessarily the case. In many instances standardized tests are developed by experts removed from any specific situation; therefore, tests may well be unrelated to the objectives adopted by any school or school system, and yet these tests are used as criteria for judging student performance. Such data may or may not be a reflection of the objectives sought.

Another major distinction between tests and evaluation as concepts is that, typically, tests are standardized on groups of children, described by the test makers, and reveal something about the progress of groups or individual students in relation to the "norming" populations. Evaluation, on the other hand, is the description of the progress of one individual toward certain objectives about which standardized information may not be available.

One more distinction is offered to clarify further the intent of the term evaluation. Quite often a test is designed to give evidence about a specific area or skill, for example, arithmetic computation or word recognition. Evaluation, on the other hand, is related to the whole array of objectives about which the school or teacher is concerned.

None of the foregoing should be taken to mean that tests and evaluation are not in any sense related. For indeed they are. Later this is dealt with in some detail.

Grading. In some cases one hears the terms *grading* and *evaluating* used synonymously. Let me quickly try to make the distinction between them. Evaluation results tell us how much progress has been made. A grade given for this progress tells the student whether the progress was enough, enough for an A or a B or even an F. The chief function of evaluation is to describe progress. Grading is an act of judging the quality or quantity of progress. Grading is sometimes done on the performance of one individual in terms of the progress of the group as a whole or in terms of the individual's progress in relation to his own ability. Evaluation yields evidence about an individual in relation to one or more objectives.

Characteristics of Evaluation

The following constitutes a description of the specific characteristics of evaluation, with illustrations of techniques where these are appropriate.

1. Evaluation, because it describes progress, assumes that knowledge is available regarding where each student began. That is, a single test at the end of a unit will not reveal much about progress unless the starting point of the individual is also known. Pre- and post-testing are sometimes done with a paper and pencil test in such an area as spelling. Initial testing is often defined as diagnosis, although the term *diagnosis* seems more negative than does the term *description* of a student's activity at the start of instruction. In "old-time" terms, this is how we find out where the student is so that we can take him as far as he can go. Without such initial information we cannot have evaluation.

2. Evaluation is a continuous process. If our interest is progress and not some sort of terminal behavior, or the acquisition of certain behaviors within a specified period of time, then we must collect evidence on student progress continuously. Only then are we sufficiently aware of the nature and direction of progress to be in a position to alter instructional strategies and environment so that progress for any individual student may be optimum for him.

3. Evaluation requires adequate samples of a student's work. For example, if we are concerned with a student's acquisition of particular physical skills, then we must have more than pre- and post-teaching data. For obvious reasons, what a student does today, because of a cold or virus, may not be representative of what is actually able to do. Therefore, many samples of his efforts must be collected.

4. An evaluation technique must offer some promise that the student will be able to engage in the behavior called for by the objective toward which the learner is to be

making progress. Tyler uses somewhat stronger language in saying that the evaluation situation must evoke or cause the student to emit the behavior under consideration (5). However, because certainty in such situations is a rarity, it seems sufficient that such a situation, at least upon close examination and logical analysis, could allow the student to engage in a given behavior.

This is not meant to interpret the term *behavior* in any narrow, restricted, or terminal sense. Nor is it intended to imply that behavior must be acquired in a specified time. Nor is it to ascertain what constitutes the behaviors anyone must accept as desirable. This is a question to be left to individuals who are responsible for curriculum planning and the actual instruction of particular students.

Within this framework, behaviors may include inquiring, valuing, enjoying, communicating, loving, appreciating, as well as memorizing and comprehending. Parenthetically, recent studies tend to confirm earlier work which indicates that approximately 90 percent of teachers' classroom questions require students to engage in memorization and regurgitation of isolated information. Only 8 percent of the time, then, is available for having students engage in other behaviors, some of which were listed above.

If we are concerned in some fashion with learners' behavior (whatever behaviors are agreed upon by those whose responsibility it is to make such determinations), then the classroom environment must provide opportunities for the learner to engage in the behavior about which we claim to be concerned. Classroom environment includes materials, equipment, lighting, as well as the nature and quality of discourse between students and teacher and among students. While we can and consciously do control the more obvious aspects of this environment, research suggests that we do not, as teachers, consciously control the dialogue in relation to the behaviors we say learners should acquire. What we say, both in classroom discussion and on examinations, tends to ignore many of the behaviors in which we claim to be interested.

This point seems too obvious to belabor; yet it is likely violated more frequently than any other requirement of evaluation. That is, regardless of what we claim to be interested in having youngsters accomplish —whether it be critical thinking, analysis, synthesis, or appreciation—the evaluation situations into which we put them require them to spout back to us, usually in the same form, bits and pieces of information. Furthermore, in far too many cases we insist that the information be acquired by a certain time in the child's school career or, if not, that he be required to repeat a grade. It is difficult to square this practice with the notions of progress and continuity mentioned earlier.

5. Evaluation is, in itself, a learning situation. An evaluation situation must allow a student to see himself in a new light, to learn something new about what progress he has made and in what new directions he might move. This implies that he in some fashion shares in the evaluation and the results thereof.

6. Finally, evaluation is open-ended. That is, an evaluation situation or technique opens new doors and points ahead rather than backward. It does not allow a learner to feel, "Now, that's finished." These final two points are directly related to the whole concept of continuous evaluation.

To summarize the characteristics of evaluation, it describes beginnings as well as progress; it is continuous; it utilizes many samples of a learner's work; it allows the student to engage in the particular behavior or behaviors toward which he is assumed to be moving; it constitutes a learning situation; and it is open-ended, indicating new directions.

Some Illustrative Evaluation Techniques

It is impossible to enumerate all evaluation techniques here. Among the wide variety available are tests, situations, anecdotal records, measurement, and other paper and pencil items.

Tests. In almost any area one can find tests designed to measure achievement of students. One only need take a superficial look through any edition of the *Mental Measurements Yearbook* to see what is available. In many cases, more than one form of the same instrument is published. Where this is true, it is somewhat simpler to determine where an individual is at the outset of instruction and where he is at the conclusion. One must be certain that the test measures those factors which are considered to be important by the school system and which are, in the estimation of those responsible for evaluation, related to those behaviors toward which the schools are working. In some instances, an examination of a test, or tests, may disclose that the school is, in fact, overlooking some areas to which it thought it was giving attention.

If it is possible to locate a test which is a true "fit" in a given situation, and if individual students do not do well after instruction, evaluation, and judgment, it could be the case that what is sought is not clear to teachers or that instruction has been inadequate or that a given student has a problem heretofore unrecognized.

The foregoing has related to commercial tests. Much the same could be said for teacher-made tests of a paper and pencil variety.

If one accepts the description of behaviors in the Cognitive Taxonomy, then it is possible to develop paper and pencil items for all six behaviors listed. This is not as true for affective behaviors. One might hypothesize that we've had a great deal more practice in testing mental behaviors than we have had in testing appreciations, values, and the like; thus we are infinitely more proficient at describing and/or agreeing upon definitions of the more "mental" behaviors. It should be recalled that the cognitive behaviors are knowledge of specifics, comprehension, application, analysis, synthesis, and evaluation.

Since we claim to be concerned with something more than cognitive learning; that is, we speak often of values, appreciations, interests, attitudes, skills, and the like, then one might raise a question as to the appropriateness of paper and pencil tests in relation to these behaviors.

Situations. Let us consider for a moment the question of appreciation of "good" literature. What kind of evaluation situation or technique makes sense in this context? What kind of question on a paper test would measure a student's appreciation? This is not to say that such is impossible. I would, however, raise a question as to whether we know any more than what a student is willing to write. And certainly we have all heard about the test-wise student. If we can believe what students state at the college level, they have learned to play the game and quite honestly inquire as to what is wanted. Once they have found out what is wanted, they will then do it. Or if we can believe some research, we might be concerned to learn that somewhere during third grade children show evidence of ceasing to be question askers and become question answerers. All this is to intimate that in some instances, paper and pencil tests are not reliable indicators of student attitudes, values, etc.

What constitutes a reasonable alternative when we are concerned with such attributes as interest? One is to arrange situations in which a student can choose from among a variety of activities. For example, a teacher may set up a music listening center, a "free reading" table, a science table, and a filmstrip center. If a student consistently chooses one, the teacher might conclude that the student is interested in that activity.

The problem here is reaching some agreement as to what sorts of behaviors we are willing to say make up an attitude, a value, or an interest. Since evaluation is largely a description of an individual, a teacher might include in the student's record that he is interested in music and then give reasons why the teacher thinks so. Others may not agree with what the teacher reports as evidence of interest on the part of the student, but at least persons reading the report will have some basis for agreeing or disagreeing and will have some description of the way in which a given student acts in relation to music.

Anecdotal Records. These records constitute another evaluation technique. Such records must meet the conditions of evaluation spelled out earlier, including initial information, continuity, open-endedness, and the others.

One factor related to anecdotal records is critical-objectivity. Frequently, the social behavior of youngsters is of importance in a school situation, important enough to be graded on a report to parents. The grade may be a check or a minus; it may be a U for unsatisfactory or an S for satisfactory; or it may be a 1, 2, or 3. Whatever the grading system, the specific grade should be based upon evidence which is relevant to the behavior under consideration. Such evidence should be as free as possible from judgment. That is, the record should be as objective as it is humanly possible

to make it. The time for judgment is when the grade is awarded, not when evidence is being collected. In such records, one should not find such words as *good* or *bad* or *trouble maker* or *a joy to have in class*. As with the question of interest, the particular behaviors which lead one teacher to the conclusion that a child is *bad* may well lead another teacher to the conclusion that the child is *exciting*. Thus, records should include description, not judgment. They should also be kept on a continuing basis, and should include many samples of what a given student does so that his behavior in many situations is recorded. I have yet to see a child who is never acceptable to me. If, however, his behavior is usually disturbing to me, I am liable to overlook the times when he is not disturbing. He is entitled to have me sample all his variety of behaviors.

Measurement. Related to testing, in a sense, is measurement. As the term is used here, it entails records of a different sort. Whether one keeps such records depends to a large extent upon what is seen as desirable in a given situation. In any case, such records as height, weight, vision, hearing, and the like are appropriate. Assuming that growth is important, without determining the precise amount to be exhibited, then records showing such progress can be useful in the overall picture of an individual.

Other Paper and Pencil Instruments. There are other paper and pencil instruments which are different from the tests mentioned above. These include interest inventories, actual written work of individuals, art work, and lists of books read. These may be useful as evidence when identifying interests or attitudes.

Where at all possible other sources of evidence (and that is all any technique is) should be employed. These new sources include films, audio tapes, and video tapes. The appropriateness of these in relation to speaking, reading, and self-expression in dramatics is clear.

Certainly there are other techniques available. The ones mentioned here are intended to indicate the breadth of possibilities and to underscore the need for a wide variety of techniques of evaluation.

Responsibilities in an Evaluation Program

The first step in building a program of evaluation is to determine to what extent evaluation is desired. In this context evaluation is not testing alone, nor is it grading, nor is it reporting. While all these may be related, they are not identical unless they happen to be defined as such in a local situation. The questions related to grading and reporting, along with promoting and retaining, require answers to a different set of questions. Therefore, for example, to plan a rather broad program of standardized testing is not to plan a comprehensive program of evaluation unless the standardized tests measure those factors and all those factors described in the objectives. Further, it should be remembered here that evaluation relates more directly to individual progress than to group progress. Another element in taking the first step is to stipulate what use will be made of evaluation results. Examples of such use include appraisal of teacher effectiveness, appraisal of objectives (are they realistic for this system), appraisal of materials, appraisal of class size or grouping practices, reporting to parents, and perhaps most important, working with each individual so that his educational environment is tailored to his needs. These decisions will determine what kind of records and how many need to be kept and by whom; where records are to be sent or kept; and who needs what information and in what form.

Here it is important to recognize and maintain a distinction between evaluation itself and the use to be made of the evidence collected during evaluation. While the distinction seems obvious, it is nonetheless the case that often the two terms are telescoped and the individual student is lost in the total program.

The following serves to illustrate. If evaluation data are to be used in appraising a total program within a school system only, then such data should be sent to a central office evaluator who might then appraise the total system and make such recommendations as "too much anxiety," "too little attention given to the arts," or to "independent reading," or to "physical education," or to some other objective which the system has established as desirable. If, on the other hand, teachers alone are to use evaluation data, such information can be kept by the individual teacher for use with individuals within his class. Obviously, these are not necessarily exclusive; evaluation data may be used in all the ways mentioned in any one situation. The point is, the use must be determined in each situation. With clarification comes an understanding of where responsibility lies for collection and use and a specification of areas where mutual use of data is to be made in the interest of each individual student. If a child's progress is minimal in one area but extensive in another, his achievement is not averaged. By analyzing a wide variety of evaluation data on an individual, there is less probability that undue pressure will be put on a student to make progress in one area when progress in another area might be more important for him. However, unless a wide spectrum of data is collected, there is little assurance that such pressure will not be unconsciously exerted. Although school systems assert an interest in the all-around development of individuals, information about individuals is typically limited to academic achievement, social behavior, and work habits. Exceptions to this over-generalization are those students who exhibit behavior or learning problems.

Because of the nature of evaluation, and

its close relation to objectives and classroom activities, it is impossible to talk about who should evaluate, and how, without treating to some extent the question of objectives.

Objectives include two elements: student behavior and content. These two terms are broadly conceived. The major function is to guide teachers in the selection of activities and evaluation techniques. If this function is to be served, it seems logical to involve teachers in the formulation of objectives. Teachers do sit on committees which are charged with stating objectives. As objectives are formulated, however, few are circulated among teachers to discover what teachers would do in the classroom in relation to the objectives. If the objectives are to communicate something to teachers then it seems reasonable to discover whether this something is in fact communicated. It matters not what the objectives are, but if they are to be emphasized in classrooms, then teachers should be able to understand the intent of an objective. The only way to find this out is to ask.

Two questions might well be asked of teachers: 1) Given a typical classroom, what *kinds* of activities would you offer to children to achieve this objective? The notion of kinds of activities in the plural is crucial; in most instances there is no one activity which will assure that an objective will be achieved nor any one activity that is appropriate for each individual as he works toward the objective. 2) What would you use as evidence to determine whether a student is making progress toward this objective? Or, how would you collect evidence to determine what progress a student is making?

Thus, the second step in building an evaluation program is to be clear about what objectives are important and whether teachers can use them as they are intended to be used. The responsibility for this step lies with the person responsible for curriculum development *and* teachers. It is not an either/or proposition.

The third major step in building an evaluation program is to exercise the imagination in relation to the types of techniques which are appropriate to a given objective. Certainly there are times when group tests are useful and relevant. There are, however, times when they cannot reveal what is needed. Critical to remember is that *whatever* techniques are employed, they allow only more or less sophisticated inferences to be made about an individual; conclusions, therefore, should be held tentatively. In any case, a real brainstorming session could be profitably held to suggest as many ways to evaluate, let us say, progress in art appreciation as a group can construct. Criteria for relevance of a technique will come out as the intent of the term appreciation becomes more clear as a result of the brainstorming. The responsibility for this step lies in the hands of the central office personnel who are in some way attached to program development and in the hands of teachers to whom the intent of objectives must be clear if relevant evidence is to be collected. When a satisfactory set of illustrative techniques has been established for any one or any set of objectives, they should be circulated along with the objectives to all teachers who will be expected to use them. Refinements can be made on the basis of responses. When a compilation has been made, a statement can then be accepted on a tentative basis. The basis is tentative because evaluation is continuous and, as evidence is collected, changes in objectives and techniques will be indicated.

The fourth step in building an evaluation program is to determine what kinds of data must be collected, how often it is to be collected, and with whom it is to be shared. For example, there may be certain academic skills which are acquired over a relatively short period of time. Thus, initial measures will be taken and reported, with one or more follow-up measures taken in a matter of weeks. If information about the permanence of learning or the extension of a skill is desired, additional measures, taken over a longer period of time, would be called for.

When interest is in something akin to appreciation of a certain type of literature or to the internalization of a particular value, if we can believe the evidence available to us, we need not expect rapid progress. Frequent collection of data regarding this kind of progress is not necessary. For assistance in making decisions regarding the timing of collection, a school staff might well employ the services of a psychologist. Whether data are shared only between teacher and child or are shared among teacher, child, and administrative personnel depends upon whether a particular kind of data are to be used for total program appraisal or for helping a given individual. This is a matter for local determination, but it is a question which must be raised.

The fifth step, and perhaps at once the most and least important, is to determine the form in which data should be collected and shared. One might even want to be so extreme as to standardize a form for anecdotal records or a vocabulary for describing progress in certain areas. This appears to be too confining, but some way of assuring accurate communication should be devised. The most efficient way to accomplish this is to ask those persons who are to use a document, test, or profile what it conveys to them. Since personnel changes fairly rapidly, this should be done regularly.

Finally, the last step in building an evaluation program is to *use* the data collected. No matter how specific the uses are, no matter how well documents communicate, and no matter how appropriate the particular technique, it all goes for naught unless it is used to help individuals make the progress of which they are capable.

Now to return to the beginning assertion. Hastings reports that in a study of 2,000 teachers in 591 schools, approximately 50 percent of these teachers look at test data or other information about their students. Payne's study (4) reveals that students who are unlikely to achieve acceptable levels of attainment under a given curricular arrangement can be identified and helped early in their school careers.

This study has supported the findings of other investigators who suggest that determinism does exist in schools. The relative positions of students within a group were established early and maintained over several years. Some change is necessary if the school is striving to bring all students to at least a minimal level of "satisfactory" achievement. The study has presented strong evidence that a change will not occur under the present practices in these schools . . . then a responsibility exists for identifying those students who are not likely to reach this level under existing conditions.

Thus, the rallying cry with regard to evaluation is, at the very least, to use what we already have in the way of data. Individual students, however, are entitled to better than the least we can do. Given our present sophistication, the best we can do is to collect relevant data so that conditions for individuals do not force them into slots, particularly when the slot is marked *failure*.

References

1. Bloom, Benjamin S. *et al. Taxonomy of Educational Objectives-Handbook I: The Cognitive Domain*. New York: David McKay, 1956.
2. Goodlad, John I. "The Teacher Selects, Plans, and Organizes," *Learning and the Teacher*, 1959 Yearbook, Association for Supervision and Curriculum Development. Washington, D.C.: The Association, 1959, 39-60.
3. Krathwohl, David, *et al. Taxonomy of Educational Objectives-Handbook II: The Affective Domain*. New York: David McKay, 1964.

4. Payne, M. Arlene. "The Use of Data in Curricular Decisions," unpublished doctoral dissertation. University of Chicago, 1963.

5. Tyler, Ralph W. *Basic Principles of Curriculum and Instruction.* Chicago: University of Chicago Press, 1950.

Module Competencies

The competencies specified for this module focus on the development of your ability to use a variety of techniques in collecting information that will enable you to make sound judgments concerning children's progress in reading. The purpose reflected in competencies 1 and 2 is that of helping you to develop an understanding of the types of tests and other techniques that can be used in evaluating reading growth. Competency 3 is directed toward providing you with a means of determining the level at which each child can be expected to achieve in reading, based on his potential for learning. The purpose in competencies 4 and 5 is to help you develop the ability to use tests and other evaluation techniques as a basis for evaluating children's growth in reading.

Instructional Activities

Three categories of standardized tests are identified and differentiated in activity 2. Following this, you are asked to examine tests using specific questions as a guide (competency 1). The concept of reading expectancy is introduced and discussed in activity 3. Two formulas are provided for your use in computing reading expectancy levels (competency 3). A procedure for you to follow in administering a standardized test and interpreting the results in terms of reading expectancy level is also provided in this activity (competency 4). In activity 4 informal techniques that can be used in evaluating reading growth are identified and described (competency 2). You are encouraged in this activity to apply informal techniques in obtaining information that can be used in evaluating one child's reading progress (competency 5). Determining the nature of the evaluation program in the school in which you are working through interviewing teachers and other personnel is the focus in activity 5 (competencies 1 and 2). In activity 6 you are encouraged to design activities of your own which will enable you to develop competence in evaluating children's growth in reading.

Competencies

1. Differentiate categories of standardized tests used in evaluating reading growth.
2. Differentiate informal (nonstandardized) techniques used in evaluating reading growth.
3. Determine reading expectancy level.
4. Administer standardized tests and interpret the results.
5. Use informal evaluation techniques and interpret the information obtained through their use.

Instructional Activities

Select from the following learning experiences those which you feel will enable you to achieve the competencies stated for this module:

Activity 1

Attend a seminar for orientation to this module.

Activity 2

Standardized (or norm-referenced) tests represent one type of instrument that can be employed in collecting data to be used in evaluating children's growth in reading. Three categories of standardized tests will be discussed in this activity: survey tests, diagnostic tests, and tests which focus on one skill area only.

The procedures used in the standardization of a test result in test *norms* which are used to compare an individual's score with the scores attained by a sample of children who have been given an initial form of the test. Norms are established by averaging the scores of this sample of children within each of the grade levels for which the test is designed. The norms for a test are presented in tables that are used by the teacher to convert each child's test score (raw score) to a grade score or percentile rank.

A frequent criticism of test norms is that the population sample does not represent a true cross-section of children throughout the country, and that as a result, the norms may be biased against children in particular communities. It is important, therefore, to determine the nature of the population sample in considering a test for possible use. This information is usually included in the teacher's manual or in the technical manual provided with the test. The following description of the population sample used in establishing norms is given by the authors of one series of reading tests:

Establishing Norms

After the items had been selected and parallel forms constructed, norms for the *Gates-MacGinitie Reading Tests* were developed by administering the tests to a new nationwide sample of approximately 40,000 pupils in 38 communities. The communities were carefully selected on the basis of size, geographical location, average educational level, and average family income. . . Within each community, testing was carried out in one or more schools, judged, by the school officials, to be representative of the community as a whole. At the elementary level all children in the selected school were tested, while in the secondary schools approximately three classrooms per grade in each selected school were tested.[2]

Survey Tests

Survey tests provide a measure of children's general reading ability. These tests typically include subtests in three areas: (1) vocabulary, (2) comprehension, and (3) speed or rate. The cover page of the test booklet for the *Gates-MacGinitie Reading Tests,* Survey D, Form 1 is shown in figure 9.1. After the test has been administered and scored, the results are recorded here.

Frequently, the grade scores obtained from the vocabulary and comprehension subtests are averaged, resulting in an overall grade score for each child. In the teacher's manual which accompanies their tests, Gates and MacGinitie point out why they do not recommend this practice:

> . . . It should be pointed out . . . that where a Vocabulary score and a Comprehension score are significantly different, averaging them obscures the very information the teacher needs and gives a misleading impression of the student's reading ability.[3]

In their discussion of the interpretation of test results, Harris and Sipay identify the kinds of information the teacher can derive from comparing a child's subtest scores. If, for example, a child's comprehension score is significantly higher than his vocabulary score, this indicates that he is weak in the area of vocabulary and is relying heavily on context as he reads. On the other hand, a vocabulary score that is higher than a comprehension score is indicative of comprehension difficulties that require additional analysis. Harris and Sipay suggest, also, that comparing rate

---

2. Arthur I. Gates and Walter H. MacGinitie, Technical Manual, *Gates-MacGinitie Reading Tests,* Survey D (New York: Teachers College Press, Columbia University, 1965), p. 2.
3. Ibid., p. 7.

FIGURE 9.1.
Cover Page of the pupil test booklet. From Arthur I. Gates and Walter H. MacGinitie, *Gates-MacGinitie Reading Tests,* Survey D, Form I (New York: Teachers College Press, Columbia University, 1964). Reprinted by permission of the publisher.

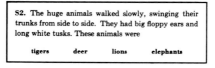

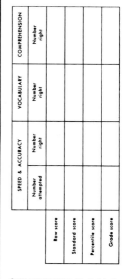

HAND-SCORED EDITION

Name_____
         (LAST)   (FIRST)

Birth date_____Boy_____Girl_____
         (MONTH, DAY, YEAR)

Grade_____Testing date_____

Teacher_____

School_____

City_____

DIRECTIONS: Read sample paragraph S 1. Under it are four words. Find the word that best answers the question.

> **S1.** Mary pulled and tried to turn the knob. She could not turn it. It was a cold day to be locked outside. What was Mary trying to open?
>
> box   bag   door   safe

The word **door** is the best answer to the question. Draw a line under the word **door**.

Now read paragraph S2. Find the word below the paragraph that best completes the paragraph, and draw a line under it.

> **S2.** The huge animals walked slowly, swinging their trunks from side to side. They had big floppy ears and long white tusks. These animals were
>
> tigers   deer   lions   elephants

The word **elephants** best completes paragraph S2. You should have drawn a line under the word **elephants**.

On the next two pages are more paragraphs like these samples. When you are asked to turn the page, read each paragraph and find the word below it that best answers the question or completes the paragraph. Draw a line under the best word. Mark only *one* word for each paragraph. Do the paragraphs in the order in which they are numbered: 1, 2, 3, etc. If you can't answer a question, go on to the next one. Work as fast as you can without making errors.

GATES — **D FORM 1**
MacGINITIE
READING TESTS

SURVEY D, FORM 1

Speed & Accuracy
Vocabulary
Comprehension

TEACHERS COLLEGE PRESS
TEACHERS COLLEGE
COLUMBIA UNIVERSITY
NEW YORK

To the Teacher:
BE SURE to follow the directions in the Manual (included in each test package) when giving these tests. The directions will tell you how to explain the tests and how to work the sample items with the students. Allow the exact time specified in the Manual.

© 1964 by Teachers College, Columbia University
Printed in U.S.A.
10   9   8

and comprehension can be useful, especially in the intermediate grades. A child whose rate is lower than his comprehension can be provided with instruction in faster reading. A child whose rate is higher than his comprehension needs instruction that emphasizes reading accuracy.[4]

4. Albert J. Harris and Edward R. Sipay, *Effective Teaching of Reading,* 2d ed. (New York: David McKay Company, 1971), p. 168.

The comparisons of subtest scores suggested by Harris and Sipay represent one use of test results. Survey tests are often used in the following additional ways: (1) as an initial screening device in identifying those children who appear to have problems that will require further analysis, (2) as a means of determining the range in reading ability represented in a class, (3) as a tool for measuring children's overall progress over a period of time, and (4) as a basis for making initial judgments concerning reading group placements at the beginning of the school year. With regard to this last use, teachers generally find that survey test scores tend to overestimate general reading ability. Since this tendency can result in inaccurate group placements, many teachers prefer to use the results of an informal reading inventory as a basis for grouping.

Two frequently stated limitations of survey tests have been identified thus far: (1) the possible lack of representativeness of the population sample, and (2) the tendency of test results to overestimate general reading ability. Additional limitations often identified include the following: (1) subtests may not include sufficient items to obtain adequate samples of the skills being measured, and (2) because comprehension varies with the type of material being read, a high comprehension score on a particular test does not necessarily indicate that the reader will comprehend other types of material at the same level; it indicates only that he has been successful in comprehending the type of material included in the test.[5]

Concern for the reading achievement (as measured by survey tests) of children who speak black dialect has, in recent years, resulted in the raising of another issue concerning the use of standardized tests. Many of these children, especially in urban areas, score below national norms on survey tests.[6] The question being raised is whether this is happening because the tests are inappropriate for speakers of black dialect. Hutchinson has reported the results of one effort to answer this question. In this study, test scores on the Metropolitan Reading Test were obtained for a group of children. Following this, items which were considered to be "dialect-prejudiced" were eliminated from one section of the test. The test was then scored again with these items omitted. On the second scoring, only 6 percent of the children were reading one full year below grade level, while on the first scoring 20 percent of the children were reading one full year below grade level. On the basis of these data, Hutchinson concluded that the Word Discrimination Subtest of the Metropolitan Achievement Test is not appropriate for children in urban areas who speak black dialect.[7] In

---

5. George D. Spache and Evelyn B. Spache, *Reading in the Elementary School*, 3d ed. (Boston: Allyn & Bacon, 1973), p. 550.
6. June O'Shields Hutchinson, "Reading tests and nonstandard language," *The Reading Teacher* 25 (February 1972):430.
7. Ibid., pp. 430-37.

another study concerning the same issue, Hochman investigated the effects of specific dialectal changes in an upper primary reading comprehension test. Stories included in the test were rewritten in black dialect, and both the original stories and the rewritten ones were read by black children and by white children. The results indicated no significant differences in test scores on black dialect items for either black children or white children.[8] It seems obvious, therefore, that further research is needed in this area. The question of the appropriateness for black dialect speakers of current standardized tests has been raised; it is far too critical to be left unanswered.

Because of the number of survey tests available, it is important that teachers, administrators, and reading specialists apply specific criteria as a means of determining which test will be most appropriate for use in their school. Harmer suggests that a number of questions need to be asked, both about the school's testing program and about the tests being considered, before a final selection is made:

1. *Why is a test to be given?*
   If the response to this question is centered more around determining a pupil's past progress than on determining his present status, a reexamination of the relation of a testing program to instruction is necessary.

2. *How will the test results be used?*
   Unless a specific instructional answer is made to this question, the administration, scoring, and recording of the results may have become a meaningless exercise in conformity.

3. *Is the test appropriate for the pupils?*
   This is a rather broad question and its facets include chronological age, intelligence, culture, and previous instruction. One basic question to be answered is: "Did the standardization of the test include groups whose characteristics are the same as those of the pupils with whom the test will be used?"

4. *Does the test assess those pupil competencies which are the teaching objectives?*
   If the testing is not directly related to what is being taught, what purpose does it serve? If, for example, comprehension is being stressed in instruction, a test of word pronunciation skills may be of some value but will not provide an adequate assessment.

5. *Is the test valid and reliable?*
   Does the test measure what it is supposed to measure and can it be depended upon to be consistent in that measurement? Such information may normally be found in technical manuals which often are available from the publishers. In addition, it is strongly recommended that a cur-

8. Carol H. Hockman, "Black dialect reading tests in the urban elementary school," *The Reading Teacher* 26 (March 1973):581-83.

rent edition of the *Mental Measurements Yearbook* be consulted for additional evaluations.[9]

The following is a list of selected survey tests which are frequently used:

California Reading Tests. Grades 1-12. Subtests measure vocabulary and comprehension.

Gates-MacGinitie Reading Tests. Grades 1-12. Subtests of *Primary A, B,* and *C* (grades 1-3) measure vocabulary and comprehension; subtests of *Primary CS* (grades 2 and 3) measure speed and accuracy; subtests of *Surveys D, E,* and *F* (grades 4-12) measure vocabulary, comprehension, and speed and accuracy.

Metropolitan Reading Tests. Grades K.7-9.5. Subtests of *Primer* (grades K.7-1.4) measure listening for sounds, word knowledge and comprehension; subtests of *Primary I* (grades 1.5-2.4) and *Primary II* (grades 2.5-3.4) measure word knowledge, word analysis and comprehension; subtests of *Elementary* (grades 3.5-4.9), *Intermediate* (grades 5-6.9) and *Advanced* (grades 7-9.5) measure word knowledge and comprehension.

Nelson Reading Test. Grades 3-9. Subtests measure vocabulary and paragraph comprehension.

Stanford Reading Tests. Grades 1.5-9.5. Subtests of *Primary I* (grades 1.5-2.4), *Primary II* (grades 2.5-3.4), *Primary III* (grades 3.5-4.4), *Intermediate I* (grades 4.5-5.4), and *Intermediate II* (grades 5.5-6.9) measure vocabulary, reading comprehension, word-study skills, and listening comprehension; subtests of *Advanced* (grades 7-9.5) measure vocabulary and reading comprehension.

Diagnostic Tests

The second category of tests to be considered in this activity, the diagnostic test, provides more detailed information concerning reading performance than does the survey test. While survey tests provide a measure of reading ability in broad areas, diagnostic tests attempt to measure ability in specific skill areas. As a result, these tests contain a greater number of subtests than are found in survey tests. The range of available diagnostic tests includes both those that are designed for group administration and those that are designed for use with individuals.

The Graphic Profile shown in figure 9.2 is from the Bond-Balow-Hoyt *New Developmental Reading Tests for the Intermediate Grades.* This is a group diagnostic test. Notice that while survey tests measure comprehension broadly, this test measures the ability to read for a variety of specific comprehension outcomes.

9. William R. Harmer, "The Selection and Use of Survey Reading Achievement Tests," in *The Evaluation of Children's Reading Achievement,* Perspectives in Reading, No. 8; ed. Thomas C. Barrett (Newark, Del.: International Reading Association, 1967), p. 63.

FIGURE 9.2.
Graphic Profile. Reprinted with permission of the publisher from *New Developmental Reading Test,* Intermediate Level, Bond, et al., developed by Lyons & Carnahan, copyright © 1970 Rand McNally & Company.

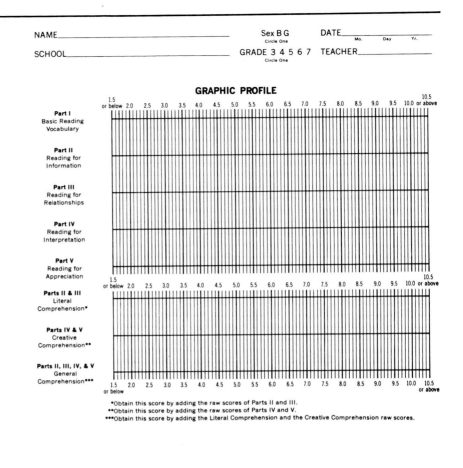

The completed Graphic Profile shown in figure 9.3 presents a summary of test results for one child who took the Bond-Balow-Hoyt *Silent Reading Diagnostic Test,* which is also a group test. As you can see, this test separates the area of word recognition into specific skills. It should be pointed out that although the Profile provides space for recording literal and creative comprehension, these subtests are not included in the test—the scores could be obtained from administering the Bond-Balow-Hoyt *New Developmental Reading Tests.* Note the horizontal "lines of importance" on the Profile. Scores outside these lines indicate the child's specific strengths and weaknesses.

Group diagnostic tests can provide useful information concerning the

Silent Reading Diagnostic Tests
GRAPHIC PROFILE

Name *James York*   School *John F. Kennedy*

Grade *4*   Teacher *Eleanor Johnson*   Date *Oct. 9, 1969*

FIGURE 9.3.
Graphic Profile. Reprinted with permission of the publisher from *Silent Reading Diagnostic Tests*, Bond, et al., developed by Lyons & Carnahan, copyright © 1970 by Rand McNally & Company.

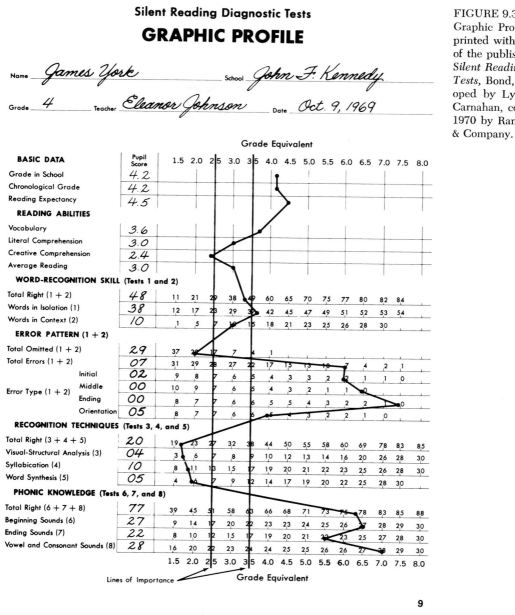

BASIC DATA	Pupil Score	Grade Equivalent
Grade in School	4.2	
Chronological Grade	4.2	
Reading Expectancy	4.5	
READING ABILITIES		
Vocabulary	3.6	
Literal Comprehension	3.0	
Creative Comprehension	2.4	
Average Reading	3.0	
WORD-RECOGNITION SKILL (Tests 1 and 2)		
Total Right (1 + 2)	48	
Words in Isolation (1)	38	
Words in Context (2)	10	
ERROR PATTERN (1 + 2)		
Total Omitted (1 + 2)	29	
Total Errors (1 + 2)	07	
Error Type (1 + 2) Initial	02	
Middle	00	
Ending	00	
Orientation	05	
RECOGNITION TECHNIQUES (Tests 3, 4, and 5)		
Total Right (3 + 4 + 5)	20	
Visual-Structural Analysis (3)	04	
Syllabication (4)	10	
Word Synthesis (5)	05	
PHONIC KNOWLEDGE (Tests 6, 7, and 8)		
Total Right (6 + 7 + 8)	77	
Beginning Sounds (6)	27	
Ending Sounds (7)	22	
Vowel and Consonant Sounds (8)	28	

Lines of Importance → Grade Equivalent

9

reading needs of children. When these needs have been identified, children who are experiencing the same difficulties can be grouped together and provided with appropriate instruction.

The following is a list of several group diagnostic tests that are available:

Bond-Balow-Hoyt New Developmental Reading Tests: Primary Reading. Subtests measure basic vocabulary, general comprehension, and specific comprehension.

Bond-Balow-Hoyt New Developmental Reading Tests: Intermediate Grades (4, 5, 6). Subtests measure basic reading vocabulary, reading for information, reading for relationships, reading for appreciation, literal comprehension, creative comprehension, and general comprehension.

Bond-Balow-Hoyt Silent Reading Diagnostic Tests. Designed to be used with children reading at second- through sixth-grade levels. Subtests measure words in isolation, words in context, visual-structural analysis, syllabication, word synthesis, beginning and ending sounds, vowel and consonant sounds.

Dvorak-Van Wagenen Diagnostic Examination of Silent Reading Abilities. Grades 4-13. Subtests measure rate of comprehension, perception of relations, vocabulary, range of general information, central thought, clearly stated details, interpretation, integration of dispersed ideas, and drawing inferences.

Ingraham-Clark Diagnostic Reading Tests. Grades 1-8. Subtests measure word form and word meanings, and sentence and paragraph comprehension.

Diagnostic instruments that are designed for individual testing are used with children who are experiencing great difficulty in learning to read. Because the diagnosing of a child's reading difficulties with one of these tests is a time-consuming and detailed process, the tests are typically administered in reading clinics, or other settings outside the classroom, by trained examiners. The cover page of the Pupil Record Booklet of the Gates-McKillop *Reading Diagnostic Tests,* shown in figure 9.4, indicates the types of information that are derived from the use of this test.

Single Skill Area Tests

Instruments which measure ability in only one area of reading represent the third category of tests to be considered in this activity. Not all of these tests are standardized in the sense that norms are provided, but they can be considered "standardized" in the sense that the procedures for administering and scoring them are clearly stated and are to be followed in the same way by each person giving the tests.

Examples from tests designed to measure word recognition skills were provided in the modules dealing with phonic and structural analysis. A selected list of this type of test is provided here also.

Botel Reading Inventory: Phonics Mastery Test. Grades 1-12. The subtests measure knowledge of phonics.

Pupil Record Booklet   Form II

GATES-McKILLOP READING DIAGNOSTIC TESTS

By Arthur I. Gates and Anne S. McKillop
Teachers College, Columbia University

Pupil's Name .... School .... Date ....

Pupil's Age .... Birthday .... Grade ...... Examiner .... Teacher ....

	1 Raw Score	2 Grade or other Score	3 Rating
AGE, GRADE, INTELLIGENCE			
1. Chronological Age			
2. Grade Status			
3. Binet ____ I.Q. .....M.A.			
4. .... I.Q. ....M.A.			
READING AND OTHER TESTS			
1.			
2.			
3.			
4.			
5.			
Silent reading average			
READING DIAGNOSTIC TESTS			
I. Oral Reading			
Total Score			
a. Omissions, Words			
b. Additions, Words			
c. Repetitions			
d. Mispronunciations			
e. Full Reversals			
f. Reversal of Parts			
g. Wrong Order (e+f)			
h. Wrong Beginnings			
i. Wrong Middles			
j. Wrong Endings			
k. Wrong Several Parts			

	1 Raw Score	2 Grade or other Score	3 Rating
II. Words: Flash Presentation			
III. Words: Untimed Presentation			
IV. Phrases: Flash Presentation			
V. Knowledge of Word Parts			
1. Recognizing & Blending Common Word Parts			
2. Giving Letter Sounds			
3. Naming Capital Letters			
4. Naming Lower-case Letters			
VI. Recognizing the Visual Form of Sounds			
1. Nonsense Words			
2. Initial Letters			
3. Final Letters			
4. Vowels			
VII. Auditory Blending			
VIII. Supplementary Tests			
1. Spelling			
2. Oral Vocabulary			
3. Syllabication			
4. Auditory Discrimination			
5.			
6.			
7.			

BUREAU OF PUBLICATIONS, TEACHERS COLLEGE, COLUMBIA UNIVERSITY, NEW YORK

© 1962 by Arthur I. Gates and Anne S. McKillop

PRINTED IN U.S.A.   FIRST PRINTING, JULY 1962

Durkin-Meshover Phonics Knowledge Survey. Any grade. The sixteen subtests measure knowledge of phonics.

McCullough Word-Analysis Test. Grades 4-6. Subtests measure initial blends and digraphs, phonetic discrimination (vowels), matching letters to vowel sounds, sounding whole words, interpreting phonetic symbols, dividing words into symbols, and root words in affixed forms.

Roswell-Chall Diagnostic Reading Test. The subtests measure knowledge of phonics.

In the module dealing with reading in the content fields, the cloze procedure was presented as a tool for determining the readability of textbook material. This procedure has also been studied as a means of measuring comprehension. On the basis of his review of studies using the cloze procedure, Culhane compares this technique with other methods of testing comprehension:

> . . . One important fact that has emerged from these studies is that the CLOZE method is as good as, and in many ways better than, existing methods for teaching and testing comprehension.[10]

Tests which focus on the evaluation of oral reading are also available. Standardized oral reading tests are used to gain information of the type obtained with informal reading inventories. The child reads a series of increasingly difficult paragraphs until he reaches the point at which the material is obviously too difficult. Errors in oral reading and in responses to the accompanying comprehension questions are recorded as the child progresses through the paragraphs. Two frequently used oral reading tests are the following:

Gilmore Oral Reading Tests, New Edition. Grades 1-8. Ten reading paragraphs of increasing difficulty; scored for accuracy, comprehension, and rate.
Gray Oral Reading Tests. Grades 1-12. Thirteen graded reading passages; scored for both accuracy and rate—combined into a single score.

In order to become aware of the similarities and differences that exist among standardized tests, examine several survey and group diagnostic tests. Specimen sets of these tests are often available for examination in college libraries or instructional materials centers. As you examine the tests, use the questions regarding test selection suggested by Harmer (presented in this activity) as a means of judging the appropriateness of each test for use with the children with whom you are working. Use the following questions, in addition to those suggested by Harmer, in your examination of each test:

1. Are the test items presented in a way that is similar to a format that the children have encountered in their instructional materials? If not, do you think the children would find the test format difficult to understand?
2. Do the directions seem clear and easy for the children to follow?

---

10. Joseph W. Culhane, "CLOZE Procedures and Comprehension," *The Reading Teacher* 23 (February 1970):411.

3. Are the directions for administering and scoring the test clearly explained in the teachers' manual?
4. Are the procedures for converting raw scores to grade level or other types of scores clearly explained?
5. Is information that would be useful in interpreting the test results provided in the teachers' manual?

Activity 3

In order to make sound judgments about each child's progress in reading it is necessary to be able to estimate the level at which he can be *expected* to read. Each child's *reading expectancy level* is an estimate of the level at which he can be expected to read based on his potential or capacity for learning. It is essential that children's reading expectancy levels, not their *grade levels,* be compared with their actual reading levels in order to determine whether their progress is satisfactory or unsatisfactory. A fifth-grade child, for example, whose reading expectancy indicates that he can be expected to read at approximately the fourth-grade level, and whose actual reading level *is* fourth grade, is making satisfactory progress, regardless of the grade level designation of his classroom. Another child in the same fifth grade, on the other hand, whose reading expectancy level is approximately fifth grade, and whose actual reading level is slightly below third grade, is obviously in need of special help. Bond and Tinker suggest that the amount of discrepancy between expectancy level and actual reading level which should be considered significant increases grade by grade. They propose that the following guidelines be used in identifying those children who are experiencing serious difficulty in learning to read:

> . . . In the first grade . . . one-half year is a sufficiently large difference between reading expectancy and reading achievement to indicate a serious problem. Even children who are three-tenths of a year lower in reading achievement than we would expect them to be are considered seriously enough retarded to be studied further as having a possible disability. At grade five, the difference must be at least one and one-half years to be classified as a disability, and nine-tenths of a year to one and one-half years to indicate a possible disability if supported by other evidence.[11]

Selecting one of the available formulas is the first step in computing the child's expectancy level. Two frequently used formulas are presented here:

11. Guy L. Bond and Miles A. Tinker, *Reading Difficulties: Their Diagnosis and Correction,* 3d ed. (New York: Appleton-Century-Crofts, 1973), pp. 102-3.

Harris-Sipay Formula[12]

$$\text{Reading Expectancy Level} = \frac{2MA + CA}{3} - 5.2$$

CA = chronological age

MA = mental age and can be estimated with this formula:

$$MA = \frac{CA \times I.Q.}{100}$$

Bond-Tinker Formula[13]

Reading Expectancy Level = years in school times I.Q. (divided by 100) + 1.0.
The 1.0 is added because the child's grade score was 1.0 when he entered school.

In a study wherein expectancy formulas were compared, Rodenborn found that marked differences resulted when three formulas were applied to compute the expectancy levels of one group of children. As a result, those children identified as being in need of remedial help through the use of one formula (based on the discrepancy between expectancy level and actual reading level) were not classified as disabled readers when a second formula was used. Rodenborn suggests that these findings emphasize the point that expectancy formulas yield only *estimates* of capacity for learning to read. He further suggests that teachers should use more than one formula to compute expectancy, so that a *range* in expectancy is obtained and used in evaluating reading progress. This range in expectancy can serve as a reminder to teachers that formulas yield estimates, not precise indications, of reading potential.[14]

Complete the following procedure in order to develop the ability to administer standardized tests and interpret the results:

1. Select one child and administer a survey reading test.
2. Score the test and convert the raw scores to grade level scores.
3. Compute the child's reading expectancy level using either the Harris-Sipay or the Bond-Tinker expectancy formula.

12. Rodenborn's use of the Harris-Sipay formula. The subtraction of 5.2 allows the reading expectancy to be expressed as a reading grade score rather than as a reading age score. Albert J. Harris and Edward R. Sipay, *How to Increase Reading Ability*, 6th ed. (New York: David McKay Company, 1975), p. 152.
13. Bond and Tinker, *Reading Difficulties*, p. 101.
14. Leo V. Rodenborn, "Determining, using expectancy formulas," *The Reading Teacher* 28 (December 1974):286-91.

4. Develop a *profile* which includes the reading expectancy level and the test results. A sample profile is provided in figure 9.5.
5. Evaluate the child's progress by comparing his average reading level with his expected reading level.
6. Analyze the test results in order to determine the child's areas of strength and/or weakness.
7. Add the completed Reading Profile to the teacher's records for the child.

Activity 4

In order to effectively evaluate each child's progress in reading as a basis for planning appropriate daily instruction, the teacher will need to collect more data than can be obtained from the administration of standardized tests. The collection of additional data is necessary for three reasons: (1) the most commonly used standardized tests, those of the survey type, measure only general reading ability, (2) standardized tests are typically administered only once or twice during the school year, and (3) standardized tests may fail to yield information that is relevant in terms of the objectives of a particular reading program.

A wide range of informal (or nonstandardized) techniques can be used to assess children's progress toward the objectives of the reading program. Making the decisions regarding the types of information that are needed to evaluate achievement of the objectives of a particular instructional program provides the basis for the teacher's selection of appropriate techniques.

Tests which accompany basal reading series, and tests developed by teachers, represent two types of informal evaluation techniques. Another type of nonstandardized test, currently receiving attention, is the *criterion-referenced* test. Millman discusses the difference between criterion-referenced (CR) and norm-referenced (NR) measurement:

> Although test experts do not agree on a single definition of *criterion-referenced* tests, all variants have in common their emphasis, in interpretation, on what a child can do relative to the subject matter of the test. Unlike NR tests, in which scores get meaning from norms indicating how well other students have performed on a test, CR measurement meaning comes from a comparison of the student's performance relative to the skills being assessed by the test questions.[15]

In contrast to norm-referenced tests, in which the focus is the individual's performance in relation to that of a norming population, the

15. Jason Millman, "Criterion referenced measurement: An alternative," *The Reading Teacher* 26 (December 1972):278.

FIGURE 9.5.

Reading Profile

Name _____   Name of Test _____

Grade _____   Date Tested _____

Age _____   Teacher _____

Summary of Test Results

Subtest	Raw Score	Grade Level Score
_____	_____	_____
_____	_____	_____
_____	_____	_____

Average reading level (average of subtest grade level scores) _____

Expectancy level _____

Formula used to compute expectancy level _____

Evaluation:

focus in criterion-referenced tests is the individual's performance in relation to the criterion score for each test item. The items which comprise criterion-referenced tests are designed to measure achievement of those skills which represent the objectives of an instructional program. Once the individual's mastery of specific skills has been assessed, the teacher can make decisions regarding the appropriate next steps in the instructional process. If the child has demonstrated mastery of the skills, he is ready to begin developing subsequent skills; if he has not demonstrated mastery, he will need to be provided with additional learning experiences that focus on these skills.

Criterion-referenced tests can be designed to measure the reading objectives within a classroom, a school, or an entire school system. In figure 9.6 are shown examples of the reading competencies that have been identified for one school district, and in figure 9.7 are the criterion-referenced test items that have been designed to measure mastery of these competencies.

Interest in criterion-referenced measurement has led to the development of a number of commercially published criterion-referenced, or objective-based, reading programs. These programs have been designed in an effort to enable teachers to establish and maintain individualized instruction in reading. In his review of several criterion-referenced reading systems, Rude identifies the components which comprise the overall structure of these programs as: (1) the identification of specific skills (objectives of the program) to be mastered sequentially; (2) assessment techniques consisting of paper-and-pencil tests which measure skill mastery; (3) a management system for recording each child's mastery of specific skills; and (4) suggested instructional activities and/or a list of commercial reading materials (basal series and supplementary materials) that have been keyed to the skills identified for the program.[16]

Many types of information that the teacher will need cannot be obtained through the use of tests. For this reason, teachers use a variety of additional techniques. In the article which introduces this module, Ammons discusses two useful informal techniques: *situations* and *anecdotal records*. Other techniques that teachers find useful are identified here. Note that the uses of workbooks and of teacher-developed activities and materials have been discussed in several other modules in relation to specific skill development.

1. *Basal reading workbooks*: workbook exercises provide information concerning children's progress in the materials of the basic reading program.

---

16. Robert T. Rude, "Objective-based reading systems," *The Reading Teacher* 28 (November 1974):169-75.

FIGURE 9.6.
Pupil Competencies.
From *Reading: Pupil Competencies—Level Nine: Book 4* (Philadelphia, Pa.: Instructional Services, The School District of Philadelphia, © 1970). Reprinted by permission of the publisher.

Reading: Pupil Competencies

Level Nine: Book 4

Pupil retains all skills of previous levels.

1. *Word Recognition*
   The pupil understands and uses:
   a. All diacritical marks
   b. All phonetic respellings
   c. Synonyms, antonyms, and homonyms
   d. All known structure elements to identify new words

2. *Comprehension*
   The pupil:
   a. Analyzes story elements in terms of main character, supporting characters, plot, and subplots
   b. Understands and uses figurative and idiomatic language
   c. Identifies:
      (1) Main idea
      (2) Supporting details
      (3) Drawing inferences
      (4) Predicting outcomes
      (5) Making judgments
      (6) Other critical thinking skills

---

2. *Teacher-developed activities and materials*: these may provide the kind of information obtained through the use of workbooks, or they may be designed to measure progress toward objectives that are not included in the basal reading program.
3. *Teacher observation*: through observation, the teacher can obtain information regarding ability to use the library, selection of material during free reading time, ability to work independently, and the presence of hearing, vision, or other health problems that may inhibit progress in reading.
4. *Interest inventories or checklists*: useful information can be obtained through the development and use of inventories in which children are asked to identify the types of reading material they enjoy, the types of activities in the reading program they like and dislike, and the types of activities, including those involving reading, in which they participate outside of school.
5. *Individual conferences*: through individual conferences, the teacher can assess not only children's progress in relation to specific skills, but also their feelings and attitudes toward reading and toward their progress in the instructional program.

FIGURE 9.7.

Reading Test. From *Reading Test—Level Nine: Book 4* (Philadelphia, Pa.: Instructional Services, The School District of Philadelphia, © 1972). Reprinted by permission of the publisher.

Lower and Middle Schools

READING TEST—LEVEL NINE: BOOK 4

	NO. OF ITEMS	NO. CORRECT	MASTERY
WORD RECOG.	27		24
COMPRE-HENSION	10		9

NAME _____   DATE _____

SCHOOL _____   GRADE _____

TEACHER _____   ROOM _____

1. Word Recognition

a. Select and underline the correct pronunciation from the two in Column B for each word in Column A.

	A	B
(1)	ghost	gōst ; gŏst
(2)	waist	wăst ; wāst
(3)	starve	stärv ; stārv
(4)	whom	ho͞om ; ho͝om
(5)	order	ōrder ; ôrder
(6)	writer	rīter ; rĭter

b. Circle the correct phonetic respelling in each row for the word in the column at the left.

(1) trudge	trŏg	trădg	trŭj
(2) carriage	cărăg	kĭroge	kărĭj
(3) rough	rŭf	rūfe	rōwf
(4) shift	shēf	shift	chif
(5) detail	dĭtāl	dĕtāle	dētăl
(6) scowl	sko͞ol	skoul	scâul

1

Evaluating Growth in Reading Ability

FIGURE 9.7. Continued.

(7) dispatch	dĭspătch	dĭspāsh	dēspáche
(8) thumb	thŏm	thŭm	thūm

c. Write <u>S</u> for synonyms, <u>A</u> for antonyms, or <u>H</u> for homonyms for each pair of underlined words in the sentences below.

(1) I <u>know</u> of <u>no</u> one who can do this job. _____

(2) The <u>fast</u> car went past the <u>slow</u> one. _____

(3) The <u>little</u> girl was caring for the <u>small</u> dog. _____

(4) Do the <u>strong</u> often help the <u>weak</u>?_____

(5) His <u>son</u> likes to play in the <u>sun</u>. _____

d. Write the root word, prefix and/or suffix for each word below.

	Root	Prefix	Suffix
(1) discolor	_____	_____	_____
(2) returnable	_____	_____	_____
(3) indirect	_____	_____	_____
(4) powerless	_____	_____	_____
(5) encircle	_____	_____	_____
(6) cheerful	_____	_____	_____
(7) unkindness	_____	_____	_____
(8) anxiously	_____	_____	_____

2. Comprehension

Read the story below.

    Many years ago, a little country needed a king. Each of the men in important positions felt that he deserved to be the ruler. Since there could be only one king, the men took to fighting among themselves. John, a young shepherd, said, "Let the people choose their ruler." But the men jeered at him and continued fighting. The people in the country were very unhappy. They gathered in front of a great stone in the courtyard to decide what should be done.

2

Like a bolt of lightning, a shining sword pierced the great stone. On the sword were the words, "The man who is able to draw this sword out of the great stone will be our new king."

All of the men stopped fighting. Each took a turn at pulling the sword free of the stone. But none could budge it. Then John, the young shepherd, said, "Let me try." The men laughed again, but the people said, "Give him a chance."

John stepped up to the stone, grasped the handle of the sword, and pulled. It came out swift as a flash. A cheer went up from the crowd. "Hail the new king!"

a. (1) Circle the main character in the above story.

     a town clerk
     a government official
     a shepherd

   (2) Circle the phrase that best describes the plot of the story.

     pulling out a sword
     choosing a king
     the great stone

b. Underline the group of words on the right that means most nearly the same as the one on the left, as used in the story.

(1) like a bolt of lightning	(with a bang)
	(suddenly)
	(quietly)

(2) draw this sword	(paint a picture)
	(pull it out)
	(find it)

(3) swift as a flash	(quickly)
	(brightly)
	(softly)

c. (1) Underline the title that best describes the story.

     A New Ruler

     John, the Shepherd

     A Pierced Stone

3

Evaluating Growth in Reading Ability

FIGURE 9.7.   Continued.

Lower and Middle Schools

(2) Underline the statement below that was most important in determining the new ruler.

There was fighting in the courtyard.

"Let the people choose their ruler."

John pulled the sword out of the stone.

A cheer went up from the crowd.

(3) Underline the reason you think the men jeered at John's suggestion for choosing a ruler.

It was a joke.

They didn't approve of this way of choosing a ruler.

They enjoyed fighting.

(4), (5), (6)

(a) Choose the statement which best describes the kind of ruler John would probably make and underline it.

a dictator

a democratic king

a fighter

a weak king

(b) Underline the statement which would be a reason for your choice.

He wanted the people to choose.

He pulled the sword from the stone.

The crowd cheered.

John was a shepherd.

4

Complete the following procedure as a means of developing your ability to use informal evaluation techniques:

1. Identify one child and use two informal techniques to collect data relative to his progress in reading.
   a) consult the child's teacher in order to determine what information, of the type that can be collected through informal techniques, he would find it useful to add to the data he already has for that child.
   b) use your discussion with the child's teacher as a basis for selecting appropriate techniques.
   c) evaluate the child's progress in the areas for which you have collected data.
   d) add the data you have collected to the teacher's records for the child.

Activity 5

In order to determine the nature and extent of the reading evaluation program in the school in which you are working, request interviews with teachers and other personnel who are involved in that evaluation program (e.g., reading teacher, principal). Ask the persons you interview to respond to the following questions:

1. What standardized tests are administered on a total school or grade level basis? What skills are measured by these tests?
2. How often are standardized tests administered during the year? Are the tests administered by classroom teachers or by other personnel?
3. In what ways are standardized test results used?
4. What informal techniques are applied on a total school, grade level, or individual classroom basis? What types of information are obtained through the use of these techniques?
5. How is the information that is obtained through the use of informal techniques put to use?

Activity 6

Design activities of your own which you feel will enable you to achieve the competencies stated for this module.

Preassessment and Postassessment

    A. Knowledge Level

        1. Identify two categories of standardized tests. Differentiate the two categories in terms of the types of skills typically measured by tests in each category.

        Criteria for successful performance:

        a) the two categories of standardized tests are accurately identified:

        b) the types of skills measured by tests in each category are accurately identified.

        2. Identify two informal techniques that can be used to collect information concerning progress in reading. Differentiate these techniques in terms of the types of information that can be obtained through their use.

        Criteria for successful performance:

        a) the two informal techniques are accurately identified;

        b) the types of information that can be obtained through the use of these techniques are accurately identified.

    B. Performance Level

        1. Administer to one child (a) a survey or diagnostic test, and (b) one additional test (e.g., phonic inventory, cloze test, oral reading test). After the tests have been administered and scored, complete the following procedure:

        a) determine the child's reading expectancy level.

        b) develop a profile of the type shown in activity 4 which includes the reading expectancy level and the results of the tests you administered.

        c) evaluate the child's progress in reading by responding to the following questions:

        (1) In your judgment, is the child's progress satisfactory? Support your answer with references to the information included on the profile.

        (2) What appear to be the child's areas of strength and/or weakness?

        Criteria for successful performance:

        a) the raw scores have been correctly converted into grade scores, and the expectancy level has been correctly computed;

        b) the evaluation of the child's progress is defensible in terms of the information included on the profile.

        2. Select one child and use two informal (nonstandardized) techniques to collect and record data relative to his progress in

reading. Ask the child's teacher for additional information (e.g., test results, expectancy level) regarding the child's reading ability. Evaluate the child's progress by responding to the following questions:

a) How does the information you obtained from the child's teacher compare with the data you collected using informal techniques?

b) What appear to be the child's areas of strength and/or weakness?

c) What is your judgment of the child's overall progress in reading?

Criteria for successful performance:

a) the data collected through the use of informal techniques have been objectively and systematically recorded;

b) the evaluation of the child's progress is defensible in terms of both the data collected through the use of informal techniques and the information obtained from the child's teacher.

References

Bond, Guy L., and Tinker, Miles A. *Reading Difficulties: Their Diagnosis and Correction.* 3d ed. Chap. 4, "General Nature of Reading Disability." New York: Appleton-Century-Crofts, 1973.

Bond, Guy L., and Wagner, Eva Bond. *Teaching the Child to Read.* 4th ed. Chap. 15, "Appraising Reading Growth." New York: Macmillan Company, 1966.

Bush, Clifford L., and Huebner, Mildred H. *Strategies for Reading in the Elementary School.* Chap. 14, "Methods of Appraisal." New York: Macmillan Company, 1970.

Culhane, Joseph W. "CLOZE Procedures and Comprehension." *The Reading Teacher* 23 (February 1970):410-13, 464.

Dallmann, Martha; Rouch, Roger L.; Chang, Lynette Y. C.; and DeBoer, John J. *The Teaching of Reading.* 4th ed. Chap. 12, "Classroom Diagnosis of Reading Ability." New York: Holt, Rinehart and Winston, 1974.

Durkin, Dolores. *Teaching Them to Read.* 2d ed. Chap. 16, "Classroom Diagnosis." Boston: Allyn & Bacon, 1974.

Harris, Albert J., and Sipay, Edward R. *Effective Teaching of Reading.* 2d ed. Chap. 6, "Determining Learning Needs in Reading." New York: David McKay Company, 1971.

———. *How to Increase Reading Ability.* 6th ed. Chap. 8, "Assessing Reading Performance, 1"; chap. 9, "Assessing Reading Performance, 2." New York: David McKay Company, 1975.

Heilman, Arthur W. *Principles and Practices of Teaching Reading.* 3d ed. Chap. 8, "Diagnosis of Reading Ability." Columbus, Ohio: Charles E. Merrill Publishing Company, 1972.

Hockman, Carol H. "Black dialect reading tests in the urban elementary school." *The Reading Teacher* 26 (March 1973):581-83.

Hutchinson, June O'Shields. "Reading tests and nonstandard language." *The Reading Teacher* 25 (February 1972):430-37.

Millman, Jason. "Criterion-referenced measurement: an alternative." *The Reading Teacher* 26 (December 1972):278-85.

Otto, Wayne; Chester, Robert; McNeil, John; and Myers, Shirley. *Focused Reading Instruction*. Chap. 11, "Organizing Learning Situations for Individual Differences." Reading, Mass.: Addison-Wesley Publishing Company, 1974.

Rodenborn, Leo V. "Determining, using expectancy formulas." *The Reading Teacher* 28 (December 1974), pp. 286-91.

Rude, Robert T. "Objective-based reading systems: an evaluation." *The Reading Teacher* 28 (November 1974):169-75.

Russell, David H. *Children Learn to Read*. 2d ed. Chap. 16, "Evaluation of Growth in and Through Reading." Waltham, Mass.: Blaisdell Publishing Company, 1961.

Stauffer, Russell G. *Teaching Reading as a Think-ing Process*. Chap. 11, "Evaluation." New York: Harper & Row, Publishers, 1969.

Tinker, Miles A., and McCullough, Constance M. *Teaching Elementary Reading*. 3d ed. Chap. 17, "Appraisal of Reading Growth." New York: Appleton-Century-Crofts, 1968.

Veatch, Jeannette. *Reading in the Elementary School*. Chap. 12, "Evaluation, Record-Keeping, and Testing." New York: Ronald Press Company, 1966.

Walcutt, Charles C.; Lamport, Joan; and McCracken, Glenn. *Teaching Reading*. Chap. 16, "Evaluation for the Reading Program." New York: Macmillan Company, 1974.

Zintz, Miles V. *The Reading Process: The Teacher and the Learner*. 2d ed. Chap. 21, "Evaluation in the Reading Program." Dubuque, Iowa: Wm. C. Brown Company Publishers, 1975.

Index

suggestions for student use, 5-7
Morpheme, 116
Morphology, 115
Morrison, Coleman, 226
Murphy-Durrell Diagnostic Reading Readiness Tests, 22

"Needing a Friend," 153-55
Nelson Reading Test, 319
New Developmental Reading Tests for the Intermediate Grades, 319-20, 322
New Developmental Reading Tests: Primary Reading, 322
Non-graded classes, 231-32

O'Leary, Helen F., 193
    "Preserve the Basic Reading Program," 194-98, 199
Olson, Willard C., 55
Oral reading, 192, 196-97
Oral reading tests, 324

Payne, M. Arlene, 312
"Pete Wants To Whistle," 206-11
Phoneme, 83
Phonemics, 82
Phonetics, 74-75, 82
Phonic analysis
    activities for skill development, 104-5
    analytic approaches, 73-74
    guidelines in teaching, 76-77
    inductive approach, 84-89
    instructional materials, 102-4
    synthetic approaches, 73-74
Phonic generalizations, 91, 93-100
Phonics, 74-75, 82
"Phonics Mastery Test," 91-94
Phonogram, 83
Phonology, 81-82
"Picking Locks and Cracking Safes For Honest Money," 217-18
Prefix, 110, 112, 116, 118-20
Pupil Checklist (Skills), 55-56
Pupil-team study, 231

Questioning (*See* Comprehension)

Ramsey, Wallace, 227
Readability formulas, 273, 275

Readiness
    activities for developing, 31, 33
    assessment of, 21-27
    factors related to, 18-20
    inventories, 23, 25-28
    tests, 21-23
    traditional interpretation of, 12-13
    workbooks, 28-30
Reading expectancy level, 325-26
Reading process
    fixations, 43
    nature of, 43-50
    pattern perception, 44
    regression, 45
    unanswered questions, 49
Robinson, Helen M., 229
Rodenborn, Leo V., 326
Root word, 116
Roswell-Chall Diagnostic Reading Test, 323
Rude, Robert T., 329
Rupley, William H., 262-63
Russell, David H., 255

Sartain, Harry W., 223
    "Specific Patterns of Current Interest," 223-36, 237, 239, 252
Schell, Leo M., 109
    "Teaching Structural Analysis," 110-14, 118, 121
Semantics, 81
Sequence
    development in comprehension, 157, 164-65, 169-74, 176-79
    development of in readiness program, 33
Seymour, Dorothy Z., 121, 128, 248
Shane, Harold G., 80, 115
Shapski, Mary, 231-32
Sheldon, William D., 52-53
Shuy, Roger W., 80
Silent reading, 192, 196-97
Silent Reading Diagnostic Tests, 320-22
Sipay, Edward R., 21, 23, 82, 315-17, 326
Smith, Helen K., 157, 164
Smith, James A., 104
Smith, Nila Banton, 134-35
    "The Many Faces of Reading Comprehension," 135-43, 149, 192, 222, 251
Spache, Evelyn B., 21, 118, 124, 149-50, 255